Helsinki, Human Rights, and European Security

HELSINKI, HUMAN RIGHTS, AND EUROPEAN SECURITY

Analysis and Documentation

Vojtech Mastny

Duke University Press, Durham 1986

© 1986 Duke University Press. All rights reserved.
Printed in the United States of America on acid-free paper ∞.
Library of Congress Cataloging-in-Publication Data appear on the last printed page
of this book.

Permission to reprint the articles and book excerpts contained in this volume has
been granted by the following publishers, journals, periodicals, individuals, and organizations. Full bibliographical information is given with each numbered article or
excerpt.
[1] and [4] Lexington Books; [3] Rand Corporation; [6] *Encounter*; [9] Institut
Universitaire de Hautes Etudes Internationales; [10] Sijthoff and Noordhoff (Martinus Nijhoff/Dr W. Junk publishers); [14] Temple Smith; [21] and [50] *New
York Times*; [24] Allen & Unwin; [30] *Intereconomics*; [40] Center for Strategic
and International Studies; [41] Zbigniew Brzezinski (Farrar, Straus & Giroux); [49]
MIT Press (*Washington Quarterly*); [59] *Foreign Policy*; [78] C. C. van den Heuvel;
[84] *The Economist*; [92], [94], and [95] Freedom House; [93] Kenneth A. Adelman (*Christian Science Monitor*); [102] Nijhoff (Martinus Nijhoff/Dr W. Junk
publishers); [126] *Europa-Archiv*; [142] *Revue roumaine d'études internationales*

CONTENTS

**PART TWO   Human Rights, Trade, and Security:
From Belgrade to Madrid**

The Favorite Soviet Basket

The Western Approaches

The Decline of Détente

PART THREE   Human Rights in the Shadow of Military Rivalry: From Madrid to Vienna

Accent on Military Security

Accommodating the Incompatible

PREFACE

Like the Helsinki agreement itself, this book had a history long before it materialized. It dates back to the initiative by the Twentieth Century Fund whose Assistant Director, Joel Blocker, suggested in 1982 that I write a history of the Helsinki Conference for the tenth anniversary of the Final Act. Although the project was never undertaken in its original form, I remained interested in it and hoped to return to it later. The opportunity presented itself during my stay in Europe in the summer of 1985 when Joel, meanwhile appointed Deputy Director of Radio Free Europe in Munich, and George Urban, RFE's Director, offered to put at my disposal the impressive files their organization had assembled on the Conference on Security and Cooperation in Europe (CSCE). And although the timetable involved in preparing an analysis and documentation of the ten years of the Helsinki process was exceedingly tight, I drew encouragement from the readiness of Duke University Press to publish the resulting book in time for the third CSCE review conference in Vienna in the fall of 1986.

A particular attraction of the project for an historian was the availability of a complete set of dispatches by correspondents of Radio Free Europe/Radio Liberty, amounting to some three thousand closely teletyped pages. Although the CSCE does not keep official minutes, it offers persistent and skillful reporters many ways to penetrate the intricate details of its semipublic proceedings. And RFE/RL has the distinction of being the only news organization that has kept its correspondents present at all the CSCE meetings at all times. It has also been fortunate enough to find highly competent professionals, notably Roland Eggleston, for the assignment. The extensive use of their writings in this book is a tribute to both their journalistic standards and the unique quality of the dispatches as an historical source.

During the less than five months I had in which to undertake the necessary research and prepare the complicated manuscript for the publisher in addition to my regular academic duties, I received support from many quarters. Particularly crucial was that extended in old friendship by William Buell, Vice President of RFE/RL for U.S. Operations, and his assistant, Jane Lester. The research assistance provided by the staff of the Commission on Security and Cooperation in Europe of the U.S. Congress, notably by Lynne A. Davidson, was indispensable. The Helsinki process was brought to life in the interviews granted by the leading American participants, Ambassadors Arthur Goldberg, James Goodby, Max Kampelman, Richard Schifter, and Warren Zimmermann, as well as by other members of the U.S. delegations—Dorothy Goldberg, John Maresca, Spencer Oliver, Martin Sletzinger. The European participants who provided valuable help at various stages of my research include Jürgen Kalkbrenner, Consul General in Boston of the Federal Republic of Germany; Jaakko Laajava, head of the arms control and disarmament section of the Finnish Ministry of Foreign Affairs; Ingemar Lindahl, political counsellor of the Swedish Mission to the United Nations in New York; Björn Skala, Swedish minister in Paris. For incisive comment and criticism, I am indebted to the reviewers of the Duke University Press and to my colleagues from the Harvard University Seminar on European Society and Western Security, to whom I presented the draft of my introductory essay for discussion on January 30, 1986.

Boston University's Center for International Relations provided, as usual, an excellent research environment and superb clerical assistance, particularly from my secretary Kathi Kehoe. Stephanie Usry deserves gratitude for preparing the index in the very short time available to her. Finally, without the special patience, efficiency, and friendship of Richard Rowson, director of Duke University Press, this project could never have been completed on schedule.

Vojtech Mastny
Cambridge, Massachusetts

INTRODUCTION
The CSCE and Expansion of European Security

Ten years after the conclusion of the Helsinki Final Act, the Conference on Security and Cooperation in Europe (CSCE) has become a well-established feature of the international scene. Yet it remains widely ignored or misunderstood in the United States, which along with Canada is its only non-European participant. In view of America's extensive and growing involvements outside of Europe, this ignorance is perhaps understandable but hardly excusable. For the CSCE *is* important—ultimately because all the other participants *think* it is, and behave accordingly. To understand their reasons is to grasp some of the critical differences that distinguish the American and European thinking on security.

THE NONMILITARY ASPECTS OF SECURITY

Bearing the brunt of the East-West military competition, the United States has been more preoccupied than its allies with the balance sheet of troops and weapons. In contrast, the CSCE has been mainly about politics. Although some of the military aspects of security have figured on its agenda, the thrust of its deliberations has been toward nonmilitary questions. This may seem misguided in dealing with a continent loaded with weapons of mass destruction where the most powerful military forces the world has ever seen have been facing each other at the closest range. Yet, whether despite or because of this extraordinary situation, Europe has also been an eminently stable place, enjoying the longest period of peace in its history. And while this desirable condition should not be taken for granted, neither should it be forgotten that so long as military strength is not subjected to the ultimate test of war or otherwise directly employed in pursuit of political goals, other attributes of power tend to predominate in the actual conduct of international relations.

The CSCE has been addressing the nonmilitary aspects of security systematically and comprehensively for the first time. Employing the method of multinational diplomacy, it has posited the sovereign equality of all its thirty-five participating states. This formal equalization of the strong and the weak may seem evocative of some of the familiar deficiencies of the United Nations. Moreover, like the UN, the CSCE has been notable for its propensity to generate torrents of words and mountains of paper in many languages, quite apart from perpetuating a constituency of diplomats with a vested interest in such ostensibly inconsequential pursuits. Nor does the CSCE's requirement that all decisions be adopted by consensus expedite matters. And the agreements reached at this unique forum are not binding under international law, anyway.

Yet these appearances are deceptive of the actual performance of a mechanism that is in important ways more productive than the mechanism of the United Nations. Lacking a permanent institutional framework, the CSCE has certainly been far less expensive. At the UN the exclusive great power veto has tended to accentuate divisions; in the CSCE the universal consensus rule has fostered interests held in common. And the ingenious concept of a conference in stages, which requires agreement on one set of issues before proceeding to the next, has been conducive to thoroughness.[1] Though Byzantine, the system has made the negotiators almost "condemned to succeed."[2]

A CONFERENCE ABOUT POLITICS

Nor has the political rather than legal character of the Helsinki agreements—something that the United States, aware of the absence of an enforcement authority, has wisely favored—detracted from their value. Since they are statements of intent voluntarily arrived at, their fulfillment is a matter of political prestige and credibility rather than merely an exercise in finding legal loopholes. This has been particularly true about "human rights," the code words referring to all those nonmilitary and nonmaterial aspects of security that prompt governments to repress their citizens. How has this new prominence of human rights, which gives the CSCE its peculiar distinction, influenced their actual condition in East and West and the relations between the two parts of Europe that are the essence of its security?[3]

A rare conference on security matters that was not convened to resolve a crisis, the CSCE has made a virtue of its lacking a sense of urgency. It has taken time to look at problems that require time. Rather than a passing affair, it has evolved into a process. And, as is to be expected from a process extending over more than a decade, it has also changed by evolving. This book examines how much Helsinki in changing itself has changed the world around it.

I. The roots and results of Helsinki

The CSCE was originally a Soviet idea.[4] Quite secure militarily thanks to the favorable strategic position it had established in Europe as a result of its victory in World War II, the Soviet Union has nevertheless remained insecure for other reasons: the dubious legitimacy of its government unwilling to submit itself to approval by its constituents; the inherent fragility of its authoritarian procedures not upheld by the rule of law; the recurrent instability of its heterogeneous East European empire; the relative backwardness of its economy; the diminishing appeal of its ideological values. As a result, the Soviet rulers, while far from averse to the use of force as an instrument of policy, have also been exceptionally well-attuned to the nonmilitary aspects of security. These larger considerations determined their campaign for a European security conference ever since Foreign Minister Viacheslav M. Molotov had first proposed it soon after Stalin's death in 1953.

A PRODUCT OF DÉTENTE

Revived in the very different milieu of the latter 1960s, the campaign at first seemed an exercise in futility. The vague, verbose, and self-serving Soviet proposals for a European security system from which the United States would be excluded were too transparently designed to split NATO to be seriously considered. That they were nevertheless being advanced testified to Moscow's ever-present proclivity for wishful thinking, its reputed pragmatism notwithstanding. Only after the proposals dropped the demand for America's ejection from Europe did the onset of East-West détente give them a chance.

At the end of the 1960s, foremost among the forces of détente was West Germany's new Ostpolitik of Chancellor Willy Brandt. His principal aide, Egon Bahr, summed up its long-term objectives as "change through rapprochement." This strategy presupposed gradual transformation of the Soviet orbit in a manner more congenial to Western—and East European—preferences. For its part, Moscow envisaged in Western Europe internal developments (referred to as "social progress") conducive to the growth of Soviet power and influence.[5] These were ambiguous but ambitious bets, for they nibbled at the premises of the "Yalta system" of divided Europe on which the security of the continent was widely believed to be resting.

Unlike in the heyday of the Cold War, neither side defined its expectations in radical terms. Responsible Western officials rarely mentioned the wiping out of communism as a desirable goal—whatever communism meant after having become polycentric. Nor did Moscow harp on the supposed "general crisis of capitalism" that would send the enemy's walls crumbling down. Amid détente, the prospects were for the coexistence of the adversary political and social systems for as long as specific policies could be reasonably devised. In the early 1970s the conclusion of the set of treaties normalizing relations between West Germany and the Soviet bloc finally made the security conference topical.

LIMITED AMERICAN EXPECTATIONS

The United States valued the planned gathering considerably less than did most of its European allies. Reaffirming its preoccupation with the military rather than political determinants of East-West rivalry, Washington linked its consent to the CSCE with the convening in Vienna of talks on mutual and balanced reduction of conventional armed forces in Europe (MBFR), a forum presumably more germane to the substance of security. Yet the progress at Vienna soon proved negligible compared with the momentum the CSCE gathered once it had been launched at Helsinki in 1973 and continued at Geneva afterward. A casualty of the abortive linkage, the American attachment to the seemingly more promising but actually less productive MBFR accounted for Washington's low profile during most of the CSCE deliberations until 1975.

In a manner full of irony, Helsinki reversed the traditional stereotypes of American and European diplomacy. Henry Kissinger, America's first European-born secretary of state, injected into the U.S. policy his particular brand of European realpolitik that sought to incorporate the best of his two idols, Metternich and Castlereagh. And the West Europeans appropriated to themselves something of that American predilection for high-sounding but ineffectual phrases about peace and international cooperation, which was evocative of the worst of Woodrow Wilson and Franklin D. Roosevelt. Not until after the Helsinki process confounded the expectations of America and Europe alike would a middle ground between the two extremes be found.

SOVIET HOPES FOR SHAPING THE AGENDA

Having devised the conference, Moscow badly wanted it to succeed. General Secretary Leonid I. Brezhnev invested much of his personal prestige in it, viewing it as the crowning piece of his "peace program" and a major claim to fame in history. This alone was enough to make Washington worried lest the Russians somehow exploit the CSCE to their advantage. Most Europeans worried less; they saw, or perhaps merely sensed, an opportunity to turn the tables on Moscow. At issue was no more and no less than influencing perceptions of security at a time when a military confrontation in Europe, while always possible, had become considerably less probable. This rendered topical "contextual" security, which takes into account both the tangible and the intangible determinants of the international climate, and which, while no substitute for "substantive" military security, is its desirable outgrowth.[6]

In their quest for contextual security, Europeans in East and West agreed with Moscow, although their perspectives decidedly differed. They saw the time ripe for reasserting their international identity—less against the respective great power they had to heed than with its connivance. For its part, the Soviet Union sought to enhance its superpower status to become the arbiter of European security. It envisaged broad, general agreements that it could interpret at will rather than any precise, specific commitments that lesser nations could invoke for their protection. Hence Moscow originally advocated periodic follow-up conferences where the interpretation would presumably take place. The CSCE was also to be anchored to a permanent "consultative committee" that the Soviet Union could hope to dominate. By shaping the agenda of European security, the Soviets could more easily impose the terms of European security.[7]

There was nothing inherently sinister about this idea of an international *Ordnungsmacht*; a hundred years earlier, Bismarck's "satiated" Germany had performed that role admirably. But there was something disturbing about the same role being coveted by the Soviet Union, which did not act satiated. Its meddling in the 1973 Middle Eastern crisis, which all but provoked a clash with the United States, differed markedly from Bismarck's restraint in regions not vital to his country's security. Nor did Moscow's fishing in the troubled waters of revolutionary Portugal, where Western Europe's most fanatically pro-Soviet Communist party strove for power, indicate a spirit congenial to the conservative German statesman. And the self-appointed and self-perpetuating Soviet oligarchy, responsible only to itself in defining the interests of the state, made the prospect of its management of the European order more problematic still. After all, similar abuses of power, only less blatant, had been what eventually proved the undoing of Germany's benign international role under Bismarck's successors.

The CSCE therefore appropriately focused attention on the internal preconditions of Soviet security, or insecurity, which were subsumed under the rubric of human rights. And the more the attention became focused on this subject, the less interest did the Soviets show in the conference's institutionalization that they had initially envisaged. Instead, the idea of follow-up conferences came to be most vigorously embraced by some of the smaller countries, particularly Yugoslavia and others in the category of neutrals and nonaligned, which saw in a continuing process a guarantee of their greater say in matters of European security.[8]

Lacking the safeguards—and constraints—that accrue from membership in an alliance, these countries proved in important ways the CSCE's most faithful and creative constituents. Finland, perhaps the most faithful of all, introduced the concept of "sovereign equality," which entitled the participants to act and be treated as states in their own right rather than merely as members of the blocs. Romania, the member of the Warsaw pact most inclined to use this opportunity, would have preferred even stronger wording than the Finns. And the Swiss invented the "baskets," an arrangement of the agenda which insured that the specifics of human rights could be singled out for attention despite the Soviet penchant for generalities.[9]

At the preliminary procedural negotiations in the spring of 1973, Moscow reluctantly agreed to the "Basket Three" agenda of topics bearing on its domestic security—from the right of its citizens to emigrate to the free flow of information—that would subsequently dominate the Helsinki process. Having originally favored but a cursory, vague, and altogether noncommittal reference to the desirability of human contacts, the Soviet representatives became drawn into protracted and detailed discussions instead. During its Geneva stage, the conference that Brezhnev had hoped to finish quickly and climax in a glittering summit, with himself as the superstar, turned into a two-year diplomatic marathon instead. Branching off in different directions, it moved from the specific to the general rather than the reverse. Its outcome depended on the balance of its three baskets.[10]

THE THREE BASKETS DEFINED

The first included the central Soviet demand for a European settlement. This was to be met by the acceptance of general principles implying Western recognition of not only the territorial but, by extension, the political order that Moscow had imposed on Eastern Europe as a result of World War II. Anxious to protect the integrity of its domain, the

Soviet Union deemed inadequate the signatories' pledge to merely abstain from challenging the existing order by force. It pleaded additional need to insure the "inviolability" of frontiers, a formula intended to sanctify especially the division of Germany. In the semantic haggling that ensued, the Soviets defended the status quo, while the West tried to keep the door open for change.[11]

Basket One also contained military items of a special kind—the politically significant "confidence-building measures" aimed at reducing the suspicions that inhibit cooperation in security matters. Foremost among such measures was the call for advance notification of maneuvers that would make the use of military force for political pressure more difficult. The Soviet representatives accepted this originally Norwegian idea only after its implementation had been made voluntary—as if the whole of Helsinki had not been a voluntary test of goodwill. They initially argued that the military and political aspects of security were separate,[12] thus trying to shelter Moscow's expanding war machine from outside interference. Judging substantive military matters a superpower prerogative, the Soviet Union sought to keep them out of the multilateral Helsinki process—but only so long as the global trends appeared to favor the East.

Basket Two addressed East-West economic relations. It impinged directly on military security in the Soviet demand for the abolition of Western restrictions on strategic exports, an area of considerable disagreement between the United States and its allies and hence open to exploitation by Moscow. For the Soviet Union, the ultimate prize was easier access to the economic bounties of the West, particularly high technology, without a political price to pay. Although Helsinki did not prompt the upsurge of East-West trade that had been under way ever since the onset of détente, it brought the political implications of expanded economic contacts into sharper focus.

The contacts also raised the question of greater accessibility of the Soviet bloc to Western businessmen inhibited by its excessive regulations. The CSCE introduced the useful distinction between "structural" obstacles to trade, which the communist regimes could not afford to dismantle without risking their stability, and "contingent" obstacles, which presumably entailed no such risk.[13] The larger issue was the influence that the free, open, and stronger economic system of the West could exert on the regimented, secretive, and weaker system of the East, a question all the more important because of the intimate relationship between economic and political control in communist states.

The discussion about the third basket vibrated the most with "innovative tension," resulting from efforts to reconcile Europe's traditions of freedom with its present realities.[14] The debate on human rights was introduced by Austria, the country that had established its reputation as the continent's foremost haven for refugees. The debate then received its particular thrust thanks to the contribution of Italy, which focused attention on the relevance of individuals to relations among states.[15] This countered the excessive preoccupation of nations with security rather than with order, a tendency evident since their consensus on a generally acceptable international order had disintegrated during the twentieth century. At the CSCE, the West linked the security of states with the security of the individuals that compose them, and the security of the individuals with the free development of their personalities.

FUNDAMENTAL ISSUES BETWEEN EAST AND WEST

Moscow's alternative version dwelt on the security of the state or, more precisely, of its ruling elite. Linking security with international cooperation, the Soviets pleaded their supposed "right to equal security"—as if a government as prolific in making enemies as theirs were entitled to special consideration for having to deal with the consequences. The May 1972 American-Soviet declaration on the principles of mutual relations had all but conceded this specious "right";[16] the CSCE did not. It more aptly addressed the causes of insecurity inherent in the Soviet system.

To protect itself from international scrutiny, Moscow invoked the principle of nonintervention. Generally understood as referring to the use or threat of force, the Russian term is conveniently undifferentiated from noninterference, thus presumably extending to political intercourse as well.[17] At Helsinki, Soviet Deputy Foreign Minister Valerian A. Zorin insisted that human contacts across national boundaries are fully subordinated to the relations between states.[18] He was suggesting that in their pragmatic pursuit of foreign policy, sovereign governments might foster such contacts at their discretion but without deference to any higher principle.

Craving to be accepted as a European power, the Soviet Union nevertheless could not afford to reject outright the libertarian postulates cherished by peoples on both sides of the ideological divide. Even in trying to nullify them, it felt compelled to pay lip service to them. In this, the language of liberty it spoke at Helsinki was truly the tribute that tyranny is obliged to pay freedom. Rather than opposing the principles, the Soviets were exploring loopholes. They sought qualifying phrases to limit compliance to "mutually agreed measures," resisting Western demands for "new ways and means" to promote human rights.[19] Although the debates seemed arcane, the issues were fundamental, for Western critics of Helsinki argued that bestowing legitimacy on the tyranny in the East put the values of freedom in the West at peril.[20]

At the CSCE, those values proved resilient enough to generate the necessary unity of purpose among West Europeans, increasingly accustomed to cooperate in many fields. Now their need to act as an entity in dealing with the economic issues of Basket Two prompted the nine member states of the Common Market to coordinate their policies in other areas as well.[21] As a result, they, rather than the United States, emerged as the Soviet Union's opposite number during the crucial Geneva negotiations. Basket Three was largely their accomplishment.

But the United States was indispensable in bringing this accomplishment to fruition. It had to assume an active role by dealing directly with the other superpower before final agreement could be reached. In February 1975, Kissinger and Andrei A. Gromyko, his Soviet counterpart, laid the groundwork in bilateral talks. The result was a compromise about frontiers that satisfied both the Soviet yearning for their inviolability and the Western desire for peaceful change.[22] It made the key Helsinki bargain between Basket One and Basket Three possible.

AN OPEN-ENDED FINAL ACT

In the Final Act, signed on August 1, 1975, the West pledged its respect for the geopolitical realities Moscow deemed essential for its security. For its part, the Soviet Union subscribed to texts that made its domestic conduct a legitimate subject of international scrutiny. It received a better title to something it already had—control of its East European empire. But the West was given a means to facilitate transformation of that empire. The distinction was between the static and the dynamic components of the Final Act, between present and future deliveries, between security as a condition to be achieved and security as a process to be maintained, between an order built on power alone and an order with justice.[23] An open-ended product of unconventional diplomacy, Helsinki was the beginning rather than an end.

A contest in contextual rather than substantive security, Helsinki could not satisfy critics inclined to mistake Soviet military strength for real strength. Concerned about the effects of such setbacks as the oil embargo and the Vietnam debacle on Western self-confidence, such critics saw the contest inevitably redounding to Moscow's advantage simply because of its determination to seek the advantage—as if the Soviets also had been gaining in the struggle of ideas.[24] Alone among the chiefs of state assembled to sign the Final Act, Austrian Chancellor

Bruno Kreisky welcomed the "clarification . . . that coexistence . . . cannot be understood as being valid for the ideological sphere." Echoing Brezhnev's challenge that détente did not preclude increased competition in that sphere, Kreisky expressed the belief that the "democratic states are also firmly determined to obtain a bigger and bigger breakthrough for the idea of democracy."[25]

Profoundly Western in letter and in spirit, the Final Act did not warrant Moscow's claiming Helsinki as a triumph of its diplomacy.[26] The Soviets hailed the outcome as the substitute for the European peace settlement that had failed to take place after World War II and as framework for the progress of détente as they understood it: a gradual but irreversible shift in the international "correlation of forces" in their favor under the conditions of low rather than high tension. But doubts evidently lingered when barely two months later the Soviets deemed it necessary to reaffirm their interpretation of the "inviolability of frontiers" by a special treaty with East Germany. As a guarantee of East German security, the treaty ignored Helsinki, citing only Soviet determination to uphold the integrity of the "socialist commonwealth"— the "Brezhnev doctrine."[27]

THE HISTORIC TURN OF EVENTS

In its concern with territorial safeguards, Moscow misjudged the real thrust of Helsinki: the destabilizing potential of Basket Three for domestic politics. The Soviets had apparently taken its provisions as so many empty words that no one could seriously expect them to honor. They seemed genuinely surprised when those words did assume political substance when invoked by dissidents throughout the Soviet bloc as a charter of human rights.[28] Although not all of the new ferment could be directly attributed to Helsinki, its growth reversed the pattern of quiescence that had prevailed in the region before. And while the scope of dissent would subsequently fluctuate from country to country, the aftermath of the accords certainly disproved the prediction that they would strengthen Moscow's hold on its empire.[29]

This historic turn of events highlighted the CSCE's relevance to societies rather than merely to states, thus establishing in reality the connection between international and domestic order that the Final Act had proclaimed in theory. The effect was all the more remarkable since the individualistic Western concepts of freedom that inspired the Helsinki principles did not necessarily conform with the prevalent traditions of political culture in a part of Europe where individual rights and obligations had been more typically derived from belonging to a group.[30] The regimes in the Soviet bloc, to be sure, did not terminate their repressive policies. Given the nature of the Final Act as a declaration of intent rather than a legally binding document, the West therefore faced the problem of whether it should insist on compliance and, if so, how. Having so adroitly set the Helsinki process in motion, the West Europeans were not so adequately equipped to manage its destabilizing consequences; neither was the United States immediately ready to do so.

Whatever the mounting East-West strains—already in March 1976 President Gerald Ford formally banned the word "détente" from his vocabulary—Kissinger at least concurred with the Moscow view in regarding the CSCE as an exclusive concern of governments. In the spring of 1976 the revelation of the "Sonnenfeldt doctrine" further seemed to confirm the administration's unwillingness to tamper with the internal problems of the Soviet empire.[31] The loose language of this confidential statement by the State Department counselor at a briefing of American ambassadors in London could be read as suggesting that Soviet hegemony in Eastern Europe was indispensable for international stability, although Sonnenfeldt rather meant the opposite. Nor did the president's subsequent gaffe about Poland's alleged independence during his television debate with Jimmy Carter show a keen appreciation of what that hegemony really means.[32] In Europe, what the Viennese wit dubbed the "Brezhfeldt doctrine" came to epitomize the shortcomings of the American realpolitik that Helsinki sought to mitigate, particularly Washington's preference for dealing with Moscow bilaterally rather than multilaterally.

THE UNITED STATES BECOMES CHAMPION OF HELSINKI

American critics, too, deplored what they perceived as the administration's excessive readiness to ignore the plight of Soviet dissidents for the sake of businesslike relations with Moscow. The new public concern for human rights had already produced in 1974 the Jackson-Vanik Amendment that made American trade concessions contingent on liberalized Soviet emigration policies. The growing congressional influence on the conduct of foreign affairs, precipitated by the government's mismanagement of the Vietnam war, could be praised or condemned but not ignored. It was this new fact of political life, sharpened by the president's domestic exigencies, that transformed the United States into a vigorous champion of Helsinki. Among those exigencies during Ford's campaign for reelection was his need for votes in New Jersey whose congressional representative, Millicent Fenwick, headed the campaign to make Moscow observe the Final Act. Supported by New Jersey Senator Clifford P. Case, she was the force behind the establishment in 1976 of the Commission on Security and Cooperation in Europe.[33]

Consisting of members not only from the House and Senate but also from the executive branch, this unique creation embodied the expanded concept of security prompted by the CSCE. It was an institutional expression of the Helsinki notion that the multiple facets of security required attention not only from governments but also from individual citizens. The administration initially tried to resist this novel idea, reasoning that implementation of the CSCE requirements was sufficiently served by diplomatic means and resenting the commission as an unwarranted invasion of the executive's constitutional prerogatives in the conduct of foreign policy.[34] Kissinger even reportedly colluded with Soviet Ambassador Anatolii Dobrynin to have Soviet visas denied to commission members traveling to Europe to monitor the observance of the Final Act on the spot.[35]

Confounding the expectations of both friend and foe, the CSCE had in less than a year established beyond any doubt the linkage between human rights and international order. This certainly made matters more difficult for governments, which had to worry about the consequences for policy, but it did not discourage growing numbers of people on both sides of the Atlantic, who bore no such responsibilities, from strengthening the linkage. The notion that sovereign states be held accountable for the treatment of their own citizens to other sovereign states and their citizens amounted to nothing short of a revolutionary innovation in the conduct of international relations. As the détente that had bred it continued to crumble, the question remained whether the innovation would last and to what effect. The future of Helsinki depended on the answers.

II. Human rights, trade, and security

No sooner did Basket Three reveal its destabilizing potential than the Soviet Union set out to divert the Helsinki process in a more harmless direction. Taking the otherwise unexceptionable position that no principles of the Final Act may be emphasized at the expense of others, it in fact singled out for special attention the economic provisions of Basket Two. This conveyed the Marxist notion that material things come first and ideas only second; the Soviet motives, however, were more pragmatic than ideological.[36]

THE SOVIET EMPHASIS ON BASKET TWO

As early as December 1975, Brezhnev in a speech in Warsaw proposed to enhance the CSCE by convening under its auspices special conferences on energy, transportation, and environmental protection.[37] Their relevance to security was tangential but not unimportant. The first concerned the rare area of economic endeavor where the Soviet Union possessed real strength because of its ability to make European countries substantially dependent on its supplies of oil, natural gas, and electricity. The second topic was germane to the increased penetration of Western markets by low-cost transport enterprises of the Soviet bloc, particularly in maritime shipping, movement of goods on inland waterways, and trucking. Finally, a conference on environmental protection—a topic of special appeal to those segments of Western public opinion that were usually also opposed to high defense spending—promised to make advanced Western conservation technology more readily available to the East where the destruction of the environment proceeded at an even faster pace than in the West. Of the projected conferences, only one on transboundary pollution actually took place, though not as part of the Helsinki process.[38]

The Soviet Union and its allies had always shown greater interest than their Western partners in East-West trade. The tiny share that the Soviet bloc held in the total volume of world trade indicated how much more the East needed the West than vice versa in economic terms. However, for some Western countries, such as West Germany, trading with the East was less dispensable than for others. And for some individual firms and businessmen, it could actually seem to be of considerable merit.[39] Inclined to put business above politics and free to do so, they were sometimes the "soft underbelly of freedom"[40] predisposed in favor of the Soviet-style stability that Helsinki sought to alter.

Moscow lured West Europeans as their supposedly "natural" supplier of energy, positing a contrast between its reliability and American unpredictability. It campaigned at international forums that were lacking a human rights dimension, particularly the United Nations Economic Commission for Europe.[41] It also sought closer links between COMECON, the Soviet bloc's agency for economic cooperation, and the Common Market. But the disparity of needs, quite apart from the incompatibility of a free association of sovereign nations and a device for the regimentation of dependent ones, inhibited accord.[42]

THE DISPUTED ECONOMIC LEVERAGE

As long as prospects of substantial economic benefits accruing from détente remained open, the Soviet Union abstained from jeopardizing them by too drastic new steps defying the Helsinki human rights provisions. It even facilitated in small ways the flow of information mandated by the Final Act—by making life somewhat less difficult for

Western correspondents and by making Western newspapers somewhat less inaccessible to Soviet citizens.[43] And while indignantly rejecting the conditions stipulated by the Jackson-Vanik Amendment, it in effect took them into account by keeping the levels of emigration, particularly Jewish emigration, higher than before. But enough other violations of Basket Three persisted to keep alive the debate about how the West might use its economic leverage to promote human rights in the East.[44]

The debate remained inconclusive because the pluralistic Western societies could never manage to consistently apply leverage to the Soviet superpower, for which trade with the West was only desirable, not imperative. The situation was different with those countries of Eastern Europe that depended more extensively on East-West trade. Among them, Romania could always be moved to improve its deplorable human rights performance at the eleventh hour whenever Congress during its annual reviews threatened to terminate its most-favored-nation status in trading with the United States.[45] Other communist regimes also were disposed to trade human rights for material rewards, notably emigration permits for specified amounts of cash. They tended to be the regimes, like East Germany and Cuba, that combined a relatively high degree of domestic repression with a relatively active foreign policy.

THE CARTER ADMINISTRATION'S PURSUIT OF HUMAN RIGHTS

The Helsinki process took a new turn with the advent in January 1977 of the Carter administration, committed to integrate human rights objectives into the formulation and execution of American foreign policy. This commitment influenced the concept of differentiation between the Soviet Union and Eastern Europe, as well as among the countries of Eastern Europe, which presumed their independence as sovereign states—the useful fiction that President Ford had found too subtle to grasp in his campaign remark about Poland. Previously, the extent of the Eastern bloc nations' dissociation from the Soviet Union had been the overriding consideration; under the influence of Carter's Polish-born national security adviser, Zbigniew Brzezinski, the new administration placed greater emphasis on the Helsinki requirement of maintaining minimum standards of decency in the Eastern nations' domestic conduct.[46]

Accordingly, Washington singled out for special attention not so much the increasingly repressive Romania as Hungary and Poland, whose human rights records at the time were the best. Romania's semi-independent foreign policy had been yielding fewer tangible dividends to the West or the Romanian people—as distinguished from the ruling autocracy—nor was there reason to expect a change for the better. Such a change could well be expected in regard to Poland and Hungary, despite their toeing the Soviet line in foreign policy. The president's state visit to Warsaw and the ceremonial return by the United States of the Crown of St. Stephen to Hungary underlined this expectation.[47]

In its quest for diversity, Washington did not neglect Moscow's staunchest allies, who also happened to be the worst human rights violators. In March 1979, bilateral talks with the GDR prepared the ground for the later expansion of U.S. relations with this increasingly self-confident Soviet ally. As a follow-up to the CSCE, similar talks took place with the Bulgarians, who were eager to counter their reputation as Moscow's most subservient clients.[48] Only the relations with Czechoslovakia, which more properly deserved that subservient reputation, remained notoriously bad, even after the American return of its gold seized by the Nazis in World War II. In its disregard of Helsinki, the Czechoslovak regime was second only to the Soviets, and the language of its CSCE representatives, who preferred to deliver their speeches in Russian, was usually at least as abusive.

THE EFFECTS ON EASTERN EUROPE

In Poland the rise of Solidarity in 1980 amply justified the expectation of change, the country's later relapse into repression notwithstanding. So did subsequent developments in Hungary and East Germany, which in 1984 together reaffirmed their interest in salvaging their Western contacts while the Soviet Union was doing the opposite. Their insistence that smaller countries in both parts of Europe have a special role to play in keeping détente alive precisely at a time of high tension between the superpowers rang the authentic note of Helsinki. Moscow rejected the theory but tolerated the practice.[49]

On this increasingly diversified East European scene, the correlation between human rights and security was by no means straightforward.[50] Of the two countries with the best human rights standing in the 1970s, Hungary and Poland, the former was perhaps the most secure because of the degree of legitimacy its pragmatic regime enjoyed in the eyes of its people. But the latter was, on the contrary, the most insecure because of the rising tide of discontent its demoralized establishment had to face. Moreover, both the increasingly secure East German leadership and the perennially insecure Czechoslovak one had execrable human rights records. And regarding the two communist states of Eastern Europe that—apart from Albania—had distanced themselves the most from Moscow, the record was deteriorating in both the autocratic, stable Romania and the pluralistic, shaky Yugoslavia.

This elusive correlation between human rights and security could not resolve the debate about whether quiet diplomacy or public confrontation better served the cause of human rights; the answer evidently depended on the time and place.[51] Rendered topical by the approaching CSCE review conference at Belgrade, the debate was a variation on the theme of whether making Moscow feel more secure or insecure caused it to be more accommodating. Most advocates of quiet diplomacy tended to favor the first answer, their opponents the second, while the latter interpretation was also more likely to be heard from Americans—and East European dissidents—than from West Europeans. The differences in outlook permeated Belgrade.

THE BELGRADE REVIEW CONFERENCE

In the early stages of the conference the Soviets gave the impression that they might consider concessions on Basket Three if induced by Western concessions on Basket Two.[52] But by then human rights had become too much of a public issue to be so traded, and no bargaining ensued. Instead, the conference evolved into a confrontation about the Soviet violations of the Final Act, which prevented consensus on any but a brief and unsubstantive concluding document.[53] This meager outcome raised questions about the wisdom of "roasting the bear in Belgrade," as one American journalist characterized the Soviet predicament there.[54]

This retrospective criticism was aimed at the conduct of the chief United States representative, Arthur Goldberg, whom the Carter administration unexpectedly dispatched to Belgrade after the preparatory first stage of the conference. His confrontational posture conveyed the preferences of the key members of the Congressional Helsinki Commission and of Brzezinski, who had commissioned a special study about the merits of confrontation for the National Security Council.[55] But neither had the idea of a thorough and critical review of the Soviet human rights abuses elicited disapproval from America's European allies with whom Washington had consulted in advance. Before Goldberg's arrival, when career diplomat Albert W. Sherer was still presiding over the U.S. delegation, the French, Canadians, British, and Dutch exceeded the Americans in castigating Moscow.[56]

Goldberg, a distinguished jurist and advocate of public causes but not a professional diplomat, initially appeared to some of his Belgrade audience more conciliatory than expected. He became more outspoken later, but still less so than would be his successor at the Madrid conference, Max Kampelman. Goldberg's tone did not always contrast with that of other Western delegates; their pronouncements, however, often went unreported, while those of the chief U.S. representative invariably

attracted attention. And even critics conceded that the Soviets overreacted to his strictures.[57]

It was not so much the manner of Goldberg's criticism of the Russians as the conditions in his delegation that mattered. He and Sherer,
now his deputy, were hardly on speaking terms. Beyond personal differences, there was the deeper difficulty of reconciling the two requirements of the semipublic Helsinki process: the expertise of professional
diplomats necessary to manage it and the commitment of concerned
citizens indispensable to consummate it. Alone among the participating
nations, the American delegation included a large contingent of "public" members, representing the nation's extraordinary variety of pressure
groups concerned with human rights in general and their fate in the
East in particular. The role of these part-time diplomats next to the
full-time professionals was never adequately defined.[58]

Regrettable though it was, the disarray within the U.S. delegation
did not fully explain the Americans' growing isolation at Belgrade.
More important were the differences of outlook that became evident
once the prospect of the conference's failure began to loom. This was
something that most Europeans simply found more painful to contemplate than most Americans, even though they realized that the blame
was of Soviet origin. They were outraged at Moscow's contention that
Helsinki entitled each country to review only its own record of compliance. And they were under no illusion that the staging during the conference of a show trial of Czechoslovak dissidents was anything but a
deliberate provocation. They still would have preferred, as the Soviets
always did, to concentrate on the CSCE's "positive" accomplishments,
and they were profoundly disappointed when hardly any such accomplishments could be registered.[59]

A MEAGER HARVEST

Having pressed hard for a substantive concluding document, the neutrals and nonaligned were the most disappointed. Switzerland's chief
delegate, Rudolf Bindschedler, an authority on international law, estimated the conference was a 99 percent failure and only a 1 percent
success.[60] The latter reference was to the agreement to meet again in
another two years, which alone qualified as something definite in a
strictly legal sense. But the CSCE was about politics, not law. Taking the
view that negotiation had not been the main purpose, the Carter administration praised the political value of publicly airing Soviet noncompliance. The value was in impressing on Moscow that the times had
passed when the domestic misconduct of governments was their own
affair.[61]

The Soviets, though the ones who had been on trial, did not altogether deprecate the results of Belgrade either. They regarded the preservation of the Helsinki process as a positive accomplishment, for which they claimed credit. Their human rights performance did not immediately plummet, thus defying the theory that public criticism of it is always counterproductive. Indeed, the meager harvest of the conference was due not so much to anything that happened there as to the decline of détente that was accelerating for other reasons. As the chief Yugoslav delegate, Milorad Pešić, observed, "the CSCE process cannot be carried on outside the context of the existing political, military, and other realities in Europe."[62]

THE DECLINE OF DÉTENTE

This critical connection was confirmed at the first CSCE meeting of experts, convened in October 1978 at Montreux to discuss procedures for peaceful settlement of disputes, a subject particularly close to the hearts of the Swiss and other neutrals. The conference revealed an insuperable conflict between the Western advocacy of compulsory arbitration and the Soviet insistence on compulsory consultation. Opposed to having its freedom of action limited by any procedural framework it could not control, Moscow was thus seeking a means to control others whom it would be able to force into consultations whenever it deemed security to be threatened. As with its earlier proposal for the CSCE "consultative committee," such consultations would enable the Soviet Union to set the agenda and dominate the proceedings. Bearing on the very essence of Europe's power relations, Montreux predictably failed, and six years later a follow-up meeting at Athens buried the subject by adjourning without even so much as an agreement to meet again.[63]

As East-West tension continued to mount, thus further reducing Moscow's incentives to accommodate Western sensibilities, the Soviet human rights record took a decisive turn for the worse in 1979, one year after Belgrade.[64] The best indication was the precipitous decline of Jewish emigration, which, as a critical issue in relations with the United States, had until then served as something of a showpiece of Soviet compliance. The systematic repression of dissidents that followed did not preclude occasional concessions in individual cases. In accordance with the Soviet view, however, these concessions were determined by the momentary exigencies of Moscow's relations with particular countries rather than by any greater respect for the philosophy of the Final Act. Indeed, if the progress of human rights in the Soviet realm were the only measure, by 1980 Helsinki would have had to be judged a failure.

PREPARATIONS FOR THE SECOND REVIEW CONFERENCE

But regardless of the plight of the dissidents, the approaching second review conference, scheduled to meet in Madrid in November 1980, indicated if anything a growing relevance of human rights to the conduct of international relations. More Eastern European activists addressed their pleas for intercession to Madrid than to Belgrade.[65] And the growing numbers of their Western sympathizers were more successful than before in spotlighting the situation in the East.[66] All these activities helped shape the negotiating positions of the Western allies who, judging the forthcoming conference as an important test of their solidarity, consulted to coordinate their policies more effectively. So did the neutrals and nonaligned, although, unlike the members of the two blocs, they did not arrive in Madrid with a common strategy.

The abiding importance of the human rights issue could be judged by Moscow's prodigious effort to prevent its performance from being examined at Madrid. During the preparatory meetings the Soviet representatives used elaborate procedural maneuvers to whittle away at the time allotted to the review of implementation. Instead they urged that the time be used for discussing new proposals, thus enabling them to seek modifications of the provisions their government did not wish to honor.[67] The dispute marked a reversal of roles since 1975, when the Soviet Union had hailed the accomplishment while the West had put its hopes in evolution; with evolution now justifying its hopes, the West tried to consolidate its gains while Moscow did its best to undo them.

In the fall of 1980 the future of the Helsinki process seemed in jeopardy. The Soviets cultivated the impression that their cooperation in keeping the process alive should not be taken for granted. And in the United States the presidential election had brought victory to Ronald Reagan, who had publicly expressed his doubts about the expediency of American participation.[68] But the danger to the CSCE, as it had been before and would be again, was more apparent than real.

The eventual solution to the impasse was bizarre. When even stopping the clock in the meeting hall the day before the scheduled opening of the conference failed to produce agreement on the agenda, Spanish Foreign Minister José Pedro Pérez Llorca proceeded to declare the conference open anyway. He thus implemented the Belgrade consensus that the Soviet Union was unable to block. This fait accompli soon led to a compromise about the agenda, which, by allowing six weeks for the discussion on implementation, amounted to a Western victory. The NATO states also unilaterally reserved to themselves the right to extend the discussion if new violations were to occur later, as it indeed happened.[69]

Although formally launched, the Madrid conference nevertheless faced an uncertain future. The neutrals and nonaligned who, more than the NATO group, saw the CSCE's main merit in communication rather than in castigation were especially chagrined. For it was obvious—although among the Warsaw Pact members only Hungary was prepared to admit it[70]—that the communist states could not afford to implement Basket Three without endangering their domestic security. And the neutrals and nonaligned tended to believe more strongly than others that Moscow must feel secure to be benevolent.

No Western nation had more of a vested interest in fostering Soviet benevolence than Finland. At Madrid it submitted a proposal to strengthen the CSCE by creating a standing committee that would meet regularly between the review conferences.[71] This again echoed the Soviet idea of a "consultative committee," with its concomitant suggestion of Moscow's acting as a privileged, though presumably benevolent, guarantor of the European order. Such a prospect could have possibly served to enhance Finland's precarious security; it would certainly have diminished the security of countries less dependent on Soviet goodwill. In any case, the diminishing evidence of that goodwill made the neutrals' independent role in the CSCE increasingly difficult.

With détente dealt a coup de grâce by the Soviet invasion of Afghanistan and by the incoming Reagan administration's refusal to resuscitate it, little but hostile dialogue took place in the Spanish capital. Yet even that dialogue was important at a time of rising tension when other channels of communication were being severed; the CSCE remained the unique forum where any concern could be aired. However, the Soviet military buildup that the United States now vowed to match added particular prominence to the arms race at the expense of other aspects of security. After the successful trade-off of Basket One for Basket Three and the unsuccessful trade-off of Basket Two, the efficacy of the Helsinki process as a vehicle for human rights now depended on whether its "militarization" could be avoided.

III. Helsinki in the shadow of military rivalry

Back in 1973 the Soviets had tried to exclude military matters from the CSCE by insisting that the military and political aspects of security are separate. But no sooner did détente begin to unravel than they ardently began to advocate a supposed enhancement of the Helsinki process by including in it so-called "military détente."[72] This postulated an international climate that would compel the West to reduce its military outlays drastically and by necessity, while making the Soviet Union comfortable enough to reduce its own armaments only moderately and by choice. Moscow would thus be better able to enjoy the political benefits of the massive military investment it had undertaken at the time when America's resources and morale were being dissipated by the effects of the Vietnam war.

SOVIET INTEREST IN "MILITARY DÉTENTE"

The initial Soviet opposition to talking about military matters at the CSCE conveyed the sound view that the conference should not duplicate the Vienna talks on Mutual and Balanced Force Reduction. The United States and France, too, had wanted to keep these ventures separate, though each for different reasons. Considering the MBFR the more substantive of the two, the United States had hoped to achieve progress there in return for agreeing to the Soviet CSCE project. In contrast, France had viewed the MBFR as a superpower forum discriminating against the lesser powers, among which she arguably stood out as the greatest.

As the tenuous link between the CSCE and MBFR withered away, the former assuming a dynamic life of its own and the latter lapsing into stupor, Moscow's advocacy of military détente took on another dimension. In their quest to render harmless the human rights postulates of the Final Act, the Soviets maintained that détente was the precondition of compliance.[73] They implied that only if the West accepted their version of détente—which meant acquiescence to expanded use of Soviet military power for political gain from Angola to Afghanistan—could they be reasonably expected to feel secure enough to begin honoring their Helsinki commitments. Soviet spokesmen therefore consistently rejected the reverse Western argument that without compliance with those commitments there could be no détente.

In the later Carter years and especially under the Reagan presidency, when the United States responded to the Soviet military challenge by a massive armaments program of its own, Moscow's pursuit of military topics in the CSCE finally became mainly significant as an attempt to hamper the resurgence of NATO defense efforts. The foremost Soviet aim at Madrid was to convene under CSCE auspices a "Conference on Military Détente and Disarmament in Europe" where topics relevant to the effort would be introduced in a manner suitable to turn the West Europeans against the U.S. policy. To be included were such politically enticing themes as the abolition of the "capitalist" neutron weapon—which kills people but keeps property intact—nuclear-free zones, and nuclear freeze.

To gain consent for the conference, Moscow signaled a readiness to bargain about human rights, thus highlighting the third type of a CSCE linkage, next to those concerned with territorial settlement and East-West trade. But there was not much to be said for the idea of making better treatment by the Soviet government of its own citizens contingent on Western concessions of a military nature, thus in effect holding the dissidents "hostages to détente."[74] Nor did the proposed intrusion of the intractable disarmament agenda into the delicate Helsinki process augur well for Helsinki's future health. Throughout the conference, Western representatives took turns impressing on the Soviet Union how much its abuse of military power, notably in Afghanistan, damaged the climate of East-West relations essential for that health to thrive.[75]

THE IMPACT OF AFGHANISTAN

Even before Madrid, Afghanistan had cast a shadow over the CSCE's Scientific Forum, convened in Hamburg in February 1980. Both security and human rights permeated the key topic of scientific exchanges, which the United States had curtailed to protest the Soviet aggression. Moscow valued the exchanges as a means of gaining access to Western science and technology for the price of tolerating strictly controlled activities of Western exchange scholars, preferably in the humanities. At the forum the Eastern concept of science as a subject of governmental policies clashed with Western insistence on free inquiry. But so eager were the Soviets to salvage the exchanges from the wreckage of Afghanistan that in the conference's final document they endorsed an explicit reference to human rights as a prerequisite for scientific progress.[76]

Afghanistan expanded the relevance of Helsinki. Having adopted the principles of the Final Act without geographical limitations, the signatories had also opened to each other's scrutiny their policies outside of Europe. By incorporating the principles into its 1976 constitution, the Soviet Union itself had unwittingly strengthened their universal validity as standards of international conduct.[77] Certainly the subsequent emergence of the CSCE as a stage where Moscow's own misconduct was being exposed and branded before an attentive international audience finally disposed of the fallacy that Helsinki was somehow playing into Soviet hands.

If at Belgrade candor had still been apt to raise many a Western eyebrow, at Madrid its merits were more readily appreciated. Max Kampelman, the U.S. delegation chief, won respect and admiration despite, or possibly because of, his candid eloquence. No conference may be belittled as insignificant that is capable of inspiring superior oratory, and the CSCE abounded in it. Kampelman's condemnation of the Soviet annexation of the Baltic states in 1940—which the United States had specifically exempted from its Helsinki recognition of the status quo[78]—was but one of many examples:

> I am well aware that the Soviet Union calls itself a "socialist" state and that by definition, *its* definition, it can never be guilty of imperialism, regardless of what it may do. There is an American saying: "If it walks like a duck, talks like a duck, and looks like a duck—it's a duck." Some may wish to call the duck a goose, or a chicken, Mr. Chairman. But it's still a duck. The acts of aggression against the three Baltic states were acts of imperialism.[79]

Nor did the Soviets, habitually given to invective in their own political pronouncements, find its use by the West an insuperable obstacle to dialogue. At Belgrade they had already reciprocated the censure of their human rights abuses by reciting alleged Western violations rather than merely taking shelter behind the Final Act's noninterference clause.[80] By accepting the challenge, they reconfirmed the Helsinki proposition that human rights are indeed everybody's business.

THE NEW WESTERN SOLIDARITY

At Madrid the West spoke more often with a single voice than at Belgrade. In its critique of Soviet implementation, the United States could count on active support from not only its traditionally close allies, among whom especially the British and the Dutch minced no words, but also from France. The growing Western solidarity at the CSCE reflected the drastic deterioration of the Soviet image among Europeans in which the Helsinki concern for human rights had played a significant role. No longer a specialty of the Right, anti-Sovietism had been embraced with gusto by the Left as well. But in addition to Moscow's conduct, the West's willingness to apply the Helsinki yardstick to its own human rights record—the United States, for example, publicized both its achievements and shortcomings in a massive congressional publication[81]—had contributed to this historic change. And nowhere was the change more striking than in France, whose newly elected socialist government of President François Mitterand found its views of the Soviet threat compatible with those of the Reagan administration.

When Kenneth Adelman, in September 1980, described Madrid as a congenial place for the nation's "fiery pro-Americanism that cries for manifestation," his was still the voice of a prophet in the wilderness among American conservatives.[82] Reagan himself had yet to be converted. Once in power, however, his administration proved more adept than its predecessors in managing the Helsinki process in the West's best interest. Already the reconfirmation of Kampelman as the chief U.S. representative attested to the grasp of the CSCE's importance by an administration otherwise not noted for its disposition to keep Carter's political appointees in office.

The confluence of French and American views made the plan for a disarmament conference that Paris had originally conceived to supersede the MBFR into a suitable means to resist the attempted Soviet transformation of Helsinki into a "peace" forum. Endorsed by Washington within a month after Reagan's inauguration, the plan anticipated a conference in two stages. Substantive progress on the "binding, verifiable, and militarily significant" confidence-building measures that the West desired was made a precondition for the disarmament discussion coveted by Moscow. But the French envisaged a discussion limited to conventional weapons.[83] This distinguished their proposal from a Swedish variant, whose suggestion to include nuclear arms was closer to the Soviet than to the NATO position.[84]

THE THREAT TO POLAND

In 1980–81 the threat of Moscow's military intervention in Poland, implied in the Soviet troop movements along its borders, dramatized the practical importance of confidence-building measures, while the Madrid condemnations of the Afghanistan aggression conveyed the warning to desist.[85] In more than one way the Polish upheaval was an offspring of the Helsinki spirit and an object lesson in the primacy of political security in contemporary Europe.[86] As elsewhere in Eastern Europe, Helsinki had fostered dissent in Poland; more than elsewhere, the country's opposition had been gaining ground against an increasingly demoralized ruling establishment. The demoralization was closely related to the East-West economic interaction that Helsinki was also meant to foster. By borrowing Western money without restraint and then squandering it with breathtaking incompetence, Poland's rulers were given a unique opportunity to demonstrate their inability to rule. The demonstration did not prompt the Solidarity opposition to supplant the regime but rather to influence its exercise of power by imposing certain standards on it. And foremost among these were the standards of the Final Act, which Solidarity demanded to be printed and disseminated throughout the nation as a charter of its rights.[87]

At no time during the crisis were considerations of military security superior to those of political security. The presence of Soviet garrisons in the country was all but irrelevant to the course of events. Nor did Poland's demise as an effective member of the Warsaw Pact, while painful and humiliating to the Soviets, upset Europe's military balance. Indeed, an armed intervention would have only accentuated the liability that Poland was for Moscow. By keeping the Polish developments in the limelight at Madrid while avoiding any suggestion of seeking military advantage, the West may have marginally helped to deter the Soviet temptation to invade. Yet all this did not prevent the coup by Polish generals, which Moscow abetted but the generals had their own political reasons to execute.

The imposition of martial law in Poland on December 10, 1981, plunged the csce into the worst crisis of its existence.[88] The immediate casualty was the almost completed draft of a concluding document. The more important gain was a demonstration of how deeply the Helsinki consciousness had become ingrained in European thinking on security. Even more than the endemic Soviet abuses of human rights, their calculated, sudden, and massive violations in Poland proved how drastic changes in the domestic conditions of a nation affected the perceptions of security among nations—not in any palpably military sense, but in a profound political and moral sense. This had not been so obvious in 1968, when outright Soviet intervention in Czechoslovakia had no comparable effect. The 1981 events added fresh substance to the old adage that without a free Poland there cannot be a secure Europe.

REPUDIATION OF THE "YALTA ORDER"

Beyond Poland, the adage attested to the inherent instability of Moscow's East European order that Helsinki had so conspicuously failed to prop up. Five years earlier Helmut Sonnenfeldt had postulated in his "doctrine" that the instability might lead to World War III. But although the political crisis had worsened, this did not make a military confrontation any more probable; it did make repudiation of the "Yalta order" more topical. This suited the Reagan administration's anti-Soviet militancy, with its ideological accent on the East-West rivalry as a contest of values. Yet the repudiation of the Yalta order, far from frivolously undermining the realities of power on which Europe's stability was presumably resting, also conveyed the sound recognition that regardless of the preferences of the superpowers, the internal dynamics of the Soviet empire made Yalta increasingly obsolete.

At Madrid, Kampelman rejected the "myth" that equates Yalta with spheres of influence, insisting that change "will come to the East as it comes to all of us, because life requires change."[89] He was merely stating the obvious. Later on, Vice President George Bush declared that "we recognize no lawful division of Europe,"[90] a far cry from President Nixon's reassuring the Soviets in 1970 that it was not possible to exploit the situation in its Eastern part against them.[91] Nor was the United States alone in rejecting the notion of a divided Europe; Yugoslavia had done so even before Helsinki, which it welcomed mainly as a means to liquidate the blocs.[92] And, in 1982, President Mitterand of France added his voice by stating publicly that "anything that will allow us to get away from Yalta will be good."[93]

The repression in Poland made the CSCE truly a battlefield in the "struggle for hearts and minds."[94] When numerous foreign ministers converged on Madrid to underscore their governments' concern about the situation, the representative of the Warsaw regime, who happened to chair the plenary session on February 9, 1982, resorted to dubious procedural maneuvers to prevent them from speaking. He could not prevent the speeches from being delivered later anyway, and the infuriating spectacle only helped gain support for the West's demand that the conference be adjourned in protest against the Polish excesses.[95]

THE STRUGGLE FOR ADJOURNMENT

The demand did not immediately resolve the perennial question of how useful it is to keep talking to the Soviets while they do not seem to be listening. The United States strongly favored the adjournment, but West Germany, among NATO members the CSCE's staunchest supporter, initially opposed it.[96] The high value that the Germans placed on dialogue, even for its own sake, suggested how their possession of Western Europe's strongest army did not suffice to offset the peculiar insecurity they felt as a divided nation. No such insecurity inhibited the Swiss who, combining both defense-mindedness and political cohesion in high degrees, sensed more deeply the affront to Western notions of freedom and human dignity that the pretense of conducting business as usual in Madrid would have meant. Along with Austria, another nation remarkably secure politically though feeble militarily, Switzerland took the lead in rallying the neutrals behind the demand for adjournment.[97]

The subsequent weeks highlighted the political value of the procedural maneuvering of which so much of the CSCE stuff is made. The Soviet Union urged the conferees to proceed with dispatch toward completion of the final document from the draft prepared by the neutrals, although it had previously found the document deficient and although now some of the draft's original sponsors disowned it as obsolete.[98] While Moscow assumed an uncharacteristically businesslike posture, the West resorted to the more typically Soviet tactic of stonewalling, denouncing the Polish situation at the plenary sessions and ignoring what Kampelman called the constant "chirping" to get down to work.[99] But without Moscow's granting consensus, the conference could not be adjourned. In this war of nerves with the regimented East, the pluralistic West had to rely on voluntary discipline.

THE NIGHT OF SILENCES

The solution devised by the deputy chief of the U.S. delegation, Spencer Oliver, tested that discipline. It envisaged refusing approval to the weekly working schedules of the drafting group. There was no precedent for such a move and little likelihood that conference meetings could thus be prevented. During White House consultations, Kampelman had already informed the president that he saw no possibility to adjourn by breaking the procedural deadlock. But now West German representative Jörg Kastl and his British colleague John Wilberforce came out in support of the plan, and together they swayed the rest of the NATO group.[100]

The result was a triumph of Allied solidarity. During the "night of silences" on March 5, 1982, all Western delegates responded with silence to repeated calls by Soviet bloc representatives to schedule further meetings of the drafting group. The conference came to a halt, and after three days the Soviet Union yielded. A face-saving agreement provided for three more meetings, at which the West kept its silence. Afterward the conference was adjourned for eight months. More than a mere tactical victory, the outcome attested to the growing common ground that NATO shared with the neutrals and nonaligned because of their affinity of values.[101]

When the delegations reconvened in November 1982, the conditions in Poland had not substantially changed. Neither had the protracted leadership succession crisis in the Kremlin that inhibited substantive decisions. These circumstances made a breakthrough at Madrid unlikely. The West had to wait until such time when the Soviets, for reasons independent of the conference, might be ready to negotiate. It had nothing to lose and possibly something to gain by introducing additional proposals on human rights. These proposals called for the Soviet bloc to end the jamming of Western broadcasts, improve working conditions for foreign journalists, lift restrictions on Western publications, facilitate family reunification, and simplify emigration procedures. With an eye on Poland, they proclaimed the right of workers to form free trade unions. They also included a demand for the convocation of meetings of experts on human rights and family reunification as part of the expanding Helsinki process.[102]

TOWARD A COMPROMISE DOCUMENT

The Soviet yearning for a disarmament conference remained the principal Western leverage. With the debate about deployment of NATO missiles to offset already installed Soviet missiles gaining momentum in Western Europe and the deadline for a decision approaching, Moscow's stake in the conference that was to influence the decision grew proportionately. Whether by design or by default, the Soviets still resisted the condition that confidence-building measures be given priority on the agenda.[103] But time was on the West's side, and the compromise that eventually ensued in July 1983 qualified as its success.

Responding to a direct appeal by Spanish Prime Minister Felipe González to the governments concerned rather than their Madrid representatives, Moscow reluctantly accepted at least some of the Western amendments—those about trade unions, journalists, and prospective emigrants.[104] And although the formulations that won consensus proved characteristically ambiguous, they were somewhat less so than had been the formulations of the Final Act. But compared with such distinctly modest results after more than three years of excruciating negotiations, the agreement to continue and expand the Helsinki process was of greater significance.

In a further trade-off between military security and human rights, the Concluding Document provided for both Moscow's pet disarmament conference and the experts' meetings on human rights and family reunification that the West desired. Yet the mandate for the conference expressed Western rather than Soviet preferences despite Moscow's last-ditch attempt to insert seemingly innocuous but potentially substantive revisions. The Soviet success in keeping the provisions about the two meetings separate from the main agreement as "chairman's statements," thus according them lesser dignity, was a matter of face rather than of substance.[105]

THE OUTCOME OF MADRID

Even this limited East-West consensus remained blocked for nearly another three months by a bizarre interlude reminding the Europeans of their vulnerability to pressures from the Third World. Aspiring to an intermediary role between them and the Arab world, tiny Malta sought to blackmail the conference into accepting proposals that would have shifted the focus from the security of continental Europe to that of the Mediterranean.[106] As their reason for doing so, the Maltese professed to be threatened by superpower rivalry, although the more immediate threat came from the support of international terrorism by their close

Libyan friend Muammar Qaddafi. The Maltese also tended to downgrade the CSCE's human rights dimension by trying to bring in through the back door the Palestine Liberation Organization as a "non-participating Mediterranean state." East and West together wisely joined in keeping the Pandora's box of Middle Eastern problems out of the Helsinki process. Serving notice of their readiness to implement their consensus even without Malta, the thirty-four other participants finally moved the maverick to bring the conference to a conclusion in September 1983.[107]

On paper, the results of Madrid were more substantive than those of Belgrade. But would no written agreement have not been preferable to one unlikely to gain Soviet compliance? Would a lack of consensus on substantive matters have not reflected more faithfully the realities of East-West relations at the time and the CSCE's dependence on improvements outside of its scope? Moreover, did the planned proliferation of experts' meetings—which, in addition to the three already mentioned, included a Mediterranean seminar in Venice and a cultural forum in Budapest, besides the ill-starred Athens talks about the peaceful settlement of disputes—presage dilution of the Helsinki process?[108] Was the process not being diverted from the review of human rights to preoccupation with military matters? Soon the disarmament conference that convened in Stockholm in January 1984 provided some answers.[109]

THE STOCKHOLM CONFERENCE

The Stockholm conference proved less of a Soviet forum than anticipated. Surprisingly dilatory in submitting its proposals, Moscow defied its previous practice by presenting them separately rather than in conjunction with its allies. It predictably hammered on such extraneous themes as the nuclear freeze, no-first-use of nuclear arms, and abolition of chemical weapons. But it seemed to lack faith in pursuing them, thus enabling the NATO and neutral countries to seize the initiative with specific proposals of their own to promote confidence-building. These included demands for compulsory notification of not only maneuvers but also other military movements and for reduction in the size of forces subject to notification.[110]

Along with the continued paralysis of the superannuated Kremlin leadership, the failure of Moscow's "peace" offensive in November 1983, when the German Bundestag finally voted for the stationing of Euromissiles, accounted for the peculiar Soviet passivity. Once the deployment decision had been made, it was considerably more difficult to wage a campaign for its undoing. The Soviet Union compounded its setback by walking out of the Geneva arms control talks and suspending the MBFR in Vienna as well. By January 1984, Stockholm remained the only functioning East-West conference on military security. As a multilateral forum, however, it could not substitute for the superpower dialogue the Soviets had broken off. When they eventually reversed themselves, their return to Geneva in 1985 was unrelated to anything that had transpired at Stockholm. However, their miscalculation about the West's resolve to proceed with its rearmament did not make the linkage between military power and human rights irrelevant.

THE OTTAWA MEETING OF EXPERTS

Acknowledging its relevance, the Soviet representatives prepared themselves better than before for discussions at the experts' meeting that opened in Ottawa in May 1985. Besides more ingenious procedural maneuvers to limit the time for review, they argued their own concept of human rights more coherently and vigorously. Consistent with their Marxist premises, they posited the supremacy of man's material rights, concerned with his physical welfare, over those safeguarding the free development of his personality that are the essence of the Western liberal tradition.[111]

The Soviet emphasis was on rights to be granted man as a member of a society governed by an arbitrary authority; these were to take precedence over the rights man asserts as an individual to protect himself from abuse by any authority. But beyond exalting the rights that offer security rather than freedom, Soviet spokesmen introduced new ones of a "third generation," needed to guarantee man's survival against the supposedly rising threat of nuclear annihilation.[112] Rendering most topical the right to mere existence, Moscow pressed the message that peace is to be valued above freedom—as if the choice were either security on Soviet terms or nuclear holocaust.

While the concepts were persuasive, the supporting evidence was not. At Ottawa, Soviet spokesmen were hard-pressed when the discussion extended to comparing the "quality of life" in East and West.[113] That such a discussion, exploring at length the conflicting systems of values involved, could take place at a security conference gave an indication of how far the subject matter of security had expanded in the ten years of the CSCE's existence. It lent further support to the notion that security is not mainly or even primarily a question of weaponry.[114]

Pursuing the theme of human rights and weaponry, the Americans sought to impress on Moscow how its disregard of Basket Three dimmed the prospects for Senate approval of arms control agreements. The congressional delegation that came to Ottawa stressed how Helsinki violations prejudiced any belief that the Soviets could be trusted to keep the agreements.[115] In a special way the appointment of CSCE veteran Kampelman as the chief U.S. delegate to the strategic arms talks that had resumed at Geneva underlined the connection.

THE BUDAPEST CULTURAL FORUM

Ending without consensus, Ottawa presaged the outcome of the Budapest Cultural Forum six months later. This again highlighted the fundamental insecurities underlying the tensions in a divided Europe. If at Ottawa the Soviet thrust had been mainly defensive—to protect the integrity of arbitrary rule from nonconformist individuals—at Budapest the Soviets and their allies went onto the offensive with their totalitarian concept of culture as a tool bending peoples to the needs of the state. In describing the duty of the writer, Soviet delegate N. T. Fedorenko postulated that "nothing else is worth writing about except peace." He ruminated that "the role of the writer is to tell the truth about war and about the rising threat of nuclear disaster."[116]

Again, procedural disputes assumed political meaning. The Soviets insisted on an agenda that would give them ample time to dwell on their quantitative cultural accomplishments—the number of books printed or films shown—while limiting the discussion on such qualitative aspects of culture, favored by the West, as the creative process or the dissemination of ideas. Moscow wanted a forum of cultural bureaucrats, and only reluctantly agreed that independent writers and artists be represented as well. Their presence made Budapest different from other CSCE conferences. It reaffirmed the Western notion that cultural creativity is the business of individuals rather than of governments. But it also made a coordinated Western strategy more difficult.[117]

If the West nevertheless scored a success at Budapest, this was due mainly to the concurrent unofficial symposium rather than to anything that happened during the stilted official proceedings. The Hungarian authorities at first tried to prevent the nongovernmental Western organizers of the symposium from holding it by denying them access to the public facilities already reserved for that purpose. But they did not interfere with the symposium's being held in private apartments where free and spirited discussion between the visiting Western intellectuals and their Hungarian counterparts ensued. An unprecedented sight in a Soviet bloc nation, it juxtaposed the security the West derives from its commitment to cultural freedom with the insecurity that both breeds and is bred by cultural repression.[118]

That the incompatible concepts of culture would prevent the Budapest participants from reaching consensus on any substantive final document was predictable. More surprising was their failure to produce even a short statement, which Hungary had proposed but Romania blocked—

presumably because of Romania's pique at having been censured for its mistreatment of its Hungarian minority. Here an ostensibly cultural feud between two "fraternal" allies gave but one sample of Europe's human rights and security problems unrelated to East-West rivalry. At Ottawa the gratuitous persecution of Bulgaria's Turkish minority had prompted the participants to tackle another such problem.[119]

The CSCE's growing propensity to end its meetings without formally agreeing on anything was a doubtful innovation to the Helsinki process. Nor did the accession of Mikhail Gorbachev to supreme power in the Kremlin necessarily bode well for continued Soviet commitment to the CSCE as a prominent part of the Brezhnev legacy, other parts of which were under review. Yet both during the celebrations of the Final Act's tenth anniversary and again at the end of the Budapest meeting, consensus prevailed that the Helsinki experience was worthwhile.[120] With the third follow-up meeting in Vienna a year away, at issue was the accommodation of a living organism to changing circumstances, not its demise.

The Helsinki balance sheet

To a demanding observer, the tangible results of Helsinki may seem meager, and indeed they are if compared to what they ought to be. Certainly respect for human rights in most of the Soviet bloc has not significantly increased and at times may have even diminished. Nor, for that matter, has the CSCE had a measurable impact on human rights imperfections in the West. The achievement of the Helsinki process has rather been in its adding importance to intangibles. Kampelman, a Washington lawyer hardly short on pragmatism, once stated at Madrid his belief in the "importance of words."[121] And the Soviets have evidently shared the belief if their proverbial concern with wording is an indication. But in the end, what is the value of words if the deeds are missing?

An all-inclusive gathering of European and North American states, the CSCE has been addressing at length a growing variety of security concerns in a very special part of the world. Europe has been unique in both the subtlety of its political thought and the sobering experiences of its history, which accentuate the elusive nature of security. In countless ways the CSCE has tested the meaning of security in the crossfire of adversary opinion as never before. The record of the conference has been a compendium of the security aspirations that constitute the building blocks of Europe's evolving international order.

REDEFINING THE CONCEPTS OF SECURITY

The decade since Helsinki has cast growing doubt on the permanence of that order, a legacy of World War II. The passing of a generation has blurred the premises on which it was originally built. Meanwhile, having survived the rise and fall of détente, the CSCE has brought the perennial tension between order and change into a new focus. By extending the frame of reference to the internal aspects of security, it has made just domestic order an indispensable ingredient of any stable international order. The Soviets have been strenuously resisting this revolutionary idea. But in doing so, they have been resisting a reality. And, as Marx has taught, when reality and "false consciousness" clash, the latter ultimately has to yield.

The open-endedness of the Helsinki process has not been congenial to the American mentality, with its penchant for instant problem-solving. It has had greater appeal for Europeans, better attuned by their history to the notion that some problems may be insoluble yet manageable by redefinition. Security is one of them; it can either grow or diminish but can never be attained. The Soviet Union has tried to pursue the chimera of absolute security, and failed. However unwillingly, its successive leaders have been compelled to increasingly adjust this unattainable ideal to political realities. The CSCE has been an outstanding expression of those realities. It has served to expand the substance of security by inducing its participants to redefine their concepts of security and relate them to human rights. For that reason alone, it is indispensable.

NOTES

1 On the CSCE's procedural innovations, see Jan Sizoo and Rudolf Th. Jurrjens, *CSCE Decision-Making: The Madrid Experience* (The Hague: Nijhoff, 1984), pp. 56–68.
2 Luigi Vittorio Ferraris (ed.), *Report on a Negotiation: Helsinki-Geneva-Helsinki, 1972–1975* (Alphen aan den Rijn: Sijthoff & Noordhoff, 1979), p. 79.
3 Alexandre Charles Kiss and Mary Frances Dominick, "The International Legal Significance of the Human Rights Provisions of the Helsinki Final Act," in Mary Frances Dominick (ed.), *Human Rights and the Helsinki Accord: A Five-Year Road to Madrid* (Buffalo: Hein, 1981), pp. 47–69.
4 Doc. No. 1.
5 Doc. No. 5
6 Doc. No. 4.
7 Ferraris (ed.), *Report on a Negotiation*, pp. 18, 28. Doc. Nos. 3, 10.
8 Doc. No. 10.
9 Sizoo and Jurrjens, *CSCE Decision-Making*, pp. 56, 73.
10 Doc. No. 9.
11 John J. Maresca, *To Helsinki: The Conference on Security and Cooperation*

in Europe, 1973–1975 (Durham, N.C.: Duke University Press, 1985), pp. 73–116.

12 Ferraris (ed.), *Report on a Negotiation*, pp. 23, 45.

13 Ibid., p. 48.

14 Ibid, p. 53. Doc. No. 9.

15 Ibid, p. 18.

16 Alexander L. George, "The Basic Principles Agreement of 1972: Origins and Expectations," in A. L. George (ed.), *Managing U.S.-Soviet Rivalry* (Boulder, Colo.: Westview Press, 1983), pp. 107–17.

17 Sizoo and Jurrjens, *CSCE Decision-Making*, p. 87. The word is *vmeshatelstvo*.

18 Ferraris (ed.), *Report on a Negotiation*, p. 28. Doc. No. 9.

19 Ibid., p. 30.

20 Doc. No. 6.

21 Doc. Nos. 7–8.

22 Doc. No. 11.

23 Doc. Nos. 12, 13, 19. The text of the Final Act is in Maresca, *To Helsinki*, pp. 226–83.

24 Doc. No. 14.

25 Doc. No. 16; also Doc. Nos. 17, 18.

26 Doc. Nos. 15, 20.

27 *Neues Deutschland*, October 8, 1975. Doc. No. 2.

28 Doc. Nos. 22–24.

29 Doc. No. 25.

30 Doc. No. 38.

31 Doc. No. 21.

32 *New York Times*, October 7, 1976.

33 Doc. No. 26.

34 Doc. Nos. 27–28.

35 Doc. No. 29. Interview with Spencer Oliver, Washington, D.C., October 31, 1985.

36 Doc. No. 30.

37 *Pravda*, December 10, 1975.

38 *The Helsinki Process and East-West Relations: Progress in Perspective: A Report on the Positive Aspects of the Implementation of the Helsinki Final Act, 1975–1985* (Washington, D.C.: Commission on Security and Cooperation in Europe, 1985), pp. 107–8.

39 Doc. No. 33.

40 The phrase is that of Lane Kirkland, "A Reminder of the Government's Bounty," *New York Times*, January 26, 1986.

41 Doc. No. 31.

42 Doc. No. 32.

43 Doc. No. 22.

44 Doc. Nos. 34–36.

45 Doc. No. 37.

46 " 'Mischief' in Moscow's Front Yard," *Time*, June 12, 1978, p. 19. Raymond C. Garthoff, "Eastern Europe in the Context of U.S.-Soviet Relations," in Sarah M. Terry (ed.), *Soviet Policy in Eastern Europe* (New Haven: Yale University Press, 1984), pp. 325–26.

47 Doc. No. 38.

48 Doc. No. 39.

49   Vojtech Mastny (ed.), *Soviet/East European Survey, 1983–1984* (Durham, N.C.: Duke University Press, 1985), pp. 227–36, 244–57.
50   Doc. No. 38.
51   Doc. Nos. 40–43.
52   Doc. No. 46.
53   Appendix B.
54   "Roasting Bear at Belgrade," *Baltimore Sun*, February 28, 1978.
55   Doc. Nos. 41, 43, 59.
56   Doc. No. 44.
57   Doc. Nos. 45, 47, 48.
58   Interview with Spencer Oliver, Washington, D.C., October 31, 1985. Doc. Nos. 49–50.
59   Doc. Nos. 48, 50–52, 56. Interview with Arthur Goldberg, Washington, D.C., December 10, 1985.
60   Doc. No. 54.
61   Doc. Nos. 55, 58.
62   Doc. No. 57.
63   Doc. Nos. 60–63.
64   Doc. Nos. 64–66.
65   Doc. Nos. 67, 68.
66   Doc. Nos. 69, 70.
67   Doc. Nos. 71–73.
68   "An Interview with Ronald Reagan," *Time*, June 30, 1980, pp. 15–16.
69   Doc. Nos. 74–76.
70   Sizoo and Jurrjens, *CSCE Decision-Making*, p. 192. Doc. No. 134.
71   Doc. No. 77.
72   Doc. No. 78.
73   Doc. No. 123.
74   Doc. No. 79.
75   Doc. Nos. 83, 84.
76   Doc. Nos. 80–82.
77   Robert Sharlet, *The New Soviet Constitution of 1977: Analysis and Text* (Brunswick, Ohio: King's Court Communications, 1978), p. 85.
78   Statement by Warren Zimmermann, Madrid, December 15, 1980, *World Affairs*, no. 4 (Spring 1982): 360–65.
79   Statement by Max M. Kampelman, Madrid, March 3, 1982, ibid., pp. 497–98.
80   Doc. Nos. 55, 138.
81   *Fulfilling Our Promises: The United States and the Helsinki Final Act: A Status Report* (Washington, D.C.: Commission on Security and Cooperation in Europe, 1979).
82   Doc. No. 93.
83   Doc. Nos. 89, 90, 92.
84   Doc. No. 91.
85   Doc. Nos. 86, 87.
86   Doc. No. 85.
87   Speech by Max M. Kampelman, Madrid, November 16, 1982, in Max M. Kampelman, *Three Years at the East-West Divide* (New York: Freedom House, 1983), p. 93.
88   Doc. No. 88.

89 Doc. No. 95.
90 Mastny (ed.), *Soviet/East European Survey, 1983–84,* p. 213.
91 "U.S. Foreign Policy for the 1970s: A New Strategy for Peace," Report by President Nixon to Congress, February 18, 1970.
92 *Yugoslavia and European Security and Cooperation* (Belgrade: Jugoslovenska Knjiga, n.d.), pp. 31–33, 41–44.
93 *Le Monde,* January 2, 1982, p. 10.
94 Doc. Nos. 94, 96.
95 Doc. Nos. 97, 99.
96 Doc. No. 98.
97 Doc. No. 100.
98 Ibid.
99 Statement by Max M. Kampelman, Madrid, February 24, 1982, *World Affairs,* no. 4 (Spring 1982): 491.
100 Interview with Spencer Oliver, Washington, D.C., October 31, 1985.
101 Doc. Nos. 101, 102.
102 Doc. Nos. 103–7.
103 Doc. Nos. 108–10.
104 Doc. Nos. 111–14.
105 Doc. Nos. 115, 116. Appendix C.
106 Doc. No. 117.
107 Doc. No. 118.
108 Appendix A.
109 Doc. No. 133.
110 Mastny (ed.), *Soviet/East European Survey, 1983–84,* pp. 97–109, and *Soviet/East European Survey, 1984–85* (Durham, N.C.: Duke University Press, 1986), pp. 90–95.
111 Doc. Nos. 119–22.
112 Doc. No. 126.
113 Doc. No. 125.
114 Doc. Nos. 123, 124.
115 Doc. Nos. 134–37.
116 Doc. No. 131
117 Doc. Nos. 127, 128, 130.
118 Doc. Nos. 129, 132.
119 Doc. No. 121.
120 Doc. Nos. 138–42.
121 Kampelman, *Three Years at the East-West Divide,* p. 122.

NOTE ON SOURCES

Although more accessible to the public than most international conferences, the Conference on Security and Cooperation in Europe is not easy to document. The speeches, draft proposals, and formal documents adopted by its participating states are voluminous and sometimes important but often also tedious, excessively technical, and not very illuminating by themselves. They present an incomplete picture of a conference that conducts most of its business at closed sessions and informal meetings where no official record is kept. The accounts of the discussions prepared by the different delegations for their governments remain classified.

Rather than relying on any particular type of source, the following documentation consists of a variety of items, including mostly contemporary and sometimes retrospective accounts by individual CSCE participants, transcripts of interviews and discussions outside the conference, correspondents' reports and editorials, statements by human rights activists, and assessments by scholars. The reports by RFE/RL correspondents described in the Preface figure prominently among the sources and are also the reason why the names of some of their authors appear so frequently in the Table of Contents.

The documents have been chosen to convey both the facts and the significance of the main aspects of the Helsinki process, particularly the connection between human rights and security. Since the goal is to grasp within a limited space the many ramifications of the process rather than to provide a scholarly edition of texts, almost all the sources have been abbreviated by deletions, though not rewritten, paraphrased, or otherwise amended. However, the four crucial documents from the Belgrade, Madrid, Ottawa, and Budapest conferences included as appendixes are printed in their entirety. Full bibliographical references are given at the beginning of each selection.

The sources are to be read in conjunction with the introductory essay that refers to them in its footnotes. They are divided into three broad sections, each concerned with a period when the relationship of human rights to another aspect of the csce—European political settlement, East-West trade, military affairs—assumed particular prominence. The subdivisions concern specific themes developed in the Introduction.

The events leading to the conclusion of the 1975 Final Act, which have been dealt with in the seminal study by John Maresca, *To Helsinki* (Duke University Press, 1985), are addressed only to the extent necessary to understand what followed. Since the csce is to be seen as a process, of which the actual conferences are but a part, many of the documents concern its wider implications. Thus, for example, selections from congressional hearings sponsored by the Commission on Security and Cooperation in Europe illustrate both the crucial American role in the process and the significance of nongovernmental influences in shaping that role. With the emphasis on concepts and policies, less attention is given to specific human rights cases that have been amply documented elsewhere.

Because of the particular American insistence to keep the csce as open as possible and because of the extensive publicity sought by the Congressional Helsinki Commission, sources of U.S. origin are by far the most readily available, as well as the most informative. To help offset the resulting imbalance (within the time limits imposed by the publisher's tight production schedule), special effort has also been made to document the variety of European positions—nato, Common Market, Warsaw Pact, neutral, and nonaligned. At least a few documents from among several supplied to the author by the foreign ministries of Finland and Sweden are included.

While the Soviet Union looms large in the book, the number of sources of Soviet origin is limited—partly because of the extreme scarcity of any unpublished documents, partly because of the verbosity and repetitiveness of those intended for public consumption. Aside from speeches and other official statements, the selection nevertheless includes authoritative accounts by Moscow's spokesmen concerning Soviet concepts of human rights and security, as well as all three of the csce's principal human rights linkages. Soviet positions at the different stages of the Helsinki process are further documented in numerous Western sources, which, besides being the only ones available, often also have the virtues of clarity and conciseness that are usually missing from the Soviet documents for which they have to substitute.

For reference purposes, the appendixes include a listing of all the csce conferences with the appropriate dates, the concluding documents of the first and second follow-up meetings (Belgrade and Madrid), and, in the absence of consensus on any common texts, the Western summaries of the results of the two meetings of experts concerned most directly with human rights (Ottawa and Budapest). The complete text of the 1975 Helsinki Final Act, to which references are frequently made, may be found in Maresca, *To Helsinki*, on pp. 227–83.

PART ONE

HUMAN RIGHTS AND POLITICAL SECURITY:
FROM HELSINKI TO BELGRADE

THE SOVIET ORIGINS

The Road to Helsinki

1

The CSCE and the Development of Détente, by Stephen J. Flanagan.
In Derek Leebaert (ed.), *European Security: Prospects for the
1980s* (Lexington, Mass.: Lexington Books, 1979), pp. 190–94.

The concept of a European security conference had been a recurrent
theme in Soviet foreign policy since 1954, but it was advanced with
greatest determination in the late 1960's. There were considerable shifts
in Moscow's aspirations for the conference over the years in response to
the exigencies of international developments and the advance of bilateral diplomacy. The Kremlin's early pronouncements envisioned such a
parley yielding a surrogate peace treaty which would affirm the postwar
frontiers, legitimize the status of East Germany, and recognize its hegemony in Eastern Europe. Moscow also hoped the fallout from such a
pact would arrest the development of West European military integration and the acquisition of nuclear weapons by West Germany. In the
late 1960's the Soviets sensed that emerging strains in NATO foreshad-
owed a major crisis in the West. Moscow believed a major offensive for
relaxation of tensions, with the security conference as its leading edge,
would expand Soviet influence throughout Europe. To understand the
development of CSCE it is essential to review Moscow's basic security pre-
occupations before the multilateral talks convened. The Kremlin's proposals for the all-European conference reflect these evolving concerns.[1]
 In his March 1966 address to the twenty-third Congress of the CPSU,
Brezhnev revived the conference idea and urged the convocation of an
all-European meeting on political détente and economic cooperation.
This trial balloon was enlarged upon by the Warsaw Pact Political Con-

sultative Committee (PCC) at its July 1966 Bucharest meeting. The Bucharest Declaration suggested that such an all-European gathering could ratify the territorial status quo, undertake the dissolution of at least the military organizations of NATO and the Warsaw Treaty Organization (WTO), replace the European Community with all-European trade associations, and foster continental cooperation in science, technology, and culture.[2] While U.S. participation was not excluded, this parley was clearly designed to be a European enterprise.

The April 1967 conference of twenty-four European Communist parties at Karlovy Vary reformulated some of the Bucharest proposals and affirmed the centrality of resolution of the German question. The conference's concluding statement berated both Bonn and Washington for pursuing aggressive policies.[3] Brezhnev called on his colleagues to mobilize broad political support in Western Europe for dismantling NATO and establishing a pan-European collective security system. It was explained that this system would evolve from an expanding web of bilateral East-West treaties. Because of their propagandistic criticisms of the United States and West Germany and their explicit assault on NATO, these proposals were never seriously entertained in the West. Moreover, the Kremlin was somewhat wary of undertaking an opening to the West at that time, fearing an erosion of its control over developments in Eastern Europe.

The invasion of Czechoslovakia smothered any chances of convening a security conference, and exacerbated Western suspicion about the meaning of détente. Thus, a major demonstration of Soviet goodwill became even more urgent. The suppression of Prague's experimentation and the general consolidation imposed on Eastern Europe enabled Moscow to feel more secure in pursuing a *Westpolitik*.[4] Moreover, since relations with China were deteriorating at this time, a relaxation of tensions in the West assumed even more importance.

The PCC advanced a more conciliatory version of the security conference proposal at its March 1969 meeting in Budapest. This new formulation did not suggest abolition of military blocs, allowed for U.S. participation, and removed recognition of the territorial situation as a precondition for initiating talks.[5]

The NATO foreign ministers remained highly skeptical of the purpose of a multilateral conference, although they agreed to review possible topics for discussion. NATO members preferred the resolution of several outstanding issues through bilateral diplomacy. At its December 1969 meeting, the North Atlantic Council linked commencement of the security conference to progress on other East-West issues including the

Berlin situation, other problems related to the division of Germany, and talks for mutual force reduction.[6] NATO's determination in this regard forced the Soviet Union to refocus its détente campaign during the next three years on improvement of relations with individual West European states. This task was somewhat facilitated by the FRG's broadening of its *Ostpolitik* after Willy Brandt's assumption of the chancellorship in October 1969.

During this period, the purview of the multilateral conference was debated in a series of communiqués following NATO and WTO meetings. While NATO wanted to probe the Pact's willingness to expand the conference agenda, the Pact leadership endeavored to keep it to a minimum. First the East bloc declared that the conference would have to address questions of security in Europe, including affirmation of the territorial status quo, trade, and economic, scientific, and technical cooperation.[7] Then in May 1970, two months after the Quadripartite talks on Berlin had commenced, the NATO foreign ministers went so far as to discuss plans for preparatory talks on the security conference, but also noted that the subjects of "freer movement of people, ideas and information" should be on any such parley's agenda.[8] A final item was added when the Warsaw Pact ministers proposed that the conference might establish a permanent organ to expedite East-West cooperation and implement conference decisions.[9] Moscow believed this last point to be a perfect compromise between its desire for a hasty European summit to ratify general principles of relations and the West's demand for substantive negotiations.

By the end of 1971, the time for the security conference seemed at hand and the general issues to be addressed were understood. With the conclusion of the Moscow and Warsaw treaties, the Quadripartite agreement on Berlin, and the impending normalization of relations between the two Germanies, several of NATO's preconditions for the commencement of the multilateral talks had been met. The Soviets launched one final drive for the all-European parley; however, they persisted in ignoring the importance of discussion of humanitarian cooperation and of the force-reduction talks.

The relationship of MBFR to the security conference was the last hurdle the Soviets had to confront. NATO demanded at least concurrent conduct of MBFR and CSCE. Initially averse to even a loose linkage of these two negotiations, the Kremlin finally succumbed to Henry Kissinger's persuasiveness and threats of further delay of CSCE by accepting the concept of parallelism. Dates and places were established for the initiation of CSCE and MBFR. While progress in one forum was in no way tied to developments in the other, NATO expressed the view that the two parleys were mutually reinforcing.

Yet, by this time, many of Moscow's initial goals for the security conference had been realized through bilateral diplomacy. West Germany's treaties with Moscow and Warsaw had resolved the most contentious border issue in Europe, the Oder-Neisse line. East Germany was on the road to recognition by the world community and an era of East-West cooperation in the commercial sphere was blooming. Nonetheless, the Kremlin attached considerable importance to multilateral endorsement of the territorial status quo, as a further legitimization of its hegemony in Eastern Europe. The basic Soviet goal in CSCE remained the same: broader relaxation of tensions to allow for an enlargement of Soviet influence throughout Europe.

Preparatory negotiations for the CSCE began on November 22, 1972, and dragged on for more than eight months. During the tedious wrangling over the agenda, which often involved semantic or procedural questions, the Soviets made numerous tactical concessions to expedite the proceedings. While Moscow sought a one-stage conference in Helsinki focused on the code of interstate relations and expansion of economic and technical cooperation, it accepted multi-staged deliberations in both Helsinki and Geneva with a greatly enlarged agenda.[10] To further complicate matters for Moscow, Romania joined Yugoslavia in a surprisingly independent stance from the outset of these talks, and Poland and Hungary quietly evinced similar proclivities. As these undesirable developments accelerated during the substantive "second stage" of the negotiations in Geneva, Soviet diplomats acknowledged privately that many of their original aspirations for the conference, particularly the permanent political body, had evaporated.[11] However, abandoning the parley at that point would have been impossible because of the Kremlin's tremendous investment, including the personal prestige of General Secretary Brezhnev, in its successful conclusion.

As the Geneva deliberations droned on for two years Moscow recognized that CSCE was not the ideal instrument for furthering its diplomacy. Nonetheless, it hoped that perseverance would allow realization of the following goals:

> Multilateral recognition of the inviolability of the post-World War II borders in Europe;
> Codification of the principles of relations between states with *different social systems*;
> Expansion of institutionalized cooperation in industry, science, and technology.

This scheme would preserve Moscow's hegemonial position in Eastern Europe, suggest durable stability in Europe—hence undermining the impetus of West European integration and "Atlanticism"—and allow for realization of the benefits of exchanges with the West while insulating the Eastern bloc from pressures for liberalization. As Robert Legvold so aptly noted, the Kremlin sought to employ CSCE as a "medium for healing Europe's economic division while sealing its political division."[12]

NOTES

1   For a thorough examination of Soviet views on European security see: Robert Legvold, "The Problem of European Security," *Problems of Communism*, January/February 1974, pp. 13–33.
2   Marshall D. Shulman, "Soviet Proposals for a European Security Conference, 1966–1969," *Studies for a New Central Europe*, No. 3-4 (1968–69), pp. 70–71; "Declaration on Strengthening Peace and Security in Europe," in United Kingdom, Secretary of State for Foreign and Commonwealth Affairs, *Selected Documents Relating to Problems of Security and Cooperation in Europe, 1954–1977*, Command Paper 6932 (London: H.M. Stationery Office, 1977), pp. 38–43.
3   "Statement on Peace and Security in Europe Issued by a Meeting of European Communist Parties in Karlovy Vary, Czechoslovakia, 26 April 1967," in *Documents Relating to Security and Cooperation in Europe*, pp. 44–47.
4   Pierre Hassner, "Europe in the Age of Negotiation," *Washington Papers*, No. 8 (Beverly Hills: Sage, 1973), p. 67.
5   Mojmir Povolny, "The Soviet Union and the European Security Conference," *Orbis*, Spring 1974, pp. 210–211.
6   "Declaration of the North Atlantic Council, Brussels, December 4–5, 1969," *Documents Relating to Security and Cooperation in Europe*, pp. 61–62.
7   "Statement of Warsaw Pact Foreign Ministers, Prague, October 30–31, 1969," *Documents Relating to Security and Cooperation in Europe*, pp. 61–62.
8   "Communiqué of the North Atlantic Council, Rome, May 26–27, 1970," *Documents Relating to Security and Cooperation in Europe*, pp. 73–75, par. 16.
9   "Memorandum of the Warsaw Pact Foreign Ministers Meeting, Budapest, June 21–22, 1970," *Documents Relating to Security and Cooperation in Europe*, pp. 77–78.
10 For a fuller discussion of these sessions by a member of the FRG delegation, see Götz von Groll, "The Helsinki Consultations," *Aussenpolitik*, 2/1973, pp. 123–129, and "The Foreign Ministers in Helsinki," *Aussenpolitik*, 3/1973, pp. 255–274.
11 This is noted in an article by one of the U.S. delegates. See Harold S. Russell, "The Helsinki Declaration: Brobdingnag or Lilliput," *American Journal of International Law* 70 (April 1976): 246.
12 Legvold, "The Problem of European Security," p. 26.

Shaping European Security

2

The "Brezhnev Doctrine," by Leonid I. Brezhnev.
Speech by the Soviet Communist Party General Secretary at
the fifth congress of the Polish United Workers' Party,
Warsaw, November 12, 1968, *Current Digest of the Soviet
Press* 20, no. 46: 3–4.

Socialist states stand for strict respect for the sovereignty of all countries. We resolutely oppose interference in the affairs of any states and the violation of their sovereignty.

At the same time, affirmation and defense of the sovereignty of states that have taken the path of socialist construction are of special significance to us Communists. The forces of imperialism and reaction are seeking to deprive the people first in one, then another socialist country of the sovereign right they have earned to ensure prosperity for their country and well-being and happiness for the broad working masses by building a society free from all oppression and exploitation. And when encroachments on this right receive a joint rebuff from the socialist camp, the bourgeois propagandists raise the cry of "defense of sovereignty" and "noninterference." It is clear that this is the sheerest deceit and demagoguery on their part. In reality these loudmouths are concerned not about preserving socialist sovereignty but about destroying it.

It is common knowledge that the Soviet Union has really done a good deal to strengthen the sovereignty and autonomy of the socialist countries. The c.p.s.u. has always advocated that each socialist country determine the concrete forms of its development along the path of socialism by taking into account the specific nature of their national conditions. But it is well known, comrades, that there are common natural laws of socialist construction, deviation from which could lead to deviation from socialism as such. And when external and internal forces hostile to socialism try to turn the development of a given socialist country in the direction of restoration of the capitalist system, when a threat arises to the cause of socialism in that country—a threat to the security of the socialist commonwealth as a whole—this is no longer merely a problem for that country's people, but a common problem, the concern of all socialist countries.

It is quite clear that an action such as military assistance to a fraternal country to end a threat to the socialist system is an extraordinary measure, dictated by necessity; it can be called forth only by the overt actions of enemies of socialism within the country and beyond its boundaries, actions that create a threat to the common interests of the socialist camp.

Experience bears witness that in present conditions the triumph of the socialist system in a country can be regarded as final, but the restoration of capitalism can be considered ruled out only if the Communist Party, as the leading force in society, steadfastly pursues a Marxist-Leninist policy in the development of all spheres of society's life; only if the party indefatigably strengthens the country's defense and the protection of its revolutionary gains, and if it itself is vigilant and instills in the people vigilance with respect to the class enemy and implacability toward bourgeois ideology; only if the principle of socialist internationalism is held sacred and unity and fraternal solidarity with the other socialist countries are strengthened.

3

International Relations during the 1970s, by N. N. Inozemtsev.
In Lilita Dzirkals and A. Ross Johnson (eds.), Soviet and
East European Forecasts of European Security: Papers from
the 1972 Varna Conference (Santa Monica: Rand, 1973),
No. R-1272-PR, pp. 11–13.

During the 1970s, the dominant trend of European developments will be further progress toward détente and cooperation between East and West Europe. This trend could be undermined by a West European political-military integration of antisocialist coloration, as promoted by Western military-industrial and financial interests. The Conference on Security and Cooperation in Europe could play an important role in the creation of a correctly conceived all-European security system and the evolution of a stable détente and cooperation among the European states.

Economic development in both parts of Europe will continue along present lines with industrial production in the East increasing at a faster rate than in the West. Common Market states are likely to experience instability in industrial production and finance, and their exports could suffer because of U.S. and Japanese competition. Nevertheless, subsequent to Great Britain's accession, the role and importance of the European Economic Community (EEC) in world economy will increase. The EEC is one of the concrete economic and political realities of Europe.

The prospects for creating a West European monetary union in the

1970s will be impaired by renewed disagreements over monetary and financial questions flaring up during the first half of the decade. The EEC will not succeed in creating a "political community," but by the end of the decade progress will be made toward creating a mechanism for coordinating major foreign policy lines of the EEC countries.

Military détente will unfold against the background of an equilibrium between the military forces of the two systems, those of the U.S. and the USSR in particular. New agreements on strategic arms limitation between these two powers will create favorable conditions for European agreements on armed forces and arms reduction. Such agreements would still be accompanied by an overall rise in European military potential due to qualitative improvements in armament. Yet, "perfecting military force will not increase the possibilities of its direct employment; the contrary will rather be the case. Use of military force as well as its uncontrolled development will be increasingly restricted by a system of political accords." This benign process could, however, be brought to a halt by Western attempts to attain "superior strength."

In all probability, both NATO and the Warsaw Treaty Organization will continue to exist through the 1970s. It is possible that the military functions of the blocs will recede. It is also not impossible that in the last half of the decade plans will be made for the dissolution of the entire bloc structure.

If all goes well, negotiations on forces and arms reduction will take place—in a forum separate from the Conference on Security and Cooperation in Europe—and, over the span of several years, will produce an agreement on criteria for the actual reductions. The ensuing comprehensive reductions will significantly reduce force levels while maintaining proportions that afford equal security and no advantages to either side.

In principle, one must consider the eventuality of the gradual formation of a pan-European security system during the 1970s. The most likely development, one that is both objectively necessary and "ripe," is that the fundamental elements of this system will undergo full maturation during this period. Should the rhythms of the formation of the pan-European security system be abruptly slowed down or its construction proved infeasible, reactionary and bellicose elements could gain political power in some Western countries and proceed to exacerbate international tension, thus increasing the possibility of conflicts in Europe.

If détente continues its favorable progress, the intensified integration proceeding apace in both parts of Europe would not lead to mutual isolation. Barring EEC's evolution in an antisocialist direction and given its renunciation of discriminatory practices vis-à-vis the socialist countries and adherence to the principles of all-European security, the decade could witness the appearance of new forms of multilateral cooperation between the EEC and the socialist community.

4

The Soviet Union and Western Europe, by Robert Legvold.
In William E. Griffith (ed.), *The Soviet Empire: Expansion and Détente* (Lexington, Mass.: Lexington Books, 1976),
pp. 227, 229–31, 243–44.

The Soviet dilemma is in the contradiction between its desires for and apprehensions about Western Europe. For, basically, Soviet leaders would prefer to face a Western Europe divided into a loose configuration of "subregions," composed of states dealing for themselves alone, and generously dotted with permanently neutral governments. Given the existence of the Common Market, their instinctive choice is for a slow, ambiguous, troubled, and, ultimately, limited integration capable neither of overcoming the competing foreign and domestic policies of members nor of attracting outsiders.

At the same time, a fragmented Western Europe with only rudimentary structures of cooperation must inevitably remain under the shadow of the United States—what Soviet leaders have lamented most for the last twenty-five years. Despite the conflicts between Western Europe and the United States, their greatest concern is still over the ease with which the United States can turn European cooperation to its own advantage.

Two fundamental challenges are likely to persist for a long time. The first is the challenge of drawing the United States into an active role in the politics of European détente. Without American leadership to give sanction and coherence to the West's part in the dialogue, the process of altering the character of relations across the divide will be diffuse and halting. On the other hand, it was extraordinary to imagine that the United States would serve as the counterpoint providing European détente its coherence. Neither Republican Administration—even while the executive retained control over foreign policy—had any interest in assuming the lead in Europe's diplomacy. In the brief time between its own original skepticism over German *Ostpolitik* and the later skepticism that its own Eastern policy stirred at home,[1] the Administration never went beyond supporting positions determined in Bonn, Brussels and Paris.

The proposition was all the more extraordinary in view of the Soviet

Union's basic set of assumptions (that the imperialist nations were falling out and American leadership was discredited) and its basic set of objectives (to break the link between American and West European power and to reduce the American hold over this area, admittedly while also averting an acceleration of West European integration). Perhaps not in a crudely calculated fashion, but in essence nonetheless, the Soviets wanted the Americans to facilitate a process that they, the Soviets, expected would lead to an erosion of imperialist solidarity and the paralysis of alternative forms of union; in the meantime, they counted on them to lend stability and restraint to relations between Eastern and Western Europe.

The second challenge generated by *Ostpolitik* or, more precisely, by the détente that it spurred, was more fundamental and more permanent, for with the fruits of economic involvement came the perils of political penetration. Détente opened the way to levels of cooperation unimagined for twenty-five years; it posed equally unfamiliar threats to the Eastern bloc's carefully preserved insulation. True, détente seemed to end the tendency of Bonn, Paris and Washington to vacillate between a policy strategy addressed to Moscow and subordinating relations with Eastern Europe and one pressuring Moscow by dealing behind its back with the most receptive of these governments. But in its place the Western powers now deliberately sought to use improved relations to force their ideas, tastes, and practices on the Socialist societies. It was a new and delicate balance that the Soviet leaders were obliged to maintain between interdependence and isolation.

The first outstanding characteristic of Soviet strategy is its emphasis on what might be called "contextual" over "basic" security. The difference is in the content that Soviet leaders give to the European part of détente. In Europe the Soviet Union tends to lump all of its initiatives and aims under the single rubric of promoting continental security. But because Soviet insecurity is political, not military, its definition of European security tends to be political rather than military. That is, the Soviet stress on setting down the principles of East-West relations (including the principles of the inviolability of frontiers and nonrecourse to force), on creating permanent consultative organs and on fostering economic cooperation stems from the Soviet Union's primary interest in consolidating the Eastern status quo and controlling the revision of the Western status quo. It is less concerned with remodeling the underlying (military) structure of security. In fact, it clearly feels that the existing military balance ought to be kept intact, if détente is to be safely pursued and Central Europe to be protected should détente collapse. Like France, the Soviet Union believes in "armed détente."[2]

The second noteworthy characteristic of Soviet strategy is its emphasis on security as a process. Most national leaderships deal with détente as a process, but it is somewhat more unusual to define security primarily as a process. In the Soviet view "security should not be regarded as an abstract and static thing in itself, but as a dynamic evolutionary process and a function of the existing and developing internal and external ties.[3] There is obvious good sense in recognizing that security, being a state of mind, cannot be fixed, but the Soviet approach carries this insight to an extreme. It is, as a result, not the end product but the process of building security that Soviet policy seeks to structure—for the same reason that it concentrates on "contextual" security. At the moment, Soviet leaders have no particular reason to labor on behalf of a new European security system; their interest is in enhancing the condition of their existing security system.

NOTES

1 After the May 1972 summit in Moscow, Soviet commentators implied that the United States had at last caught up with the West Europeans. As one of them reported after the summit, now the ground has been cut out from under "the opponents of relaxed tensions . . . between the FRG and the socialist countries," who "before were able to speculate on a certain ambiguity and contradictoriness in Washington's attitude." See E. N. Novoseltsev, "Sovetsko-amerikanskie peregovory v verkhakh i evropeiskaia bezopasnost," *SShA: Ekonomika, Politika, Ideologiia*, no. 12 (December 1972), p. 44.
2 The phrase is Michel Tatu's.
3 M. Dobrosielski, "Peaceful Coexistence and European Security," *International Affairs*, no. 6 (June 1972), p. 35. Dobrosielski is the director of the Institute of International Affairs in Warsaw, but the journal is Soviet and so, unquestionably, is the view.

5

European Security and "Social Progress," by Charles Andras.
Radio Free Europe Research, RAD Background Report/117
(East-West), July 21, 1975, pp. 1–2, 5–8, 15.

Judging by their political-ideological activity, most of the socialist regimes entered on the preparatory work for the proposed conference with fairly clear ideas about what to do with a post-CSCE Europe and what role the Communists should play in it.

According to the socialist media, the advance of peaceful coexistence, of détente, and the holding of the CSCE also demonstrate that capitalism has lost its paramount position in shaping the fate of the Western world, particularly Europe, and that it must now share power with the forces of socialism. To some authors there has been a "change in the international power ratio" in favor of socialism, which has become the more dynamic, the better organized, the more promising social force of the present and of the future, steadily and rapidly gaining in power and influence among the working population of the West.

The regimes' overwhelmingly optimistic picture of East-West relations and the situation in Europe turns out to be somewhat ambiguous when it is examined more closely, however. While they speak of unprecedented socialist victories and a superior socialist position, they also discover and accentuate the survival and vigorous activity of an allegedly powerful "capitalist reaction" which constitutes a real threat to the broadening of détente and what it is supposed to facilitate: the construction of socialism. This attitude seems to be motivated by a concern lest the mere fact of détente and a "successful conclusion" to the CSCE create a false impression in the minds of many people that the case of Europe has been settled and the fighters for peace can relax. In the view of the Soviet alliance such a vision of the future is wrong. Even with a European summit as the culmination of the CSCE the continent will only be on the threshold of its new life, constantly exposed to internal and external dangers. Hence, this will not be a time for complacency; rather, the struggle for a new Europe must be continued with even greater determination and the CPS must assume a leading role in it, in order to bring about a "Europe of peace, security, co-operation, and social progress."

The key element is the term "social progress"—a relatively new formulation indicating the nature of the final stage of the long campaign to achieve peace, security, and co-operation. The socialist community's concept of peaceful coexistence does not imply maintaining the social *status quo*, or providing a safe-conduct for the capitalist system. Peaceful coexistence means continuing the class struggle using different means; it is a process designed to prepare the way for "social progress" which figures as the ultimate assurance, the main pillar, of peace and security in a new Europe. These three—peace, security, and social progress—are seen in a dialectical relationship: the struggle for peace and security paves the way for social progress, and vice versa. What is necessary is a "combination of the struggle for a lasting peace with the struggle for social progress in capitalist countries." This is pictured as a complex, multilateral struggle conducted on more than one level. Among other things, it must inspire, further, and accomplish the following actions and aims:

(a) A "successful conclusion" of the CSCE. In this connection the regimes are particularly interested in the 10 principles regulating future interstate relations in Europe, which they claim will stabilize political détente.

(b) The stabilization of détente in the political field should be followed and complemented by military détente. This means completion of the Vienna force reduction talks along the lines proposed by the socialist countries.

(c) The ultimate aim, of course, is to eliminate the division of Europe into opposing blocs. For the time being, however, the blocs will stay, and at the present stage the forces of progress should concentrate on dissolving the military alliances. If NATO disbands, the Warsaw Pact will follow suit. The struggle against military alliances should gradually broaden into a general campaign of disarmament.

(d) Meanwhile, it is imperative to intensify the struggle against revanchist, reactionary, and revisionist forces, and to promote the cause of social progress everywhere.

For all practical purposes, "social progress," or what it is purported to accomplish, comes very close to socialism as implemented in the countries of Eastern Europe. At the same time the regimes want to assure everyone that what they have in mind is not an endorsement of the "export of socialism." In each country, they repeat, it is up to the working class and the mass movement to decide when to enter on the road to socialism. But it is also correct to say, they add, that such a decision will rarely result from a "spontaneous act." What is needed is "energetic political action," "concerted action," led—but not monopolized—by Communists and aimed at the "liquidation of the system of exploitation."

The "European concept" of the Soviet Union and its East European allies does not exist as a final, definite project, at least not for public consumption. Its main contours and guiding ideas can be discerned in many pronouncements, statements, and articles related to East-West co-operation, to the CSCE negotiations, to the European CP conference, to peaceful coexistence, to the Western economic "crisis," etc. Among the numerous elements of the concept the regimes seem to be especially interested in "social progress." Other aspects of Europe's future and organizational questions connected with the establishment of a collective security system attract much less attention. "Social progress" emerges from the campaign as a magic cure for the ills of Europe. Obviously, it is expected to bring about a breakthrough toward socialism in the West and to gradually surmount all the differences between East and West in the spirit of socialism.

Asserting Western Values

6

Shadows over Helsinki, by Leopold Labedz.
Encounter, June 1973, pp. 80–81, 88.

The achievement of nuclear parity between the USA and the USSR, international recognition of the two German states, the end of American military involvement in Viet Nam, the rise of China and Japan, the emergence and enlargement of the community of West European nations—these are the main elements which form the background to the current preparations for a Conference on European Security and Co-operation. One issue in the negotiations perhaps transcends in historical importance the immediate balance-of-power considerations. The question of the "free movement of people and information" which is being discussed at the preparatory talks in Helsinki, goes to the roots of the problem of Europe's historical identity and indeed of the Western cultural tradition.

The prospect of a détente in Europe raises different hopes and fears in the East and in the West. The very existence of negotiations on an overall European basis would seem to imply the recognition of the historical unity of Europe, but the contrasting interpretations of the issues under discussion—particularly in the question of "cultural contacts"—only emphasize the continent's continuing division. This division is based on political systems whose chief characteristics still remain essentially unchanged. Would détente between East and West offer hope or bring despair? Would it be a step towards an evolution of a new Europe in line with its own cultural tradition, or contribute to the demise of this tradition?

The resolution of conflicts in Europe in the past provides no parallels to the present situation. Ideological conflicts can no longer be assuaged by such a formula as *cuius regio eius religio* because even if it were acceptable, it would not be workable in the age of mass cross-frontier communication. Hence the historical importance for Europe in general (and for Western Europe in particular) not only of considerations of strategic security, but also of questions concerned with "the flow of ideas and information." The idea of freedom of thought and expression has been the cornerstone of the European cultural tradition at least since the Renaissance, if not since Hellenic times. Surely, if this tradition is to be preserved it must remain the cornerstone.

What risks and opportunities present themselves in the current talks and how do they bear on this issue? The negotiations in Helsinki and the intensified campaign for ideological purity in the Soviet bloc indicate that its leaders are more anxious to reinforce the present ideological divisions than to facilitate any real lowering of political and cultural barriers in Europe. As the London *Economist* (17 February) put it, although

> the Russians have shown so much enthusiasm for the Conference on European Security and Co-operation, they have also shown great reluctance to agree to anything that would actually help Europeans to feel secure or to co-operate at all closely.

The Soviet Ambassador, Viktor Maltsev, explained in Helsinki that in the proposed greater exchange of ideas "there can be no room for the dissemination of anti-culture—pornography, racism, fascism, the cult of violence, hostility among peoples and false slanderous propaganda." This is a formula which can easily be made to exclude any and all ideas to be "exchanged." Yuri Zhukov, the official Soviet commentator, provided earlier (in *Pravda*, 12 January) an authoritative explanation of what Mr. Brezhnev meant when he said (speech of 21 December 1972) that the acceptance of a wider exchange of ideas, information, and personal contacts in Europe must be limited by "the sovereignty, laws and customs" of each country. In Zhukov's blunter formulation, the socialist countries are not going to open their doors to "bourgeois ideological invasion," because such "ideological disarmament" would lead to the re-establishment of bourgeois society.

Although the internal effects of détente are not uniform throughout the Soviet bloc, they are far from producing the expected relaxation necessary for "a free flow of ideas, of information, and of people." But it is now argued that neither *Ostpolitik* nor détente were supposed to produce immediate results (although the Western public was led to believe that there would be improvement rather than deterioration in this respect). The optimistic view is that the positive and beneficial effects will come later. In the long run, the policies adopted (such as endorsement of the legitimacy of the Soviet position in Eastern Europe, relaxation of trade and technological barriers, and even the real risks which political concessions entail for the West) would be justified. As Dr. Roger Morgan has succinctly put it, "the lesson of the 1960s, now being drawn by the West, is that the best hope of changing the status quo lies in accepting it."

Optimism can be the basis of political dynamism or of wishful thinking, just as pessimism can lead either to realism or to despair. From an analytical viewpoint they are both irrelevant. What is important are the actual policies applied to the present situation which the West has adopted, for better or for worse, and which may turn out to be either relatively successful or absolutely catastrophic but, as the optimists hope and the pessimists fear, their results will only be apparent "in the long run." It would seem logical, therefore, considering the historical nature of the challenge, to approach the problems which form the subject of détente negotiations by adopting a long-term perspective, however difficult it may be for the usually short-sighted pragmatism of Western foreign policy. The West both lacks cohesion and fears the loss of military security, particularly in Europe. The Soviet Union, while increasing its military might, remains in many ways politically vulnerable. But the historical prospects of the challenges present in the East-West negotiations in Helsinki (and elsewhere) are not limited to the question of the immediate military and political equilibrium. Whatever the formula arrived at on the basis of these undoubtedly important considerations, it is the factors pertaining to the question of legitimacy which are decisive in the long run; and in this respect the West simply cannot afford to give up its assets. Just as the Communist countries are afraid of the political consequences of cultural relaxation, so the West would become peculiarly vulnerable if it betrayed its own cultural tradition. Hence the importance of emphasizing in this context the role of cultural factors and of their long-run effect not only for the East but also for the West. If it does not defend its cultural values, if it fails to stand firm on the question of cultural freedom in general, the West will not only throw away the chance of the eventual evolution of the Communist regimes but will also gravely jeopardize the chances of survival of these standards in the West. Freedom is not always "indivisible," but surely compromise on cultural questions may well lead to a decline of intellectual freedom in the West.

7

EEC Stresses Common Approach, by Russell Dybvik.
Report by RFE correspondent, Brussels,
June 8 and September 28, 1973.

The nine Common Market governments have stressed at the Helsinki
preparatory talks that Community procedures must be applied in dealing with any East-West trade program emerging from the conference.

This position was made clear by Belgian Ambassador Jacques Eggermont, speaking for the nine-nation Community, at Thursday's plenary
session in Helsinki.

"It especially concerns commercial exchanges about which the Community holds a common policy," the Belgian ambassador said. "The
nine states have examined the mandate concerning commercial exchanges also in their quality as members of the European Community.
The Belgian delegation, in the name of the Community, is able to give
its agreement to this mandate," he said.

Eggermont was speaking for the Community as a whole because
Belgium currently holds the presidency of the EEC Council of Ministers.

European Commission Deputy Secretary General Klaus Meyer today
told newsmen in Brussels that Eggermont's intervention was "a first
step toward normalization" of the problem of EEC representation at the
security conference.

"Since it is known that economic questions will be raised in the European Security Conference," he said, "it has been asked whether the
Community will be present to defend and talk normally of its competence as it does in other international organizations.

"As you know, there was a political problem, in that the Eastern
[European] countries do not recognize the Community and also that
this conference is considered as a conference of states.

"Yesterday, a first step toward normalizing this situation was made in
the sense that a spokesman made a declaration in the name of the members of the Community," Meyer said. . . .

The nine—first in the Helsinki Preparatory consultations, then at
the Helsinki ministerial first phase of CSCE and again on the opening day
of the Geneva phase of CSCE—have made it clear that a Community
spokesman will handle affairs within the Community's competence. It
was only Wednesday that the first formal reaction emerged.

The Czechoslovak and Soviet delegates questioned the propriety of
five Commission officials being contained within the Danish delegation.
Their titles clearly show them to be officials of the European Commis-

sion and are in the Danish delegation only because Denmark currently holds the presidency of the Common Market Council of Ministers.

8

On Behalf of the European Communities, by Aldo Moro.
Speech at the CSCE meeting, Helsinki, July 30, 1975. "Verbatim Record of the First Meeting," July 30, 1975, CSCE/III/PV.1, pp. 27–28.

It is within this framework of a dynamic perspective and an enrichment of the very fabric of political and human relations that, as Chairman of the Council of the European Communities, I would like to recall the declaration made in Helsinki on 3 July 1973, by the Minister of Foreign Affairs of Denmark on behalf of the European Communities. Mr. Andersen drew the attention of his colleagues to the fact that, according to the subjects, the Communities could be involved, in conformity with their competences and internal procedures, in the work of the Conference and that the implementation of the results of the negotiations on these subjects would depend on the agreement of the Communities. The latter have considered the conclusions of the Conference on these matters and I have the honour to inform you that these have been accepted.

Consequently, I shall sign the Final Act of the Conference in my dual capacity: as representative of Italy and as President in office of the Council of the Communities respectively.

Third countries will have the assurance therefore that the conclusions of this Conference will be applied by the Communities in all matters which are within their competence, or which may come within their competence in future.

I would like to recall that in terms of economic and social development, and also with a view to greater and improved international economic relations, the European Communities have already made a significant contribution to the objectives of this Conference. The Member States of the European Communities, recalling the evolving nature of their institutions, consider that the results of the Conference will not provide a hindrance to the process of European integration which they intend freely to pursue. This process, which is a factor of peace and security, constitutes a positive contribution to the development of co-operation in Europe. The Member States intend to continue together to co-operate with all participating countries in order to achieve this objective.

The cohesion of the nine countries of the European Communities has proved useful in the work of the Conference and this is indeed a constructive contribution in trying to find points of common agreement with the participating States. In fact it is a testimony to the open spirit with which these countries intend to continue their multilateral dialogue for the purpose of détente, peace and co-operation.

The Creation of Basket Three

9

Human Contacts and the Spread of Information, by Luigi V. Ferraris. In Luigi V. Ferraris (ed.), *Report on a Negotiation: Helsinki— Geneva—Helsinki 1972–1975* (Alphen aan den Rijn: Sijthoff and Noordhoff, 1979), pp. 53–56, 299–305, 308–12, 321–27. Translated from the Italian by Marie-Claire Barber.

Negotiations regarding the various topics of the Third Committee started on 28 March 1973 and concluded on 8 June, resulting in four working documents preceded by a preamble. The four documents contained the mandate for the four Subcommittees, which during the course of the Conference's second stage were to prepare the proposals for improvement of human contacts and for wider dissemination of information and greater exchanges in culture and education. The preamble stated the general objectives of the Third Committee and the ways in which these objectives were to be attained.

The first impression of the preamble and mandate was one of concreteness and innovative tension. The final result was far from what the Soviets had hoped for at the beginning of the preliminaries. Ambassador Valerian Zorin, head of the Soviet delegation during the preliminaries, arrived in Stockholm on a working visit at the beginning of November 1972 and reconfirmed Moscow's feelings on the length of time the Conference should last—not more than two or three weeks. He also reconfirmed that, other than the declaration on principles, the agenda should concern questions of economic, technical, and cultural cooperation, but that any reference to the exchange of people and ideas should be excluded. In substance, Moscow expected a very short final document that would outline some fundamental directives for future inter-European cooperation, aimed at maintaining the status quo.

Later on, these concepts were carried forward by the head of the Soviet delegation, Ambassador Zorin, in two interventions on 3 and 4

April. In these he emphasized, with great singlemindedness, that because human contacts constituted a part of cultural cooperation, they could not be placed in the mandate for the Third Committee; moreover, they should be discussed and resolved bilaterally.

These strongly held points of view make possible a clearer outlining of the views of the USSR and its allies.

(A) The search for a multilateral understanding in the fields of "cultural cooperation," based on a series of "fundamental directives" that each country would put into effect in accordance with its own legal system;

(B) The availability for talks on some of the humanitarian problems (for instance, the reunification of families), in which only the states concerned could take part, and, in any case, this could be done only outside of the Conference.

These objectives are highlighted by the intention of the USSR and its allies, shown on various occasions even if indirectly, to exclude every possible modification of national legislation in the field of human contacts.

The Western standpoint at the preliminaries was based on the view that in Europe there is a divergence between the universally accepted rules and the situation as it actually is—and in gradual decline—typified by obstacles that prevent talks and the establishment of improved relations between individuals or institutions. To be innovative with respect to this situation, the Western countries were asking the Conference for a series of specific measures that would give a new priority to contacts between people and to cultural exchanges.

In the case of the Eastern countries the Conference was to stop détente from being a monopoly of the governments, replacing it instead by the spontaneous product of contacts between individuals. In the case of the Eastern countries—détente being an instrument of a definite state objective—contacts among individuals and cultural cooperation should be seen and dealt with in the light of such objectives.

It is necessary to understand the big difference that exists between the expression "work out new ways and means appropriate to these aims"—an expression that demands adoption of a series of concrete measures that would be implemented by all thirty-five Conference participants—and the adoption of a series of "fundamental directives" (this was a viewpoint defended by the Eastern European countries at the preliminaries), which each country would put into effect, choosing the moment and the means.

On 19 September 1973, in the formal opening of work on the second phase of the Conference, the Swiss Ambassador, Bindschedler, made an indirect allusion to what was to be the Third Committee's real negotiating problem: "Attention, Messieurs, le diable est dans les détails." The drama of all the working organs of the Third Committee was, in fact, in the very "detail." The Western delegations insisted on detailed proposals; the Eastern European delegations, on the other hand, refused to deal with details or tended to water them down into general directives.

The coordination among the Nine was excellent, even though their emphasis sometimes differed. Holland's firmness contrasted with the Federal Republic of Germany's caution. France enjoyed emphasizing the importance of the search for "that which unites us, leaving aside that which divides us." Italy was no less firm than Holland, although she expressed her ideas in more sober terms. Among the NATO countries, the United States showed itself to be extremely discreet, while Canada and Turkey played an active and brilliant role in a search for a solution to the negotiating problems. Finland was able to maintain her rather difficult position with great dignity. Austria always offered her contribution with highly honest intentions and with courage. There were, of course, moments of uncertainty in the face of the monolithic negotiating posture of the Eastern European delegations. But the strong line assumed by the Nine was not excessively undermined, even when, outside of the Conference, positions were taken on the inopportuneness of upsetting the process of East-West détente, which seemed to contain an invitation to moderation for the Western negotiators.

During the course of a working lunch on 5 December, given by the Soviet delegation for the Italian delegates, the Deputy Foreign Minister of the USSR and Leader of the Soviet delegation at the Conference, Kovalev, plainly stated:

(A) The Third Committee would have only one final document "drawn up so as to be understood by public opinion." This was a typical expression that the Soviet delegation resorted to in order to indicate that the Conference should conclude with a single general document, since it would be based on general directives and not on specific proposals.

(B) The USSR did not intend to relent on the question of the preamble to the final document of the Third Committee.

(C) Standing firm on these two conditions, the USSR was willing to search for acceptable solutions to the various questions that came under the Third Committee's jurisdiction.

Thus, long and exhausting negotiations began on the question of the preamble, about which the Nine were uncertain as to which path they should follow. Was it better to accept a preamble that included a gen-

eral reference to the principles, or should possible safety clauses be negotiated within the introductory paragraphs of the Subcommittees? In
other words, should they accept a safety clause of a general nature, or
should they accept single clauses for the different subjects?

May, June, and July 1974 were characterized by almost total stagna-
tion since the USSR and its allies had blocked the work of drafting in
the Subcommittees with pretexts and cavils of every sort. During informal contacts the Eastern European delegates did not hide their profound dissatisfaction over the lack of any progress in drafting the preamble of the Third Committee. This was also discussed during the
meeting between Kissinger and Gromyko, which took place at the end
of April. Apparently Gromyko raised the problem of the preamble,
pointing out the principles that interested the USSR, and Kissinger replied, insisting on the fact that some progress should be made in the
humanitarian and other sectors. The two interlocutors appear to have
adhered to their own points of view; at any rate, no date was considered
for a final meeting of the Conference.

During the middle of June, Finland put forward a compromise proposal on the problems pending in the First and Third Committees (the
"all-embracing package"), which provided that "cooperation should
take place in the full respect of the principles." This meant that the
criteria agreed upon during the course of negotiations could not be considered definitively accepted but were subject to a sort of "permanent
control" on the part of the states before the Conference's decisions
could be implemented. Thus, it is no longer the human contacts and
their improvement, in themselves, that favor détente, but it is the State
that judges when human contacts are admissible or when they should
be curbed in carrying out their strategic objectives in any given historical moment.

The "all-embracing package" was approved on 26 July, the last work-
day of the Conference before the summer break. On the same day an
attempt was made to complete drafting of the document on access to
printed information, which, in the translation worked out by the Soviet
experts, meant access to journals and periodicals from other countries,
by "organizations" rather than "individuals." The negotiations dragged
on uselessly until late evening in a tired and emotional atmosphere.

During October and November, discussion of the safety clause requested by the USSR ("reciprocally acceptable conditions") continued
in the Subcommittee for Human Contacts.

The efforts of the Western delegations were aimed at opposing the
Soviet definition, which intended giving the clause an interlocutory

character, subordinating to its solution all other progress in the sector on Human Contacts.

It was, in fact, the consensus of the Western delegations that accepting such a clause would have legitimized the right of every state to refuse to implement the decisions agreed upon at the Conference.

On 3 December—after more than eight months of negotiations—the document on the reunification of families was approved. This constituted an important step forward in the negotiations on Human Contacts.

The document did, in fact, clearly and originally establish the rules of conduct that states should follow on bilateral and multilateral levels in regulating a subject about which it had been recognized that humanitarian needs prevail above any other consideration.

It was only at the end of April 1975, when a situation of total stalemate became clear, that it was decided, as a first step, to work out a complete document of all the registered and nonregistered texts of the two Subcommittees. With regard to the problems still pending, this would safeguard the basic Western positions, while at the same time it would naturally contemplate certain necessary concessions so the document could be given serious consideration.

The document that had been set down was basically satisfactory. The texts relating to Human Contacts—the preamble and formalities for travel—were slightly weakened with respect to the original Western proposals; the texts relating to Information and in particular to the working conditions of journalists remained more or less faithful to the original requests.

On 19 May, Kissinger and Gromyko met in Vienna. On this occasion it appears that Kissinger praised the Western document to his Soviet colleague, leading Gromyko to clearly understand that it was an important and serious step that the Socialist delegations had taken.

On 28 May, at a working lunch, Deputy Minister Kovalev and ambassadors of the United States, Great Britain, and France discussed the questions not connected to the Third Basket. During the course of the lunch (which, according to Conference rumors, was interrupted by telephone calls from Moscow) the Soviet delegates asked for a confrontation on Third Basket problems. Additionally, in order to try to sweep aside a few of the more serious reservations put in the way of the Western document, they clearly indicated that they agreed to start negotiations on the basis of the "global" idea requested by the Western delegations.

The immediate impression among the majority of Western delegations was that the signal expected for so long from the Soviet delegation had finally arrived. Certain delegations still called for caution, but undoubtedly a general feeling prevailed that the Soviet move should be interpreted as a decisive and true desire to search for an agreement that would lead toward meeting many of the Western requests. The withdrawal of certain important reservations from the Western document considerably reduced the points that the Soviet delegation had said they still wished to negotiate: of the twenty-seven problems brought up by the Soviets in the texts on Human Contacts, only nine remained; and of the nineteen points raised in the texts on Information, fourteen remained.

In spite of the major openings in the Human Contacts part of the document—which was, in fact, the weakest part of the entire package—the distinct impression arose that even on the other points it would be possible to find solutions satisfactory to the West. The Soviet delegation, in fact, had let it be known that they wished to conclude the Conference. Thus the West found itself in a privileged negotiating position.

On the afternoon of 29 May the first informal meeting among the delegation leaders took place, coordinated by the Austrian representative (for Human Contacts) and the Swiss representative (for Information). Two of the Western leaders, Denmark and Great Britain, immediately took the floor to express their satisfaction with the constructive interest shown by the Eastern countries in the Western document. Dubinin and the Polish representative, Dobrosielski, replied, expressing their willingness to negotiate.

It is interesting to point out that, right from this first meeting, the Romanians, followed by the Yugoslavs and the Spanish, were keen to stress that they intended to participate in all the negotiating sessions, and they did not intend—and the Romanian delegate strongly pointed out his view—to delegate the protection of their interests to anyone else, adding that the negotiations should not assume the nature of an East-West meeting.

During the course of this first meeting there occurred what for months had seemed impossible: the Polish ambassador, on behalf of the Socialist delegations, accepted the entire preamble to Human Contacts in the version that had been presented in the Western document, with the exception of the last paragraph where there remained the well-known difficulty of indicating the nature of the participating states' commitment. They accepted all the titles and subtitles requested by the West.

The meetings then followed one after another, with the sessions stretching into the night and always within the same room (jokingly called "the room of miracles"). During the days immediately following, the other important question to which a satisfactory answer was found was the text relating to journalists. A few days after 29 May, the Soviet delegation began to appear more flexible in this sector as well, and realistically positive solutions were found to such problems as the reference to technical personnel, which the Soviets had maintained, up till that moment, not to even wish to negotiate.

The paragraph concerning the nonexpulsion of journalists was accepted in its entirety in the Western version; the paragraph relating to contacts with information sources did not retain the explicit reference to individuals—which was objectively impossible to obtain—but was formulated in such a way as not to exclude such a possibility.

At the same time the Americans presented another version of the paragraph on broadcast information to the Soviet delegation. This version did not receive the total and general consent of certain delegations of the Nine, but later, during the last days of the negotiations, it was accepted by all the delegations.

On 6 June, during the course of a lengthy night meeting, an agreement was reached on the introductory text to the information based on a satisfactory balance that—as always required by the West—separated the safety clause, introduced by the Eastern countries, from the final paragraph, which contains the list of objectives that the states intended pursuing.

Many meetings followed for the tedious verification of the translations. (Certain delegations, including the Soviets and Americans, were very careful about this aspect of the work.) Finally, on 4 July came provisional registration in the Third Committee of all the texts jointly.

On this occasion various delegations took the floor to mark the important event and to make general comments. The first to speak was Ambassador Dubinin who underlined the important "step forward in quality," which took place with the registration of the Third Basket texts; from a confrontation of different points of view, they had arrived at co-authorship of a common text.

Immediately afterward, Ambassador Farace took the floor to point out the constructive presence of the Nine at the Third Basket negotiations and to stress faith in the political responsibility and goodwill with which the participating states would have to implement the measures envisaged by the texts.

Security as a Process

10

Follow-Up to the Conference, by Ljubivoje Ačimović. In
Ljubivoje Ačimović, *Problems of Security and Co-operation in
Europe* (Alphen aan den Rijn: Sijthoff and Noordhoff, 1981),
pp. 270–74, 278–82.

From the very first steps taken to convene the Conference on Security
and Cooperation in Europe, the question arose of what would happen
afterwards and how provision would be made for a continuation of efforts. However, the ideas and policies of various participating states, and
even the terminology used, underwent a certain evolution.

At first, even before the preliminary consultations at Helsinki, there
was much thought and talk about institutionalizing the Conference by
setting up bodies authorized to deal with questions of European security.

Later there were certain shifts in the positions taken by various participating states and subsequent terminological changes: especially during the last phase of the multilateral preparatory talks in Helsinki, the
phrases "institutionalization" or "creation of an organ for questions of
security and cooperation in Europe" were dropped in favor of the phrase
"follow-up to the Conference."

Views gradually evolved on whether or not the momentum created
by the Conference should be maintained: before and during the preparatory consultations in Helsinki opinion in the West finally swung over
to a negative position regarding the idea of any follow-up (especially
under the influence of France and the United States); during the second
stage of the Conference the Soviet Union gradually lost its original enthusiasm for the institutionalization of the Conference and substantially
modified its policy on the follow-up; in the middle of the second stage,
the non-bloc countries and Romania mounted a strong campaign in
favor of a follow-up to the Conference and with the indirect support of
some smaller western countries (notably Norway) managed to overcome all opposition and achieve their goal.

At the ministerial meeting in Helsinki (first stage), the Soviet Union
and its allies included within the Czechoslovak proposal a draft document on the follow-up which provided for the creation of a consultative
committee which would act in the period between future conferences.
The basic weakness of this proposal was that the main function of the
envisaged mechanism was not focused on the implementation of the
decisions of the Conference, i.e., the provisions of the Final Act, and

on the promotion of the multilateral effort initiated by it, but rather on it being a body to oversee peace and security in Europe (in practical terms, to act as an institutional watchdog for the territorial and political status quo in this continent). This plan was unacceptable to the other participating states, including Romania. Also there was a prevailing belief that nothing should interfere with the general jurisdiction of the UN Security Council, and that consequently no parallel body on a regional level should be created.

However, this initiative reflected only the initial position of the Soviet Union and its allies, and it was gradually abandoned in the course of the Geneva talks; indeed, the idea of any genuine follow-up to the Conference on Security and Cooperation in Europe was dropped altogether. This change of heart could be accounted for by the evolution of the Conference itself during the Geneva negotiation, which went far beyond the scope envisaged by the Warsaw Pact countries when they first called for the convening of such a conference. The wide range of issues discussed and the substantive nature of the impending resolutions (for instance, in the third basket, and as regards the military aspects of security of the Mediterranean question) discouraged these countries from insisting that this multilateral undertaking be continued. This change could first be sensed at Geneva, when these countries stopped pushing so hard for a follow-up to the Conference and then revised their original demand by seeking merely the occasional convening of further conferences on security and cooperation in Europe (presumably at the summit level). The East thus withdrew from the first ranks of the battle for a follow-up to the CSCE, leaving as the main antagonists the non-bloc countries and Romania on one side and the NATO countries (including some smaller countries which were more inclined to support the position of the non-bloc countries) on the other side.

In line with their general attitude towards the Conference on Security and Cooperation in Europe, the non-bloc countries and Romania immediately felt that it would be an essential part of the expected results of the Conference to secure a genuine continuity. Only on a long-term basis, as a sustained all-European effort, could it perform its historical function. These countries insisted the entire time, from the Helsinki consultations to the last days of the second Geneva stage, that this idea be incorporated in the Final Act. They enjoyed a varying degree of support from countries such as Norway, Spain and Canada, and had unspoken sympathy from some East European countries, for instance Poland.

The basic policy and bargaining position of the non-bloc countries regarding the follow-up to the CSCE were embodied in the proposal on

this issue submitted by Yugoslavia in March 1974. The gist of this proposal—which emphasized that the Conference as an active factor in improving security and cooperation in Europe must make sure that the
multilateral effort which it initiated be continued if its goals were to be
achieved—was that a permanent all-European body to be called the
Continuing Committee be set up for the purpose of coordinating, initiating and reviewing activities involved with the implementation of the
decisions of the Conference, and also to further the cooperation begun
between participating states as well as prepare for new conferences of
this kind. There was no question of setting up a regional international
organization to deal with questions of security and cooperation in Europe, but rather of establishing this form of European consultation
through periodic meetings of representatives of the participating states.

The position of the NATO member countries and especially of the EEC
in its compromise form was set forth in the Danish proposal submitted
in April 1974. Its main feature was the rejection of the system of regular (periodic) meetings and thereby of any genuine follow-up to the
Conference. As conceived in this document, the work of the CSCE would
be sustained through two types of measures: first, unilateral, bilateral
and multilateral measures to implement the decisions (embodied in the
provisions of the Final Act) of the Conference; and second, the convening in 1977 of a meeting of high officials of the participating states
to review the progress made both in implementing these decisions and
in improving relations among participating states and, in the light of its
findings, to submit proposals outlining the appropriate measures still
required in order to achieve the goals set by the Conference on Security
and Cooperation in Europe—measures such as (i) additional meetings
of experts, (ii) subsequent meetings of high officials, (iii) a new conference.

The compromise was reached at two levels: in the conception of the
basic parts of the follow-up document—the preamble representing the
views of the non-bloc countries and the main body reflecting the policies of the western countries, and secondly, within the main body of the
document where the position of the West is modified in favor of certain
concessions to the concept of the CSCE follow-up as envisaged by the
non-bloc countries. By its very nature, the compromise on this question
was not a sound solution because of the discrepancy between the introductory part and the main body of the follow-up document.

The document first sets forth the purpose of further meetings at a
European level and then prescribes its organizational aspect. The purpose of such meetings is described as a "thorough exchange of views"
both on the implementation of the provisions of the Final Act and on

measures to promote security and cooperation in Europe. As we can see, the purpose of further action is fairly clearly stated, but the details are missing. The adopted compromise wording reflects the twofold opposition to a follow-up: first, because of the objections of the eastern bloc there is no specific mention of an evaluation of the implementation of the provisions of the Final Act but only a thorough exchange of views, and second, because of the opposition of both blocs, especially the West, there is no specific reference to consideration and adoption of new measures, but, again, only to a thorough exchange of views "on the deepening of their mutual relation, the improvement of security and the development of cooperation in Europe, and the development of the process of détente in the future." The doors are thus left ajar for any later attempts to restrict or check the follow-up activities, but on the other hand, the text as a whole provides sufficient grounds for opposing such attempts. In other words, the restrictive approaches were not accepted, but they were given some leeway, which, if used, is bound to lead to disagreements and disputes.

The organizational aspect of the CSCE follow-up, which is of vital importance for the practical implementation of the very idea of the continuity of the CSCE process, is precisely that part of the compromise in which the West gained the upper hand. Instead of the establishment of a system of regular meetings at a European level, the possibility was only envisaged of meetings of representatives of the participating states to carry out the aforementioned "thorough exchange of views," and the time and place were specified for the first meeting only, which was also charged with the task of defining the modalities of similar meetings and a new Conference.

The proponents of a genuine continuity of the CSCE process nevertheless succeeded, albeit in an indirect way, in securing a foothold in the text that would give them scope for further action in that a provision was included which speaks in plural of the organization of meetings of representatives of participating states. The Belgrade meeting is described as the first of this kind and is given the task of deciding on the modalities for similar meetings to follow. These clauses, backed in the preamble to this chapter of the Final Act by clear provisions generally endorsing the idea of the continuity of the CSCE process, provide a good basis for further efforts to ensure this continuity.

The importance of the follow-up to the Conference on Security and Cooperation in Europe is related to the very nature of this all-European undertaking, and to the fact that the Conference forms an integral part of a broader process of a positive transformation of contemporary international relations and that, consequently, it cannot remain as a single, once-only act but must take on the aspects of a process or of a sustained action. Therefore, any interruption of this process would amount to a denial of the Conference itself, and if it is implemented on a provisional, ad hoc basis, this would again make its achievements unstable and uncertain. This fact implies further considerations which determine the importance of the follow-up to the CSCE.

First, the Final Act as a political instrument for achieving the aims adopted at the Conference will be politically viable only so long as there is an appropriate sustained all-European action. Any interruption in this multilateral process will make the Final Act a document more of historical interest than of any relevance to current political affairs, a document that may be cited but that will not serve as an instrument for action, and objectively it will become a dead letter. Thereby the Conference would become an event of ephemeral importance.

Second, the long-term changes that are desired and that should be gradually effected on the basis of the results of the Conference on Security and Cooperation in Europe imply the elimination of the bloc system of relations, and this cannot be achieved in a world in which only bloc institutions are operating, i.e., without a non-bloc all-European context. The blocs cannot be expected to dig their own graves, nor can the efforts initiated by the CSCE be carried out by individual states or in a piecemeal fashion. If there is no follow-up to the CSCE, Europe stays with all its previous divisions and bloc machinery, without any organized all-inclusive undertaking. The assumption was that this new, all-European organized effort should not only become a practice but should grow and with time assume a dominant place in the context of European association.

Third, if it is correct, as we believe, that a resolution of the problems of security and cooperation in Europe requires first and foremost qualitative rather than quantitative changes in international relations, then the implementation of the provisions of the Final Act cannot be seen as a mechanical sum of individual unilateral, bilateral or multilateral activities, but must necessarily be a concerted effort to achieve the desired goal. The general regular meetings of representatives of the participating states would have precisely the function of coordinating and guiding the numerous wide-ranging activities involved in implementing the provisions of the Final Act. These meetings would provide the auspices for the necessary political synthesis of all the individual ongoing work and would give the entire undertaking a new, all-European and non-bloc character.

Fourth, from the standpoint of security, the very fact that there would be a regular gathering of European countries based on the Final

Act, with all its politically extremely important content and form, would undoubtedly exert a positive influence—the awareness that a meeting of the "European plenum" is imminent might for instance to some extent deter a potential aggressor. Without overestimating this effect, we must assume nevertheless that a country would be more prone to resort to force when it could expect to face only individual protests and complaints than when such an action would automatically, at the next CSCE follow-up meeting, be entered into the general balance sheet of the results in implementing the Final Act. At any rate, these regular gatherings would have a positive, stimulating effect as regards compliance with all the assumed obligations.

Inviolability of Frontiers

11

The Inevitable Conclusions, by John J. Maresca.
In John J. Maresca, *To Helsinki: The Conference on Security
and Cooperation in Europe,* 1973–1975 (Durham, N.C.: Duke
University Press, 1985), pp. 110–16.

If the Final Act has a claim to being a substitute for a peace settlement
following the Second World War, it is principally because of the agreement it contains on frontiers in Europe. This compromise between the
concept of inviolability of frontiers and the possibility of peaceful change
is a carefully balanced one and is the CSCE's attempt at a rational approach to the territorial questions left over from the war. In declaring
that the present boundaries of states in Europe are inviolable, the CSCE
confirmed multilateral acceptance of the changes resulting from the
war; the geopolitical status quo in Europe was accepted with a number
of unresolved issues left intact. At the same time the peaceful change
language preserved positions of principle about future revisions; the
possibility of a physical evolution of the territorial situation was thus
also accepted, provided it occurs peacefully.

For the Soviets, the principle of inviolability of frontiers was—in the
private words of one of their delegates—"the key to European security,"
since it would permanently fix all European frontiers, particularly the
division of Germany. Not only would this protect the status of the
GDR, the USSR's strongest ally; it would also prevent a united Germany from again threatening the Soviet Union, and would facilitate the
growth of Soviet influence in Western Europe. The Soviets also had an

interest in obtaining language recognizing their incorporation of the Baltic states (Latvia, Lithuania, and Estonia) into the USSR.

The Soviets regarded as a major achievement the agreement reached during the Helsinki preparatory talks to include inviolability as a separate and distinct principle on the list of ten principles to be drafted during Stage II of the Conference. The nearest precedent for the CSCE principles, the UN Friendly Relations Declaration, contains the following language on inviolability of frontiers: "Every state has the duty to refrain from the threat or use of force to violate the existing international boundaries of another State. . . ." However, in the UN document this phrase is contained in the principle of refraining from the threat or use of force, and is not a separate principle.

From the outset of the Geneva phase of the CSCE, the Soviet delegation stressed the need for a "crystal clear" principle of inviolability and asserted that they would not budge from their own proposed language on inviolability: "Inviolability of frontiers, in accordance with which the participating States regard the existing frontiers in Europe as inviolable now and in the future, will make no territorial claims upon each other and acknowledge that peace in that area can be preserved only if no one encroaches upon the present frontiers."

In addition to the Soviet-proposed version of the inviolability principle, there were also FRG and French versions, which were very similar and had U.S. support, and a Yugoslav draft. The key element in the FRG (and French) draft was inclusion, in the inviolability principle itself, of language specifying that peaceful changes in frontiers were not excluded and were in keeping with international law: "The participating States have the duty to refrain from the threat or use of force against the existing international frontiers of another participating State or for the settlement of territorial disputes and questions relating to State frontiers. The participating States regard one another's frontiers, in their existing form and irrespective of the legal status which in their opinion they possess, as inviolable. The participating States are of the opinion that their frontiers can be changed only in accordance with international law, through peaceful means and by agreement with due regard for the right of the peoples of self-determination."

Like the establishment of inviolability as a separate principle, the inclusion of language specifying that peaceful change is possible was a novel idea. No such language appears in the Friendly Relations Declaration, which because of its universal acceptance was regarded as a model for work on the CSCE principles.

When the drafting of the principles began in early February, 1974, the Soviets undertook a concerted drive for acceptance of their inviolability language. The inviolability principle was the third on a list of ten, and drafting on it began in March, after completion of drafting on the first two principles. This timing was unfortunate for the FRG; their leverage would have been stronger if this key Soviet desideratum had come under negotiation later, simultaneously with other major Conference issues.

As drafting work proceeded, it became clear that the Soviets would accept language on peaceful changes of frontiers provided it was separate from the principle of inviolability. The first of several key negotiating compromises on the inviolability/peaceful change issue came as the result of the Spanish suggestion that language on peaceful change be drafted on a separate piece of paper simultaneously with drafting of the inviolability principle itself. The text of the principle, as it emerged from the final drafting process, was brief: "The participating States regard as inviolable all one another's frontiers as well as the frontiers of all States in Europe and therefore they will refrain now and in the future from assaulting these frontiers.

"Accordingly, they will also refrain from any demand for, or act of, seizure and usurpation of part or all of the territory of any participating State" (Final Act [FA] 31–32).[1]

The floating sentence on peaceful change read as follows: "The participating States consider that their frontiers can be changed only in accordance with international law through peaceful means and by agreement."

The FRG had no problem with the first paragraph of the inviolability language; Bonn accepted that frontiers should not be altered by force, that they were therefore "inviolable," and that they should not be "assaulted." The second paragraph, too, was generally acceptable; the FRG, like other CSCE participants, agreed that there should be no "act of seizure or usurpation" of territory. But the inclusion of the phrase, "any demand for" seizure and usurpation was less clear. It was thought that this phrase might be read as excluding even reiteration of the FRG's position of principle that the reunification of Germany should one day be possible in peaceful circumstances.

To clarify the point, the German delegation sought Soviet views on the meaning of the phrase. On the final day before agreement, after difficult discussions, the question was put to Kovalev: What was the Soviet interpretation of the significance of the phrase "demand for"? Kovalev's response was rambling and ambiguous. He was then pressed to cite an example of what the Soviets would view as a "demand for" seizure and usurpation of territory. Finally, Kovalev gave an example: an "ultimatum" would, in Moscow's view, constitute a "demand for" territory.

The German delegation told Kovalev that the Bonn government would record this interpretation with their negotiating history of the inviolability clause, and if there were ever a dispute on the issue, the FRG would publicly cite Kovalev's example as the accepted Soviet definition of what constituted a "demand for."

This information was conveyed by phone to Bonn. Most senior officials were unreachable, and final authorization to accept the compromise was difficult to obtain. Late in the evening, telephonic instructions were given, including the five conditions that were later met, and the principle of inviolability, along with the "floating sentence" on peaceful change, was approved.

Agreement was "subject to subsequent decision on location in final document/documents and to agreement on texts as a whole." This meant that the phrase on peaceful change could theoretically be included in any one of the ten principles, including inviolability of frontiers.

The Western delegations felt that the inviolability language as agreed conveyed the idea that only violent changes in frontiers were excluded and that, with the phrase on peaceful change to be inserted in the list of principles providing specific acknowledgment of the possibility of peaceful change, an acceptable balance had been struck. The word, "assaulting," was particularly thought to convey the sense of the type of violent change that should be excluded, even though this word was translated into Russian as "posegat," which conveys a less violent impression.

Following registration of the principle of inviolability of frontiers and the enunciation of the FRG's reservations, Chancellor Schmidt and Foreign Minister Hans-Dietrich Genscher, perceiving that the FRG's negotiating position with regard to language on peaceful change had been considerably weakened, approached Kissinger seeking active American assistance in negotiating a peaceful change clause that would more effectively balance the inviolability language and preserve the FRG's position of principle on German reunification.

The United States could hardly refuse such a request from a key ally, and agreed to put forward the FRG's preferred peaceful change language as a U.S. proposal. This "U.S." proposal on peaceful change was tabled in the full CSCE on July 26, 1974: "In accordance with international law, the participating States consider that their frontiers can be changed through peaceful means and by agreement." About four months had passed since registration of the so-called "floating sentence" on the same subject.

The "U.S." formulation was intended for placement elsewhere than the principle of inviolability of frontiers, probably in the principle of sovereign equality, and it was therefore necessary that the phraseology be similar to that of the other attributes listed; it could not be phrased negatively by inclusion of the word "only," since the other attributes were phrased positively and such a juxtaposition would have stressed the fact that peaceful change can occur solely in certain narrow circumstances.

The Soviet reaction to the U.S. proposal was decidedly cool, not only to the substance of the new phrase, but also to the fact that the United States was acting on behalf of the FRG. The Soviets became even more annoyed when they tried to discuss this new language and were referred back and forth between the West Germans and Washington.

The U.S. action set off a series of contacts and exchanges on the peaceful change sentence, which was a subject of discussion at or on the fringes of virtually every high-level U.S.-Soviet or U.S.-FRG meeting during the following six months, in New York, Moscow, Vladivostok, Washington, and Geneva. The Soviets produced an alternative text that was very close to the "floating sentence" phraseology, and the United States, again acting with and for the FRG, presented another variant to the Soviet embassy in Washington in January 1975: "The participating States consider in accordance with international law that their frontiers can be changed by peaceful means and agreement." The Soviets rejected this new variant in mid-February.

On February 17, Kissinger arrived in Geneva on short notice for one of his periodic meetings with Gromyko. This two-day visit would dramatically affect the negotiation on frontiers.

Both men wanted to resolve the peaceful change issue. It had become important to Kissinger because of his promise to the Schmidt government in Bonn to attempt to obtain Soviet agreement to language that would balance inviolability of frontiers. It was important to Gromyko because, ever since the inviolability language had been agreed, the FRG had maintained that it would not go to a Stage III Summit without a satisfactory phrase on peaceful change. Although the United States and the USSR were close to finding a formulation that would satisfy them both, the precise phraseology remained elusive.

In agreement with the FRG, the United States handed the Soviets yet another version of the peaceful change language on February 17: "The participating States consider that, in accordance with international law, their frontiers can be changed by peaceful means and by agreement."

The new formulation was delivered to the Soviet mission late in the morning and was handed immediately to Gromyko. When he met

Kissinger for lunch, Gromyko scribbled two changes on the proposed formulation. He suggested moving the phrase, "in accordance with international law," so that it would appear after the word "changed," and wanted to reintroduce the word "only." The phrase then read: "The participating States consider that their frontiers can be changed in accordance with international law only by peaceful means and by agreement."

At a meeting with Kovalev after lunch, the U.S. side told the Soviets that inclusion of "only" was not possible, since it would appear to restrict the circumstances in which frontiers can be changed. This was especially true if the sentence were to be fitted into the principle of sovereign equality. (The other possible placement discussed was in the principle of territorial integrity of states.)

It was agreed that the other suggested change would be tried out on the FRG. Both sides were to reflect on the situation.

Kissinger and his party left Geneva in the afternoon, but Gromyko remained one day longer. At nine in the evening Kovalev asked to see U.S. delegation chief Sherer. The meeting was arranged for ten o'clock. Kovalev handed over a new formulation, similar to Gromyko's latest suggestion, but without the word "only": "The participating States consider, that their frontiers can be changed in accordance with international law, by peaceful means and by agreement." (Placement of the first comma in this version may have been a simple punctuation error by the Soviets in their use of English.)

The FRG's reaction to this language was that, though elimination of the word "only" was significant progress, the sentence still had faults. As now drafted, it would make peaceful changes in frontiers subject to three conditions: they should be (1) in accord with international law, (2) by peaceful means, and (3) by agreement. Bonn felt that peaceful change was by definition in accordance with international law and that the text would reflect this fact.

To stick as closely as possible to the compromise sentence that was now emerging, the FRG suggested simply moving the erroneously placed first comma so that it would appear before the phrase, "in accordance with international law." The phrase would then read as though it was taken for granted that peaceful change was in accordance with international law: "The participating States consider that their frontiers can be changed, in accordance with international law, by peaceful means and by agreement."

This change was proposed to the Soviets, who made a swift and dramatic decision: they accepted it. Two weeks later the U.S. delegation announced to a surprised NATO caucus that agreement had been reached with the Soviets on this key Conference issue. "I would like to extend my congratulations to the negotiators," said the Canadian delegate, "whoever they may be."

When it was finally accepted by the full csce, the peaceful change sentence was included in the principle of sovereign equality, and it appears in FA 25 as negotiated between the United States and the Soviet Union.[2] To complete the balance between the inviolability and peaceful change formulations, it was also thought necessary to insert a phrase somewhere in the principles stating that all the principles are of equal weight. Such a phrase appears in FA 70: "All the principles set forth above are of primary significance and, accordingly, they will be equally and unreservedly applied, each of them being interpreted taking into account the others."[3]

When Kissinger, in a press conference on February 25, 1975, referred to issues in the csce that had "become so abstruse and esoteric" that they depended on the placement of a comma, he was referring to this episode, but while the issue of peaceful change had indeed become somewhat abstruse following lengthy and esoteric negotiations, it was, and remains, the heart of the territorial compromise that made it possible for the Conference to reach agreement.

NOTES

1   Maresca, *To Helsinki*, p. 230.
2   Ibid., p. 229.
3   Ibid., p. 233.

Freedom and Security

12

Real Security in Europe, by *The Times* (London), July 7, 1975.

Western governments have been right to insist that security in Europe depends not only on accepting existing state frontiers but also on meeting the widespread desire for freer movement of people and information. A Europe in which families are divided, in which people cannot travel and meet each other easily or inform themselves properly about what is going on, may be a secure Europe in Russian eyes but it cannot be a secure Europe in Western eyes.

This basic difference remains. The Russians continue to equate freedom with insecurity. The West continues to equate it with security. The conference has not removed the disagreement or substantially changed anybody's views. Nor will its final texts be legally binding. It has, however, been valuable in putting the issue firmly on the conference table and demonstrating that Western countries take political freedom seriously. It has shown that the future of Europe depends on very much more than endorsing the *status quo*.

13

Pledges without Restrictions, by the Ministry of Foreign Affairs of the Netherlands.
Memorandum presented to the Lower House of the States
General of the Kingdom of the Netherlands, May 3, 1979,
Human Rights and Foreign Policy (The Hague:
Ministry of Foreign Affairs, 1979), pp. 116–20.

The central passage on human rights in the Final Act is the seventh principle in the Declaration on Principles Guiding Relations between Participating States.[1]

The pledges on human rights given by the participating States in the seventh principle are formulated without restrictions. Besides, the right of the individual to know and act upon his rights and duties in this field is confirmed. Not only is this provision of great importance for the observance of the provisions of the Final Act and for the involvement of the public therein, but moreover this provision and the statement that all human rights derive from the inherent dignity of the human person emphasize that the rights in question are not granted to people by the State but are inherent in their person and that the State must respect these rights.

The importance of the reference to the International Covenants on Human Rights in so far as the participating States may be bound by them lies in the fact that now that the Covenants have been ratified by most of the CSCE countries these countries can call upon one another to observe the Covenants by virtue of this pledge to the co-signatories in the Final Act.

Finally, reference is made to the passage in which the thirty-five countries state that respect for human rights is an essential factor for the peace, justice and well-being necessary to ensure the development of friendly relations and cooperation among States. This confirms what successive Governments of the Netherlands have also maintained, namely that if détente is to develop further it cannot be restricted to relations at government level. For if human rights are trampled underfoot, tension may arise leading to repercussions in international relations. Avoiding such situations of tension is therefore an essential precondition for lasting progress in détente.

However, this in itself is not enough. Another important source of tension is mutual distrust between peoples. Breaking down distrust between the peoples of East and West is therefore of great importance if détente is to continue. In order to improve mutual understanding, the two sides must get to know each other better. The Western countries therefore opted for as much openness as possible in the CSCE negotiations. Much of this is reflected in the Final Act, for example in the confidence-building measures in the military field and in the "third basket" which, in point of fact, is concerned with breaking down barriers to freer movement of persons, ideas and information. Examples of this are the provisions on reunification of families, facilitating wider travel abroad, improving the dissemination of foreign newspapers and other publications and cooperation in the fields of education and culture.

Since the respect for human rights contained in the seventh principle relates mainly to the internal order of the participating States, it is worthwhile to consider the relationship between this principle and the sixth principle, concerning non-intervention in internal affairs.

Where the text speaks of "non-intervention," the Eastern European countries had originally proposed using the word "non-interference." In the course of the negotiations the word "non-intervention" was adopted instead, because "intervention" is more limited in scope and refers only to armed intervention, coercion or violent subversion. "Interference" on the other hand does not necessarily involve violence or coercion, but can also take place through diplomatic channels or radio broadcasts for example. The sixth principle thus does not exclude involvement of the latter kinds. This is confirmed by the second, third and fourth paragraphs of the sixth principle, where the words "accordingly" and "likewise" indicate that these paragraphs go on to define what is meant by "intervention" in the first paragraph.

The sixth principle therefore cannot correctly be invoked in order to keep other countries from commenting on inadequate observance of the provisions of the Final Act. Besides, it is not logical to try to avoid debate on the implementation of the Final Act by invoking the sixth principle. The Final Act, after all, is a series of mutual pledges which would become meaningless if the parties were not permitted to remind one another of them.

A less conspicuous passage, and one which in practice is less frequently used in defense, occurs in the first principle and states that the participating States will respect each other's right to determine its laws and regulations. This is presumably used more sparingly as an argument because of the second paragraph of the tenth principle. Here it is stated that in exercising their sovereign rights, including the right to determine their laws and regulations, the participating States will not only conform with their legal obligations under international law but will also pay due regard to and implement the provisions in the Final Act. It follows from this that if national laws or regulations conflict with the Final Act, States which maintain such provisions contravene the Final Act and are therefore answerable to the co-signatories for doing so.

In view of the above, the conclusions must be that the Final Act contains nothing which stands in the way of full implementation of the human rights norms subscribed to in it.

NOTES

1 For the full text, see John J. Maresca, *To Helsinki: The Conference on Security and Cooperation in Europe, 1973–1975* (Durham, N.C.: Duke University Press, 1985), pp. 231–32.

The Conflicting Judgments

14

The Masterly Ambiguities, by George R. Urban et al.
Symposium conducted by Radio Free Europe, December
1973–August 1975. In George R. Urban (ed.), *Détente*
(London: Temple Smith, 1976), pp. 23–25, 237, 300–320,
343–45.

Urban:[1] We have, in this symposium, repeatedly raised the question whether a declaration on European security would make any difference either to the present state of East-West relations, or to the internal status quo in Eastern Europe or Western Europe. I am curious to know in what way the Soviet and western sides are likely to harness the Helsinki document to their particular political strategies.

The interpretation of the masterly ambiguities written into the document is manifestly important. Barely two weeks after Helsinki, Brezhnev told a group of visiting US congressmen that different parts of the document required different interpretations. He said the inviolability of frontiers and non-interference in internal affairs were "points of a binding nature," whereas those contained in Basket Three were subject to further agreements.

On Portugal, too, we have seen some surprising exegeses. Within three weeks of Helsinki, *Pravda* commented that the EEC countries' decision to postpone considering (until the autumn of 1975) whether to offer economic aid to the communist-dominated Portuguese Government was "to interfere directly in the internal affairs of the Portuguese." "Is it not time," *Pravda* asked, "to begin fulfilling the obligation undertaken by the representatives of the western powers at the conference in Helsinki concerning non-interference in the internal affairs of other people?"

Labedz:[2] I am not sure that, from the western point of view, the ambiguities of the Helsinki declaration are as masterly as Urban has indicated. They are more likely to rebound against the West than against the East. Basket Three, which was the main western concern, is no more specific than the Universal Declaration of Human Rights, and can be no more effectively invoked. I am sure that Brezhnev would have readily signed the Ten Commandments if no specific clauses were to be attached to them on how exactly they must be expressed in concrete policies. The main Soviet concern—western confirmation of the existing frontiers of the Soviet empire—is also somewhat ambiguously formulated but easier to interpret as conferring international legitimacy on Soviet political and territorial expansion since the second world war. Solzhenitsyn called it the final betrayal of Eastern Europe by the West.

Western Europe conveys a message to Eastern Europe by its very existence. It makes Soviet insecurity in Eastern Europe permanent and all-pervasive. This, if nothing else, makes it imperative for the Soviet leaders to gain maximum de jure recognition for their hegemony over Eastern Europe, and to do what they can to remove the politico-cultural menace implicit, not in this or that piece of West European policy, but, as I say, in the fact that Western Europe exists. If we were not so influenced by Soviet Orwellian double-think, we would have called the Security Conference by one of its two proper names—either Soviet Security Conference, or European Insecurity Conference.

The western powers tried to limit the damage by stressing the importance of freer communications, but by putting on paper how little they were prepared to accept, they have also implicitly stated how much the Soviet side will be allowed to get away with. Also, the American apologetics of the Helsinki document would—if their logic were to be taken seriously—lead to some strange conclusions. For example, Ford assured the American public that the Helsinki document does not imply the recognition by the USA of the incorporation of the Baltic states in the USSR. But what then does it mean? The answer that it confers "only" moral but not legal recognition amounts to saying that aggression is acceptable morally but not legally—which is like refusing to condone rape in law, while condoning it in morality. This is neither good ethics, nor good jurisprudence. Is it good politics?

Urban has rightly mentioned that almost immediately after signing the Helsinki declaration, Brezhnev applied to the document the usual Soviet double standard by announcing that some of its points, which he likes, are binding, while others, which he dislikes, are not. Historically, this is just another example of the Soviet interpretation of "peaceful co-existence": you must grant *us* freedom on *your* principles—we will deny *you* freedom on *our* principles; *you* must not interfere in Eastern Europe—*we* will have a free hand in Western Europe; "arithmetic majorities" apply to missiles but not to elections, and so on.

Nor is there anything unexpected in *Pravda's* invoking the Helsinki declaration in support of communism in Portugal. What amazes me are the reactions of those supposedly shrewd western politicians and publicists who, unmindful of the political experiences of recent history, still hope (or say they hope) that the Soviet Union will somehow conform to *their* interpretation of the Helsinki declaration. There is no excuse for such naivety, self-induced or real.

Whatever uncertainties about Soviet behavior after Helsinki some western observers may entertain, the fundamental question in the late 1970's and 1980's will be exactly the same as it was after Yalta: what opportunities will Moscow be permitted to exploit? Unless there is a general re-evaluation of our foreign policy, that is to say, unless our foreign policy stops being a record of unilateral western concessions to the rising Soviet power and an open-ended promise of more to come, the pseudo-détente which led up to Helsinki will eventually lead to the Finlandization of Western Europe as surely as Yalta resulted in the satellitization of Eastern Europe.

Ball:[3] Anything that comes out of the Security Conference is likely to be utilized by the Soviet Union for its own propaganda purposes. Brezhnev certainly looks forward to the declaration emanating from that Conference and the summit meeting that follows as vindicating his policy of détente. He can effectively use that at the twenty-fifth Communist Party Congress in February 1976—which will presumably be the climactic moment of his career. Perhaps the best we can do is to make sure that the propaganda is not too disadvantageous for the West.

Urban: The European Security Conference has three main problem areas on its agenda: security in terms of the present European status quo, economic and scientific co-operation, and Basket Three—the free flow of people and ideas across ideological frontiers. Can agreement on the first two of these lead to a genuine détente without agreement also being reached in the free flow of persons and ideas?

Pitterman:[4] Détente would certainly lack credibility if the first two conditions were met but the third wasn't, for how could we trust the words of a power that has renounced the use of force in its "foreign" relations but goes on using it internally? Nevertheless, one should aim high but be content with the best bargain one can strike in the circumstances. Stability in Europe *will* mean a certain progress. We are asked to underwrite the status quo in Eastern Europe. But isn't this a fact of life anyway? Could we change it short of going to war? And would anyone want to risk universal destruction so that Kaliningrad may revert back to Königsberg?

It may well be that the Security Conference will, in effect, not be able to progress beyond dealing with the first "basket" of problems, in which case we shall simply be putting our names to Europe's present frontiers and going home, knowing perfectly well that not much has been achieved. However, it is possible and highly desirable, that the Conference should proceed to finding answers to the second and third "baskets" of problems. But these are inter-related. If the Soviet side is serious about wanting both peace and loans, investment, know-how and all the rest of the things it needs, it must be prepared to match the free flow of western capital and technology with the free flow of people, information and ideas. Progress in one must bring with it progress in the other.

Urban: But wouldn't a free flow of people, books, newspapers, radio and television programmes undermine Basket One—that is to say, the security of the Soviet system—by altering Russia's and Eastern Europe's present social order, and thereby changing the status quo? This is what the Soviet spokesmen really mean when they protest that they will not permit the nefarious products of bourgeois culture to be smuggled in under Basket Three. In a sense I can see their point: you can't ask a partner, with whom you are negotiating a declaration of security and co-operation, to sign his own death warrant.

Pitterman: A free flow of people and ideas would surely change the Soviet system: the people would press for more freedom and democracy. But for this change to happen you need no declaration on security or anything else for that matter—it is happening anyhow, and it will be happening faster as the Soviet system gets technologically more sophisticated. You can't run computer-based industries with morons. A successful implementation of Basket Three would, of course, further accelerate this process, which is desirable.

The effects of a declaration on European security and co-operation would, of course, be a long time in coming. But it is not delay—it is much rather undue haste—that gives me cause for concern. The main danger that I see emerging from an ill-considered and over-hasty détente is an unholy alliance between capitalists and commissars. The capitalists are so anxious to do business with the commissars that they may conveniently forget to make the necessary conditions.

Urban: With all that said, you are nevertheless for détente rather than against it?

Pitterman: I most definitely am, but we must have our wits about us. There is a Negro proverb I have seen quoted in an American congressional testimony: "Cheat me once—shame on you: Cheat me twice—shame on me." That sums it up.

NOTES

1   British author, interviewer, specialist in East-West relations.
2   Editor of *Survey*, British journal on East-West affairs.
3   Formerly U.S. Undersecretary of State.
4   Former Social Democratic Vice Chancellor of Austria.

15

Summing Up the Outcome of World War II, by Leonid I. Brezhnev. Speech by the Soviet Communist Party General Secretary at the CSCE meeting, Helsinki, July 31, 1975. "Verbatim Record of the Third Meeting," July 31, 1975, CSCE/III/PV.3, pp. 14–17.

The Soviet Union regards the results of the Conference not merely as a necessary summing up of the political outcome of the Second World War. This, at the same time, is an insight into the future in terms of the realities of today and of the age-old experience of European nations.

One could hardly deny that the results of the Conference represent a delicately weighed balance of the interests of all participating States and, therefore, should be treated with special care.

We can say that a difficult road has been travelled so far, from the time when the idea of the European Conference was first advanced, to its culmination—conclusion at the highest level. The Soviet Union, in assessing soberly the correlation and dynamics of various political forces in Europe and the world, holds a firm conviction that the powerful currents of détente and co-operation on a basis of equality, which in recent years have increasingly determined the course of European and world politics, will gain, thanks to the Conference and its results, a new strength and an even greater scope.

The experience of the work of the Conference provides important conclusions for the future, too. The major one which is reflected in the final document is this: no one should try to dictate to other peoples on the basis of foreign policy considerations of one kind or another the manner in which they ought to manage their internal affairs. It is only the people of each given State and no one else, who have the sovereign right to resolve their internal affairs and establish their internal laws. A different approach would be perilous as a ground for international co-operation.

16

Coexistence Not Valid for the Ideological Sphere, by Bruno Kreisky.
Speech by Chancellor of Austria at the CSCE meeting,
Helsinki, July 31, 1975. "Verbatim Record of the Fourth
Meeting," July 31, 1975, CSCE/III/PV.4, p. 30.

It would not make sense to minimize or even ignore the fundamental differences of these diverse political and social systems. I greatly welcome, therefore, the fact that the clarification is often made that coexistence—the notion under which we understand the form of peaceful relations at present possible—cannot be understood as being valid for the ideological sphere. I welcome this clarification because the democratic states are also firmly determined to obtain a bigger and bigger breakthrough for the idea of democracy and we think that democracy is in itself such a creative form of government that, within its framework and while strictly observing its principles, major social reforms have taken place and will take place in the future.

17

Frank Criticism Must Be Allowed, by Olof Palme.
Speech by the Premier of Sweden at the CSCE meeting,
Helsinki, July 31, 1975. "Verbatim Record of the Fourth
Meeting," July 31, 1975, CSCE/III/PV.4, p. 26.

Respect for one another's social systems and the principle of non-intervention should not be taken to mean that this exchange will be restricted to assent and joint declarations. Frank criticism must also be allowed to make itself heard in the face of phenomena such as the oppression of dissidents, torture and racial discrimination. Moreover, the process of détente should in my view offer increased possibilities for an open and freer debate on fundamental political and ideological questions.

18

Profoundly Western Orientation, by Gerald R. Ford.
President Gerald R. Ford to Rep. Dante B. Fascell,
December 3, 1976, *First Semiannual Report by the
President to the Commission on Security and Cooperation
in Europe* (Washington, D.C.: U.S. Government Printing
Office, 1976), pp. viii–ix, 4.

The Final Act has not transformed the behavior of signatory nations overnight, but it has committed the national leaders who signed it to standards of behavior which are compatible with Western thoughts about the relationship of people to their governments. With its profoundly Western orientation, the Final Act reflects the great importance that the West attaches to human rights and the self determination of peoples. . . . the United States rejected in the negotiations and rejects in principle the concept of hegemony. Rather than freezing the political face of Europe the Final Act expresses the determination that Europe should again become a continent of nations free to choose their own course, both domestically and internationally.

The Helsinki document provides an agenda and a detailed framework—accepted at the highest political level by both East and West as well as by the neutral states of Europe—for addressing the problems which led to the division of Europe. In other words, we and our Allies have, with CSCE, added a dynamic new dimension to our efforts to reduce the barriers between East and West, a dimension which is based on peaceful contacts between both governments and peoples in Europe and North America.

The CSCE in fact became a negotiation about the manner and pace of breaking down the division of Europe and alleviating the human hardships engendered by it. The addition of Western Basket Three initiatives gave concrete meaning to commitments on human rights. CSCE thus must be seen against both this larger diplomatic background and in terms of the real opportunities to bridge the postwar divisions between East and West in Europe.

A Framework for Change

19

The Helsinki Decalogue: Hope or Reality? by Jacques Andréani.
Speech by the Ambassador of France to Italy at the
conference on CSCE at the Institut Universitaire de Hautes
Etudes Internationales, Geneva, June 21, 1985, manuscript,
pp. 3–9, 12–13. Translated from the French by Anne-Marie
Burley.

The question, essentially, is the following: if it is true that the security of Europe assumes that the territorial and political realities that were established at the end of the Second World War are universally admitted, must one then conclude that all change is impossible, or at least inadmissible? This controversy is particularly well known with regard to frontiers: should one speak of their intangibility or their inviolability? We know that the question was resolved very clearly by strongly affirming elsewhere that, in conformity with international law, these frontiers can be modified by peaceful means and by agreement. A reasonable compromise was thus reached on this critical point, between the idea of the status quo and the idea of change.

A second essential theme of the debate was to decide whether, since we were enacting rules of conduct between States in their relations with one another, we should refer to thirty-five states, each one endowed by law with the rights of sovereignty, territorial integrity, and nonintervention in its internal affairs, or on the contrary to two blocs facing each other across the line which divides Europe. Should we establish rules of conduct for states of one bloc vis-à-vis the other bloc, or should we consider each one of the thirty-five states, regardless of its membership in a bloc, to be legally bound to respect the Ten Principles in relations to each of the thirty-five others, including those states that are its proper allies and partners? In other words, is Helsinki to sanction the existence of different rules within a bloc—rules that do not conform to those generally established? No one could deny the existence of the political and military configuration. For our part, we have never considered that our belonging to the Atlantic alliance modifies our sovereignty in any way. As a result, we have insisted with our allies that the Declaration of Principles should not serve to reinforce the cohesion of a bloc so as to strengthen coercive elements over the sovereignty of the small states that make up its members.

The rejection of a bloc approach has been part of the philosophy of the Helsinki process from the very beginning of the consultations. This approach has been greatly facilitated by the eminent role played since the beginning of the process by neutral and nonaligned countries, which have had no desire to appear as minor partners in a dialogue between the two alliances.

And the question was very clearly resolved by the provision that the enunciated principles must be respected and implemented "by each one of the participating States in its relations with all the others."

The third leading theme of the debate was the question whether the code of conduct should be limited to interstate relations in the strict sense, regardless of the domestic situation obtaining within different states, or whether one should not recognize that the field of interstate relations is subtended by, in some sense, the network of relations between states and the individuals over whom these states exercise their authority. The argument, in sum, is as follows: it is not enough to say that if states abstain from the threat or use of force against one another, respect one another's frontiers and hold them to be inviolable, and refrain from intervening in one another's internal affairs, international security will be assured. One of the essential sources of bad relations between states, and hence of insecurity, stems from the fact that in certain states human rights are violated, and the right of self-determination is insufficiently respected.

Concretely, the question was whether to include in the list of principles these two fundamental elements: the respect for human rights and the right of self-determination. It is important, it is essential that the question was resolved in the affirmative. Recognition that respect for human rights is a part of the context of international relations, and that it constitutes one of the factors necessary for an improvement of this situation, represents an important advance.

Everyone acknowledges the existence of political regimes, because one signs a solemn declaration with them on the highest level, but it is recognized that a profound improvement of European relations assumes that these regimes respect human rights. A particular type of integration has been instituted in one part of Europe; this is a fact, but it does not justify the sacrifice of the sovereignty of small states to ideological solidarity. The frontiers are those that were fixed after the war, but their peaceful change is a possibility. A people may be divided, but its aspirations to unity, as long as they are affirmed peacefully and with regard for the security of others, may rest on the right of peoples to self-determination.

I think that we must rid ourselves of the widespread idea, to my mind disastrous, that accepts as a normal and admitted fact the notion that the same concepts authorize different interpretations by East and West.

There are not two types of democracy. Democratic principles are the same for all. There are simply countries that respect these principles, and others that respect them less.

There are not two concepts of political freedom, or of religious freedom. There is the fact that in certain countries these freedoms are not assured.

Similarly, when one country imposes its code of conduct on others, and uses pressure or threats to constrain them, one cannot say that this country is manifesting its attachment to a different conception of state sovereignty, of nonintervention, of nonrecourse to the threat or use of force. It must be said that such a country is violating sovereignty, intervening in internal affairs, infringing the principle of nonrecourse to force.

One of the benefits of the debate at Geneva and Helsinki must be the casting off of this dubious relativism, this form of mental weakness, by which we prevent ourselves from using the instrument that the Final Act represents for what is precisely its primary purpose—that is to say as an objective standard by which it is possible to measure the contribution—or lack thereof—of different states to the cause of improving international relations.

All this is the significance of the Helsinki text on Principles. It in no way guarantees that Europe "will overcome Yalta" in the near future. But it gives us an instrument that allows us, over the long term, to appreciate movements in that direction and to encourage them.

20

Results of the Conference, by the Politburo of the CPSU
Central Committee.
Moscow, August 7, 1975, *Current Digest of the Soviet Press* 27, no. 31:14–15.

The outcome of the conference is the end result of understandings reached on the basis of consideration for the opinions and interests of all and on the basis of general agreement. These agreements correspond to the interests of all the peoples of our continent without effacing differences in ideologies and social systems. There are no victors or vanquished, no winners or losers. The conference is a victory of reason, the prize of all who cherish peace and security on our planet.

The conference creates opportunities for substantially strengthening peace and security in Europe. The principles of relations among states agreed upon by the conference participants are intended to create a reliable foundation for excluding aggression and any type of violence from European international relations. They reaffirm corresponding provisions, which already have the force of law and were previously included in bilateral agreements between states and in other documents signed in the past few years.

The results of the conference create the necessary preconditions for a substantial expansion and intensification of cooperation among European states in the areas of economics, science, technology, environmental protection and other spheres of economic activity, as well as in the sphere of humanitarian questions, such as exchanges in the areas of culture, education, information and contacts among people. The development of cooperation on an all-European scale and on the basis of the observance of the laws and traditions of each country will promote the strengthening of the foundations of peace and security on the European continent and the consolidation of mutual understanding among the states and people of Europe. On the other hand, the development of this cooperation will enable the peoples of the continent to make more successful and rational use of the material and spiritual values at their disposal.

International détente is becoming increasingly substantive. The materialization of détente is the essence of everything that is designed to make peace in Europe truly lasting and unshakable. It is, of course, extremely important to proclaim correct and just principles of relations among states. But it is no less important to establish these principles firmly in present-day international relations, to put them into practice and make them a law of international life not to be broken by anyone.

The all-European conference is the culmination of everything positive that has been done thus far on our continent to bring about the changeover from the "cold war" to détente and the genuine implementation of the principles of peaceful coexistence. At the same time, it is the point of departure for Europe's consistent all-round progress toward lasting peace and the exclusion of war from the life of the peoples.

The main thing now is to see that political détente is supplemented with military détente. One of the primary tasks in this area is to find ways to reduce armed forces and armaments in Central Europe without detriment to anyone, but, on the contrary, to the benefit of all.

The decisions of the conference have great significance for people outside Europe as well. The right to peace belongs to every man on our planet. Détente must be expanded, deepened and extended to all parts of the world.

21

The "Sonnenfeldt Doctrine," by Helmut Sonnenfeldt.
Remarks by the counselor to the Department of State at a
meeting of U.S. ambassadors in Europe, London, December
1975, official State Department summary, *New York Times,*
April 6, 1976.

We are witnessing the emergence of the Soviet Union as a superpower on a global scale. This will be a long-term process. It is a process
that is just beginning in global terms as the Soviets are just now breaking out of their continental mold. They are just now developing modalities for carrying out such a global policy.

The reason why it is possible for the United States and its Western
European allies to develop the policies that will allow us to cope with
this situation is that Soviet power is developing irregularly. It is subject
to flaws and to requirements which in some cases only the outside world
can meet.

Their thrust as an imperial power comes at a time well after the
period when the last imperial power, Germany, made the plunge, and
it hence comes at a time when different rules and perceptions apply.
The Soviets have been inept. They have not been able to bring the
attractions that past imperial powers brought to their conquests. They
have not brought the ideological, legal, cultural, architectural, organizational and other values and skills that characterized the British, French
and German adventures.

In addition, there are serious underlying pressures and tensions in the
Soviet system itself.

The base from which imperialism asserts itself has serious problems
in the economic and social sectors. There are also internal nationalist
groups which are growing. Non-Russian nationalist groups in Russia
are growing at a disproportionally faster rate, which will add to these
tensions in the base whence springs Soviet imperialism.

The Soviets have been particularly unskilled in building viable international structures. They have nothing approaching the European Community or the many other successful Western institutions. In Eastern
Europe particularly, the single most important unifying force is the
presence of sheer Soviet military power. There has been no development
of a more viable, organized structure.

If anything, the last 30 years have intensified the urges in Eastern
countries for autonomy, for identity. There has been an intensification
of the desire to break out of the Soviet straitjacket. This has happened

in every Eastern European country to one degree or another. There are almost no genuine friends of the Soviets left in Eastern Europe, except possibly Bulgaria.

The Soviets' inability to acquire loyalty in Eastern Europe is an unfortunate historical failure, because Eastern Europe is within their scope and area of natural interest. It is doubly tragic that in this area of vital interest and crucial importance it has not been possible for the Soviet Union to establish roots of interest that go beyond sheer power.

It is, therefore, important to remember that the main, if not the only, instrument of Soviet imperialism has been power.

The reason we can today talk and think in terms of dealing with Soviet imperialism, outside of and in addition to simple confrontation, is precisely because Soviet power is emerging in such a flawed way. This gives us the time to develop and to react. There is no way to prevent the emergence of the Soviet Union as a superpower. What we can do is affect the way in which that power is developed and used. Not only can we balance it in the traditional sense, but we can affect its usage—and that is what détente is all about.

It is often asked how détente is doing. The question itself evades the central issue we are trying to pose, that is, what do you do in the face of increasing Soviet power? We will be facing this increased power if our relationship with the Russians is sweet or our relationship with the Russians is sour. The day when the U.S. could choose its preferences from two alternatives is over: That is, turning our back on the world—usually behind the protection of another power like the British Navy—or changing the world.

That choice no longer exists for us. There is too much power in the world for us to ignore, not just the Soviets, but other industrial powers, raw material producers, and even the combined political power of the dwarf states. Nor do we today have enough power to simply overwhelm these problems.

So the Soviets will be seen and heard on the world stage no matter what we do. Therefore, the question of whether or not détente is up or down at a particular moment is largely irrelevant. We Americans like to keep score cards, but the historic challenge of the Soviet Union will not go away and the problem of coping with the effects of that growing Soviet power also won't go away.

We don't have any alternative except to come to grips with the various forms of power which surround us in the world. We have to get away from seeing détente as a process which appeases or propitiates Soviet power. We have to see our task as managing or domesticating this power.

That is our central problem in the years ahead, not finding agreements to sign or atmospheres to improve, although those have some effect. Our challenge is how to live in a world with another superpower, and anticipate the arrival of a third superpower, China, in 20 years or so.

The debate in the United States on détente is illustrated by comments that Soviet trade is a one-way street. It seems that today you can't just get payment for the goods you sell—you must get Jewish emigration, or arms restraint, or any number of other things.

Our European friends have extended considerable credit to the Soviets and Eastern European countries, while the U.S. does not extend lines of credit but, rather, approves financing on the basis of each project. That feature gives us some control over the direction of Soviet economic development. The Europeans have surrendered on this point. While not falling into the trade trap, we have seen trade as a set of instrumentalities to address the set of problems we face with the Soviets. We have to find a way to develop a coherent trade strategy that goes beyond the commercial views of individual firms.

The grain agreement is a good but narrow example of what I am talking about. The Soviets were forced to accept that they need substantial imports from the United States. That gives us leverage, but only if it is done within a coherent framework of policies to achieve certain objectives. M.F.N. (most-favored-nation treatment) has been considered a concession to the U.S.S.R. and in a sense it is. The Soviets don't like paying interest—they prefer to earn their way as they go.

If this is an accurate assessment, then with M.F.N. and credit policies we can get the U.S.S.R. to be competitively engaged in our U.S. markets. If done skillfully, this forces them to meet the requirements of the sophisticated U.S. market. M.F.N. entry into U.S. markets can have an impact on Soviet behavior. This is not a trivial matter.

It is in our long-term interests to use these strengths to break down the autarchic nature of the U.S.S.R. There are consumer choices being made in the U.S.S.R. that, although more below the surface than those in the United States, can be exploited.

This is just one illustration. There are many assets in the West in this area and instead of looking at them as just commercial sales, we need to be using them to draw the Soviet Union into a series of dependencies and ties with the West. It is a long-term project.

When we lost the M.F.N. battle with Congress, we lost our ability to impose a degree of discipline on the Soviet Union, as we were able to do in the case of the grain deal. This is the real tragedy of losing that trade issue. In the long term, we have suffered a setback.

With regard to Eastern Europe, it must be in our long-term interest

to influence events in this area—because of the present unnatural relationship with the Soviet Union—so that they will not sooner or later
explode, causing World War III. This inorganic, unnatural relationship
is a far greater danger to world peace than the conflict between East and
West. There is one qualification to this statement. If Western Europe
becomes so concerned with its economic and social problems that an
imbalance develops, then perhaps the dangers to the United States' interests will be endangered by the simple change in the balance of
power.

So it must be our policy to strive for an evolution that makes the relationship between the Eastern Europeans and the Soviet Union an
organic one. Any excess of zeal on our part is bound to produce results
that could reverse the desired process for a period of time, even though
the process would remain inevitable within the next 100 years. But, of
course, for us that is too long a time to wait.

So our policy must be a policy of responding to the clearly visible
aspirations in Eastern Europe for a more autonomous existence within
the context of a strong Soviet geopolitical influence. This has worked
in Poland. The Poles have been able to overcome their romantic political inclinations which led to their disasters in the past. They have been
skillful in developing a policy that is satisfying their needs for a national
identity without arousing Soviet reactions. It is a long process.

A similar process is now going on in Hungary. János Kádár's performance has been remarkable in finding ways which are acceptable to the
Soviet Union which develop Hungarian roots and the natural aspirations of the people. He has conducted a number of experiments in the
social and economic areas. To a large degree he has been able to do this
because the Soviets have four divisions in Hungary and, therefore, have
not been overly concerned. He has skillfully used their presence as a
security blanket for the Soviets, in a way that has been advantageous
in the development of his own country.

The Romanian picture is different, as one would expect from their
different history. The Romanians have striven for autonomy, but they
have been less daring and innovative in their domestic systems. They
remain among the most rigid countries in the internal organization of
their system.

We seek to influence the emergence of the Soviet imperial power by
making the base more natural and organic so that it will not remain
founded in sheer power alone. But there is no alternative open to us
other than that of influencing the way Soviet power is used.

Finally, on Yugoslavia, we and the Western Europeans, indeed, the
Eastern Europeans as well, have an interest which borders on the vital

for us in continuing the independence of Yugoslavia from Soviet domination. Of course we accept that Yugoslav behavior will continue to be, as it has been in the past, influenced and constrained by Soviet power. But any shift back by Yugoslavia into the Soviet orbit would represent a major strategic setback for the West. So we are concerned about what will happen when Tito disappears, and it is worrying us a great deal.

So our basic policy continues to be that which we have pursued since 1948–49, keeping Yugoslavia in a position of substantial independence from the Soviet Union. Now at the same time we would like them to be less obnoxious, and we should allow them to get away with very little. We should especially disabuse them of any notion that our interest in their relative independence is greater than their own, and therefore, they have a free ride.

Basket Three Assumes Political Substance

22

Soviet Attitudes and Policy toward Basket Three,
by F. Stephen Larrabee.
Radio Liberty Research, RL 135/76, March 15, 1976,
pp. 5–10, 12.

A striking feature of the Soviet approach to the Helsinki agreement has been the noticeable shift of emphasis and change of tone in Soviet commentary about the conference. Initial Soviet comments were marked by an exuberance and optimism that seemed to reflect a belief that Moscow could exploit the atmosphere of détente created by the conclusion of the conference in order to further its foreign policy goals in Europe.

By September 1975, however, much of the enthusiasm for Helsinki had become more restrained and was replaced by a new defensive tone as (1) Western leaders such as Harold Wilson and Giscard d'Estaing began to remind Moscow that its commitment to détente would be judged to a large degree by the manner in which it implemented the provisions of Basket Three; and (2) as its own citizens began to cite Moscow's signature on the Helsinki agreement as justification for greater freedoms at home.[1]

The new tone was signaled by an article in *Izvestiia*[2] by Georgii Arbatov, Director of the USA Institute and one of the Soviet Union's foremost experts on international affairs. The article calls for elaboration because it sets forth what have since been the main features of the Soviet response to Basket Three. In his article Arbatov makes several important points:

1. Détente does not mean that the Soviet Union has pledged itself to

accept the *social* status quo in the world or halt its support for national liberation struggles—a point amply demonstrated by recent Soviet behavior in Angola.

2. It is wrong for the West to think that the Soviet Union "owes" them anything in return for accepting the present European borders, particularly in regard to the implementation of Basket Three.

3. The Soviet Union has far outstripped the West in terms of concrete fulfillment of the Helsinki agreement.

4. The West is trying to use Helsinki as a wedge to interfere in Soviet internal affairs, even though the Final Act strictly prohibits such attempts.

5. Although Moscow intends to implement the pledges undertaken at Helsinki, this does not mean that it will fling open its doors to "anti-Soviet, subversive propaganda, materials preaching violence or stirring up national and racial strife, and pornography."

6. Détente does not mean that the ideological struggle has ended, but it does necessitate a renunciation of "ideological diversions and subversive methods of 'psychological warfare'."

7. In the light of Watergate, Vietnam, and a host of other well-publicized scandals, what "moral right" do US politicians have to talk about "eternal values of freedom and democracy"; before lecturing others on these values, the US ought to "put its own house in order first."

Arbatov's article marked the beginning of an increasingly vociferous "counter-offensive" aimed at combating Western criticism of the Soviet position on Basket Three and at demonstrating that the Soviet Union has been more scrupulous in implementing the Helsinki agreement, particularly Basket Three, than the West. The award of the Nobel Peace Prize to dissident scientist Andrei Sakharov appears to have been one of the major developments that prompted the Soviet authorities to step up this counter-offensive. One of its main elements has been an increasing emphasis on the fact that détente does not mean an end to the ideological struggle—a point that Brezhnev sought to make particularly clear during Giscard d'Estaing's trip to Moscow in October by openly rejecting the French President's calls for "ideological détente."

Another element of the Soviet counter-offensive that has taken on greater prominence lately has been the attacks made against the Western news media. While Radio Liberty and Radio Free Europe have been the main targets,[3] the Deutsche Welle and the BBC have also been subject to sharp criticism. The recent, successful Soviet attempt to obtain the revocation of RFE's accreditation to the Winter Olympics in Innsbruck is indicative of this stepped-up campaign. As Secretary of State Henry Kissinger has emphasized, the revocation is a clear violation of the Helsinki agreement.[4] The action establishes an ominous precedent.

In the last several months, however, Moscow has undertaken a number of measures aimed at demonstrating that it intends to comply:

On January 21 TASS declared that eighteen Western newspapers, among them the *New York Times, Frankfurter Allgemeine Zeitung,* and *Corriere della Sera* would go on sale in the Soviet Union some time in 1976; these, TASS stressed, were in addition to newspapers such as *Le Monde, The Times,* and *Neue Zürcher Zeitung,* which were already on sale in the Soviet Union. However, it should be noted that the latter papers are only available in small numbers—in the case of *Le Monde,* for instance, the number of copies available is about forty—and then only in tourist hotels where they are not on open display but hidden under the counter.

Helsinki has brought some moderate improvements in the working conditions for foreign journalists who represent a number of Western countries, including the United States and France. They have been granted multiple entry visas, allowing them to travel in and out of the Soviet Union more freely; also, as of March 1, Western journalists will no longer have to apply for a special permit if they wish to visit an area outside the restricted forty-kilometer limit. As is presently the case with diplomats, they will simply be required to give notice of their travel plans twenty-four to forty-eight hours in advance, specifying the reasons for their journey, their destination and exact route, their proposed means of transportation and any expected stopovers or breaks. However, since the state holds a monopoly on most facilities, the authorities can still prevent visitors from traveling to certain places, by exploiting technicalities such as lack of accommodations or unavailability of required means of transportation. On the whole, it would seem that openness in, and accessibility to news remains as difficult as before.

Recently the Soviet Union has indicated a relaxation on its part in some of the rules and regulations related to emigration. According to Western sources, some of the measures taken so far have included:

1. Reduction of the fee for obtaining an exit permit from 400 rubles ($540) to 300 rubles ($405).

2. Relaxation of the requirement for a character reference from the applicant's supervisor and Party secretary at his place of work. This document was often difficult to obtain because applicants may have been dismissed from their jobs or hostile officials were unwilling to issue the document.

3. Provision for review of cases every six months instead of every year.

4. Provision for appealing refusals within the state visa system.

Despite Soviet footdragging and evasion, however, some changes have occurred. They have come slowly and grudgingly, and by Western standards they have been far too few and limited; but they have nonetheless occurred. Moreover, it is clear from the increasingly defensive reaction of the Soviet Union in recent months that the Soviet leadership is under considerable pressure to at least give the appearance of carrying out the provisions of Basket Three. In other words, the leaders of the USSR clearly recognize that they cannot ignore the issue even if they cannot afford to go about fully implementing the provisions.

NOTES

1   In the last six months Radio Liberty's *Arkhiv Samizdata* has received more than fifty documents that refer to the Helsinki agreement and call on the Soviet government to implement the provisions contained in Basket Three. See also Peter Osnos in the *International Herald Tribune*, October 8, 1975, on Moscow's internal problems with the Helsinki agreement.
2   September 3, 1975. An abridged version of the article was published in the *New York Times* on October 8, 1975.
3   See *Pravda*, January 15, January 30, and February 2, 1976; also *Izvestiia*, February 1976.
4   In a cable sent to Julian K. Roosevelt, the U.S. member of the International Olympic Committee. See Henry Bradsher, *Washington Star*, February 14, 1976.

23

Moscow Group to Promote Observance of Helsinki, by
Iurii Orlov et al. "On the Formation of the Public Group
to Promote the Observance of the Helsinki Agreements
in the USSR," Moscow, May 12, 1976, *Reports of Helsinki Accord
Monitors in the Soviet Union* (Washington, D.C.: Commission
on Security and Cooperation in Europe, 1977), pp. 2–3.

On May 12, 1976, The Public Group to Promote the Observance of the Helsinki Agreements in the USSR was formed in Moscow.

The aim of the group is to promote observance of the humanitarian provisions of the Final Act of the Conference on Cooperation and Security in Europe. We have in mind the following articles of the Final Act:

1. The Declaration of Principles, which the participating states will follow in their mutual relations: Point VII, "Respect for human rights and fundamental freedoms, including freedom of thought, conscience, religion or belief."

2. Cooperation in humanitarian and other areas. (1) Contacts between people (in part, point V on the reunification of families). (2) Information. (3) Cooperation and exchanges in the area of culture. (4) Cooperation and exchanges in the area of education.

The Group to Promote considers that its first goal is to inform all Heads of State which signed the Final Act on August 1, 1975, and also to inform the public about cases in direct violation of the articles named above. With this aim, the Group to Promote:

(1) accepts directly from the Soviet citizens written complaints about personal experiences which relate to violations of these articles, and in a concise form will readdress them to all Heads of State which have signed the Act and also to public opinion;

(2) collects with the help of the public any other information about violations of the above articles, will rework this information and will give a detailed evaluation of its reliability, and will then send it to the corresponding Heads of State and public.

In some cases, when the Group comes across concrete information about special manifestations of inhumanity, for example:

—the taking away of children from religious parents who wish to educate their children according to their beliefs;

—forcible psychiatric treatment with the purpose of changing thoughts, conscience, religion or beliefs;

—the most dramatic instances of divided families;

—cases which reveal special inhumanity in regard to prisoners of conscience.

In its activity, the members of the Group to Promote proceed from the conviction that the issues of humanitarianism and free information have a direct relationship to the problem of international security and they call for public opinion of other participant countries of the Conference at Helsinki to form their own national Groups to Promote in order to assist a complete fulfillment of the Helsinki Agreements.

24

Charter 77 Declaration. Prague, January 1, 1977.
In H. Gordon Skilling (ed.), *Charter 77 and Human Rights in Czechoslovakia* (London: Allen & Unwin, 1981), pp. 209–13.

In the Czechoslovak Collection of Laws, no. 120 of 13 October 1976, texts were published of the International Covenant on Civil and Political Rights, and of the International Covenant on Economic, Social and Cultural Rights, which were signed on behalf of our Republic in 1968, were confirmed at Helsinki in 1975 and came into force in our country on 23 March 1976. From that date our citizens have the right, and our state the duty, to abide by them.

Their publication, however, serves as an urgent reminder of the extent to which basic human rights in our country exist, regrettably, on paper only.

The right to freedom of expression, for example, guaranteed by article 19 of the first-mentioned covenant, is in our case purely illusory. Tens of thousands of our citizens are prevented from working in their own fields for the sole reason that they hold views differing from official ones, and are discriminated against and harassed in all kinds of ways by the authorities and public organizations.

In violation of article 13 of the second-mentioned covenant, guaranteeing everyone the right to education, countless young people are prevented from studying because of their own views or even their parents'. Innumerable citizens live in fear that their own or their children's right to education may be withdrawn if they should ever speak up in accordance with their convictions.

Freedom of public expression is repressed by the centralized control of all the communications media and of publishing and cultural institutions. No philosophical, political or scientific view of artistic expression that departs ever so slightly from the narrow bounds of official ideology or aesthetics is allowed to be published; no open criticism can be made of abnormal social phenomena; no public defense is possible against false and insulting charges made in official propaganda; the legal protection against "attacks to honor and reputation" clearly guaranteed by article 17 of the first covenant is in practice non-existent; false accusations cannot be rebutted and any attempt to secure compensation or correction through the courts is futile; no open debate is allowed in the domain of thought and art.

Freedom of religious confession, emphatically guaranteed by article 18 of the first covenant, is systematically curtailed by arbitrary official action; by interference with the activity of churchmen, who are constantly threatened by the refusal of the state to permit them the exercise of their functions, or by the withdrawal of such permission; by financial or other measures against those who express their religious faith in word or action; by constraints of religious training and so forth.

Responsibility for the maintenance of civic rights in our country naturally devolves in the first place on the political and state authorities. Yet, not only on them: everyone bears his share of responsibility for the conditions that prevail and accordingly also for the observance of legally enshrined agreements, binding upon all citizens as well as upon governments. It is this sense of co-responsibility, our belief in the meaning of voluntary citizens' involvement and the general need to give it new and more effective expression that led us to the idea of creating Charter 77, whose inception we today publicly announce.

Charter 77 is a free informal, open community of people of different convictions, different faiths and different professions united by the will to strive, individually and collectively, for the respect of civic and human rights in our own country and throughout the world—rights accorded to all men by the two mentioned international covenants, by the Final Act of the Helsinki conference and by numerous other international documents opposing war, violence and social or spiritual oppression, and which are comprehensively laid down in the United Nations Universal Declaration of Human Rights.

Charter 77 is not an organization; it has no rules, permanent bodies or formal membership. It embraces everyone who agrees with its ideas, participates in its work, and supports it. It does not form the basis for any oppositional political activity. Like many similar citizen initiatives in various countries, West and East, it seeks to promote the general public interest. It does not aim, then, to set out its own programs for political or social reforms or changes, but within its own sphere of activity it wishes to conduct a constructive dialogue with the political and state authorities, particularly by drawing attention to various individual cases where human and civil rights are violated, by preparing documentation and suggesting solutions, by submitting other proposals of a more general character aimed at reinforcing such rights and their guarantees, and by acting as a mediator in various conflict situations which may lead to injustice and so forth.

By its symbolic name Charter 77 denotes that it has come into being at the start of a year proclaimed as the Year of the Political Prisoners—a year in which a conference in Belgrade is due to review the implementation of the obligations assumed at Helsinki.

Catalyst of Destabilization

25

A Framework for Helsinki Watchers, by James F. Brown.
Statement by Director of Radio Free Europe, Washington,
May 9, 1977. *Basket Three: Implementation of the Helsinki
Accords*, Hearings before the Commission on Security and
Cooperation in Europe, Ninety-Fifth Congress, May 9, 1977
(Washington, D.C.: U.S. Government Printing Office, 1977),
pp. 280–87.

All Helsinki watchers must be aware that genuine differences can exist
between East and West (and even within each of the two camps) about
how some agreements should be interpreted and some results assessed.
The most basic of these differences shows itself in the dichotomy between state and society so manifest in the Helsinki document.

Two levels: state and societal

Western policy toward the communist countries, particularly toward
Eastern Europe, must be conducted at two levels: the state level and
the societal level. The reason is obvious: in the majority of the states
concerned there is still little basic identification by most of the population with either rulers or their governing institutions.

It was only in the last few months of the CSCE negotiations in Geneva
that the West pressed determinedly for the societal dimension in East-
West relations to be recognized. Until then it had appeared that the
conference would be almost exclusively a state-to-state affair. But in the
months leading up to Helsinki the interaction of Leonid Brezhnev's
eagerness to get an agreement signed with the newly found societal concern of some Western negotiators resulted in a final document that displayed some balance between the state and societal dimensions of East-
West relations. Generally speaking Baskets I and II of the Final Act
encompass state relations; the crowded Basket III has very much to do
with societal relations.

As for Basket III, the Soviet and East European leaders had always
envisaged this as comprising officially sponsored and conducted human,
cultural, educational, social, and sporting contacts. They were apparently unprepared for the West's eleventh-hour insistence that it should
provide for genuine human contacts—the "freer flow" of people, information, and ideas. That they were prepared to modify their stand was

due to Soviet, and particularly Brezhnev's impatience to achieve the consummation of what they perceived as a diplomatic triumph and to their confidence that the dangers inherent in this Western initiative could be minimized or contained.

This confidence must have seemed well founded in mid-1975. For the previous 4½ years, after the upheavals in Poland which Moscow handled with great skill, Eastern Europe had been politically stable and economically prosperous, with all its countries enjoying the highest living standards in their history. Soviet leadership in the region had been decisive and, though the integrative processes the Soviets had initiated might be working too slowly to satisfy them completely, some progress had been made toward creating an infrastructure of cohesion dominated by Moscow. The situation looked safe enough, therefore, to weather the dangers of Basket III. And Western policy seemed sufficiently passive and "State-oriented" to occasion little foreboding.

Stability disrupted

Unfortunately for the Soviet leaders, this period of stability and prosperity in Eastern Europe was in fact coming to an end by the time of the Helsinki conference. At the beginning of the year the USSR itself had dealt the fabric a damaging blow by drastically raising the prices of its raw material exports on which almost the whole of Eastern Europe is so dependent. At about the same time several East European economies began to suffer the effects of the recession and inflation in the West—in itself a reflection of the degree to which East-West economic relations had developed.

At the same time an element of political uncertainty was beginning to disturb the previous placidity. The fragility of Brezhnev's health made East European elites suddenly aware that the Soviet Union was nearing a comprehensive change of leadership involving not just one leader but most of the group that has dominated the Soviet Union for over a decade. There has also been the quite new phenomenon of Euro-communism with all its attractions for elites both inside and outside the ruling communist parties.

Helsinki as a catalyst

It was into this Eastern Europe, with its uncertainties and fears, that Helsinki was injected. The result was unexpected, incalculable ferment. Four years earlier, Helsinki's impact would have been slight; now it was quite shattering because the East European situation had changed so remarkably. This is not to dismiss the Western role entirely. It is simply to say that the dominating political (as opposed to cultural) force in, and influence on, East European societies is not of Western provenance but is either indigenous or, more often than not, Russian. The West is not a prime mover in Eastern Europe: Helsinki, American policy, Radio Free Europe, can and do exert their influence, but its degree is largely dictated by the situation actually prevailing in the region concerned.

It follows that the ultimate "destabilizing force" in Eastern Europe is not imported from the West, as the officially controlled media repeatedly charge: it is of domestic or Soviet origin. The strongest destabilizing force in Eastern Europe is, in fact, the Soviet Union and the manner in which it has exercised its hegemony there since World War II. Hence Eastern Europe's history over the last 30 years has been punctuated by crises, and a "Pax Sovietica" has never existed. It would have required three things: (1) harmony between each East European government and the Soviet Union; (2) harmony between each East European government and its own population; (3) acceptance by the East European populations of Soviet hegemony.

For all three preconditions to be met much would have to change in Eastern Europe, most of all Soviet policy—and there appears little hope of this in the near future. But, in the meantime, the instability that has recently developed and is at the root of the strong societal response to Helsinki is likely to grow. It will present that Soviet leadership, old or new, with two alternatives—although the choice would, of course, be affected by domestic difficulties or by relations with China: to seek to enforce cohesion by ever more repressive measures, or to allow the Finlandization of Eastern Europe.

The societal response to Helsinki should be seen, therefore, against this rapidly changing East European background. The Final Act with its enumerations of elementary freedoms, signed by all the East European leaders, became a rallying point, a symbol to be invoked amid the growing dissatisfaction. And those invoking Helsinki knew they were not just embarrassing their own communist leaders but gaining publicity in the West, popularizing their cause there and often insuring themselves against harsh repression. The role of the Western press since Helsinki has often been vital. After several years of neglect interest quickened in 1976, and an unpremeditated interaction developed between Western publicity and Eastern dissent—greatly to the wrath of Eastern officialdom.

It would be pointless to catalogue here all the occasions on which Helsinki has been invoked by groups and individuals in East European societies demanding greater freedoms or protesting their denial. Helsinki has caught the imagination not only of intellectuals acting singly or together, or of powerful pressure groups like the Catholic Church in Poland, but also of simple individuals with a grievance never redressed or a request never granted. A catalogue would in any case be defective since, despite the vigor of the Western media, those specific examples of a response to Helsinki that are on public record would surely give no indication of the total response, group and individual, throughout Eastern Europe. Alongside Polish intellectuals protesting constitutional changes or denials of civil rights, Polish bishops magisterially enunciating their demands, the massive gesture of Charter 77, and the courageous battle of Paul Goma, there have undoubtedly been countless cases through Eastern Europe, totally unreported, in which the Helsinki freedoms have been invoked.

The Eastern response

Again, we return to the two dimensions of state and society. East European society's reaction to Helsinki has been extraordinary, and the response of the East European states (like that of the Soviet Union) has consequently been nervous, guarded, essentially negative. A fascinating chain reaction can be observed here: Eastern Europe started to pass from a period of stability to one of instability. The self-confidence of its rulers was impaired accordingly. This helped produce manifest dissatisfaction and restlessness in its societies. These societies thus became far more responsive to the Basket III sections of the Final Act—the "essential" Helsinki then became anathema to communist officialdom—a demon to be exorcised.

In public, of course, the East European authorities are never as blunt as this. In fact, in seeking to explain Helsinki away, to demonstrate what it does not mean rather than what it does mean, they have sometimes displayed considerable sophistry. One of the most persistent of their recent ploys—taking their cue from Brezhnev himself—has been to argue that the Final Act must be taken as a whole, with no undue stress on any of its parts. To emphasize Basket III, it is charged, at the expense of Baskets I and II—i.e., the "state controllable" baskets—is to pervert the true meaning of security and co-operation in Europe.

But the unexpected mushrooming of the civil rights movement in Eastern Europe caused the authorities to erect new defenses against the dangers of Helsinki and deliver a few counter-attacks. Against the civil rights leaders a curious logic was invoked: these men and women are seeking to disrupt the national and international harmony that is the essence of Helsinki. Although they may invoke Helsinki, they are in league with cold war forces in the West which are seeking to undermine its achievements. Therefore, to suppress them, far from contravening Helsinki, is actually to implement it in the fullest sense of the word. The most repeated and shrillest use of this argument has undoubtedly been made by Czechoslovakia.

Emigration

A serious problem for some of the East European states has been posed by the provisions of the Final Act regarding emigration and family reunions. The countries most affected are the GDR, Poland, and Romania, and there is no doubt that large-scale emigration could damage the economies of these—and indeed of all—East European states. In Poland and Romania, a mass exodus of citizens of German stock (real or claimed) would mean a loss of skilled workers and efficient farmers; and the East German authorities put up the Berlin Wall in 1961 precisely to stop the hemorrhaging of the population. This is a genuine problem, and the valid reluctance of East European leaders to open the flood gates should not be brushed aside, still less smugly condemned. In these circumstances the steps taken by the Polish and Romanian governments to permit increased emigration over the last half year should be recognized and valued. (The almost total refusal of the GDR authorities to process the mounting number of applications to emigrate to the FRG—variously put at between 100,000 and 200,000—can best be put down to the haunting fear of a reversion to the pre-Berlin Wall situation.)

The eventual Polish and Romanian decision to allow increased emigration should not be seen simply as a gesture to Helsinki. Polish Germans are being reunited with their families in West Germany mainly because Bonn has agreed to make massive credits available to Warsaw. This agreement has often been hailed as a symbol of the "spirit of Helsinki" but its origin and fulfillment owe little to the CSCE. Similarly, Romania's readiness to step up emigration—particularly of Germans and Jews—owes more to the bargaining levers of the American Congress than to the humanitarian appeals of the Final Act. Indeed Romania, a multinational state determined to become an integral one, has recently become the most frenetic supporter of a meeting so as to strengthen the bargaining posture of the Eastern alliance. Accordingly, emigration from Poland and Romania, for example, may well be accelerated in the short-term future, more Western newspapers may be put on sale throughout Eastern Europe, etc. Czechoslovakia, hardly in the van of fulfilling either the spirit or the letter of Helsinki, has in fact recently increased the number and range of Western periodicals available to its citizens.

Individual case histories

A valid caveat that can be entered against the preceding analysis is that it has generalized too much, tending to treat Eastern Europe as a homogeneous whole rather than the patchwork quilt it remains in spite of the Soviet Union's efforts at integration. National differences at once become apparent when one attempts to assess which East European states have "fulfilled" Helsinki more effectively than others. But even here a general rule might be hazarded, one that follows from what has been argued above and that again demonstrates the crucial importance of the societal factor. The two states that have "implemented" Helsinki most fully are those with the closest rapport with their societies, or which are seeking to strengthen, or repair, that rapport.

If the six East European members of the Warsaw Pact were conceived as race horses competing for the Helsinki Stakes, how would they look as they entered the final straight before Belgrade? Hungary would be well up in front with Poland lying second. Several lengths behind would be Romania. After that, sadly out of the running, would come Bulgaria, followed by the GDR. Czechoslovakia, cantering lamely along and showing little interest in the race, let alone in winning it, would bring up the rear.

Before taking a quick look at the individual form sheets of these entries, a word first about form requirements. What does "fulfilling Helsinki" mean or involve? This is what Belgrade could be all about and what could make Belgrade a totally inconclusive encounter. The crux of the matter is that there are virtually no objective criteria acceptable to both sides. Where public values are broadly similar, as in Western Europe and North America, this would cause difficulty; where they are basically different it is impossible. That being said, here are some totally arbitrary and obviously "society-oriented" criteria by which the performance of the East European states might be judged, always bearing in mind that the success or failure of each in meeting some of them over the last 21 months has probably owed very little indeed to Helsinki.

(1) Responsiveness to internal societal pressures including dissent;
(2) A liberal attitude to emigration and family reunion;
(3) A relatively relaxed policy on censorship and intellectual freedom;
(4) Concessions to domestic ethnic minorities;

(5) A liberal attitude to Western travel;
(6) A willingness to permit human, social, educational, and cultural exchanges of a private, as well as a state-controlled, nature.

Obviously no East European state gets full marks on these points. By absolute standards all fall short of the ideal (as, of course, do most or all non-Communist states), but assessments must be relative. For example, the Polish workers beaten or harassed by the police after June 1976 must be surprised to see their government so well placed in the Helsinki ratings; so must a fairly large group of Polish intellectuals, whether members of the Committee for the Defense of the Workers or not. Yet the fact is that the Polish authorities, subject to much stronger societal pressure than those of any other country in Eastern Europe, have responded with relative restraint. This becomes strikingly evident when a comparison is made with the Prague leadership's response to Charter 77 and official Romanian viciousness against the protest group around Paul Goma after early efforts at conciliation had failed. This is not to suggest that Gierek's restraint has been due to any perceived need to fulfill the spirit of Helsinki; it is attributable mainly to consideration prompted by the Polish domestic situation—and at the time of writing there are signs that the official line may be hardening. But to assess what aspects of a state's behavior are due to any particular constraint, such as Helsinki, and in what degree, is impossible.

Now let us take a closer look at individual performances in the Helsinki stakes.

Hungary—With a political touch amounting to genius, Kádár has established rapport with most of the population that permits a relaxed, "live and let live" atmosphere found nowhere else in the Warsaw Pact. Result: Societal pressures on the state have been slight, and there has been little demand for emigration. Helsinki has been handled calmly, its dangers recognized but contained; a letter of 34 intellectuals supporting Czechoslovak Charterists caused little official consternation. Dissident intellectuals in general and revisionist philosophers in particular have been handled firmly but not repressively by Warsaw Pact standards. Hungary has been more liberal than others in importing Western culture. Outstanding example: A Hungarian edition of Paul Samuelson's famous "Economics" has appeared in Budapest, accompanied by reviews attesting its importance. (In terms of the Helsinki "spirit," one Samuelson is worth a hundred Dickens and Jack Londons. This one example, incidentally, makes nonsense of the whole score-card approach to Helsinki.)

Poland—Incredible blunder of abortive food price increases in June

1976 shattered confidence of Gierek leadership and showed that remarkable advances in Polish living standards since Gierek assumed power had not generated firm rapport between rulers and ruled. Since then, despite police harassment of the dissident intellectuals and still defiant workers, Gierek has sought to throw out more lines to the people, to open more societal safety valves. Media are often harsh, sometimes frenetic, re: Western "saboteurs" of Helsinki, but Poland's Basket III fulfillment, partly because of safety valve tactics, is not discreditable by general East European standards. Prevailing wind may be backing, however: At Central Committee plenum on April 14, 1977, Gierek spoke sternly of limits to criticism and attacked dissenters as class enemies. But Polish society—with Roman Catholic Church as alternative power center—is more independent than any other in the region. In certain instances it dictates policy to the state rather than vice versa.

Romania—Internal regime here has always been hardest, apart from Albania and perhaps Bulgaria. Ceauşescu leadership totally out of sympathy with societal provisions of Helsinki but very concerned about its image in West—not just for economic reasons: Romania's policy of independence from Soviet Union necessitates Western support. Hence concessions on emigration despite genuine fears this could lead to mass demands for exodus from Germans and, above all, worldwide sympathy. Shortly after this media began tremendous barrage against Western "perverters" of Helsinki. Main fear seemed to be emigration. In early April authorities switched from leniency to harsh repression of dissent.

Bulgaria—Has played minor role in Helsinki interaction; official reaction to Basket III negatively rigid. Authorities in firm control although civil rights movement in Czechoslovakia has caused some restlessness in intellectual circles. Bulgaria has largest "non-Warsaw Pact" ethnic group in Eastern Europe—800,000 Turks. Little desire for mass repatriation, however, and Ankara is not forcing issue: if it did, serious difficulties possible, although Bulgaria's record with minorities traditionally good.

German Democratic Republic—Pankow's hope (and some Western analysts' belief) that loyal East German consciousness was developing after 1961 realized only within confines of sports stadiums. When Final Act signed, it was clear even to optimists that East German "miracle" was part of history. Societal restlessness aggravated leadership nervousness already aroused by dangers of Bonn-Moscow "détente." Under Helsinki rubric mass influx of visitors from FRG—3,500,000 in 1976 alone—has had unsettling effect on workers and technical intelligentsia. Note also that over 60 percent of East German population can tune in to West German TV; many do so. Perhaps even more unsettling is mass contact with Poles (in 1976, 5,600,000 East Germans visited

Poland and 7,100,000 Poles visited GDR). Much more relaxed atmosphere in Poland and lack of party control at lower levels have apparently impressed many East Germans. Nervousness of SED leadership most evident recently in Biermann case, but more important is tightening of security precautions throughout GDR.

Czechoslovakia—Well known in West that only in economic sphere has Husák normalization policy succeeded. By mid-1975 it was apparent that growth in standard of living was slowing. This further undermined confidence of already divided leadership. Helsinki greatly feared because trauma of 1968 still strong in leaders' minds: which explains hysterical overreaction to Charter 77. Persecution of signers of charter has been worst violation of Helsinki spirit of Eastern Europe and has further tarnished image of Czechoslovakia abroad. Its drama should not distract attention from persecution of Catholic Church, particularly in Slovakia, also unexampled in Eastern Europe.

Congress Takes the Initiative

26

A Commission to Monitor Compliance, by Millicent Fenwick. Statement by U.S. Representative from New Jersey, Washington, May 6, 1976, *Conference on Security and Cooperation in Europe: Part II*, Hearings before the Subcommittee on International Political and Military Affairs of the Committee on International Relations, House of Representatives, Ninety-Fourth Congress, May 4, 1976 (Washington, D.C.: U.S. Government Printing Office, 1976), pp. 6–10.

Mr. Chairman, last August Speaker Albert asked me and 17 other Members of the House to go on a working trip to the Soviet Union and Romania. We departed for Leningrad just a few days after the Helsinki accord had been signed. There was speculation that this was going to be just a verification of the post–World War II European borders. Others felt it was a hope for change in these closed systems in Communist Europe. The risk, of course, was that the countries would disregard the provisions of the accord that they felt were uncomfortable and would simply not implement them.

During our travels in the USSR the congressional delegation found many Soviet citizens hopeful that the accord would finally help them obtain a measure of freedom in the USSR or would give them means to leave and find freedom elsewhere. Congressman Yates and I cochaired an ad hoc committee of the group which met with dissidents and refuseniks and people of all faiths, Jews, Christians, and agnostics. Through all of our conversations, the one consistent thread was that the West must not forget the third basket of the Helsinki Accord which addresses itself to human rights. Leonid Plyushch, when asked by the subcommittee what could be done in the West to promote the observance of human rights in the Soviet Union, urged that the West should "strive to have the Helsinki accord implemented not only in words, but in reality." Dr. Sakharov has also spoken in this vein. The Judiciary Committee's report, "Emigration of Soviet Jews," presents a summary of the committee's conversation with Dr. Sakharov, and he stressed that détente should not "divert our attention from the issue of human rights."

Congressman Yates and I and other members of the congressional delegation spoke with numerous individuals and groups who repeated this theme. We pursued it with officials. When we met with Mr. Brezhnev we spoke to him about this and rather resignedly he sighed and said this was the 150th time the basket three provisions had been brought to his attention and he pointed out there would be an international commission meeting in Belgrade in October 1977. That Commission, I'm sorry to say, will only begin to study ways in which these accords can be monitored. So it's quite a long way off from any implementation. We must follow through, I do believe, with the international agreements we have signed. As President Ford said in Helsinki, history will judge the effectiveness of the Conference "not by the promises we make, but by the promises we keep."

The monitoring Commission which is suggested in the bill would embody those principles which have distinguished this Nation above all others: our respect for human dignity, the importance of the individual and the freedom to pursue one's own thoughts and beliefs and religion. This is what America does best, Mr. Chairman, and I feel strongly that we should emphasize these values in our international relations.

The structure of the Commission calls for 11 members including three from the executive branch appointed by the President, but this would be above all, a congressional unit. The chairman is to be appointed by the Speaker and I expect the Commission Chairman would select the director. The Commission would be physically located on Capitol Hill, in close proximity to the House and Senate Members it is to serve.

This unique composition acknowledges one important factor—success of any monitoring depends on executive-legislative cooperation. Congress cannot duplicate the representatives that the departments have overseas who are in a position to follow more closely contract negotiations, visa applications and so on. On the other hand, Members of the Congress are perhaps more aware of the individual cases and group assessments developed by associations in this country. Congressional participation will help agencies like the State Department to speak more forcefully for human rights in dealing with the Communist countries. It will, in effect, indicate to all the signatories that with our signature on the accord, we earnestly expect implementation of the provisions.

I look upon this joint legislative-executive endeavor to produce not only a meaningful and accurate record of European compliance or noncompliance, but also as an example of intergovernmental cooperation in a most important human field.

27

Regular Procedures Have Been Established, by Robert J. McCloskey.
Letter by Assistant Secretary of State for Congressional Relations
to Sen. John Sparkman, Chairman, Committee on Foreign
Relations, U.S. Senate, Washington, January 19, 1976,
Conference on Security and Cooperation in Europe: Part II,
Hearings before the Subcommittee on International Political
and Military Affairs of the Committee on International Relations,
House of Representatives, Ninety-Fourth Congress, May 4, 1976
(Washington, D.C.: U.S. Government Printing Office, 1976),
pp. 3–5.

The Department of State has instructed our embassies in the Soviet Union and Eastern Europe to report regularly on implementation and compliance with the freer movement provisions and other aspects of CSCE. Regular procedures have also been established here in Washington to compile and analyze all relevant information on CSCE compliance. The CSCE action office within the European Bureau of the State Department has established contact with all U.S. Government agencies concerned with any aspect of CSCE, including the Departments of Defense and Commerce.

Furthermore, we have already taken up with the Soviet Union several specific provisions of the Final Act which relate to long standing U.S.-Soviet problems, including multiple entry/exit visas for American journalists and reunification of divided families.

We believe that we have taken all appropriate steps to encourage observance of CSCE provisions, to ensure the collection of the maximum information on CSCE compliance, and the regular compilation and analysis of such information. We welcome Congressional interest in this process and stand ready to cooperate with your committee and other committees of the Congress with an interest in csce, and to consult closely with all members of Congress who express such an interest.

The commission envisaged in S. 2679 would not appear to be equipped to add significantly to the action already being taken or the information being compiled; nor would it appear able to exercise a more effective monitoring role than existing committees or subcommittees of the Congress. Furthermore, its extraordinary composition would not seem to provide an appropriate or effective means for coordinating or guiding our efforts.

28

The Administration's Objections, by Robert Lyle.
Report by rfe correspondent, Washington, October 1, 1976.

The administration has never liked the idea of a "Helsinki Watch" Commission established by Congress. It considers it an encroachment on the prerogatives of the executive branch to conduct foreign affairs.

When the legislation that set up the Commission was passed, President Gerald Ford took the unusual step of signing it in private. The press was not invited to watch, nor did he make any public statement as the bill became law.

Congressman Dante Fascell, the Commission Chairman—as well as Senators Clairborne Pell and Clifford Case and Congresswoman Millicent Fenwick, its chief architects—became so concerned over administration inaction that they met for breakfast with Secretary of State Henry Kissinger on August 24.

Kissinger raised several objections to the Commission itself and to administration participation. The Congressmen said the Commission will go ahead with or without administration cooperation.

Kissinger foresaw the possibility that executive branch representatives—asked to vote publicly on sensitive foreign policy questions—might be outvoted by Congressional members. That could be embarrassing.

He said the Commission could be used by one executive branch department—such as defense—to interrogate another executive department in any policy dispute.

Commission officials say the value of the Commission is that it will be the only visible agency publicly monitoring compliance with the Helsinki Accords.

29

State Department's Collusion with the Soviets? by Michael Bartholomew.
Report by RFE correspondent, Washington, November 1, 1976.

The chairman of a congressionally mandated commission for monitoring compliance with the Helsinki Accords said today the Soviet Union and the U.S. State Department have joined in preventing commission officials from visiting eastern Europe and the U.S.S.R.

Congressman Dante Fascell, a Democrat from Florida, said three members of the executive branch who serve on the commission were instructed today by Secretary of State Henry Kissinger to go only to Brussels and not enter communist countries.

Fascell said a group will visit Romania from November 11 to 14 and Yugoslavia from November 17 through the 20th. He said the commission has not received visas to enter the Soviet Union, Hungary, Bulgaria, Czechoslovakia, Poland or East Germany.

Fascell called Kissinger's decision a "deeply regrettable, last minute policy reversal." He noted that Kissinger and Soviet ambassador Anatolii Dobrynin both objected to the establishment of the commission by Congress last June.

PART TWO

HUMAN RIGHTS, TRADE, AND SECURITY:

FROM BELGRADE TO MADRID

Shifting Focus to Economics

30

The Relevance of Economic Issues, by Bettina S. Hass-Hürni. "The Relevance of Economic Issues at the Belgrade Conference," *Intereconomics*, May–June 1978, pp. 142–43, 145–46.

Since Geneva there has been a significant change in the role of economic issues, which has been barely noted in the mass media, although it is felt that it could be of decisive importance for the process of détente. Questions of "cooperation in the fields of economics, science and technology and the environment" (Basket II) did not occupy a central position in Geneva and were regarded by the Eastern European countries as of secondary importance. It is not an exaggeration to say that in Belgrade, Basket II, i.e. East-West trade and general economic issues, could be regarded as a *basis and at the same time* as a *barometer* for détente. This enhancement of the role of Basket II was due to three factors.

Firstly, the USSR was urging the convening of the so-called "Brezhnev conferences," three pan-European meetings to discuss energy, transportation and environment, respectively. From the first of these gatherings the Soviet Union hoped to create political tensions among the allies in NATO, a continuation of its traditional policy; from the second, the USSR hoped to obtain Western capital for the expansion of its economic—and hence strategic—infrastructure, while the third is a fashionable subject for conferences and is politically harmless, even though it does offer the opportunity to gain technological know-how from the West.

Secondly, the member countries of the Council for Mutual Economic

Aid (the official title of COMECON) have heavy foreign debts with the West. This put Eastern Europe in the position of a "demandeur" in Basket II, and thus *compelled* it to display interest in intensifying trade and cooperation.

Thirdly, the Eastern countries—Hungary, Poland and Yugoslavia in particular—are beginning to realize that their economies cannot and will not develop without Western technology. In ideological terms, Eastern Europe can assume that the technological gap can be narrowed by cooperation with the West, and that increased economic relations will expand political relations. As the next step, this might be a way of exerting direct influence on the capitalist market economies.

A *fourth* reason for the greater role of Basket II also emerged in the political tactics being pursued in Belgrade: since questions of security must first be tackled bilaterally, i.e. particularly in the MBFR and SALT discussions, before arms control in Basket I can make progress, and Basket III ("human rights") was to be downplayed, attention could usefully be focussed on Basket II to divert attention away from military and humanitarian issues, both of which were at the very least unpleasant for the East.

The West too had good reasons for seeking to expand its economic relations with the East: a desire to open up new markets, the pressure of public opinion in favor of a further "opening" to Eastern Europe, possibly as a consequence of the "development weariness" resulting from all the economic and political disappointments in the Third World, together with a belief in the superiority of the free-market system strengthened by the fact that Europe has withstood the economic effects of the oil crisis quite well. For all these reasons, European economic relations can be regarded as a "neutral" factor of equal interest to the East and to the West and at the same time as a barometer for détente.

As in every round of negotiations, classical negotiating procedures have already evolved in the five years the CSCE process has been in progress. The Western countries, for example, always started by saying that the governments of the free-market countries have much less control over their private industry than the Eastern European governments have over their state-controlled enterprises—a good argument against unwelcome proposals.

Secondly, Eastern Europe's familiar demands for most-favored nation treatment (which would amount to a gift from the West worth some $2 bn), and the removal of obstacles to trade (e.g. admission of drugs and medical instruments free of duty) are countered with references to the recession and high rates of unemployment; similarly, criticism of insufficient interest in industrial cooperation is countered with a reference to surplus capacity in Western countries. The familiar Western arguments against the "new international economic order" are also trotted out each time.

Thirdly, praise was heaped on the work of the UN Economic Commission for Europe—in order to avoid institutionalization of the CSCE. But few mentioned that this Commission is *not* a negotiating body, i.e. that it is not always able to solve practical problems.

Fourthly, the West took the view that the Belgrade meeting did not have to reach agreement on a new Final Act—which would detract from the Helsinki Final Act—but was merely required to record shortcomings and successes in the implementation of the Final Act. No *new* obligations should be assumed until the old ones had been performed satisfactorily.

Getting the parties used to discussions which could move forward from ideological confrontation to true dialogue—this evolution is already detectable in the CSCE negotiations—may well form a useful basis for the establishment of economic equilibrium in Europe. Getting the parties used to discussing things in the CSCE can certainly be regarded as a "confidence-building measure," to employ a concept from Basket I taken from the military field. For this it would be essential that the CSCE retain powers of political decision and not fall prey to groups of experts or the influence of technocratic organizations such as the UN Economic Commission for Europe.

31

The Second Basket for Europe, by Vladlen Kuznetzov.
New Times (Moscow), May 1980, no. 18, pp. 10–11.

The United Nations Economic Commission for Europe is a unique organization—in fact, the only one where the linking up and mutual adjustment of the mechanisms of East-West cooperation in the economic and adjacent fields is conducted on a really big scale. Here in Geneva this is called co-operation between countries with market economies and countries with centralized planned economies. The ECE is a kind of laboratory, the experimental base and workshop of co-operation. Here experience is born which is of interest to other countries and regions and, in the first place, to the developing states. It is one of the few bodies where the recommendations of the Final Act are being implemented today to a greater extent than anywhere else. This is of special importance at a time when the anti-détente forces are clamoring about sanctions and embargoes, which are contra-indicated in the world of today where the economic interdependence of countries and regions is constantly growing.

The oft-used comparison to a brain trust suggests itself, but it would be an exaggeration: ideas are generated primarily not in the Geneva headquarters (although there is no ban on this, of course), but in the capitals of the ECE states; they are to be found in the Helsinki Final Act. The numerous initiatives, projects and recommendations contained in it will suffice for many years to come and the ECE figures not infrequently as their direct addressee and executor. It has been estimated that in that part of the Final Act entitled "Co-operation in the Field of Economics, of Science and Technology and of the Environment" (known as the "Second Basket"), the forum of European regional economic co-operation is mentioned fourteen times. This is not an exercise in arithmetic, but an indication of the role the ECE plays in Europe and beyond it.

And it was not fortuitous that the Geneva session spoke primarily about the Helsinki accords, which were the main subject of the speech made by the head of the Soviet delegation, Zoya Mironova, and of the speeches of the representatives of many other countries.

The discussion centered on how to materialize the recommendations of the Helsinki charter of peaceful co-operation and the good-neighbourliness and the valuable ideas that were advanced after the all-European conference with a view to ensuring the triumph of the spirit of Helsinki. Foremost among them is Leonid Brezhnev's proposal, put forward in 1975, for holding three European congresses or conferences—on environmental protection, energy, and transport.

The participants in the 35th session noted with gratification that one of the suggested undertakings had already been carried out. In November 1979 Geneva hosted a high-level conference, held under ECE auspices, on environmental matters. It was of benefit to all the participants, and became a weighty argument in favor of holding other similar conferences. Its success takes the wind out of the sails of the skeptics who still doubt whether the triad of congresses suggested by the U.S.S.R. is needed at all.

The Soviet Union proposed holding a forum on energy not because it expected to reap some special benefits or privileges. The greatest beneficiaries will be precisely those who cannot boast of a robust energy health. But there is something in which the Soviet Union is vitally interested, and that is peace and stability in the continent, preventing Europe from sliding down into confrontation and strife, and ensuring its confident advance along the route charted in Helsinki. Moscow proposes that the problem be solved radically, by linking up power systems and jointly carrying out major projects for the tapping of energy resources.

West European countries export to the U.S.S.R. considerably more industrial goods than the United States does. The greater the volume of export, the more fully the production capacities are utilized, the higher the income and the lower the unemployment rate—hence, the stronger the West Europeans countries' positions in the competitive struggle. By demanding that its NATO partners curtail their trade and economic ties with the U.S.S.R., Washington is out to deprive them of the advantages of economic co-operation with the East and above all of its large and stable export market and rich sources of raw materials—a market which enables them to reduce idle plants, lessen unemployment and conduct business systematically, on a stable long-term basis. While itself losing on this, Washington wants others to lose still more: the worse things are for the West European competitors, the better it is for the U.S.A.

32

COMECON and the European Community, by Raymond Broger. "Implementation of the Final Act of the Conference on Security and Co-operation in Europe," report on economic cooperation presented by the Committee on Economic Affairs and Development, Parliamentary Assembly, Council of Europe, Strasbourg, April 19, 1977, Doc. 3953, pp. 6–7.

In February 1976 the Chairman of the COMECON (CMEA) Executive Committee sent a letter to the Chairman of the Council of the European Communities to propose "the examination of the question of the conclusion of an agreement between COMECON and the EEC on the basis of mutual relations." The draft agreement which was appended contained proposals, inter alia, on the mutual application of the most favored nation clause (Article 6), on non-discrimination in trade (Article 7), on trade in agricultural products (Article 9), on monetary and financial questions (Article 10) and on co-operation in the field of standardization, environment, statistics, economic forecasts, etc. (Article 3).

Although these proposals have not been accepted by the Council of the European Communities, it seems useful to sum up briefly some of the problems which their implementation would have raised:

a. Lack of equivalent reciprocity. Even by limiting matters to the tariff field, the mutual granting of the most favored nation clause would not permit a fair balance of concessions because the customs tariffs do not fulfill the same function for the EC and for the state trading countries. The resulting tariff advantages for COMECON countries' exports should be offset by some form of concession which could be considered as equivalent by the Community.

b. Non-respect for Community competences. There are many provisions in the draft which would not respect Community competences. The most favored nation clause would be granted by member states and not by the EC as such. "Application agreements" would have to be concluded between each country of the EC and each country of COMECON, which would run counter to the EC exclusive competence in the trade field.

c. Extension of "generalized preferences." The draft lays down that the EC should grant the benefit of its preference scheme to COMECON countries which are at a level of economic development justifying such treatment. (Romania benefits already of the EC generalized system of preferences.) The EC, however, has always considered that generalized preferences are subject to its autonomous decision. In this respect it does not wish to be bound by any contractual link.

In November 1977 the Council of the European Communities replied to the COMECON proposal. It offered to open negotiations with a view to concluding a co-operation agreement establishing "working relations" between the two parties. At the same time the Council approved a preliminary draft agreement so as to indicate what in the Council's opinion the agreement should entail. It aims at establishing working relations for the exchange of contacts and information covering various fields such as trade and economic statistics, forecasts, environmental co-operation etc. As regards trade relations, the Council has affirmed its offer already made in 1974 that it is willing to enter into trade negotiations with each of the member countries of the COMECON.

Patterns of Interdependence

33

Compliance with Basket Two, by John Hardt.
Statement by senior specialist in Soviet affairs, Library of
Congress, *Basket II—Helsinki Final Act: East-West
Economic Cooperation,* Hearings before the Commission on
Security and Cooperation in Europe, Ninety-Fifth Congress,
January 13, 1977 (Washington, D.C.: U.S. Government
Printing Office, 1977), pp. 5, 7–10.

Although the Helsinki Final Act was signed by 35 nations two—the Soviet Union and the United States—are the pacesetters—especially in economic policy. If we may liken the relationship of the two powers to a joint airflight, this Helsinki period might be likened to a "holding pattern." After the Trade Act and the Export Import Ban Act amendments had been passed by Congress and signed by the President in January 1975, MFN status was offered to the USSR in fulfillment of the commercial agreement arrangements. The Soviet Union did not accept the conditions of the Jackson-Vanik amendment and the treaty did not then go in force. However most of the arrangements on business facilities (i.e., the Trade Center in Moscow), exchange of information, third country arbitration, terms of settlement of Lend Lease debts, anti-dumping and market disruption understandings continued without rupture. But the political propulsion was lacking for change in the areas of agreement and was absent at the time the Final Act went into force in August 1975. The impetus for change resulting from adoption of the Final Act thus had to rely on the incentives below the superpower and governmental level. The governments of many of the signatory nations in Western and Eastern Europe were relatively more active than the United States and the Soviet Union during this period in fostering economic and commerical relations. The private and public commercial interests in the participating nations were similarly more active than their government counterparts.

A number of principles have been stated and accepted in the Final Act and subsequent documents. One overarching principle as yet unsettled relates to the definition of the general criteria for change: Is change to take place in the economic and commercial practices of all countries on the basis of common interest and benefit, or, are the Eastern countries to change toward Western principles and institutions? It is important to clarify this principle especially if the Eastern signatory countries adhere to the former interpretation and some of the Western nations—including the United States—adhere to the latter.

The states which participated in the All-European conference decided that they each will build relations with other participating states on the basis of the following principles: sovereign equality, respect of the rights inherent in sovereignty; non-use of force or the threat of force; inviolability of frontiers; territorial integrity of states; peaceful settlement of disputes; non-intervention in internal affairs; respect of human rights and fundamental freedoms; equality and the right of peoples to settle their own destinies; cooperation between states; and a good neighbor policy of fulfilling obligations under international law. *The trends and forms of development of mutually advantageous cooperations were defined and concerted.*

The Final Act has not transformed the behavior of signatory nations overnight, but it has committed the national leaders who signed it to standards of behavior which are compatible with Western thoughts about the relationship of people to their governments. *With its profoundly Western orientation, the Final Act* reflects the great importance that the West attaches to human rights and the self determination of peoples.

The terms "mutually advantageous cooperation" and "profoundly Western orientation" seem to connote the difference in basic perspectives, even though the latter phrase is directed specifically to "Basket Three." There is no question that the structure of government in the Eastern and Western nations is different and that these differences influence the attainment of the goals of the Final Act. Clarifying this concept is important. If the changes in institutions are primarily or solely on the part of the Eastern nations, then their motivations will be different for compliance than if the required changes are to be reciprocal.

Even assuming reciprocal change, the costs of change will have to be assessed in each case as less than the expected benefits. The exchange rate in these dynamic calculations would seem to differ from country to country in both East and West. Perhaps a useful guiding principle for all participating nations would be concentrating on those areas of change where the net benefits are perceived as greatest in both East and West. One example might be the provision of detailed planning data by Eastern nations in the interest of obtaining Western credits at world market rates. The cost to Eastern leaders might be a more relaxed disclosure policy than is traditional or deemed desirable, and a greater exposure of their economies to the involvement of Western decision-makers. The Western banks and commercial interests may, in turn, have to accommodate to the uncertainty and cost of operations in unfamiliar Eastern environments and/or possibly longer or more risky patterns of repayment. Each side presumably would benefit more than the perceived cost of change if the accommodations were made. Western nations would benefit by obtaining a greater understanding of Eastern economies which could result in the opening up of new markets and Eastern countries would benefit by obtaining valuable, and much needed, Western credits. At the same time benefits in economic affairs, in tariff and credit across the board, and changes in emigration and other policies of concern might not be as easily balanced.

The principle of world economic interdependence was stated in the Final Act. Complementarity of resources—natural and capital—adds to production and efficiency of economic performance. Eastern nations now refer to the international division of labor. Western countries restate the notion of comparative advantage. The flow of resources restricted only by production and transportation costs is to the general economic interest of all participants in the world market. However, some advantages or disadvantages to Eastern and Western perspectives may be contrasted by reference to selected aspects of more economic interdependence. These are illustrated below:

Technology transfer

Western—Sales of plant and equipment to Eastern nations may broaden the future sales base of technologically advanced product lines by large scale production, keep unit costs down, and research and development budgets up: however, some sales may be risky in maintaining future global competitive positions through patents and other contracts and risk through the technology transfer a significant contribution to the military-related production of possible adversaries.

Eastern—Western technology effectively absorbed may be the critical margin in key sector performance, however, the political and institutional changes conducive to effective technology transfer may weaken the traditional Eastern system of planning and management.

Improved reporting and dissemination of economic information

Western—More and better economic information is the basis of expansion of economic ties. Stable markets and less risky relations are more likely to result in an economic environment in which knowledge of available economic opportunity is full and accurate. However, private commercial and banking information—industrial secrets, privileged market forecasts, etc.—are critical for maintaining competitive market positions.

Eastern—Generation of more uniform, reliable data may improve Eastern planning and management and if supplied to Western users may assure lower prices and more favorable credit terms; however, information control is a form of political control and a security measure. Wider, foreign dissemination of key economic data may weaken Party control of the economy, foster debate among resource claimants, and provide information to those who may use it for purposes otherwise adverse to Eastern State interests.

Trade development

In principle most countries now favor increased trade.

Western—Freer trade may encourage substantial long run expansion of markets in the Eastern nations and provide cheaper, better sources of raw materials and manufactured goods. However, a sharp change in commercial markets may lead to dislocation in the Western domestic economies in terms of employment and production, e.g., components for Western autos may be produced at lower cost in Eastern nations but the short term impact on Western employment may be deemed costly.

Eastern—Lower tariffs (MFN would especially favor Eastern industrial exports to the West), less restrictive quotas and other measures directed toward the Western principle of free trade would facilitate the expansion of East-West trade and reduce the pressures of balance of payments deficits. However, expanded exports of industrial products require some domestic priority to meet world market standards and will still leave products open to unilateral determination of market disruption or dumping. Easier credit terms or extension of cooperative agreements may mean more intrusion in the domestic information and management systems than desired.

Joining the world market

Interdependence implies some acceptance of the world market.

Western—Large scale, high technology Western enterprises require expanding markets to take advantage of economies of scale, keep costs down and stay competitive. The Eastern market appears to be the great untapped potential. However, the Eastern state control of trade isolates the Western seller from the user, long term stability of trade prospects appears somewhat unpredictable, costs in a highly bureaucratized and controlled Eastern market seem high and short term profits small.

Eastern—Access to the world market may not only provide superior goods, technology, and systems, but some guide to domestic Eastern comparative advantages in establishing production priorities. However, the world market still has the traditional Marxist disadvantages of being anarchic, subject to cycles in demand and instability in prices. The recent Eastern exposure to Western stagflation, contributing to their balance of payments deficits brought this long term problem abruptly into current focus.

Interrelationship of baskets

In general all issues of the Final Act are interrelated, but how and in what manner is under question.

Western—Progress in economic interdependence may shift the emphasis away from security and political confrontations toward areas of mutual interest in expandable commercial and cultural relations and redirect the emphasis on military and political control. However, military preparations in the East and reduction in the cultural and political barriers may not proceed with economic improvement, e.g., resources may be released for rather than withdrawn from military programs; moderation in foreign relations may lead to more control of internal change in domestic Eastern relations.

Eastern—There may in the short run appear to be more gain from expanding economic relationships with the West and the world market in terms of advanced technology, improved systems of management, etc.; however the Western conditions may tie "Basket Two" to "Basket Three" and overbalance the economic gains by perceived losses in political terms. "Humanization of borders" or relaxed restrictions on emigration may lead to "brain drains," weakening of political control, and external criteria for decisions perceived to be domestic in character.

Wielding Economic Leverage

34

Effectiveness of the Jackson-Vanik Amendment, by Gerald L. Parsky.
Statement by Assistant Secretary of the Treasury for
International Affairs and questioning, Washington, January 14,
1977, *Implementation of Helsinki Accords*, Hearings before
the Commission on Security and Cooperation in Europe,
Ninety-Fifth Congress, January 14, 1977 (Washington, D.C.:
U.S. Government Printing Office, 1977), pp. 70–73, 76–77.

Mr. Bingham:[1] I know this hearing today is concerned with Basket
II, but obviously there is a relationship between Basket II and Basket
III. What do we do about our efforts to implement the provisions of
Basket III? Can we relate that in any way to the implementation of Basket II? You suggest that we can, but you do not suggest how.

Mr. Parsky: Congressman, I think you have touched on a very important subject, as usual. And I think, first of all, we should start with the
approach that governments should take, vis-à-vis the subject of trade and
economic cooperation. It seems to me that the principal responsibility of
governments in the process is a facilitating one and that the private sector is still the principal element of generating trade and economic development among countries, two-way in nature, benefits flowing each way.

However, the Government does have an important role to play when
impediments exist to the free flow of trade and to the free development
of economic cooperation.

Clearly, the restrictions contained in the Jackson-Vanik amendment[2]
are an impediment to the flow of trade between countries. Obviously,

the underlying basis behind that legislative restriction was a legitimate concern about a humanitarian issue.

The experience, however, that we have had since its enactment has been that the humanitarian objectives which are just and right were not served by that legislative approach.

It is going to take a certain degree of diplomacy. It is going to take utilization of the existing mechanisms that we have in place. It is going to take a coordination of our overall relationship. But as part of that overall package, I think recommendations for elimination of the Jackson-Vanik restrictions can be forthcoming and we can still satisfy legitimate humanitarian concerns.

Mrs. Fenwick:[3] It seems to me there are two impediments, not just one. One acts as an impediment, as the Jackson-Vanik amendment that you refer to. Certainly equal on the other side is the treatment of people. The impediment is that refusal to treat people decently. They ask our businesses to tell them what they need. They do not know what they need in order to make a productive plant. I have heard this over and over again. How to put it all together is what is frustrating the Soviet economy. They think they have the means of doing it, but they do not know how to put it together.

Look, if they want to find out what they need and if they want more trade, they have *got* to pay some attention to what is a basic feeling in this country. And we are shocked—at least I was, speaking for myself—with some of the testimony we heard yesterday about the official and quasi-official people who had gone to Moscow and said these humanitarian concerns were just a response to special interest groups in politics.

Mr. Bingham: If I may pursue my original question. I do not really think you answered it, Mr. Parsky. You said there are ways in which we can pursue the humanitarian goals that we are seeking. But just what, specifically, are you referring to? And do they have anything to do with the expansion of trade or the treatment of trade, or do we just simply consider these as totally separate Baskets, unrelated to each other? And do we simply reserve the right to talk about or protest violations of Basket III?

Mr. Parsky: No, I do not consider the Baskets totally separate. I do not consider the interests or the objective purposes of the Baskets as being unrelated.

What I am saying is, we have established over the recent past a network of relationships, governmental and private. It seems to me we ought to be able, we should be able, we should be pursuing through all of these networks the achievement of the humanitarian interests that we espouse. We have established governmental commissions; we have established trade councils; we have various governmental networks that I think, if properly pursued, can bring about the objectives we want.

Mr. Oliver:[4] Mr. Parsky, the Soviet Union has undertaken a significant moral and political obligation in CSCE and to carry out its provisions. What do you think we should do if they fail to carry out those obligations?

Mr. Parsky: Again, it is a question of assessment as to what failure is. That is a process of time. There are a number of different obligations, moral, economic, political, social, that are inherent in it, and it is a matter of assessment.

As part of a governmental policy, vis-à-vis the Soviet Union or any other country, we have to assess what that means and what it means to us.

Mr. Oliver: What I am saying is if they do not fulfill their political obligations, then is it unfair to use the economic lever to try to enforce those provisions or to let them know that if they do not fulfill their obligations in one area, then we may question the advisability of entering into agreements in other areas?

NOTES

1 Jonathan Bingham, U.S. Representative from New York.
2 For details, see document no. 37 below.
3 Millicent Fenwick, U.S. Representative from New Jersey.
4 Spencer Oliver, staff director and general counsel, Commission on Security and Cooperation in Europe, U.S. Congress.

35

Basket Two May Bring Intangible Benefits, by Elliot L. Richardson. Statement by Secretary of Commerce, Washington, January 14, 1977, *Implementation of Helsinki Accords,* Hearings before the Commission on Security and Cooperation in Europe, Ninety-Fifth Congress, January 14, 1977 (Washington, D.C.: U.S. Government Printing Office, 1977), pp. 94–95, 98–99, 110–11.

Secretary Richardson: The development of economic cooperation, as set forth in Basket II, may bring about intangible benefits to the United States. Increased economic cooperation necessitates many more direct contacts between Americans and people of all levels in the East. These contacts offer those in the East an opportunity to observe the personal freedoms and liberties which we enjoy, and the effective and efficient operation of Western trade, industry, and technology in a decentralized and open economic setting. Although economic cooperation alone is far too weak an instrument to achieve the economic, political, and humanitarian goals we seek, such relationships, over time, can contribute importantly to greater flexibility and more openness in the economic and social systems of the Communist countries.

Ms. Fenwick:[1] Are you suggesting that the Basket II and III—III particularly—sections of the Helsinki Accords could be used in place of title IV and that we might obtain more satisfactory results from a humanitarian point of view if we developed and leaned on the Helsinki Accord and substituted that for Jackson-Vanik and Stevenson?[2] Is that what you are suggesting?

Secretary Richardson: Yes, in substance. Not a total substitution perhaps, but nevertheless in the course of the negotiation of the overall relationship we should lean heavily on the Final Act, both Baskets II and III and their relationship to each other, as the kinds of relationships which all the signatories have said should characterize the standards which they apply internationally and to each other.

Ms. Fenwick: But, Mr. Secretary, look at the danger we expose people to who have no other protection, because then we say to every businessman conducting an agreement, deal or arrangement that it is going to be up to them to bring up the Helsinki Accords and the Basket III provisions: we leave in their hands the implementation of this international accord unless we have written legislation. Isn't that a very frail thing?

Secretary Richardson: I don't think that follows. I would not suggest that this be left to the individual businessman. I think we ought to call to the attention of the individual businessman that the other country has undertaken to improve access to end users and has talked about the exchange of information. If the countries aren't doing this, the businessman should go to the commercial counselor in the embassy and let him know about it. We should do a little jumping up and down, point to the Helsinki language and ask what is the matter. More broadly, however, what I had in mind was that the United States and the Western signatory countries—through diplomatic processes, and through the instrumentality of this Commission—should use their positions to exert steady pressure toward the implementation of the provisions of the Final Act.

What I am saying, is that we don't need to improvise the orchestration here. However, orchestrated through a range of channels and approaches and voices, the Helsinki Final Act is and can be, I think, of significant value.

NOTES

1   Millicent Fenwick, U.S. Representative from New Jersey.
2   The Stevenson Amendment to the Export-Import Bank Authorization Bill of
    1974 set a limit of $300 million in credits over four years to the Soviet Union
    and further limited to $40 million credits for energy exploration.

36

The Economic Bargaining Chips, by Gregory Grossman.
Statement by Professor of Economics, University of California
at Berkeley, *Implementation of Helsinki Accords*, Hearings
before the Commission on Security and Cooperation in
Europe, Ninety-Fifth Congress, January 14, 1977 (Washington,
D.C.: U.S. Government Printing Office, 1977), pp. 140–41.

In the economic area, there has been a marked advance in at least one
respect—the sheer turnover of East-West trade, and especially in the
value of imports of the European COMECON countries from the industrialized Western countries. This jump in imports has been accompanied by net capital inflow from the West into the USSR of five or
more billion dollars over the two years. All this is surely very much in
accord with Soviet objectives.

Unfortunately, this advance has not been accompanied by commensurate improvements in other economic areas mentioned in the Final
Act, especially those that touch on traditional Soviet secrecy and ob-
structionism. Particularly, one fails to notice over the past year and one
half any substantial widening and deepening of publication of timely
information on internal developments inside the Soviet economy, or of
more direct contacts between the producers or ultimate consumers on
the Soviet side and the interested Western firms on the other side.
(Some observers point to the start of quarterly publication of official
Soviet foreign trade statistics beginning with the first quarter of 1976 as
evidence of progress in the sense of the Helsinki Agreement. While to
some extent this is so, and is especially convenient for academic and
governmental researchers, one wonders how useful the data are for business purposes given their highly aggregated form. And in any case foreign trade data by their very nature generally have been available from
the trading partners' side already.)

In general, it would be a serious mistake to confuse the gargantuan
Soviet appetite for Western goods and capital, which has been abun-
dantly evident since at least the start of the First Five-Year Plan in
1928, for a readiness to change political spots, either internally or exter-

nally. On the contrary, the more successful the Soviet regime is in obtaining western economic co-operation without any significant political quid-pro-quos, the more freedom of action is it likely to sense in both domestic and foreign spheres. The notion that the Soviets will by means of economic ties become "enmeshed in a web of mutual economic interdependence" is conjectural at best. As we have noticed, they take the proffered benefits and are careful to avoid those steps that would "enmesh" them or change their wonted ways. As a result, "mutual interdependence" can easily turn into double dependence on our part: we could become dependent on their good will in repaying debts and shipping key materials such as energy, and at the same time also on their market for goods of interest to strong pressure groups in this country (e.g. the farmers). Moreover, once the Soviet regime feels secure in its receipt of economic benefits from the West, it will surely give shorter shrift to those at home seeking to emigrate or to uphold basic human rights. After all, it must not be forgotten that the Soviets opened their doors to Jewish emigration in 1969, not after the Nixon-Brezhnev meetings that launched the détente but in expectation of it.

To return to the Helsinki Agreement and in view of the asymmetry of economic interests between the U.S. and the USSR, it would behoove the United States to take full cognizance of its economic power in urging the Soviet Union (and other Eastern European governments) to fully comply with the political and humanitarian provisions and principles written into the Final Act. Basically, this means retaining export controls and deferring any relaxation in the present restrictions on long-term loans and credits to the Soviet Union until we are reasonably confident that the USSR is acting positively, constructively, and lastingly to an extent that is commensurate with the importance of the economic benefits to it. This mutual accommodation could, of course, be stepwise.

Just what forms this action might take, what evidence we would need, and the proper legal preparations on our side, are important questions, though not within the purview of the present statement. Yet in this connection one must bear in mind that the Soviet leadership may have only recently demonstrated its readiness to promise major political concessions in return for major economic benefits from us, and in matters that it loudly insisted to be strictly of its own domestic concern. I am of course referring to its putative acceptance of the conditions of the Jackson Amendment in regard to emigration and the treatment of applicants for emigration, as documented in the well-known Kissinger-Jackson correspondence (the *New York Times*, October 19, 1974, pp. 1 and 10). The benefits that the Soviets expected at the time were primarily large, long-term credits, and when these were virtually denied to them by the subsequent action of the U.S. Congress, they—not irrationally—renounced the 1972 Trade Agreement. But it must be stressed that it was the denial of the most coveted prize, credits, and not the terms of the Jackson Amendment, that led to the renunciation of the trade agreement, contrary to what the Soviets have been telling us since (with good purpose on their part). At first they apparently did agree to the political accommodation in expectation of economic benefits. On the other hand, we can reasonably doubt whether the Soviet authorities would have allowed emigration to continue in the event that the Jackson Amendment had been voted down by the U.S. Senate.

Thanks to the events of January 1975—the renunciation of the trade agreement and the re-suspension of long-term credits to the USSR, events that have occasioned only negligible economic costs to this country if any, as we have seen—the new Administration and the new Congress are in the fortunate position of still holding most of the economic bargaining chips for constructive influence on the course of our relations with the USSR and the rest of Eastern Europe, both within the framework of the Helsinki Agreement and on an even more comprehensive and global basis.

37

Romania and the MFN Lever, by Lynne A. Davidson.
In Lynne A. Davidson, "Tools of Human Rights Diplomacy
for East Bloc Countries," manuscript, Washington 1985,
pp. 17–29.

Romania is one of the few East bloc countries with which the United States has significant economic leverage to affect human rights conditions. The principal instrument of that leverage has been the annual review of the President and Congress to determine Romania's eligibility to receive Most-Favored-Nation (MFN) trading status in conformity with Section 402 (Jackson-Vanik Amendment) of the 1974 Trade Act.

Under Jackson-Vanik, the President must submit his recommendation on whether or not to extend and use his authority to waive Section 402 for each applicable country by June 3. Following receipt of the President's recommendation, Congress has the power to terminate a country's MFN status by taking action within 60 days after July 3. The Subcommittee on Trade of the House Ways and Means Committee and the Subcommittee on International Trade of the Senate Finance Committee traditionally schedule public hearings to afford the executive branch and interested non-governmental organizations a chance to air their views and concerns before the issue is decided by Congress.

Each year since Romania's trading status first came up for annual review in 1975, the President and Congress have concluded that, despite Bucharest's flawed record, humanitarian aims would better be served by the renewal of MFN status, than by its denial. In 1981, the MFN review was fairly routine, but by 1982, the climate for MFN renewal for Romania had darkened. After Poland's collapse, enthusiasm had lessened in the West for trade with Eastern Europe's shaky economies—and Romania was considered to be one of the shakiest next to Poland's. Also, in late 1981 and early 1982, Romania cast further shadows by taking repressive measures against activist Christians, by showing inadequate responsiveness to congressional intercessions on behalf of intending emigrants, and by letting Jewish emigration fall to unacceptably low monthly levels. Through the work of the Helsinki Commission and other organizations, this poor human rights record came to the attention of Congress in the early months of 1982, provoking several Members of Congress to collect signatures on letters to Presidents Reagan and Ceauşescu expressing concern about human rights conditions in Romania. At the same time, several private organizations geared up their lobbying efforts.

Then, on June 2, President Reagan issued a tough message to Congress concerning extension of MFN to Romania. While he recommended that the MFN status be renewed in 1982, the President stated his concern about Romania's emigration record and the need for its re-examination. The President acknowledged that emigration from Romania to the United States had increased six-fold since the waiver had been put into effect and that the maximum number of emigrants admissible under U.S. immigration procedures had been permitted to leave Romania for permanent settlement in the United States over the previous twelve-month period. However, at the same time, the President cited certain problems including the fact that the Romanian government had not improved its emigration procedures, which he called "cumbersome and plagued with obstacles for those who merely wish to obtain emigration application forms." The President said that he had weighed these humanitarian concerns within the context of the satisfactory state of overall U.S.-Romanian relations and concluded that, on balance, the aim of Section 402 would best be served by a renewal of MFN in 1982. He then added that he intended to inform the Romanian government that unless a noticeable improvement in its emigration procedures were to take place and the rate of Jewish emigration to Israel were to increase significantly, Romania's MFN renewal in 1983 would be in serious jeopardy.

Even prior to these cautionary comments from the Executive Branch, the new Romanian Ambassador evidently got the message from some quarters (not the least of which was Helsinki Commission Chairman Fascell) that Romania was in for a hard time in Congress on MFN renewal. Romanian responsiveness to expressions of U.S. concern about specific emigration cases began to improve. The Romanian Ambassador launched an intensive lobbying effort of his own on the Hill. A number of longstanding emigration cases raised by Chairman Fascell and other Members of Congress were quickly resolved. Significantly higher numbers of Jews were given emigration approval for Israel. The actual number of Jews arriving in Israel also jumped. The emigration processing of large numbers of Christian families, including activists, was stepped up appreciably. However, progress was made on a case-by-case basis, rather than in terms of systemic reform.

Despite the last-minute efforts by Romania to bolster its record, disapproval motions on Romanian MFN were lodged in both chambers of Congress and Romania's human rights record was roundly criticized during the House and Senate hearings, scheduled respectively for July 12–13 and August 10, 1982. In the interval between the House and Senate hearings, higher monthly levels of Romanian emigration were registered through July and into August and a number of cases of interest to particular Members of Congress were resolved. Then, in an unprecedented response to heightened congressional and public concern, eleven prisoners of conscience arrested for the unauthorized acquisition and distribution of Bibles were included in an amnesty of twenty-seven individuals.

The House voted down its disapproval resolution on August 18, shortly before Congress recessed. Romania's MFN status thus was permitted to continue for another twelve-month period, but with stated congressional reservations and obvious erosion of support for its extension.

Meanwhile, building on the groundwork laid during the MFN review, the Conference of Presidents of Major American Jewish Organizations began talks with Romanian officials in Washington in August and continued the discussions in Bucharest in September. Deputy Assistant Secretary for Human Rights and Humanitarian Affairs Elliott Abrams engaged in an initial round of talks in Bucharest on October 6–7. These discussions resulted in Romania's agreement to respond definitively to emigration requests within six to nine months. Romania also promised to cease harassment of would-be emigrants.

However, Romania's good faith participation in these talks was thrown into serious question when on November 1, 1982, the government issued a new "education decree," which required inter alia that emigrants reimburse the state in hard currency for the cost of education beyond the compulsory ten-year level. The decree affected all prospective emigrants from Romania, not just those destined for the United States. Ethnic German emigration to the FRG and Jewish emigration to Israel were seriously restricted by the tax and strong protests were lodged by both governments with Bucharest.

Trying to leave the door open for a change in the Romanian position, President Reagan on March 4, 1983 signalled his intention to terminate Romania's MFN status and other benefits effective June 30, 1983, if the education repayment decree were to remain in force on that date. Making the announcement several months ahead of the termination date gave U.S. importers time to protect their interests. It also gave Romania some more time to reconsider its action. Both Romania and the United States knew that once lost, MFN could not easily be rebuilt, since the initial conditions Jackson-Vanik requires a country to meet in order to acquire (or in this case, re-acquire) MFN status are much tougher than those governing its extension once gained.

In mid-May, Romanian Foreign Minister Andrei came to the United States and met with Vice President Bush, Secretary of State Shultz, and other officials. At the end of the month, FRG Foreign Minister Genscher paid a two-day visit to Bucharest for talks with President Ceaușescu. Afterwards, although he publicly denied there was any link between the two matters, Genscher announced that "a satisfactory solution" to the emigration issue had been found and that the FRG had agreed to go ahead with rescheduling Romania's bilateral debt (the FRG is Romania's largest Western trading partner). The two matters were not, as East Europeans are fond of saying, coincidental.

Then, in his annual message to Congress on MFN extension, on June 2, 1983, President Reagan similarly announced that he had "received assurances from the President of Romania that Romania will not require reimbursement to the state of educational costs as a precondition to emigration, and that Romania will not create economic or procedural barriers to emigration," and recommended that MFN be extended for another twelve months.

Another major occasion to send a message to the Romanians that U.S. interest in human rights is shared by the executive and legislative branches was the second U.S.-Romanian Human Rights Roundtable held in Washington, D.C. on February 27–28, 1984, in conformity with a recommendation in the Madrid Concluding Document. The first Roundtable, a voluntary CSCE spinoff forum, had taken place in February, 1980, in Bucharest.

In order to maximize the chances for discussion of concrete problems and minimize possibilities for Romanian philosophizing about human rights, on the advice of the Helsinki Commission the United States delegation took care to tie the agenda for the Roundtable to specific provisions of the Helsinki and Madrid CSCE documents. Accordingly, each side addressed the agenda items by relating its own domestic experience in fulfilling Helsinki and Madrid pledges on human rights. By using this approach the U.S. participants were able to draw their Romanian counterparts into extensive discussion of the full range of human rights problems in Romania. Throughout the frank exchanges the United States emphasized that the true value of the Roundtable lies less in the words that are exchanged than in the deeds that follow. In particular, Helsinki Commission Staff Director Spencer Oliver stressed that violations of the human rights provisions of the Helsinki and Madrid agreements seriously weaken the credibility of the Helsinki process in the eyes of the public.

On May 31, 1984, President Reagan issued his 1984 MFN recommendation to extend Romania's waiver for one more year. In his accompanying message to Congress, the President reported that emigration from Romania to all countries had more than doubled and emigration to the United States had increased ninefold since 1974. Progress was noted in the numbers of people receiving exit documentation and in the shortening of the processing time for passport applications. However, President Reagan acknowledged that "there are still many problems in the emigration area."

On August 10, Congress recessed until early September without having passed a bill or joint resolution of disapproval, thereby permitting the Presidential decision to stand and Romania to retain its MFN status for another year. Word subsequently reached the West that the Romanian Government had quietly released Father Calciu, Romania's most famous prisoner of conscience, on August 20, three days before Romania's National Day (August 23), an occasion around which amnesties tend to be timed. While the immediate steps leading up to Father Calciu's release have not yet become known, it is certain that the combined intercessions by a succession of U.S. Administrations, Members of Congress, Helsinki Commissioners, Western and neutral and nonaligned governments and private human rights organizations in this country and abroad finally succeeded in bringing the Romanian Government to the conclusion that its interests would be better served by setting Father Calciu free than by continuing his imprisonment.

Although it is a useful instrument, Jackson-Vanik is no magic wand. It is unrealistic to expect the annual MFN review to produce instant institutional changes in Romania. The MFN tool should not be regarded merely as a stick to brandish disapprovingly once a year. Nor should the carrot of MFN extension be regarded as an unqualified seal of U.S. approval. Rather, Jackson-Vanik is a specialized tool of leverage—an instrument to be applied with a steady hand from one MFN review to the next and in conjunction with other human rights policy instruments such as CSCE in order to accomplish concrete, if limited, objectives: the reunification of families, the release of prisoners of conscience, easements in the plight of human rights activists, and some improvements in the way the Romanian Government treats segments of the population.

Promoting Diversity in Eastern Europe

38

Human Rights in Eastern Europe, by Rudolf L. Tökes.
"Human Rights in Eastern Europe: An Overview, 1977–1980,"
statement by Professor of Political Science, University of
Connecticut, *Basket III: Implementation of the Helsinki
Accords*, Hearings before the Commission on Security and
Cooperation in Europe, Ninety-Sixth Congress, March 25,
1980 (Washington, D.C.: U.S. Government Printing Office,
1980), pp. 12–29.

The difficulties that East Europeans face today cannot and must not obscure the historic importance and profoundly positive impact of the Helsinki Conference on Security and Cooperation in Europe on the 140 million people and the governments which rule them in this part of Europe. The Helsinki Agreements, although viewed initially with considerable misgivings by many Americans, have proved to be one of the most successful, and thus far virtually cost-free, investments of United States prestige in the postwar era on behalf of noble ideals such as peaceful interaction among nations with differing political beliefs on matters as diverse as military security, international trade and human rights.

Indeed, the value and historic merit of United States participation in CSCE and its subsequent leadership of the West in efforts to implement the three main provisions (or Baskets) of the Final Act can best be appreciated if we consider what might have happened in Eastern Europe in the last five years if a multilateral agreement of this kind had not existed. Without the binding moral and legal force of the Final Act, some of the open and hidden tensions of East-West relations and of the political and societal contradictions of Communist Eastern Europe might have erupted in ways that could have resulted in sharply increased East-

West confrontations and in the drastic curtailment of the presently available modest personal autonomy of the peoples of Eastern Europe.

Without the moral (and indeed legal) authority of the Final Act behind them, the more than one hundred thousand East Germans who peacefully queued up before the regime's passport offices might, without any hope to leave for the West, have resorted to desperate measures to vent their frustrations. Although these hopes remained essentially unfulfilled (except for the GDR's contemptible trade in political prisoners for West German marks and technology), at least it was no longer deemed a political crime to seek official permission to emigrate from that country. Similarly, without the Helsinki Agreement's emphasis on national sovereignty, some East European regimes—and the Polish and the Hungarian come to mind in this connection—would have yielded to Soviet pressures to crack down on native dissidents far more severely than they have done. Moreover, without Basket II the penetration and wholesale adoption of Western technology, science and management techniques by East European states would not have taken place—nor, as a consequence, could since 1976 Poland, Hungary, Romania begin to distance themselves from COMECON and edge closer to the Western market economies. All these, therefore, have been beneficial consequences of the CSCE, and helped ameliorate East Europe's internal tensions by keeping the quality of East-West government to government relations on a correct, though far from cordial footing.

However, from the viewpoint of US concern for human rights the most important achievement of the Helsinki Agreements was the placing of this issue, as an integral part, into an interlocking and interdependent structure of commitments addressing military, economic and scientific concerns. By being linked to "Humanitarian and Other Fields," the security and economic components of the Agreements have, to this day, effectively sheltered human rights which, for the US, though somewhat less so for the Western European states, have been the heart of the Helsinki Accords. By providing material incentives to the governments of Communist Eastern Europe, the United States and its Western allies have been in the position to reward those states that have made a demonstrable effort to implement Third Basket provisions.

Through the vehicle of this Commission's Semiannual Reports the US opened a new and important channel of communication to the East European signatories of the Final Act. By establishing the set of flexible yet verifiable criteria for monitoring Soviet and East European compliance with the Helsinki Accords, the United States has succeeded in keeping the entire issue of East-West relations, and especially the question of human rights in the forefront of public attention both in this country and in Europe.

These Reports may, for all intents and purposes, be taken as unusually explicit statements of US foreign policy toward the USSR and Eastern Europe. Each of the Reports that has appeared thus far has made a careful distinction between the Soviet and East European record of compliance with the Helsinki Accords. In doing so, the US has given recognition to geopolitical and military realities and the constraints under which the governments of Eastern Europe operate. By establishing individual, though on the whole compatible, standards of compliance which the US can realistically expect of each East European state, important flexibility has been gained with respect to the judicious exercise of US influence over the conduct of these countries.

Human rights: Western theory and East European traditions

While all those who believe in freedom and democracy must applaud the judicious use of military, political and economic resources to generate philosophically desirable results, it is not entirely clear whether our definition of human rights is at all congruent with traditional East European beliefs and expectations associated with this term. On the positive side, there is absolutely no doubt that Western philosophies of human rights run counter to and help undermine the theory and practice of Marxism-Leninism in the Communist world. What is less certain, however, is whether those rights which we consider inalienable and take for granted as central to our way of life are similarly understood, with Czechoslovakia's important exception, by most East Europeans. East Europeans accord primacy to *collective* rather than individual and *socioeconomic* rather than political rights. These rights are, and have always been, administered by bureaucrats of the executive branch rather than by an independent judiciary which is without established traditions of independence in Eastern Europe. The notion of having a "buffer" between the individual and the state had been well known and protected in Masaryk's Czechoslovakia and in Germany before Hitler but elsewhere in Eastern Europe "human rights" have always been measured by different standards.

In the midst of Great Power struggles, history has taught the peoples of small East European states to place the highest value on their collective survival as viable national, economic, cultural, linguistic and religious entities. Survival means self-reliance and skepticism toward Western slogans, including those advocating human rights which, as the East

Germans, Hungarians, Poles and Czechoslovaks know from bitter experience, are not and cannot be backed up by the full military and economic might of the West. These considerations counsel patience and careful balancing of priorities by those seeking to promote positive changes in Eastern Europe.

In calling attention to the existence of historically conditioned perceptions of the substance and procedural guarantees of human rights in this part of Europe I am *not* advocating any lessening of our insistence on the full implementation of the East European regimes' delivery of these rights to their citizens. Rather, I am recommending that we employ more sophisticated techniques of analysis for the monitoring of individual governments' performance under the Helsinki Accords. For example, it would be entirely unrealistic to expect Bulgarians, with their deeply entrenched historical and cultural affinities to Russia, to suddenly turn around and embrace what most people in that country would consider alien and, in the given policy context, explicitly anti-Soviet, philosophies of liberal democracy. On the other hand, this Commission would have a sound case for insisting on meaningful compliance with the human rights provisions of Helsinki by the government of Romania which prides itself in its somewhat dubious classical Roman and, in the more modern and undeniably valid, affinities with French culture and civilization.

While it is useful and indeed essential to communicate to East European governments the views of this Commission and that of the US government, such evaluations must be informed by the area's historical and cultural traditions. As I pointed out above, the semiannual ranking of foreign countries' performance under the Helsinki Agreements has considerable value for the articulation of US policy. On the other hand, unless careful distinctions are made, it can also become a sort of beauty contest which could interfere with ongoing confidential negotiations or, conversely, arouse unrealistic expectations with respect to hoped-for policy changes in a Communist country. Too frequent public stock-taking of this kind can be counter-productive in cases when the recipients of US criticism can and do point out the rather uneven human rights record of some of our friends and allies in Asia, the Middle East and Latin America.

Human rights: the societal impact

Three years ago in his testimony before this Commission James F. Brown[1] made a most useful distinction between the "state" and "societal" levels of East Europe to which Western human rights policies are addressed. As he pointed out, the Communist states sought to limit meaningful implementation of the Helsinki Agreements to Baskets One and Two and tried to downplay Basket Three or, to use Brown's felicitous phrase, "the essential Helsinki."

It is the "societal" level and, more precisely, the dynamics of the societies of today's Eastern Europe and the way in which various social groups perceive Basket Three that deserve close attention. It may be controversial to suggest, but in my opinion it is doubtful that the daily lives, working conditions, and cultural preferences of the *average* East European have been in any immediate way affected by Helsinki—"essential" and otherwise. If the impact was not immediately perceptible by all then how did Helsinki affect the people of East Europe?

To make a judgment about the societal impact of Helsinki we must first look at how the 98 per cent non-dissident, non-activist, non-incarcerated, though certainly not apolitical, East Europeans live, think of themselves and of the society of which they are a part. It is this silent majority and the conditions under which they might respond to the western human rights message that ought to be of interest to those seeking to measure Helsinki's influence since 1977.

The first point to note is that the East European beholders of the "essential Helsinki" live in societies which have undergone major changes in the last 35 years. The image of downtrodden and bitterly anti-Communist masses was probably accurate in the darkest days of Stalinism, but today these passions are largely spent. In the last fifteen years popular concerns have focused mainly on issues of economics, welfare and social mobility within the established political framework. Economic reforms of the late 1960s produced increased living standards. The reforms also aroused expectations of higher wages, more plentiful food supply, better selection of consumers' goods, improved housing conditions and unhindered access to public and privately owned means of transportation. Moreover, the people have come to expect a fair chance to improve their income and social status through higher and specialized education and upward career mobility in the system.

The Helsinki Accords of 1975 coincided with increasing popular dissatisfaction with the East European states' economic performance and contributed significantly to the politicization of all East Europeans, regardless of class status. On the other hand, the pattern of public awareness of the political potentials of the human rights issue has been highly uneven. Because various segments of the East European societies had different stakes in and different opportunities for the realization of their concerns they reacted in a number of ways to the challenge and promise of Helsinki.

Fortunately from the Communist incumbents' viewpoint, Western governments and international broadcasters (except probably Radio Free Europe) articulated the issue of human rights in fairly abstract and philosophically absolute terms which did not directly address the issue of social and welfare rights. Most East Europeans have traditionally understood human rights to mean food, clothing, shelter, free or low cost social welfare services and guaranteed employment which the communist governments, by and large, did provide for their citizens. For the average person Helsinki meant a symbolic end to the Second World War, a vague hope for the lessening of international tensions and a chance to bring up one's children in a more peaceful world.

None of these mean to imply that the regimes have succeeded in winning the loyalties of the majority, or that the East Europeans' sense of national, cultural, linguistic and religious identity had diminished to the point of willingly accepting Communist rule and Soviet supremacy over their native land. Quite the contrary: all these beliefs and values are alive and are making themselves felt throughout the area. The point, however, is that short of grievous provocation by a desperate regime and its Soviet masters, most people would prefer to come to terms with unpleasant realities by trying to improve their lot in both legal and illegal ways rather than to take to the barricades under slogans of human rights, national independence, ethnic autonomy and religious freedoms. Surviving and coping are the oldest human rights strategies in this part of the world.

Rights and wrongs: social status, religious freedom,
ethnic autonomy and youthful self-expression

Unlike the politically passive majority, in the late 1970s there are four clearly distinguishable clusters of East Europeans who *have* reacted positively to the opportunities that Basket Three offered to citizens of the Helsinki signatory states. Among these the most visible have been the leading intellectual dissidents. The personal histories and the political message of Robert Havemann, Wolf Bierman and many others in East Germany, of Edward Lipiński, Adam Michnik and the authors of many scores of dissident journals, pamphlets, appeals and the birth and heroic struggle of the Czechoslovak Charter 77 group are well known. Similarly, the names and writings of prominent Hungarian, Yugoslav and Romanian dissidents of the late 1970s are familiar to those with genuine interest in the struggle for human rights, political and artistic freedoms in Eastern Europe. Therefore, it seems impractical, within the confines of this brief essay, to try to summarize the record of these brave and gifted champions of their nations' fundamental rights. However, what is virtually unknown to most Americans is the shared needs and concerns of those social, religious and ethnic groups for whom the well-known East European dissidents speak.

The first of these may be called the new socialist middle class of Eastern Europe. It is made up of people in the 25 to 40 years of age bracket who entered the job market in the 1960s upon acquiring specialized skills, university degrees and, with these, an opportunity for gaining material comforts and secure prospects in the existing system. Around 1975 or 1976 the era of economic prosperity came to an end and the regimes began instituting restrictive measures to control inflation and growing foreign trade deficits. Widespread concerns about the possible return of economic hardships, and fears of the reinstitution of arbitrary, and even Stalinist, political controls to combat popular unrest awakened many hitherto contented beneficiaries of welfare socialism to the need for a secure legal-institutional framework to protect their economic rights and political interests.

It was against this background of existential insecurity and sense of powerlessness of the new middle class that a quiet struggle began to codify the civil rights of members of the professional class by narrowing the scope of offenses which the authorities have the discretionary right to call "political." Fears of the revival of official lawlessness have also generated pressures for establishing rational and predictable guidelines and codes of conduct for the use of police power against suspected white collar offenders. The ratification of the Helsinki Agreements by the national legislatures as the law of the land, though it accorded no real protection for anyone and least of all the low status individual, did give a new sense of self-confidence to members of the highly educated postwar generation and the courage to assert their interests. Although reliable evidence is difficult to come by, it is said that the volume of appeals against all kinds of unfavorable official decisions involving salaries, personnel policies and requests for visas for extended trips or short vacations in the West, has increased manifold since 1977. It seems that the Final Act helped foster the development of a new, fuller sense of citizenship in Eastern Europe. This has placed the authorities on the defensive in their dealings with the younger and better educated segments of the societies who no longer live in awe of the secret police.

The other major group of individuals with the motivation to seek redress for violations of their human rights under the Helsinki Agreements are the religious believers and ethnic minorities of Eastern Europe. With ample justification, these people regard themselves as victims of anti-religious government policies and/or those of chauvinistic intolerance of the dominant ethnic majority. Measures of government repression against these groups have ranged from job discrimination to selective imprisonment and forcible resettlement to distant parts of the country. Unlike the powerful Polish Catholic Church which enjoys a virtually coequal status with the Communist party and the government, Turkish Moslem minorities in Bulgaria, German Lutherans, Hungarian Catholics and Calvinists in Romania, Catholics in Czechoslovakia, members of fundamentalist Protestant sects (Seventh Day Adventists, Jehovah's Witnesses, Pentecostalists) and isolated Jewish communities throughout the area are vulnerable to official harassment of all kinds. The election of an East European, Cardinal Karol Wojtyła of Cracow, as the Pope in 1978 was providential and gave a powerful protector for the beleaguered religious believers of Eastern Europe. Though the Pope has no divisions, his moral authority is immense, as is his influence as the ultimate guarantor of religious liberties in Communist lands.

Again, with the important Polish exception, the East European religious faithful are generally rural and socially low-status individuals whose only hope for justice lies in Western co-believers bringing their case to the court of world public opinion under the Helsinki Final Act. The Communist tactics of imposing tight controls (though certainly not imprisonment) on the persons of top clergymen but ruthlessly persecuting for alleged "common criminal" activities members of their congregations often succeed in keeping the issue out of the Western media. And this brings me to the general problem of apparent Western disinterest in the fate of tens of thousands of inarticulate, often poorly educated and underprivileged people—some of them believers, some of them ethnic minorities or both—in Eastern Europe whose human rights are routinely trampled underfoot by the authorities without any fear of adverse foreign reaction. It is somehow unfashionable to publicize the stories of old peasants, migrant workers or that of the traditionally third-class citizen Gypsies throughout East Europe who land in jail after an argument with the rural police about an anti-Communist remark, faulty work or residence papers or a missing sack of feed from the collective farm warehouse. Neither Amnesty International nor the leading Western newspapers seem to be interested in cases of this sort, though one hopes that Radio Free Europe is allowed by Congress to inform its listeners about such regime violations of the average East Europeans' human rights.

The Helsinki Accords notwithstanding, or perhaps because of them, the plight of ethnic minorities in Slovakia, Romania and in Bulgaria as well has worsened in recent years. Hungarians, Ukrainians, and Poles in Slovakia and Germans, Hungarians, Ukrainians, and Bulgarians in

Romania are subject to various kinds of discriminatory policies that the spokesmen of these groups call "second-class citizenship" and "cultural genocide." When the results of the 1980 census in Bulgaria, Romania and Czechoslovakia will be available, this Commission will have an opportunity to test the validity of the Turkish, Macedonian, and Hungarian ethnic minorities' charge of "statistical genocide" through the decennial disappearance of ten to fifteen percent of their co-nationals from the official census tolls. Although Communist governments, especially the Hungarian, tried to intercede through quiet diplomacy on behalf of their ethnic diaspora in neighboring states, such efforts are rebuffed—ironically, in the name of the "non-interference-in-internal-affairs" clause of the Final Act.

The young generation of the East Europeans—workers, high school and university students, the growing number of job dropouts and those rejected on political grounds by university admission committees—represent the fourth cluster of people who have been touched by the "spirit of Helsinki." Communist Eastern Europe is ruled by oligarchies of old men who have little understanding and no sympathy for the economic and cultural needs and concerns of the young generation. The youth of Eastern Europe, as young people everywhere, are idealistic, restless and are searching for ways to fulfill their aspirations. In terms of career opportunities they find no "room at the top," nor at "the middle" for people who have been kept out of universities and specialized training programs. And at the workplace it is most often not achievement but political loyalty which earns promotion and rewards. Millions of newly married East Europeans today find themselves completely locked out of the housing market, even though low-cost housing is to be one of the guaranteed social rights in the communist state.

University students, particularly those in the humanities and the fine arts, have been perhaps the most sensitive to the profound contradictions between the regimes' ideological pretensions and the materialistic, privilege-bound and anti-intellectual quality of life around them. In every East European state these university students are the "reserve army" of the visible dissidents. Inspired by or with the help of the prominent dissidents, these young intellectuals organize and participate in educational counter-institutions in the form of "flying universities," study circles, and discussion groups. What is striking about the political beliefs of the alienated university youth is that they manage to combine the human rights provisions of Helsinki with respect to basic political freedoms of speech, assembly, and dissemination of written material with an abiding faith in democratic socialism. Helsinki has thus given new impetus to efforts to promote peaceful "within-system" reforms and alternatives to the ideologically bankrupt system that its apologists call "real socialism."

Unlike the politically conscious university youth, there is another cluster of young people who seek personal fulfillment in religion and apolitical cultural pursuits. A closer reading of the lyrics of songs of Czechoslovak, Hungarian, Bulgarian, Polish and East German rock groups and popular balladeers can be more enlightening than ten learned dissident treatises about the human condition in Eastern Europe. The traditional Western themes of love, longing and loneliness are sharpened by words of self-destructive bitterness, political estrangement and a sense of desperation about the future. For the vast audiences of such counter-cultural messages, the matter of personal autonomy is of paramount importance, therefore they are a natural constituency to receive and possibly act upon what they perceive to be the essential meaning of Helsinki.

In sum, the beliefs and behavior of these four societal groups have been substantially, and perhaps irreversibly, influenced by the East European states' formal adherence to the Helsinki Accords. The changes in social attitudes are also symptoms of the underlying malaise of popular distrust of the governments for their demonstrated unwillingness to accommodate citizen demands for substantive and procedural guarantees of basic political and social rights. In a fundamental sense, the record of these groups is an important manifestation of a crisis of confidence in the Soviet-sponsored socio-political order in postwar Eastern Europe. The tensions are becoming severe and, in the opinion of many thoughtful East Europeans, the implementation by the regimes of the Helsinki Agreements is the only realistic way to prevent the coming crises of the 1980s in this part of Europe.

NOTES

1   See document no. 25 above.

39

Political Relations and Contacts, by Commission on Security and Cooperation in Europe.
In *The Helsinki Process and East-West Relations: Progress in Perspective: Report on the Positive Aspects of the Implementation of the Helsinki Final Act, 1975–1984* (Washington, D.C.: Commission on Security and Cooperation in Europe, 1985), pp. 8–10.

The Helsinki process has provided a valuable multilateral framework which has encouraged bilateral discussion and high-level contacts between the United States and the nations of Eastern Europe other than the Soviet Union. The commitments undertaken at Helsinki—contained in the principles and, indeed, throughout the Final Act—have facilitated the United States' pursuit of a policy of differentiation in its relations with the countries of Eastern Europe. The Helsinki framework has enabled East European nations to engage in bilateral endeavors with the West, including the United States, that were not previously possible and has given the East European states marginally greater room for maneuver vis-à-vis the Soviet Union in conducting their foreign and domestic policy. This limited increase in flexibility has been demonstrated in the series of bilateral meetings covering the broad range of CSCE issues, including human rights, held between the United States and many of the East European countries since the end of the Belgrade meeting in 1978.

These bilateral consultations provided the framework for a broader and more in-depth exchange of views on both bilateral and international issues than would ever have been possible before the initiation of the CSCE process. For the most part, these talks were held between the Belgrade and Madrid meetings as part of the bilateral approach to implementation called for in the Follow-up section of the Helsinki Final Act.

Following is a listing of the bilateral CSCE talks held between the United States and the countries of Eastern Europe between the Belgrade and Madrid meetings. The United States delegation to these talks usually consisted of representatives of the CSCE Commission as well as of the Department of State:

  —*September 1978*: United States visited Hungary and Romania
  —*November 1978*: United States visited G.D.R., Poland, and Bulgaria
  —*November 1979*: Bulgaria visited the United States
  —*March 1979*: G.D.R. visited the United States
  —*April 1979*: Romania visited the United States; and

—*May* 1979: Hungary visited the United States.

In addition to these bilateral U.S.–East European talks on CSCE issues, the Helsinki era ushered in a series of high-level talks between the United States and Eastern Europe in which CSCE issues were discussed at length. These include the visit of Hungarian Deputy Foreign Minister Nagy to Washington in June 1978, the visit of Bulgarian Deputy Foreign Minister Tsvetkov in November 1978, the visit of U.S. Assistant Secretary of State for European Affairs George Vest to Budapest and Sofia in October 1979 and the visit of U.S. CSCE Ambassador Max Kampelman to Bucharest in April 1981.

Two significant bilateral acts, consistent with the spirit of Principle IX, cooperation among states, and affecting the political relations of the U.S. with two East European nations were facilitated by the climate of cooperation established by Helsinki. The first occurred in January 1978, when the United States formally returned to Hungary the historic crown of St. Stephen which had been in American hands since the closing months of World War II. The return of this crown, the symbol of the Hungarian nation for centuries, has undoubtedly helped contribute to the development of normal and friendly relations between the United States and Hungary.

The other event took place at the end of 1981, when the United States and Czechoslovakia ended a controversy dating back to 1948 by signing an agreement on the return to Czechoslovakia of 18.4 tons of gold. This gold had been seized from Czechoslovakia by the Germans during the Nazi occupation of that country in World War II and was recovered by the United States at the end of the war. The United States sequestered the gold in 1948 when the Communists took power in Czechoslovakia and seized private property including the holdings of Americans and Czechoslovaks who had fled from Nazi occupation and later became American citizens. Under the terms of the agreement, Czechoslovakia agreed to pay $81.5 million to American claimants and, in exchange, the gold, estimated to be worth $250 million, was returned.

For and Against Quiet Diplomacy

40

From Helsinki to Belgrade, by the Williamsburg Conference.
In *From Helsinki to Belgrade: Issues and Perspectives,*
Williamsburg Conference IV (Washington, D.C.: Center
for Strategic and International Studies, 1977), pp. xi, 5,
9–12, 27–30, 33, 35, 40, 42–43.

The fourth Williamsburg conference entitled "From Helsinki to Belgrade: Issues and Perspectives" (April 22–24, 1977), sponsored by the Georgetown University Center for Strategic and International Studies, was devoted to the complex problems of implementing the Helsinki Final Act's human rights provisions and of assessing their role in the broader context of the East-West relationship. Conference participants represented the United States, Canada, the Federal Republic of Germany, France, Greece, Italy, Belgium, and the United Kingdom.

Congressman Fascell[1] observed that despite the often dramatic rhetoric attached to the Helsinki Accords, "there are not going to be any dramatic changes overnight." The process of improving rights throughout the world, and particularly in the Soviet Union and Eastern Europe, is a very long and slow one. It is to be hoped that the Helsinki Accords and the follow-up conference at Belgrade will be steps in the direction of easing tensions, although it may appear at the moment that such tension is increasing. Mr. Fascell said such apparent ironies are not unique: "In an effort to ease tension we are producing new tensions with this new emphasis on human rights, but that ought not to deter us."

Mr. Claude Marcus[2] observed that the French were cautious on the matter of human rights not because of any lack of commitment or conviction but because they were afraid there might be some damage to the positive effects of détente. "If we interfere too much in Soviet internal affairs, we fear we may lose détente," he said.

Mr. Peter Corterier[3] discussed the German position on these matters, observing that since the Helsinki Agreement some 60,000 persons have emigrated from East Germany, and that the West Germans did not want to do anything to jeopardize the success of the program. He further mentioned that the Helsinki Accords had enabled many East Europeans to stand up against their governments, which he felt was a very positive development.

Professor Bromke[4] insisted that the Western countries should not go about taking strong public postures on behalf of the freedom of the satellite countries without adding a cautionary statement reminding Eastern Europeans of the consequences of such actions. The consequences of similar inflammatory statements of the past were terribly serious, and he hoped that there would be no repetition in the future.

Congresswoman Millicent Fenwick[5] raised the broader question of the moral underpinning of U.S. foreign policy. "Either you believe in human rights or you don't," she said. While it was necessary to express our concerns diplomatically, she said that the United States must make it clear that human rights are the basic rock on which our foreign policy rests. "How can we have relationships with countries or people who do not understand what we care about most strongly?"

Mr. Simes[6] began by quoting Congresswoman Fenwick, "There must be a time when we stand up for what we believe in." But, Mr. Simes said, there is no contradiction between a moral stand and cautious diplomacy. He found the argument unconvincing that since the Soviets are preaching at us, we should preach at them, and he argued that the United States must look at the specific meaning of the human rights movement in the context of the USSR. One then discovered that there were three groups of people who were protesting against Soviet rule: real democrats (Sakharov); nationalists (Solzhenitsyn), who want a moderate authoritarian regime, and extremists of different sorts, including Russian Nazis, whose only disagreement with Hitler was over the incompleteness of the destruction of the European Jews.

Keeping this in mind, Mr. Simes suggested that we remember two other facts. First, that human rights do not mean the same thing in the Soviet Union as they do in the United States. The natural rights of man have never been accepted in Russia as they have in the West; Russia has been an authoritarian state for many centuries. People were always treated as tools of the state. Even today's more spectacular violations of human rights have historical antecedents. In the nineteenth century, for example, political dissidents were declared by the authorities to be mentally ill.

Second, we must look objectively at the nature of Soviet dissidents. Sakharov, Mr. Simes said, is "too good to be true," a moral and intellectual giant. As such, he is probably not capable of rallying mass support, any more than Milyukov—who occupied much the same position in the early twentieth century—had a real chance of winning against Lenin. Furthermore, we must not forget that both Lenin and Hitler came to power in periods of a relative relaxation of controls, when an old regime was being threatened by "dissidents" from within. Consequently, destabilization of the Soviet system in the absence of a democratic alternative had some inherent dangers. This is not to say, of course, that we should not support dissidents, but only that we must be careful before associating with them to know not only what they stand against but also what they stand for. We also should appreciate that from the dissidents' point of view, the United States is not an end, but a tool to support their cause, and Mr. Simes quoted Walter Laqueur, who ruefully observed that what hostages feel ought to be done about terrorists is irrelevant to the real situation, since they are not in the best position to judge. The same sort of thing might be said about the dissidents, who demand unrelenting pressure on the Soviet system. The heroic dissidents are quite prepared to be sacrificed, but the real question is whether the United States is prepared to sacrifice them, and whether it would serve our interests.

Consequently, we must ask the question, "Whom are we addressing in the USSR?" If we indiscriminately support the dissidents, we risk antagonizing and making life more difficult for many reform-minded people in the Soviet Union in much better positions to make a real policy input.

Mr. Simes said he was delighted by Carter's new stress on human rights, but regretted that so much was done all at once: the letter to Sakharov; the telegram to Slepak; Bukovsky's reception at the White House; urging Congress to vote more funds for Radio Free Europe, Radio Liberty, and other statements which the Soviets perceived as threatening. If the Soviets believe that we will only be satisfied with a fundamental change in the Soviet system, there will be trouble, he said. The Jackson Amendment has shown that we can achieve modest changes. "Without pressure for human rights, détente would be immoral; without détente, pressure will not work. We must constantly preserve a delicate balance between the two," he stated.

Professor Laqueur[7] regretted the limitation of the debate to human rights in the USSR and to a few thousand dissidents. He said he thought it would be better to address the question of freedom in the Soviet Union, which was quite a different subject.

There were, Professor Laqueur said, three reasons why human rights should be important in United States foreign policy:

1. It is a matter of principle. No one, however, is so naive as to claim that it should be the only principle. As Max Weber once observed, the ethics of politics are not those of the Sermon on the Mount. As soon as you indulge in politics, Weber used to say, you give a finger or hand to the Devil. But Weber did not say that the ethics of politics should be the ethics of the jungle.

Professor Laqueur observed that small countries often have a much better record on human rights than larger ones. This is particularly true in Europe, where Austria and Holland have far better records than France and England.

2. Realpolitik. Brezhnev and company have always said that, détente or no détente, the ideological struggle will continue. The Soviets, of course, have always interpreted the struggle as a one-way street, but this should not be so. While we may be isolated in the United Nations, we are not by ourselves in the world. Hundreds of millions of people support us and our ideology, particularly those who have experienced the alternatives at first hand. Moreover, he observed, Soviet ideology has lost most of its appeal. If Communist parties are prospering throughout the world, that is certainly not because of the attraction of the Soviet model or Soviet rhetoric.

3. Détente. Professor Laqueur stressed that he was speaking of something above and beyond mere rhetoric and that real détente could only be lasting and meaningful with a minimum of mutual trust. This cannot exist, he said, without some minimal democratization of Soviet society. This is not simply an abstract matter, he noted, and indeed the problem of arms control has to be viewed in this context. "It is genererally accepted that meaningful future agreements on both strategic and conventional arms have to be based on effective means of inspection. But such means do not exist, and they do not exist precisely because of the absence of democratic checks and balances in the Soviet Union and the unwillingness of the Soviet leaders to open up their country to foreign inspection and free travel in general. Thus, the prospects for genuine progress in arms control are virtually nil unless and until the Soviet system becomes more open. The movement toward the protection of human rights is an essential part of this process."

What are the arguments against actively (not stridently) pursuing freedom in the Soviet Union, and indeed in the rest of the world? Some people say that you simply cannot do it, and that any full-scale attempt to pursue freedom will only threaten peace. Professor Laqueur responded that there is no evidence that pursuit of this policy threatens peace in and of itself, and furthermore it may well be that we are moving toward increased tension in any event. Secondly, some people say that we should advocate human rights, but we should not do it provocatively. The problem here, he observed, is that the issue is itself a provocative one to nations who deny human rights to their citizens. Finally, there are those who say we should speak out on the issue from time to time, but we should not link it to other questions. However, Professor Laqueur quoted El Cid: Lengua sin manos, cuemo osas hablar? (Tongue without hands, how do you dare to talk?) It is perfectly obvious, he said, that unless the human rights records of the most powerful countries are taken into account in United States foreign policy, fine sentiments will not have the slightest impact. They will be rightly considered by friend and foe alike as a public relations exercise aimed at American domestic consumption.

Having said this, there is no guarantee such a course of conduct will work. On the other hand, the Soviet Union faces several crises at the present time: it has problems of nationalism, problems with its satellites, and a major confrontation over succession. We do not know how it will all work out. However, Professor Laqueur stressed that this policy is the only one that holds out any prospect at all for the future.

Mr. Alan Lee Williams[8] began by referring to a remark by Mr. David Owen, the British Foreign Minister, that "any approach to the USSR must be sufficiently balanced so as not to jeopardize détente." However, said Mr. Williams, there was no need to be defensive or apprehensive about it. The Soviet Union desperately needs Western technology, and there is no need for us to be timid about our values, since the Soviet Union will undoubtedly launch a massive diplomatic offensive against the West as the Belgrade Conference approaches.

Professor Pipes[9] started by referring to news stories that dealt with Soviet government protests against the showing of "Dr. Zhivago" in the American Embassy in Moscow. It appears that some Soviet citizens were invited to the showing, and the Soviets objected quite violently. The *New York Times* quoted an American diplomat, who asked, "Is it not ridiculous that a great power like the Soviet Union should feel so threatened by a motion picture?" Professor Pipes said, "I believe that the USSR is right and the diplomat is wrong." The Soviet Union is a great power by dint of its coercive strength and its military arsenal; otherwise, it is a second- or third-rate power. Consequently, Soviet experts are right to be afraid of things like movies and books, because these do indeed threaten its vitals. Professor Pipes said that the issue of human rights probably disturbs the Soviet Union far more than American ICBMS or SLBMS or bombers. Why is that?

Human rights are more important to us than questions like the Vietnam War, because Vietnam was only a sideshow in the overall strategic picture while human rights is a fundamental issue. "I would be terribly upset if human rights were used solely as a public relations device."

Professor Pipes said that human rights is a terribly serious issue, and if we undertake to make this issue a central one for American foreign policy, we must be prepared to see it through to the end. We must be prepared to embark upon a campaign that may last as long as 20 to 30 years. We must not under any circumstances pull our horns in when the USSR arrests some people. We must be prepared to pursue this policy steadily and steadfastly.

The corollary to this is that if we are not serious, it is best to do nothing. If we initiate this policy without being prepared to see it through, we will expose many to jail and even to death and we will damage ourselves. If we sign solemn documents and then do not observe them, we corrupt ourselves as a people. Moreover, quite apart from questions of strategy, if we do nothing about gross Soviet violations of human rights, we are in danger of becoming like them, regarding such questions cynically and instrumentally.

Mr. Zablocki[10] said that we should not go to Belgrade in order to rewrite Helsinki, and that we must keep the limits of what can be done clearly before us. He viewed Belgrade with considerable optimism, calling it "a chance to review Helsinki, to achieve greater cooperation in the implementation and monitoring of the final act, and a chance to discuss positive as well as negative aspects." Mr. Zablocki said that whatever was done at Belgrade had to be based on a firm consensus among Western nations, and urged that we try to uncover elements of progress in Eastern Europe as well as negative themes. He observed, for example, that the Yugoslavs were very proud that they were not criticized as much as other Eastern European parties by the Fascell committee.

Mr. Corterier said that, in preparation for Belgrade, the political Committee of the Nine had already agreed on the basic ground rules, which appear to be compatible with the goals as stated by the American speakers present at Williamsburg. He reiterated his conviction that confrontation with the Soviet Union would be useless, and indeed counterproductive; there is even some slight chance that it might drive the Soviet Union out of such conferences.

Mr. Oliver[11] said that he was worried about what appeared to be Western European concern over the U.S. emphasis on human rights. He wondered if there were not some danger that the United States might be taking an overly aggressive posture on this question, so that it risked being isolated from its allies in Belgrade. If this occurred, he said, Belgrade would turn into a superpower confrontation. He recalled that it was the Europeans, after all, who had pushed hardest for Basket Three, and therefore that a common front was terribly urgent at Belgrade.

Mr. Deshormes[12] replied to Mr. Oliver by saying that he felt there was adequate coordination between the Western powers at the parliamentary level, even though more could be done in the area of public opinion. He did not think there was any danger of the United States being isolated at Belgrade.

NOTES

1 Dante Fascell, U.S. Representative from Florida, chairman of the Commission on Security and Cooperation in Europe.
2 Claude Gérard Marcus, Member of the National Assembly, Paris.
3 Peter Corterier, Member of the Bundestag, Bonn.
4 Adam Bromke, Professor of Political Science, McMaster University, Hamilton, Ontario.
5 Millicent Fenwick, U.S. Representative from New Jersey.
6 Dimitri Simes, Director of Soviet Policy Studies, Center for Strategic and International Studies, Georgetown University.
7 Walter Laqueur, chairman, International Research Council, Center for Strategic and International Studies, Georgetown University.
8 Alan Lee Williams, Member of Parliament, London.
9 Richard Pipes, Professor of History, Harvard University.
10 Clement Zablocki, U.S. Representative from Wisconsin.
11 Spencer Oliver, staff director and general counsel, Commission on Security and Cooperation in Europe, U.S. Congress.
12 Phillipe Deshormes, Secretary General, North Atlantic Assembly, Brussels.

41

The Advisability of a Confrontationist Approach,
by Zbigniew Brzezinski.
In Zbigniew Brzezinski, *Power and Principle* (New York:
Farrar, Straus & Giroux, 1985), p. 297.

On April 22, I directed that interagency papers be prepared on Eastern Europe issues, clearly setting out the alternatives for U.S. policy. The response was received in midsummer, and on August 23 the Policy Review Committee met to consider the study. This meeting also dealt with the related Conference on Security and Cooperation in Europe. I urged that we think through all the options in CSCE and played a bit of a devil's advocate role, as my journal notes indicate. "I pushed hard and I believe effectively for a more assertive U.S. posture in CSCE. In fact, I stunned everyone there by suggesting that we have a paper prepared which deliberately examines the advisability of a confrontationist approach. The State Department types were horrified even by the thought. I suggested to them that we may not accept it, but the idea is we should consider it. My inner hope is that by considering such an approach we will help to stiffen their backs even if we end up adopting a policy which is more designed to achieve compromise. In any case, I pushed hard that the United States take the lead and be perceived as . . . pushing CSCE toward higher standards."

42

Semiprivate, Bilateral Diplomacy, by James F. Brown.
Statement by Director of Radio Free Europe, Washington,
May 9, 1977, *Basket III: Implementation of the Helsinki
Accords*, vol. II, Hearings before the Commission on
Security and Cooperation in Europe, Ninety-Fifth Congress,
May 9, 1977 (Washington, D.C.: U.S. Government Printing
Office, 1977), pp. 291–92.

I think that the problem with something like Belgrade is that it can degenerate into a circus or a gladiatorial contest, with a great number of charges and countercharges being made for show, with the result that relations between states might—because of Helsinki and even more so because of Belgrade—become worse rather than better. That was not the aim of the European Security Conference at all.

What I would think would be more effective is a private, or semi-private kind of diplomacy, bringing up these cases not on a comprehensive basis—a multilateral basis—but more on a bilateral basis or involving three or four states having a specific conference on one aspect of Helsinki—on emigration, for example, or on the exchange of scholars, exchange of students, family reunions.

The states which feel themselves aggrieved should try to get together with the states that they feel themselves aggrieved by.

43

We Will Strive for Maximum Practical Impact, by Cyrus R. Vance.
Statement by the Secretary of State and questioning,
Washington, June 6, 1977, *Basket III: Implementation of
the Helsinki Accords*, vol. IV, Hearings before the Commission
on Security and Cooperation in Europe, Ninety-Fifth
Congress, June 6, 1977 (Washington, D.C.: U.S.
Government Printing Office, 1977), pp. 86–87, 90–91, 93,
96–97, 101–2.

Mr. Vance: We seek full implementation of all the commitments contained in the Helsinki Final Act. None can be called more binding, more vital, than the others. All three of the so-called baskets are important.

We seek incremental improvements in relations between East and West on all the fronts surveyed at Helsinki: political, economic, scientific, cultural, security, and humanitarian.

We seek to move forward on all these fronts simultaneously; the freer flow of people and ideas is as important to long-term security and cooperation as, for example, advance notice of major military maneuvers; the humanitarian pledges at Helsinki are as important as, say, the promise of greater commercial cooperation.

There will be consideration of new proposals. But we must not be diverted from assessment of how fully the specific undertakings of Helsinki have been carried out by all the signatories.

At Belgrade, we will assess on the spot how best to be effective and persuasive in pursuing our objectives. Between public diplomacy and quiet diplomacy, we will strive for maximum practical impact.

We will avoid grandiose new proposals that have little chance of being acceptable. Propaganda ploys, debating points, have no place in our strategy.

We will state our goals and our assessments clearly, without polemics.

When I outlined the administration's human rights policy at the University of Georgia in April, I said that "a decision whether and how to act in the cause of human rights is a matter for informed and careful judgment. No mechanistic formula produces an automatic answer."

Our basic objective is to forward two fundamental principles: one is improving the relationship between states and the other is improving the lot of the individual citizen in each of these countries. So all of our work is directed toward achieving those basic purposes.

The question then arises of how you best do that. We think that you best do it by concentrating, as we believe is intended by the document itself, on the review of implementation. We think it is also possible, however, to discuss some new proposals in connection with that review if they be of a limited number and if they really do build upon the structure of the Helsinki Accords.

Mr. Case:[1] There is confrontation here. The ultimate confrontation is between the system of the East and the system of the West. Unless we really treat this as involving that, I do not think we are doing what at least I believe the Congress considers ought to be done.

To have this brought out in Belgrade would make the accords worthwhile. And I think not to do it would be to just go through an exercise and waste an awful lot of good people's time.

I have not talked in a precise way. I have said some things loosely, but I have stated my concern at having this thing run by a bunch of professional diplomats which is what you fellows are supposed to be. Some of you are only part time.

And I like both kinds and we need both kinds, but you are still in that spot and I do not know whether you can break free from it. Frankly I have not yet seen the kind of spirit to have the knock-down, drag-out, real confrontation that I think is called for at this stage.

We have a deep disagreement about this, and maybe that is the reason the Commission does exist and is going to be represented in Belgrade. It is not a matter of anything personal at all. It is just a matter of recognizing that there is a difference between the kind of a job that you have to do and that we have to do.

Mr. Vance: Let me assure you that we will make a real effort to carry forward on what we and you have said about our obligations in this conference. Our commitment to human rights and to reviewing the implementation of the Helsinki Accords on human rights is deep and abiding and I think it is just as deep and abiding as that of the Congress.

Now I do, however, repeat again the caution that I do not think it ought to be done in a polemical fashion and if by "knock-down, drag-out," you mean it is going to be polemical, then we do have a disagreement.

Mr. Pell:[2] Now, on the general question of the emphasis on human rights, do you feel that this is having an adverse effect on our fundamental relations with the Soviet Union in détente? My own view is that it is not, but there are two tracks here, and one is human rights and the other is the fundamental question of arms control and basic relations between the nations.

Mr. Vance: I share your views, Senator Pell. I think that there are two tracks on this and I think that the basic interest which the Soviet Union has in the problem of arms control, particularly in the strategic area, stands on its own two feet. And that, therefore, there is not the linkage that has sometimes been suggested.

Mr. Pell: Along that same line, are you concerned that our emphasis on human rights is going to cause any split with our Western allies? I did notice that while they all would come up to you in private and say fine, they did not want to particularly identify themselves as vigorously as ourselves publicly.

Mr. Vance: I think we are going to find different public responses by different countries. I think you are quite right that all of them do say in private conversations that they are very much with us on this—some of them say that for special reasons they do not feel at this point that they can be quite as outspoken as they would like to be under the circumstances. Let me say that in our preparation for Belgrade, we have coordinated very closely with our allies and will continue to do so as we move toward the fall when the substantive discussions will get underway.

NOTES

1   Clifford P. Case, U.S. Senator from New Jersey.
2   Claiborne Pell, U.S. Senator from Rhode Island.

The Manner of Disagreement

44

Design to Avoid Confrontation, by Michael B. Wall.
Report by RFE correspondent, Belgrade, June 16, 1977.

The Western countries have wasted little time in Belgrade in taking an approach carefully designed to avoid an early confrontation over human rights while at the same time securing a thorough review of that controversial issue later.

The Western approach, a combination of softness in tone with firmness in substance, also includes some changes from the attitudes taken during the original European Security Conference talks in Helsinki and Geneva.

Yesterday's opening session of this Belgrade meeting—intended to arrange the details for a review later this year of the final document signed in Helsinki—was largely ceremonial and organizational. But the British delegation quickly circulated a proposal on behalf of the Western countries and then held a press conference to outline it to the world—although the British did not speak about it in the conference hall until today.

The most interesting element in the Western approach is, of course, the role being taken by the United States. It was the enthusiastic campaign for human rights mounted by the new American President, Jimmy Carter, that led some to expect an angry clash between East and West over the issue in Belgrade.

Once in Belgrade, the United States has been playing it very low key. The American delegates have been saying consistently since they arrived that they are here only to arrange the purely technical details of the meeting later this year that will actually discuss substantive matters.

The United States also let the West Europeans take the lead on the Western proposal introduced by Britain on behalf of the Common Market and other Western countries. The intention is to avoid giving the impression that Carter is riding into battle waving a human rights spear.

The Americans refused to comment on the Western proposal yesterday—keeping it a British proposal and then waiting until a press conference and a speech at the meeting this morning by Albert Sherer, head of the U.S. delegation. And on both occasions, Sherer even said that the United States did not consider the Western proposal ideal and would have preferred a different one. He gave as an example the issue of the length of the main meeting later this year—the main procedural dispute that has arisen between East and West so far.

Asked what other faults the Americans found with the Western proposal, Sherer admitted that they were really only minor details. In essence, the Western proposal is right in line with American thinking.

Another example of the American influence is the fact that the Western proposal calls for far more public sessions than were held at the original European Security Conference. American diplomats in Belgrade have said that it was a mistake to conduct so much of the original negotiations in private. The previous Ford Administration was sharply criticized by conservatives at home for secretly negotiating concessions to the Soviet Union at Helsinki and Geneva, and Carter wants to avoid this.

The entire American role has changed. The Nixon and Ford Administrations took little interest in the Helsinki and Geneva negotiations for a long time, but this time the Americans are very clearly actively involved.

The current show of Western unity in Belgrade follows recent differences in emphasis between the Americans and West Europeans—with Carter strong on human rights and the West Germans, for example, worried about endangering détente. Now all Western governments are taking the same low-key approach.

45

Overreaction to Goldberg, by Michael B. Wall.
Report by RFE correspondent, Belgrade, November 2, 1977.

The temperature rose somewhat at the meeting in Belgrade in the first half of this week when Western delegates criticized human rights violations in Eastern Europe.

It was an event that the Soviet Union tried to avoid through various tactics, including a warning by Chief Delegate Iulii Vorontsov Monday evening that this sort of thing could lead to a break-up of the Belgrade meeting.

In addition, Soviet delegates were reportedly telling Europeans behind the scenes that the United States was endangering the Belgrade meeting by emphasizing human rights.

As it turned out, however, it was the French who first fired a broadside on human rights Monday afternoon, with the Americans holding their fire because they were presiding over the session.

François Beauchataud read a long list of human rights violations: trials of historians and artists for their views, imprisonment and other harassment of writers, intellectuals, national minorities, and religious groups such as Baptists and those who tried to emigrate such as Jews. And then in case there was anyone who had not gotten the point, Beauchataud said many of these things applied to the Soviet Union and Czechoslovakia.

Chief Canadian Delegate W. T. Delworth then said three countries harassed, exiled, arrested, tried and imprisoned citizens who wanted to open a dialogue with their governments. He concentrated on Czechoslovakia by name, especially on a law barring citizens who had corresponded with emigrants from leaving the country but his tone was quite sharp throughout.

The Americans say Chief Delegate Arthur Goldberg did not soften his prepared speech yesterday. Instead he added statements about conditions in the United States and arguments that raising human rights violations did not amount to intervention.

Goldberg has a habit of scrawling over his prepared text as he waits to speak, writing upside down and sideways in the margins and between lines—and then going ahead with further unwritten additions when he actually does speak. As a result, the United States delegation eventually gave up trying to produce a full text of Goldberg's remarks as delivered.

When Goldberg did finally speak yesterday, he accused the Soviet Union and Czechoslovakia of bringing charges against people who were merely trying to promote the Helsinki Agreement. He mentioned Czechoslovakia's Charter 77 Manifesto as well as the psychiatric treatment of persons held for their political views (without naming the Soviet Union). And he announced that the United States and other countries would submit a proposal that people monitoring the Helsinki Agreements be protected by their governments even when they criticized their governments.

But he also emphasized American shortcomings and invited other delegations to criticize the United States. And he also adopted a tactic he has used before in Belgrade, backing into the human rights violations in a legalistic speech. A main thrust of his argument was that the United States and other delegations had the right and duty to raise such things as—and then he would mention a violation or case.

As a result of the legalistic and defensive approach and his digressions, both Western and neutral delegates came out of the chamber last night remarking how moderate Goldberg's speech had been.

Vorontsov did not seem to think so, however. He linked it to the language of the Cold War.

Vorontsov also suggested that Goldberg did not understand what the Belgrade meeting was all about, and he patronizingly advised veterans of the Geneva and Helsinki negotiations to explain it to Goldberg. Vorontsov's argument that the United States stood alone on the issue of raising human rights violations came, however, after it had actually been the French and Canadians who had first done so. In fact, in view of expectations that the Dutch might make a strong statement of their own later, one European delegate smilingly commented that he hoped the Common Market would not get too far ahead of the United States on the issue.

Vorontsov's claim that the majority of delegations supported the Soviet position also seemed belied by the overall Warsaw Pact plight in Belgrade.

It had been unable to avoid the human rights debate early this week precisely because neutral countries like Sweden had stood with the West in urging that the situation be aired now.

Some of the arguments in Vorontsov's reply seemed drawn up well in advance, although both the Goldberg speech and the situation had turned out somewhat differently. But, while some European delegates felt Vorontsov had overreacted to the Goldberg speech, response was milder than Monday's and he did not repeat the threat to break up the meeting.

46

Barter Discussed, by Michael B. Wall.
Report by RFE correspondent, Belgrade, November 3, 1977.

Basket Two seems to be taking the main thrust of the Warsaw Pact offensive at the Belgrade meeting, and some Western delegates suspect that the East Europeans may have a kind of barter in mind there. According to this theory, the Warsaw Pact is pushing its Basket Two proposals on economic and technological cooperation as a reply to the Western interest in Basket One, human rights, and Basket Three, human contacts and information.

The Warsaw Pact seems to be saying that the West will have to accept its Basket Two ideas if the East is to yield on Baskets One and Three. But by making Basket Two proposals unacceptable to the West, the Warsaw Pact seems to be preparing an excuse for rejecting Western initiatives on human rights, human contacts, and information.

The link between these areas became obvious in other ways this week. Some Western delegates thought part of the East European anger on Basket Two might not have just been aimed at the Western arguments in that committee. They thought it might also have been intended as a reflection of Warsaw Pact anger at the Western attacks over human rights in Basket One.

47

Drumbeat on Human Rights, by Michael B. Wall.
Report by RFE correspondent, Belgrade, November 4, 1977.

Western delegates are satisfied that they have been able to raise the East European violations. And by doing so gradually, they have managed to widen the framework for the discussion. Comments that might have raised eyebrows a month ago are common now, and even more might become acceptable later on.

Western delegates realize that the Soviet Union is not going to accept today's proposal on universal respect for groups and people trying to monitor compliance with the Helsinki agreement. The proposal is a gesture of Western support for those activists at a time when there are hints that the Soviet Union might try some on severe charges.

The West considered the recent Prague trial a provocation. And, although diplomats from other East European delegations apologized privately, some Western delegates believe that the Czechoslovak authorities did not do this on their own. It was considered a test of Western reaction to what might happen if Moscow did the same.

American officials have indicated that they would consider any such Moscow trial very serious indeed, especially in view of personal assurances by President Jimmy Carter that Anatolii Shcharanskii was not working for the Central Intelligence Agency.

The cases of Shcharanskii and the other monitors have been raised—along with such humanitarian cases as family reunifications—in private bilateral meetings held by Goldberg and other Western delegation heads with Vorontsov and East Europeans. The Communist delegates only promise to relay the reunification lists they are given to their capitals, and Goldberg and the Western diplomats are waiting to see what happens. Such lists have been handed over before by the State Department in Washington and the American Embassy in Moscow, for example, and sometimes many of the people mentioned eventually have found their way to the West.

Although this channel is outside the debating chamber, the Western diplomats think the speeches themselves play a role—even if the concluding document turns out to be a bland mélange. They think that the constant hammering away at human rights violations must, with time, have an effect on Eastern Europe. They point out that no country or even a self-contained group like the Warsaw Pact likes to be constantly isolated and criticized in such a way. They know Eastern Europe is not going to change overnight, but they feel that the Western drumbeat on human rights will lead to some improvement.

As Goldberg said in an interview with our correspondent, the minimum goal is to ease the lot of those engaged in peaceful dissent. It may not be revolutionary, but if they accomplish it, the Western diplomats will feel that their time in Belgrade was well spent indeed.

48

Soft and Hard Europeans, by Ian MacDonald.
Report by RFE correspondent, Munich, December 1, 1977.

Soviet activists, among them Professor Andrei Sakharov, criticized some West European states for being too soft at Belgrade. While the group said the U.S., Holland, Denmark, Norway, Sweden and Belgium had taken what was termed a sufficiently consistent stand, it accused Britain, France, and West Germany of staying "quiet."

Belgrade delegates were a little mystified by this assessment, which they feel must have been based on inadequate information. The fact is that these countries have been far from quiet but, unlike speeches made by the Americans, those of other Western and neutral delegations have largely gone unreported, except in the early stages of the conference, when a large corps of newsmen was able to provide blanket coverage. The very large American delegation has been throughout the most active one in the information field and has consistently provided the news media with details of contributions made in plenary and committee sessions by U.S. members. The others have not.

One American diplomat, speaking to our correspondent by telephone, expressed the view that the criticism was unfair and that the three major West European states had all made important contributions on the human rights issue.

A member of one of the delegations under fire described the lists of "hard" and "soft" countries as "nonsense" and said that the allegedly weak delegations had often taken a tougher line on human rights than those praised by the Moscow group.

He agreed that, in the initial phase of the Belgrade meeting, there had been "certain differences of approach" between the U.S. and West European states in reviewing implementation of the Helsinki recommendations but said that the West as a whole has long been united in its attitude.

The nine EEC delegations meet every day to coordinate their line and their experts from the various committees also hold regular get-togethers to work out their cooperation in greater detail. The nine in turn coordinate their approach with that of the U.S. and the remaining NATO members.

49

Breakdown at Belgrade, by Carroll Sherer.
Washington Quarterly, Autumn 1978, pp. 80–85.

At the summer Preparatory Meeting, most of the participating states were represented by modest delegations headed by professional diplomats who, like Albert Sherer of the United States, had been the architects in Geneva of the Final Act. They knew each other, and they all understood the unique procedures which had led to its final success. With the surprise appointment of Justice Arthur Goldberg as head of the U.S. delegation just a few weeks before the Main Meeting commenced, a superaggressive new approach with the highest possible profile was suddenly adopted. In accord with the administration's new stance were presumably the "hawks" among the congressional commission who sincerely believed that Belgrade would be the appropriate place to start settling the basic ideological differences between participating states.

When the U.S. delegation finally lined up, not only was the congressional commission playing a much more active role, but there was a mind-boggling array of public members appointed by the White House, the secretary of state, and by Justice Goldberg himself. The American presence was overwhelming and ubiquitous. Over 140 people were authorized to wear official badges (while the British and French managed with a dozen each, and the Canadians had but five). They included representatives of the American labor movement, B'nai Brith, a Roman Catholic monsignor, an Eskimo, a black woman lawyer, a Polish-American political science professor, a college president, some businessmen, several professional civil rights champions, and Madames Goldberg and Sherer, just to mention a few.

Criticism of Justice Goldberg personally was not limited to the Eastern media, but those who have chosen to blame the general mess and the ultimate failure of the conference to produce a meaningful document solely on the chief U.S. delegate are taking a simplistic view. Granted, his personality is unsuited to diplomatic negotiation, especially one as tender as CSCE—but "Goldberg" was not the name of the disease; it was only a symptom. The ambassador, as he constantly reminded members not only of his own delegation but also of others', was responding to direct orders from the White House. Several times he claimed to have been telephoned by the president himself. Whether this was fact or fancy is of little importance. What *is* important is that the ambassador was acting out in his fashion what he perceived to be the chief executive's wishes. Furthermore, perhaps because of Justice Goldberg's close connection with the White House, no attempt was ever made by the Department of State to deter or temper his tactics or those of any of the other members of the giant, undisciplined delegation. The veteran diplomats among them, knowing that all too often goals matter less than the right strategy, did what they could to help the delegation function without embarrassment, but they were so outnumbered that their voices were mostly lost in the storm. However, it should be recognized that, lacking their presence, the damage to Uncle Sam's image would have been even more devastating than it was. Ambassador Goldberg himself became conscious of some need for modification of his tone, and to his great credit he made a determined effort, but the damage had been done.

Hints of the extent of disregard for accepted practices at CSCE by the American delegation came very early. Although in the Preparatory Meeting it had been agreed that, as in Geneva, the meetings would not be public, the Americans called frequent press conferences where they gave their version of what had transpired at the meetings and handed out copies of their speeches. Some public members even gave press conferences on their own. Soon, other delegations, partly in self-defense, began to follow this practice. The Eastern bloc felt betrayed, but there was little they could do to control the situation. The Soviets became progressively more sullen as speeches about "implementation" continued to be delivered while new proposals (ultimately over 100) piled up. Ambassador Marian Dobrosielski, head of the Polish delegation, in an attempt to clear the air, gave an impassioned speech in which he beseeched the delegates to acknowledge that they had deep ideological differences which would not go away being emphasized. He recommended: "Let us not concentrate on the things that divide us, but rather start to search for the many things which we as Europeans have in common. That is where we should begin."

Western delegations were becoming equally restless, wondering whether the seemingly endless parade of Americans intent on giving speeches would ever stop and when the time would come for what they considered to be the substantive work.

50

A Series of Caucuses and Conflicts, by David A. Andelman.
"Accord in Belgrade," *New York Times*, March 20, 1978.

The Soviet Union and many of its allies went into the conference determined to limit the damage caused by what they had come to see as an unequal tradeoff in Helsinki: sweeping guarantees of human rights and a freer exchange of information and people between East and West in return for de facto recognition of Europe's postwar boundaries and Soviet hegemony over East Europe. The West, particularly the United States, wanted a thorough airing of what it saw as flagrant violations of the Helsinki guarantees on human rights. The 13 neutral nations were eager for a strengthening of Helsinki's military and political safeguards, known in the code language of the conference as "confidence-building measures."

But many diplomats from all sides believe that the mechanics of how the two principal groupings—the 15-member North Atlantic Treaty Organization and the 7-member Warsaw Pact—functioned has more of an impact on the conference's rather feeble outcome than any of the broader controversies. "We went into Belgrade determined to preserve allied unity," a member of the United States delegation said bitterly last week. "But it soon became merely a mechanism to restrain the

United States leadership position. We were simply left out of the decision-making process."

"It was made clear to all of us in what direction the Warsaw Pact
grouping would be going at Belgrade," said a diplomat from a member
of the Soviet-led alliance. "But divisions did not begin to appear until
well after the start of the meeting in October—until things really began
to deteriorate."

The positions of East and West were developed far in advance. In
November 1976, East-bloc leaders met in Bucharest, Rumania. Six
months later, the foreign ministers convened in Moscow where, according to one diplomat, "mention was made of the campaign of human
rights we would likely encounter in Belgrade." Similar talks were under
way in the Western alliance and its subgroup, the nine-nation European
Economic Community. When both sides arrived in Belgrade, the lines
were already well drawn. Each morning at 9, the Common Market
members caucused to discuss the program of the day, then joined their
six Western colleagues for a full-scale planning session.

"Our problem was a complex one," said an American delegate. "We
came with the major decisions already taken [by the Common Market
group]. It took us three weeks at the outset for us to raise human rights—
until we got agreement from the whole NATO caucus to discuss this question. We never made a move without consensus from all members of
NATO. But this has left its marks."

At the same time difficulties were developing within the Soviet-led
group. Only three countries absorbed the brunt of Western criticism of
human rights, the Soviet Union, Czechoslovakia and East Germany.
For the others, a hard-line position seemed inappropriate, not only because of its negative effect on East-West relations in Belgrade but for
the impact it might have in other forums as well. President Carter's
visit to Poland, for instance, took place at the height of the conference.
So did Hungary's delicate negotiations with the United States on the
return of the Crown of St. Stephen and most-favored-nation trading
status.

Keeping the diverse and often divergent regimes of East Europe in
line became increasingly difficult for Moscow. Rumania frequently
skipped bloc caucuses. Hungary and Poland often pressed moderation
on the Soviet Ambassador, Yuli M. Vorontsov. "It's these caucuses, as
well as the more open debates, that are enabling some of these countries to assert their independence and their own voice," said a diplomat
from a "neutral" nation. "And most of them tell me they hope this will
spill over well after everyone's left Belgrade and Helsinki is only a
memory."

The Disappointing Finale

51

Two Concepts of the Final Document, by Ian MacDonald.
Report by RFE correspondent, Munich, January 18, 1978.

Soviet delegation chief Iulii Vorontsov outlined the kind of final document his government wants to see adopted while his American opposite number, Arthur Goldberg, listed the things the U.S. feels should
be included. The views Goldberg expressed are broadly shared by all the
Western states represented at Belgrade.

The Soviet draft turned out, as everyone had expected, to be short,
generalized and non-committal. It said nothing about the differences
about human rights which have been the chief hallmark of the discussions in Belgrade and it ignored all the Western and neutral proposals
designed to produce real if limited progress in this area. Indeed, the
draft disposed of the entire complex in a single sentence: "The participating states stated their readiness to expand cooperation in humanitarian fields, as provided for in the Final Act."

Reaction to the Vorontsov draft was immediate and negative—not
only on the part of the Western states but also by the neutral and non-
aligned delegations. The official Yugoslav news agency Tanjug, custom-
arily cautious in reporting the conference, noted today: "The way the
Soviet delegation prepared the proposal for the final document met
with objections and criticisms at the session yesterday. The proposal is
most often criticized for being very short and having included none of
the proposals submitted by other countries."

Both the West and the neutrals are insisting on a comprehensive and
substantive document which will record frankly the negative as well as
the positive aspects of Helsinki implementation and will contain concrete commitments to further humanitarian progress.

As usual the dissenting voice in the otherwise harmonious chorus of
the Warsaw Pact states is that of Romania. The Romanian delegation
chief, Valentin Lipatti, told yesterday's session the concluding document should be "a political document of substance which should contain specific solutions, decisions and recommendations meant to give a
strong impetus to the efforts for concretely solving the fundamental
questions of security in Europe and for translating into life the provisions of the Helsinki Final Act." Such a document would be a far cry
from the vague and anemic text tabled by Vorontsov.

On one thing at least both sides are now agreed. Belgrade will be succeeded in 1980 by another follow-up meeting in Madrid. At least the formal continuation of the Helsinki process is guaranteed.

52

Neutral Bid Fails, by Ian MacDonald.
Report by RFE correspondent, Belgrade, February 27, 1978.

What may be the last bid to avert a public admission that the Belgrade Conference has failed today ended itself in failure.

It took the form of an informal draft for the concluding document which was privately circulated to the 35 delegations late last week. The draft emanated from the nine neutral and non-aligned countries but was not publicly sponsored by them.

"It was not a commonly accepted paper by the neutral and non-aligned group," said one neutral diplomat today. "It was put together in a hurry in order to get some kind of negotiating basis because it became clear last week that we could no longer hope for a long, substantive document."

And another neutral delegate explained: "None of us identifies himself with this paper. Our views on how the concluding document should look had been laid down earlier. This non-paper, as we have come to call it, was produced as a last attempt to have a document which would merit that name and would not simply be a communiqué."

A representative of an EEC country commented scathingly: "No one wants to admit to the fatherhood."

The child, it turned out, was in any case stillborn. Intensive weekend consultation between the neutral on one side and Eastern and Western delegations on the other showed that there was no prospect of its being accepted in the consensus demanded by the rules.

The four-page draft was flatly rejected by the West because it made no mention of human rights and contained no new measures for the improvement of human contacts.

In spite of a jovial remark by the Soviet Union's Iulii Vorontsov last Friday that the non-paper looked 95 percent acceptable, it transpired that the East wanted changes which would have emasculated the draft still further.

53

A Small Harvest, by Ian MacDonald.
Report by RFE correspondent, Belgrade, March 2, 1978.

If there is one thing on which unofficial consensus reigns in Belgrade, it is the unanimous desire of the delegates to the Helsinki follow-up conference to pack their bags and go home.

Today—after five months of vociferous argument—fulfillment of that desire seemed just around the corner.

The reason is the remarkably speedy progress made by the unofficial group of eight nations which took it upon themselves yesterday to try and work out a concluding document acceptable to all.

The three-page text they produced this morning is only a basis for negotiation and many delegations, including some of the eight themselves, will do their best to amend or add to it.

Nevertheless, the general view is that the conference now has in its hands what will, with minor changes here and there, go down in the records as the official scorecard of the Belgrade Meeting.

In the view of one football-minded diplomat, it states more or less that the match ended in a goalless draw.

Certainly the three pages contain nothing of the substance for which the Western and neutral participants fought so stubbornly against a Soviet defense resolved to give nothing away.

The paper is, in content and language, a close relative of the draft put forward by Denmark two days ago on behalf of 16 Western states.

That is to say, it is a minimal text which makes no attempt to conceal the fact that an unbridgeable gulf separates Eastern and Western assessments of how the Helsinki provisions have been implemented. "Different views were expressed as to the degree of implementation of the Final Act reached so far," it states.

Nor does the paper hide the failure of the conference to accept any of the 100-odd proposals made for improving détente. It says: "Consensus was not reached on a number of proposals submitted to the meeting."

There is no mention of human rights. The responsibility for this momentous omission is placed by the Western and neutral delegates squarely on the Soviet doorstep. Humanitarian questions—in the public eye, at least, the most important aspect of the conference—have had to be left out because the Soviet Union and its closest allies refused to have them included.

The paper does, nevertheless, reaffirm the validity of the entire Helsinki Final Act. It declares: "The representatives of the participating states reaffirmed the resolve of their governments to implement fully, unilaterally, bilaterally and multilaterally, all the provisions of the Final Act."

These provisions include the commitment to observe human rights and fundamental freedoms as well as commitments to carry out a series of measures in the field of human contacts and exchange of information.

That, Western delegates emphasize, means that, although this paper adds nothing to Helsinki, it also subtracts nothing from the obligations undertaken in the Finnish capital in 1975.

The fact that both East and West are now prepared to settle for a mini-document has led to a feeling of resignation among the neutrals, who have held out to the last for the retention of at least some substance.

They have not yet abandoned the fight to expand the follow-up provisions. And in this sector the new paper shows two changes from the original Danish proposal.

First, it sets a later date for the next Belgrade-style conference in Madrid. It is now proposed that a preparatory meeting should open in the Spanish capital on September 9, 1980 with the main conference to start on November 11, 1980.

Second, the paper calls for an expert group meeting on the Mediterranean to be held in Malta—a concession made by both East and West in face of a Maltese threat to withhold consensus if it were not included. The proposed mandate for this meeting is "to consider the possibilities and means of promoting concrete initiatives for mutually beneficial cooperation concerning various economic, scientific, and cultural fields, and in addition to other initiatives relating to the above subjects already under way."

Unless the neutral and non-aligned countries succeed in winning last-minute acceptance of further expert group meetings on information and military confidence-building measures, this Mediterranean meeting can be regarded as the solitary formal fruit of these last five months.

Not only a further follow-up meeting but also the organization of the expert get-togethers on the peaceful settlement of disputes and science were things to which the Belgrade Meeting was already committed in advance.

"It is," said a neutral delegate today with diplomatic understatement, "a small harvest."

54

The Weary Consensus, by Ian MacDonald.
Report by RFE correspondent, Belgrade, March 8, 1978.

It was 1247 (CET) on the Italian-made electronic clocks in Belgrade's
Sava Center today as the massive mahogany doors to Hall Number One
swung open.

The crowd of journalists waiting outside needed no one to tell them
the result of the plenary within. The relieved smiles on the faces of the
delegates as they filed out were confirmation enough.

Five months and five days after the Belgrade Conference began, consensus had at last been achieved on its concluding document. Only its
official registration and the closing speeches remained.

When consensus was finally announced, there was a little scattered
applause—largely from members of the Conference Secretariat. Most
delegates seemed to feel there was little at the end of the conference to
cheer about. What began on October 3 with such high hopes is ending
with a non-result in an atmosphere of farce.

Many delegates would agree with the much-respected head of the
Swiss delegation, Rudolf Bindschedler, who told a press conference last
night quite frankly: "One can say that this conference is a one per cent
success and a 99 per cent failure."

The Swiss Ambassador feels that this failure can be attributed to a
number of causes. Like some other neutral delegates here, he blames
the atmosphere of confrontation which developed between the two
super-powers in which, as he put it, a real dialogue was replaced by
arguments and mutual accusations.

Like other Western and neutral diplomats, he deplores the total
absence of progress on human rights and contacts as well as on freedom
of information—a subject especially dear to Swiss hearts.

Bindschedler thinks it fair to say that the inability to make any advance at Belgrade also reflects the general state of current relations between the U.S. and the Soviet Union.

It may be expected that similar expressions of regret, perhaps wrapped
up in more diplomatic language, will be heard during the closing
speeches. And there are many here who hope that these will at least
restore some dignity to proceedings which, in the past weeks, have deteriorated to a level which one disillusioned delegate described as a
theater of the absurd.

A Postmortem

55

From Speech by Soviet Delegation Chief, by Iulii Vorontsov.
RFE report, Belgrade, March 9, 1978.

Not all have come to Belgrade with a desire to work out practical recommendations designed to strengthen security and develop cooperation in Europe, to further détente, to promote mutual understanding, and confidence among all the participants of the multilateral process which was so successfully initiated in Helsinki.

It will be recalled that some delegations from the first days and throughout the Belgrade meeting have directed their efforts to sidetrack the meeting onto the path of psychological warfare, to turn it into an arena of ideological confrontation. Instead of undertaking steps to strengthen mutual understanding and confidence among the states and peoples of Europe, attempts have been made here to sow seeds of discord and suspicion with a powerful propaganda setup mobilized to this end outside these rooms. Dodging a serious discussion of the burning issues related to European security and above all those of limiting the arms race and military détente in Europe, these delegations have sought to switch over to other subjects and to challenge the socialist countries on human rights and cooperation in humanitarian fields.

These attempts, in fact, have failed completely and it couldn't have been otherwise. Indeed, only someone who has completely lost a sense of reality would question the practice of genuine socialism where the working man is in the focus of attention and care of the state and society. And what else could be said by those who have on their hands and their conscience such problems, insoluble for capitalism, as unemployment of many millions of people, infringement on the rights of women, humiliating discrimination of national minorities and migrant workers in employment and education, in everyday life and political activity. What else could be said by those who practice racism and uphold apartheid, who victimize champions of civil rights, not stopping short of legal persecution on false charges.

As to the Soviet Union and other socialist countries—and we are proud to reiterate it once again—their citizens for the first time in history have become genuine masters of their own destiny. For many years now workers of the Soviet Union have been regarding as quite natural such fundamental rights as the right to work and free education (including higher education), free medical assistance, the right to maintenance in old age and in sickness, the right to housing, as well as the right to take part in the management and administration of the state and public affairs, in the discussion and adoption of laws of all-Union and local significance. All of these rights have not been merely proclaimed. They have been expressly written down into the USSR Constitution and are materially guaranteed by the state, which is not to be found in any of the countries in the West.

In the course of polemics on human rights forced upon this meeting the mask of hypocrisy has been torn off those who sought in vain to put up a smoke screen of unbridled demagogy on the one hand—to cover up a bleak picture of the infringement of basic human rights in a number of countries in the West and on the other—to divert the attention of the public of Europe from the build-up of the military budgets and arsenals in the West and from the plans by certain quarters to involve European states in a new, still more dangerous neutron phase of the arms race.

What in fact is going on? Those who are hawking the neutron bomb to Europe and peddle the extermination of human beings without damaging houses, cars and other property are the ones who clamor most about human rights and freedoms of the individual. Can one imagine anything more cynical than that?

56

From Speech by West German State Secretary, by Günther van Well. Report by RFE correspondent Ian MacDonald, Belgrade, March 9, 1978.

The Belgrade meeting has been an attempt at a new kind of approach in international relations. On the positive side, all participants have actively shared in an open discussion of matters which previously had to a large extent been diplomatic taboos. We shall have to continue our efforts to create conditions for the further extension of détente, for an intensive exchange of views on the need for better cooperation. If we want détente to be a dynamic process we shall have to consolidate and develop the new dimensions in mutual relations that have become visible in Belgrade.

We regret that the many millions of people in the participating states who have been following the conference ever since it opened five months ago will not find anything in the final document about the things they are so greatly interested in; in other words about what specific improvements in the whole of Europe have resulted from the Final Act of Helsinki and what improvements all participating states have determined should result from it in the future. It would have done much to enhance the credibility of the multilateral process of détente if the 35 participating states in Belgrade had specifically stated that the individual has a legitimate right to invoke the Final Act. The exercise of freedom of thought, freedom of conscience, and freedom of religion must become a key element of our efforts to shape modern and humane international relations.

57

From Speech by Head of Yugoslav Delegation, by Milorad Pešić.
Report by RFE correspondent Ian MacDonald, Belgrade,
March 9, 1978.

Through restrictive approaches on the one hand, and unrealistic expectations on the other, it appears that the ideological rivalries are being resumed. The CSCE process cannot be carried on outside the context of the existing political, military and other realities in Europe. However, its strength and substance are in the fact that it should not be subordinated to, and thus defined, by them, no matter how powerful the logic of the bloc attitude to the CSCE still may be. Our activities thus become a form of gradually overcoming the divisions and limitations present here.

58

The Belgrade Meeting, by Jimmy Carter.
Fourth Semiannual Report by the President to the Commission on Security and Cooperation in Europe, December 1, 1977–June 1, 1978, special report no. 45, Department of State, June 1978, pp. 3–7.

In evaluating the results of the Belgrade meeting, it is important to keep in mind its mandate. The Belgrade meeting was not primarily a negotiation, and it did not look toward a revision of the Helsinki Final Act. Its major task was to conduct an exchange of views on CSCE implementation since the Helsinki Summit and to examine means of deepening cooperation in the future. The views exchanged during the course of the meeting and the precedents and issues which derive from them are thus the most important legacy of the meeting itself.

The initial Soviet position on the implementation review in general and on human rights in particular was that each state should express views only about its own record in order to maintain a "positive" conference atmosphere. The Soviet Union also sought to establish a perspective that deemphasized the significance of human rights at Belgrade and in the CSCE process. Throughout the meeting, the Soviet Union returned to the theme that the real task of Belgrade was to concentrate on security issues in order to "complement political détente with military détente." The corollary to this misleading argument was that the West was distracting the meeting from its real purposes by focusing attention on human rights.

The United States attached particular importance to a thorough review of the human rights and humanitarian provisions of the Final Act because these provisions stood most in need of improved implementation. We considered all sections of the Final Act of importance, however, and worked to assure that they would also be given detailed review at Belgrade. In addition, the U.S. delegation went to Belgrade prepared to engage in a candid discussion of implementation flaws in our own country as well as elsewhere. Ambassador Goldberg said, for example, that the United States sought to discuss human rights from the point of view that no nation had yet achieved its full implementation and that "We have much to learn from that exchange of views."

The full dialogue that the U.S. delegation desired was never achieved. Soviet and other Eastern speakers adopted the line that any discussion of the implementation deficiencies of another state was barred by the sixth principle of Basket One, that of "nonintervention in internal affairs." This debate continued throughout the conference with Western and neutral/nonaligned states repeatedly refuting the notion that discussion of any aspect of CSCE implementation could constitute "interference" in a participating state's internal affairs. While insistence on the nonintervention argument limited Eastern participation in the discussion of implementation progress, it did not stifle Western objectives with regard to the implementation review. By remaining firm and making their points regardless of Eastern objection, Western and neutral/nonaligned delegations succeeded in maintaining the principle of accountability of all states for their implementation performance. Among the most important accomplishments of the review was demonstration that:

—The full implementation of all provisions of the Helsinki Final Act is essential to the successful development of détente and of security and cooperation in Europe;

—Human rights and humanitarian issues are a major, integral aspect of the CSCE process as well as of détente;

—Individual states will be held accountable for their implementation failures, both at future CSCE meetings and in the eyes of world opinion;

—The United States and other CSCE states will not hesitate, and indeed consider it important, to point out specific examples of implementation failures which threaten the health and credibility of the CSCE process;

—Efforts to mask implementation shortcomings with the cloak of nonintervention in internal affairs will not deflect legitimate criticism of a country's implementation record.

Because the CSCE is a long-term process, however, the influence of the Belgrade meeting cannot be judged in the short term or in isolation from the events which preceded and will follow it. Belgrade was an important but single step on the long road to implementation of the pledges given at Helsinki. The United States is determined to continue along this road. While the CSCE is not the only element of détente, its particular importance is in the recognition it accords to the human dimension of the process. The Belgrade meeting reiterated to all signatory states the central fact that successful détente cannot be selective and that the problems of people as well as of power remain firmly on the East-West agenda.

59

Inevitable Disappointment, by Albert W. Sherer, Jr.
Foreign Policy 39 (Summer 1980): 156–59.

Goldberg's one thought was to protect Carter's credibility on human rights. As he self-righteously hammered away at the cause of Soviet dissidents, reaping encomiums from émigré groups and the president, he progressively alienated friend and foe alike at the conference. The idea of allies and neutrals that détente in Europe offered the best hope for progress in human rights was doomed. Moreover, a golden opportunity was provided for the Soviets to drive wedges within the Western alliance and between it and the neutral states.

The delicate fabric of the CSCE should not be strained by international burdens it was never meant to carry. Inflated goals, publicly expressed, only serve to build up false hopes and result in inevitable disappointment when dramatic progress is not made.

Nothing short of a miracle will sufficiently improve the general climate in time for Madrid. Détente is now in disarray, the CSCE being but one victim.

It is quite possible for the United States to adopt a stance true to American human rights principles without jeopardizing realistic hopes of practical results. It is a question of style. Dropping its sanctimonious attitude that antagonized so many at Belgrade, the United States should revert to a lower profile and encourage the West European countries to take the lead. Press conferences for the purpose of imparting information rather than for making headline accusations could create an atmosphere that would provide smaller countries, including those of the Warsaw Pact, with room to maneuver. Human rights would be served more genuinely by such a posture than by confrontation.

THE DECLINE OF DÉTENTE

No Peaceful Solutions

60

The Montreux Conference, by Ian MacDonald.
Report by RFE correspondent, Munich, October 27, 1978.

The 35 states which signed the 1975 Helsinki Documents meet again in Montreux, Switzerland, next week to consider peaceful ways of settling international disputes.

The purpose of the meeting, which is expected to last from three to six weeks, is to agree on a form of machinery to find solutions to disputes. It will work on the basis of a Swiss "draft convention on a European system for the peaceful settlement of disputes" submitted during the Helsinki negotiations.

The Swiss distinguish between two types of disputes—those suitable for settlement by court and those which are not.

Disputes in the first category are concerned with the application of existing law or are conflicts in which one party challenges the legality of a right claimed by another.

The second kind of dispute is one in which a party demands the alteration of a situation or a legal arrangement which it regards as intolerable. The Swiss argue that, in such cases a binding court decision is impracticable and judges would be overtaxed because there would be no objective norm on which to base a verdict.

They therefore propose two types of machinery for the solution of disputes—a court of arbitration for legal disputes and an investigation, mediation and settlement commission for the other.

In both cases the procedure itself would be mandatory but only in the case of the arbitration court would the decision be binding on all parties concerned. That means that, if two governments failed to agree on an issue at dispute between them, either could insist on the case being taken before the court or commission, as appropriate, and the other would be obliged to submit itself to the subsequent proceedings.

The Swiss want both bodies to be composed of independent individuals and not of state delegates. They suggest that each state should nominate a suitable judge and commission member to hold office for a fixed and preferably lengthy period of time.

The Swiss concede that there are weaknesses in their proposals and that the weakest point is the non-binding nature of the commission's recommendations. In their view, however, this is the most which can realistically be expected in Europe's present state.

They argue that, had such a machinery existed and had all European states taken on the obligation to submit their disputes to it instead of taking unilateral action, some major European wars could have been avoided.

61

Dispute on Compulsory Mediation, by Roland Eggleston.
Report by RFE correspondent, Munich, April 12, 1984.

In Athens, the 35 states which signed the Helsinki Final Act have been negotiating for almost a month on a framework for the peaceful settlement of international disputes.

For many of the diplomats in Athens the arguments which have gone back and forth over these in the past three weeks are uncomfortably familiar. They are much the same as those which were heard at Montreux in October 1978.

That six-week long meeting ended in failure because the Soviet Union refused to make the slightest concession to the principle of legally binding agreements.

The United States and its European allies, with the support of the nine neutral countries led by Switzerland and Austria, want an agreement which will compel disputing countries to turn to an outside mediator if they cannot settle the argument themselves.

They have argued since the conference began on March 21 that an obligation to accept mediation, even if one side does not wish to do so, could make a worthwhile contribution to resolving international disputes.

But the Soviet Union and its allies reject the idea of compulsory third-party mediation. They argue that the parties to the quarrel should try to settle it themselves and bring in a third-party umpire only if both sides are willing.

The United States and West European countries consider that approach pointless because it does nothing to improve the situation as it exists now.

But the strongest opposition to the Soviet proposal has come from the neutrals Switzerland and Austria. They have argued in Athens that it opens the way for small countries to be bullied by the Soviet Union, which they say has little respect for the rights of others. They say there is no way the Soviet Union would voluntarily accept an impartial third-party mediator in any case it was likely to lose.

62

The Soviet Proposal, by Roland Eggleston.
Report by RFE correspondent, Athens, April 26, 1984.

The Soviet Union has now told the conference trying to draw up a framework for the peaceful settlement of international disputes what sort of quarrels it is prepared to admit to mediation by a third-party tribunal and what should be excluded.

The Soviet ideas appear in an unofficial working paper distributed to diplomats trying to draw up a final document. Western negotiators say it is a revealing list which exposes Soviet concern that an agreement involving the compulsory mediation of disputes could be used against it. But it also shows where they see an advantage.

The Soviet working paper says countries should resort to a compulsory conciliation procedure involving an outside mediator only when direct negotiations have failed to resolve the dispute within six to 12 months. It goes on to say that the only disputes which should go to such a tribunal at all are those concerned with "violation of international obligations in economic, scientific or technological spheres of international co-operation—in particular, protection of the environment, energy, transport connections and other cases of similar character."

Western diplomats say the Soviet Union apparently believes that such a provision would open the way for it to put the United States and other Western countries before a tribunal if they impose sanctions, as happened after the declaration of martial law in Poland.

The Soviet proposal then goes on to list matters which it wants excluded from a conciliation procedure. It begins with "disputes relating to the fulfillment of treaties of mutual assistance." The Soviet Union used such treaties to justify its invasion of Czechoslovakia and Afghanistan. It clearly does not want any agreement which would open the way to it having to explain such acts to a tribunal.

The paper also seeks to exclude disputes "relating to limitation of the armaments race and disarmament and those relating to frontiers." Western diplomats say the reference to frontiers is unclear. It could mean the Soviet Union is opposed to outside mediation when there is a dispute over the alignment of the border. But there are also other types of quarrels which arise between countries because of problems on the border.

The Soviet document rejects any form of involvement by international mediators in matters which are within a country's domestic jurisdiction. Soviet negotiators have told the West that this particularly applies to human rights issues. It does not want any system which would compel it to go before a tribunal to defend its violation of the human rights provisions in the 1975 Helsinki accords.

The Soviet working paper also proposes a couple of useful escape clauses. One says any country should have the right to refuse to enter into compulsory mediation if it believes the procedure is being used to interfere in its internal affairs. Another says a country should have the right to refuse if it does not recognize that a dispute exists. That, of course, is totally unacceptable because it could be used to wreck the whole procedure.

63

Athens Conference Fails, by Roland Eggleston.
Report by RFE correspondent, Athens, April 28, 1984.

The agreement the West and the neutrals were seeking would have meant a commitment to take almost all unresolved quarrels to the conciliation commission except those touching on national security or disarmament. But the Soviet Union, supported particularly by Czechoslovakia and East Germany, opposed the principle of compulsory recourse to a conciliation commission. Their position was that international disputes should be settled by direct negotiations—a system they call "consultation."

Of course most countries which have a quarrel with another try to start talks in an effort to settle it. But the Soviet position was that these direct talks should be compulsory. It argued that the country which considered itself to have been injured should have the right to demand obligatory negotiations with the other country and also set the date and the place for them. The West had a number of objections to this.

The final result of these six weeks of talks is a one-page document that says that discussions were held on the peaceful settlement of disputes and notes that there was particular emphasis on how to include a third-party element.

The document also says it is recognized that further discussions should be held in an appropriate framework. Whether to do so will be left to the next Helsinki follow-up conference which is to be held in Vienna in 1986. At least in the Western camp there is a feeling that there is little point in convening more talks until the Soviet Union is ready to be more constructive.

Human Rights Denied and Defended

64

Trials Cast Shadow over Bonn Meeting, by Michael B. Wall.
Report by RFE correspondent, Bonn, July 11, 1978.

The Soviet trials of civil rights activists who invoked the 1975 Helsinki Agreement have cast a shadow on the Bonn meeting which is supposed to organize a scientific forum called for in the Helsinki Accord. The outrage over the latest Soviet trials prompted British Foreign Secretary David Owen to order his delegation to raise the matter in Bonn. United States delegates have also expressed their concern.

On the surface, the Soviet trials would seem to have nothing to do with the Bonn meeting or the Scientific Forum but these gatherings are part of the Helsinki Agreement, which the West feels is being flagrantly violated by the Soviet trials. As Owen said in Parliament, the West expects all parts of the Helsinki accord to be respected—including those on human rights. He even said it was a matter for consideration whether it was worthwhile participating in a meeting under the Helsinki framework if one part of that agreement was being violated.

In Bonn, East European delegates closely questioned Westerners about the topics they were suggesting for the Scientific Forum, wanting to know what they really meant by them. The East Europeans even objected to the seemingly innocent Western suggestion for an overall theme—the role of science in meeting fundamental human needs. It seemed that fundamental human needs sounded too much like fundamental human rights.

65

Soviet Implementation of Basket One, by Jimmy Carter.
Ninth Semiannual Report: Implementation of Helsinki
Accord, June 1, 1980–November 30, 1980, special report no. 77,
Department of State, pp. 14–15, 18–19.

The Soviet human rights record continues to worsen. The relentless year-long government campaign of repression against human rights activists of all sorts remains in force. During this period, more than 150 persons in the Soviet Union have been arrested for their human rights beliefs. A temporary slowdown of this campaign during the Moscow Olympics soon stopped, and recent months have seen trials and heavy sentences imposed on many dissidents arrested earlier.

Through imprisonment, harassment, and exile, the Soviet authorities have decimated the groups founded in the USSR to monitor Soviet compliance with the Helsinki Final Act. Only a handful of members remain active. Rather than allow private citizens to monitor Soviet performance of Final Act obligations, the Soviet Government has chosen to suppress their activities. Their advocacy of human rights has been denounced and prosecuted by Soviet authorities as anti-Soviet slander and subversion. Some have been subjected to psychiatric imprisonment and abuse on the grounds that their beliefs are evidence of insanity. Many others have been sentenced to long prison terms.

The Moscow Helsinki Group's effectiveness has been undermined by the continuing persecution of its members. Since its establishment in 1976, it has issued almost 150 formal reports on Soviet compliance with Helsinki obligations. Its reports have dealt with such topics as religious freedom, emigration and family reunification, treatment of political prisoners, free dissemination of information, interference with postal and telephone communication, and repression of national minorities. The Moscow group's activities have been severely and increasingly impaired by the repression of the Soviet Government.

The co-founder of the Moscow Helsinki monitors, physicist Yuriy Orlov, continues to serve out his 7-year sentence under harsh conditions in the Perm #2 labor camp. He has been denied family visits and parcels. On September 5, 1980, he was sentenced to 6 months of solitary confinement for protesting interference with his correspondence and demanding an improvement in camp conditions.

The Ukrainian Helsinki monitoring group has been hit hard. Most members are now in prison or exile. The Helsinki monitoring groups founded in Armenia, Georgia, and Lithuania have also been systematically hounded and suppressed by the Soviet government.

The distinguished physicist and Nobel Peace Prize winner Andrei Sakharov, one of the most forceful and eloquent spokesmen for human rights in the Soviet Union, remains in exile in the closed city of Gorky where he was taken by Soviet security agents on January 22. He is cut off from most outside contacts.

Religious groups not registered with the government are subject to severe harassment. Many of their leaders have been imprisoned, and mere membership in such groups is a criminal offense. Religious activists in the Soviet Union were subjected to a wave of arrests and trials in the last 6 months.

An estimated 30,000 members of the unregistered Pentecostal Church are reported seeking to emigrate because the Soviet Government does not allow them to practice their religion freely. On November 11, some 100 Pentecostalists in the Soviet Union began a 5-day fast to dramatize their repeated demands to be allowed to emigrate. Any religious activity by the Pentecostals outside officially recognized churches is considered to be illegal, and interrogations and house searches by the authorities are commonplace.

There continue to be disturbing signs of anti-Semitism in the Soviet Union, expressed in press attacks on Zionism.

The Final Act signatories agreed to facilitate freer and wider dissemination of information of all kinds, to encourage cooperation in the field of information with other countries, and to improve the working conditions of journalists.

In the Soviet Union, the only widely available non-Communist U.S. periodical is the U.S. International Communication Agency magazine *America Illustrated*, which is distributed in 60,000 copies with the agreement of the Soviet Government. The Soviet distribution agency which handles this magazine has recently been returning approximately 10,000 copies of each issue, as compared to the 1,600 returns which were average for each issue in 1979.

In contravention of the Final Act's goal of freer dissemination of information, several Eastern countries continue to jam Western radio broadcasts. The Soviet Union took a major step backward on August 10 when it resumed jamming of the Voice of America, the BBC, and the Federal Republic of Germany's Deutsche Welle broadcasts. All VOA services directed at the Soviet Union, with the exception of the English service, are now jammed on some or all frequencies.

During the reporting period, there were a number of incidents involving American journalists. Two American correspondents were roughed up and detained by Soviet police for filming in Red Square. Several American journalists have been sharply criticized by name in the Soviet press for alleged subversive activities. Soviet authorities proposed outlandish fees for use of Soviet facilities for spot coverage of the Moscow Olympics; only 40-odd of 200 applicants received visas.

66

Belgium Charges Soviet Anti-Semitism, by Roland Eggleston.
Report by RFE correspondent, Madrid, November 27, 1980.

At the Helsinki Follow-up Conference in Madrid, Belgian delegate René Panis said anti-Semitism was showing itself more and more clearly in the Soviet press. It also took the form of harassment of Jews, administrative measures against them, deprivation of employment and the closing of educational doors. He said the main victims were those who wanted to emigrate but had been refused permission.

Panis referred to the drop in the rate of Jewish emigration from the Soviet Union, which has fallen from more than 51,000 last year to less than 20,000 this year. He said Soviet statements made in the Basket Three working group in the past few days left the impression that the way in which Moscow treated minorities, in this case the Jews, depended on the global state of détente. These statements seemed to confirm other opinions heard in the West recently that the rate of Jewish emigration was a barometer of relations between the two superpowers.

He said it was impossible that the fate of the Jews or any other minority could depend on such political consideration. He quoted excerpts from the Universal Declaration of Human Rights on the right of a person to leave and return to a country and said the Soviet Union had committed itself to honor these.

He also quoted paragraphs in the Helsinki Final Act on the right to religious freedom and said the Soviet Union was expected to honor the right of Jews to practice their religion or teach Hebrew without retribution.

After Panis' speech the Soviet delegate V. T. Chikalov said the Belgian delegate had slandered the Soviet Union. He read out loud to the working group two articles of the Soviet Union Constitution (34 and 36) banning discrimination and guaranteeing equal rights for all. He insisted there was no discrimination in the Soviet Union against Jews and no policy of anti-Semitism.

When he sat down, the Belgian delegate took the floor again and said that Belgium had a great respect for the Soviet Constitution but placed its faith in deeds rather than words.

67

Open Letter to the Belgrade Conference, by Paul Goma.
Letter by Romanian author, Bucharest, February 18, 1977,
Basket III: Implementation of the Helsinki Accords, Hearings
before the Commission on Security and Cooperation in
Europe, Ninety-Fifth Congress, vol. 3 (Washington, D.C.:
U.S. Government Printing Office, 1977), pp. 389–90.

We request that this letter, to which a copy of the Constitution of the Socialist Republic of Romania is appended, be disseminated by all possible means and particularly by press, radio and TV during the preparatory phase of the [Belgrade] Conference. Once the Conference is in session, we shall advise the participants of signers who had in the meantime adhered to our action.

1977 having been declared Human Rights Year, we, the signers of this open letter, addressed to the Belgrade Conference, consider of utmost importance the fact that it has become necessary to convene an international gathering, at the highest level, for the purpose of defending and upholding the rights of man.

Whichever may be the states whose anti-human behavior has brought about this conference, we protest against all forms of oppression—physical, moral, intellectual—in political prisons, in forced labor camps, in psychiatric wards, in older or newer gulags—which tread underfoot liberty and dignity.

In contemporary dictatorships, the essential forms of individual and social manifestations (the arts, culture, science, political and religious creeds, national consciousness) become empty words in the service of ideological propaganda of the respective dictatorship. On the other hand, the rights guaranteed by internal totalitarian states, are not respected. This is the case for the articles of the R.S.R. Constitution with respect to civil liberties, the right to work, to education, to association, the right to free speech, press assembly, meetings, and demonstrations, the freedom of conscience, the inviolability of person, home, the secrecy of correspondence and telephone conversations. Equally disregarded is the right to free movement of person, ideas, information, while the right to citizenship is perverted into an obligation which does not serve the cause of progress.

All over the world there is much talk about dignity and liberty. But how many people in the states in which dignity and liberty are genuinely respected know that there are states in which human beings are forever bound to the country in which they were born? How many people know that there are many states in which for many decades the voters unanimously cast their ballots in favor of the single candidate hand-picked by the men in power, in total disregard of the voters? How many know that there are countries in which work and not the laboring man is important? How many are aware of the fact that there are states in which citizenship is turned against the citizen and in which the principle of non-interference in internal affairs is used to deny the rights of the international community to concern itself with the non-observance of human rights and fundamental freedoms?

68

Letter to the Madrid Conference from Mírov Prisoners.
Mírov, Czechoslovakia, January 1981. *Human Rights in
Czechoslovakia: The Documents of Charter '77, 1977–1982*
(Washington, D.C.: Commission on Security and Cooperation
in Europe, 1982), p. 16.

As political prisoners of a socialist state we are forced to point out that Czechoslovak representatives in Madrid are lying when they claim that documentation and arguments presented by others with regard to human rights violations in Czechoslovakia are pure fabrications. We ourselves are testimony to judicial discrimination in prisons and are an embarrassment to justice in a state that does not observe human rights in any way. As long as agreements, already accepted, are not being implemented, it is not possible to agree to conclude new agreements. We were sentenced because we raised the question of violations of human rights. Some of us were sentenced because they returned home to their families from abroad—even though they were promised that they would not be punished.

Today, only a few citizens believe in the sort of ideological purity and humanity which is being presented to them by the media. They are being confronted at every step with the contradiction of words with reality. The same applies to equality of citizens before the law. As long as this state of affairs prevails, no citizen can be certain that his human rights will be observed and that he will not be deprived of his property and employment. This approach to a human being is in direct violation of accepted obligations in this area of human rights. Instead of implementing accepted agreements, the regime points 'elsewhere' and calls facts fabrications, in order to divert attention.

We, therefore, confirm the rightfulness of the charges brought up in Madrid and we request that the participants of the Conference, as well as the United Nations and world public opinion, condemn these actions and demand an immediate release of political prisoners in Czechoslovakia and strict observance of civil and human rights.

69

America's "Helsinki Lobby," by Robert Rand.
Report by RFE correspondent, Washington, July 31, 1980.

Representatives from over 100 ethnic, religious, and human rights groups met with leaders of the American delegation to the Madrid Conference on Tuesday to mark on August 1st the fifth anniversary of the signing of the Helsinki Final Act. For well over an hour, spokesmen from these non-governmental organizations queried, criticized, and sometimes lectured U.S. delegation chairman Griffin Bell and his colleagues about what Washington's policy toward the Madrid Conference should be.

The briefing was testimony to the considerable influence that America's "Helsinki Lobby"—as the non-governmental organizations have been called—has gained since the Final Act was signed.

The Helsinki Lobby is not a unified movement, but rather a mixed bag of organizations which share a desire to bring their special interests to the attention of governing officials responsible for CSCE affairs. They advocate a range of Helsinki-related issues, most of which center on promoting the rights of ethnic and religious minorities and on facilitating emigration.

Over the past five years, the Helsinki Lobby has vigorously pressed the White House, State Department, and U.S. Congress to invoke the Helsinki agreement in the name of dozens of ethnic, religious, and humanitarian causes. The Helsinki Lobby was particularly active during the Belgrade Conference, when leaders of these organizations urged U.S. officials to formally raise their causes at the CSCE bargaining table in the Yugoslav capital. A similar campaign is again underway this year, pegged to the opening of the Madrid Follow-up Conference in November.

While American officials cannot possibly fulfill all of their requests— the time and strategic constraints of conducting negotiations with 34 other Helsinki signatories ensure that the U.S. has sought to strike a balance between carrying out responsible diplomacy and satisfying the special interests of the Helsinki Lobby. As a result the representatives of these organizations have been fully incorporated into the CSCE process to ensure that the Helsinki Lobby, whose constituency includes millions of voters, has ample opportunity to advise American policy-makers.

President Carter has named 30 individuals representing a variety of special interest groups as public members of the U.S. delegation to the Madrid Conference. As official participants to the follow-up conference, the public members will be able to meet with U.S. diplomats on the scene, and actually take part in the conference's behind-closed-door debates. The number of public members on the Madrid delegation is six times greater than was the number of public members on the U.S. delegation to the Belgrade Conference, an indication both of widespread American concern over human rights violations of the Final Act, and of the influence that the Helsinki Lobby wields in an election year.

U.S. officials have also promised that non-governmental organizations not represented on the Madrid delegation will be able to meet with delegation members in the Spanish capital to receive briefings on the progress of the conference and to exchange views with U.S. officials.

Over fifty non-governmental organizations have participated in Congressional hearings on CSCE over the past few years. And members of the Commission on Security and Cooperation in Europe, the congressional Committee that provided the Helsinki Lobby with that public platform, were included on the U.S. delegation to the Belgrade Conference, and will be on the Madrid delegation as well. The CSCE Commission has collected mounds of information on numerous causes advocated by the various organizations, and much of this material will be available for use by the U.S. delegation in Madrid.

In advocating their special interests, some Helsinki Lobby representatives have exhibited a certain naiveté about the realities of international politics, while others have revealed a lack of sensitivity to the wider issues at stake in the CSCE process. At the State Department CSCE briefing on Tuesday, for instance, one person asked the delegation for help in setting up anti-Soviet demonstrations in front of the conference hall in Madrid. Another suggested that the U.S. Delegation ask the USSR to stop jamming Radio Liberty's Latvian Service, "at least for the duration of the Madrid Conference." A third wondered if Griffin Bell couldn't renegotiate the Oder-Neisse Line. Still others pressed the delegation to focus on such Helsinki-related issues as the plight of American Indians and alleged Romanian discrimination against the Hungarian minority in Transylvania. Nearly all of the questions asked at the briefing focused on the Helsinki Final Act's humanitarian provisions. No one seemed interested in Helsinki's other provisions, such as those on confidence building measures or scientific and commercial exchange.

70

French Activists Demand Firmness in Madrid, by Susan Ovadia. Report by RFE correspondent, Paris, November 11, 1980.

Several Eastern and Western rights activists in France have called on the West to remain firm on human freedom issues at the Helsinki Review Conference in Madrid.

One such appeal was adopted this week in Marseilles at the end of a two-day international colloquy on the current situation of Soviet workers.

The some 1,000 participants urged Western nations to insist, in particular, that the Soviets grant the right to family reunification and to free movement as stated in the Final Helsinki Act.

The Paris Le Figaro today carried three comments on the Madrid conference—by exiled Romanian writer and rights activist Paul Goma, Czechoslovak-born writer Pavel Tigrid and Alain Ravennes, the co-founder and Secretary General of the Parisian Intellectuals Committee for Freedom in Europe.

Goma severely attacked President Nicolae Ceauşescu and claimed that violations of human rights in Romania were increasing together with general repression. The West should not remain silent on these violations, Goma said, giving examples of recent persecutions of Romanian dissidents.

Tigrid said all dissidents and all peoples now obliged to live under Soviet rule should at least be spiritually represented in Madrid. The West, he said, should press for Soviet concessions where they were possible and did not directly threaten the regime. Concrete and systematic insistence, he said, could yield tangible results, in particular concerning family reunification, travel authorization and increased cultural exchanges.

Even if there was no hope to convert the Soviet Union into a democracy, Tigrid said, it was necessary for the West to participate in meetings such as the one held in Madrid.

Ravennes agreed, but warned that Madrid must not imply Western capitulation before Soviet totalitarianism. He urged the West to state, from the very opening of the conference, two conditions: first, that the Soviets withdraw all their troops from Afghanistan; and then, that all East Europeans in jail for demanding full implementation of the Helsinki accords be released.

The West, Ravennes said, should refuse to participate in any masquerade that would cover up Soviet violations of the Helsinki accords.

Dispute over Madrid Agenda

71

Soviet-Prompted Deadlock, by Roland Eggleston.
Report by RFE correspondent, Madrid,
September 12 and 17, 1980.

The meeting preparing for this year's review of the 1975 Helsinki accords adjourned unexpectedly early today to allow backroom consultations on avoiding a Soviet-prompted deadlock.

It had been expected that the nine neutral and non-aligned states would produce a working paper on the November agenda for today's session. They were asked to do so yesterday by Hungary and Norway.

It would have been based on the so-called Yellow Book. This is the booklet of rules worked out for the last Helsinki review conference in Belgrade in 1977–78. It took seven weeks of stormy negotiations to produce them.

Conference sources told our correspondent the neutrals' initiative was stillborn because of the attitude chief Soviet delegate Iurii Dubinin took in a private meeting late yesterday afternoon with the Austrian delegation leader, Dr. Franz Ceska. He apparently said in strong terms that the USSR considered the Yellow Book to be prejudiced in favor of the West and against the interests of the USSR.

Seen from Moscow one of the main problems with the Yellow Book is that it does not provide definite cut-off dates for ending discussions. The Soviet Union fears a repetition of what happened in Belgrade when it was attacked for weeks on end for its human rights record. Other East European countries were also criticized. This time, the USSR is also going to be denounced for its invasion of Afghanistan.

The Soviet Union also dislikes the Yellow Book formula worked out in Belgrade because it does not provide a definite date for ending the review conference. The appropriate paragraph sets various target dates for ending the conference but says only that "every effort should be made" to meet them. It then goes on to say "the meeting will end in any case by adopting its concluding document and by fixing the date and place of the next similar meeting."

It is innocuous only on the surface. The key fact is that all agreements at these Helsinki review meetings have to be unanimous—and that includes the concluding document. The paragraph in the Yellow Book means the conference could go on indefinitely until consensus is reached on the concluding document. . . .

Czechoslovakia inserted the first discordant note. In what delegates described as unusually blunt language, a Czechoslovak delegate spurned the working paper presented by Spain this morning as not providing a basis for discussion.

This is the key issue: Spain proposes that "Every effort should be made to agree on the concluding document" by March 5. But it makes clear that this is only a guideline. If agreement is not reached by March 5 then the conference must go until there is an agreement on the concluding document. There also has to be agreement on the date and place of the next meeting.

Similar rules applied in Belgrade. There the target date was not met and arguments went on for weeks as the West tried to get a reference to human rights into the document. Finally it admitted defeat and allowed a sentence saying that consensus had not been reached on some points.

This time, as the Soviet Union has been told quite firmly, the West is determined to get something a little stronger. There's no real hope of getting the Warsaw Pact countries to agree to a specific reference to Afghanistan and the repression of human rights groups. But the West wants wording which makes its feelings extremely clear.

The West is also determined to keep the option of raising human rights issues whenever it feels appropriate. The Spanish working paper leaves plenty of scope for this although it does not mention it directly. That's another reason for Warsaw Pact disappointment with it.

72

Discussion Reaches Bedrock, by Roland Eggleston.
Report by RFE correspondent, Madrid,
September 24 and 26, 1980.

After more than two weeks of negotiation, some of it on secondary issues, the discussions have now reached the fundamental differences separating the Warsaw Pact from the West and most of the neutral and non-aligned states.

The new atmosphere has been apparent since yesterday, when Czechoslovakia tabled a working paper on how the Warsaw Pact believes the review conference should be organized. What the Czechoslovak—or, better said, the Warsaw Pact—paper does is squeeze into five-and-a-half weeks all the most important issues, including the time the West insists on having to examine human rights violations in Eastern Europe and the Soviet invasion of Afghanistan.

In that five-and-a-half weeks the Czechoslovaks want the conference to examine how each country is living up to the Helsinki accords and to discuss new proposals to help European security, the date and place of the next meeting, Mediterranean security and the reports of the specialist meetings which have taken place since the last Helsinki follow-up conference in Belgrade in 1977–78.

The five-and-a-half weeks would also include the one week traditionally given up to opening statements and the other week traditionally devoted to general debate. It would take the conference from its opening on November 11 up to the break for the Christmas holidays on December 19. All that would be left to do when the delegates gather again on January 26 would be to begin drafting a final document. As a Dutch delegate exclaimed to reporters today: "It is indigestible!"

It is accepted around the conference corridors that not even the Warsaw Pact takes the proposal seriously. . . . Therefore its tabling was just a tactic, or "trying out the water," as Chief American Delegate Max Kampelman likes to describe it. There was a hint from the Soviet side that perhaps the West would like to trade concessions: the Warsaw Pact would give a little in return for the West surrendering some of the compromises won in the struggle to establish a similar book of rules for Belgrade. The West, however, has stood firm. It wants to keep the Belgrade book of rules and the bait dangled by the Warsaw Pact has not tempted it.

The Western reaction was probably expected. Where the Warsaw Pact miscalculated was with the neutrals and non-aligned. It seems genuinely taken aback to discover that they are as opposed to the Czechoslovak proposal as the West.

The Warsaw Pact apparently failed to take into account two points. The first is that the signatories of the Helsinki accords are sovereign states and they object to any attempt to curtail their right to speak out on subjects which interest them. The other point is that the neutral and non-aligned are extremely interested in putting forward suggestions for new projects to help European security and want these discussed thoroughly and in detail.

A strong line was taken by Austria. It is associated with a string of new proposals covering military security, wider dissemination of information, better working conditions for journalists and international co-operation on energy. In some cases it is acting together with the neutral and non-aligned group, in some with Switzerland and Spain and some are its own initiative. Its delegate, Dr. Franz Ceska, made it plain that Austria considered all these issues too important to be rushed through in the way envisaged by the Czechoslovak paper.

None of the non-communist delegations want to stay in Madrid for weeks quibbling over points they thought had been settled in Belgrade. There is a wry appreciation for those who obviously expected nothing better.

All members of the British delegation have their families with them and the Maltese are telling everyone they brought enough money for 50 days and expect to use it all. So far there have been 14 working days and the real problems have just begun to be considered.

In this mood, there was a flutter of hope yesterday when the tall, elegant head of the Soviet delegation, Iurii Dubinin, unexpectedly stood up to make a speech on the Czechoslovak proposal. Dubinin has kept in the background for most of the meeting and there were expectations that his intervention signalled a new approach.

But although he spoke for 45 minutes, the longest address made by anyone so far, he failed to make clear what he was driving at. One experienced Western diplomat described it as "Soviet baroque," which he defined as a lot of fine-sounding phrases strung together which seem impressive until the listener tries to understand what they mean. A delegate from a neutral country told our correspondent he was sure the speech was significant in some way but he did not know why.

73

Three Separate Proposals, by Roland Eggleston.
Report by RFE correspondent, Madrid, November 7, 1980.

The only thing certain about this year's Madrid conference is that it will begin as scheduled next Tuesday morning.

No one in Madrid knows what will happen after that.

At the end of the ninth week of preparatory meetings, there is still no agreement on either an agenda or a timetable for the conference. Nor has a list of speakers been prepared to follow the opening address by Spain.

As of this afternoon, the meeting has before it three separate proposals for breaking the deadlock on the agenda and the timetable. They are from the neutrals, the Warsaw Pact countries, and the Common

Market countries. There are many similarities between the neutral and Common Market proposals but the Warsaw Pact is light years away from both.

The Warsaw Pact paper was presented last night in the names of Hungary, Czechoslovakia and East Germany although it was clearly directed by the Soviet Union. As usual with East European proposals at this meeting, it was presented in Russian, which is one of the six working languages.

The paper generally repeats ideas on the timetable and the agenda submitted in earlier East European papers and rejected as unacceptable by the West, neutrals, and non-aligned.

The circumstances surrounding the introduction of the Warsaw Pact paper have deepened the atmosphere of disillusion at the preparatory meeting.

It was introduced without warning only a few hours after the neutrals had circulated a compromise proposal of their own which they believed would be considered favorably by the Communist states.

The neutrals had been encouraged and urged to bring out the paper by the Soviet number two delegate, A. S. Kondrashev. He had argued that only they were in a position to break the deadlock. He had private talks with the neutrals as recently as Monday and Tuesday of this week.

But instead of supporting the paper when it eventually appeared yesterday morning, the East Europeans brought out their own. Delegates in the meeting told our correspondent in Madrid that the neutrals were literally open-mouthed with shock when Hungary's János Petran stood up to say he was circulating a paper.

74

Conference Clocks Stopped, by Roland Eggleston.
Report by RFE correspondent, Madrid, November 11, 1980.

A new East-West row erupted tonight when the Hungarian Chairman of a plenary session declined to leave the post.

Our correspondent says the row arose over a technical maneuver which has kept Hungarian delegation leader János Petran as chairman of the plenary sessions.

The conference clocks were officially stopped at two minutes to midnight last night to enable informal negotiations on the agenda and timetable to continue under yesterday's date.

The negotiations have failed to break the deadlock and Western countries decided tonight that there should be a return to today's time. They did so because they want to formally open the conference later tonight on November 11, as scheduled.

The initiative was taken by Holland, which withdrew its consensus for the clock-stopping operation. Then Liechtenstein formally told Petran that he was no longer chairman and must make way for the new chairman, a Spaniard.

But at this point the Soviet Union stood up to say that consensus was required to appoint the new chairman and it would not give it.

At 2030 CET the argument had been going for more than 50 minutes and tempers were becoming heated.

The co-chairman of the American delegation, Max Kampelman, has intervened twice to tell Petran that his position is now illegal, but Petran and the Soviet Union have rejected the claim.

Western delegates said they were concerned that the argument was taking up time which could be devoted to getting the full conference underway tonight as scheduled.

U.S. spokesman Jaroslav Verner confirmed that the Hungarian Ambassador had refused to give up the chair.

Verner said: "It is the view of my delegation that this is a usurpation on the part of the Hungarian chairman of the chairmanship and is illegal. The Hungarian Ambassador has conducted the meeting in an arbitrary manner."

Verner said the entire session lasting about two hours covered only the procedural question of starting the clock. He gave no indication of the fate of the agenda proposals that were being considered earlier in the day.

He said also that it is the understanding of the U.S. delegation that the Spanish hosts of the conference will call an opening session to order before midnight.

75

The Conference Finally Opens, by Roland Eggleston.
Report by RFE correspondent, Madrid, November 12, 1980.

The conference finally opened in Madrid last night in a slightly incredulous atmosphere with no one quite ready to believe it was really happening.

Only an hour before Spanish Foreign Minister José Pedro Pérez Llorca stepped on to the rostrum to deliver a two-minute speech formally opening the trouble-dogged conference it seemed unlikely to happen.

Not only was there no break in the weeks-long deadlock over the agenda and timetable but the final plenary session of the preparatory meeting had deteriorated into a squabble over the chairmanship. In the conference cafeteria some delegates were discussing whether the squabble was an attempt to draw out the proceedings of the preparatory meeting so that the full conference would be unable to open on November 11 as scheduled. There was worried speculation over whether the conference would be able to continue for more than a few days without an agenda or timetable. The speculation was fueled by the repeated refusal of the Soviet Union over the previous nine weeks to the drawing of lots to decide on the order of speakers on the first working day.

But when the delegates resumed after a long coffee break the differences suddenly seemed to dissolve.

The presiding Hungarian, Petran, was allowed to remain in the chair with the friendly goodwill of everyone until the end of the session. It was agreed that the conference could open even without an agenda and then everyone also agreed to meet again after midnight to try to settle some issues in the better atmosphere. Apparently they did, because early today lots were drawn for the order of speakers at today's working session.

The change was wrought by the Spanish and Soviet delegations at a meeting during the long coffee break. Those who were there say it was agreed that the reputation of all 35 states would be damaged if the squabbling prevented the conference beginning as scheduled.

Some observers believe an important factor was the presence in the plenary of more than 20 public members of the U.S. Helsinki Committee. These people, drawn from many areas of ordinary American life but not officials, had openly expressed shock and dismay at the squabbling and the difficulties at reaching agreement with the Soviet Union and its allies.

76

The West Has Its Way, by Roland Eggleston.
RFE correspondent, Madrid, November 28, 1980.

The West has had its way and is using the Helsinki follow-up conference in Madrid to denounce the invasion of Afghanistan and criticize the Soviet and East European record on human rights.

It did so by simply rolling over a Soviet effort to stall the debate by starting a procedural wrangle over whether priority should be given to the principle supposed to govern the behavior of the countries which signed the Helsinki accord or to a discussion on disarmament and military confidence-building measures.

The West had learned a lot from the Soviet delaying tactics in the nine wearying weeks of the preparatory meeting. This time it just ignored the procedural row. It packed the list of speakers with Western delegates who went straight into Afghanistan and human rights when it was their turn to speak. Soviet Deputy Foreign Minister Leonid Ilichev, who is a small, very round man, fumed and in the words of one Western delegate, "flapped his wings like an angry penguin." But there was nothing he could do and in the end he accepted, with bad grace, the timetable enforced by the West.

The West has now exhausted almost all it wants to say about Afghanistan unless events there give cause to revive the issue. It is now concentrating on human rights and will use the next three weeks to bring up individual cases and identify people by name. The Soviet Union and its allies have a few sessions in which to push their favorite theme of disarmament and military détente but the emphasis will be on human rights, just as the West insisted it should be.

Western delegates who were at the last Helsinki review conference in Belgrade say the tone in Madrid is harder and the dialogue more direct. Confrontations between East and West occur almost daily in the plenaries and the working sessions.

"We never had too many illusions about the Soviet Union before Belgrade," a Western delegate said. "Now we have none. And the way the Soviet Union and its allies behaved in the preparatory meeting destroyed any ideas that they might be prepared to be reasonable. We know our goals and we are going for them as hard as we can. There will be no slackening."

77

To Insure Orderly Continuity, by the Delegation of Finland. Proposal by Finland, Madrid, December 17, 1980, Foreign Office, Helsinki.

The participating States

Decide to organize meetings among their representatives in the interim periods between the Follow-up Meetings of the participating States:

1. These meetings will be referred to as "the CSCE Committee" and be composed of plenipotentiary representatives appointed by the Ministers of Foreign Affairs of the participating States,
2. The Committee will carry out the following functions:
    (i) *Meetings of Experts of the participating States*
    The Committee will carry out preparatory, co-ordinating and other organizational functions, as necessary, with regard to the Meetings of Experts of the participating States, convened by the decisions of the Follow-up Meetings.
    (ii) *The preparation of the Follow-up Meetings of the participating States*
    The Committee will carry out the preparatory functions with respect to the Follow-up Meetings. For this purpose, the Committee will constitute itself into a Preparatory Meeting not later than three months prior to the opening of the Follow-up Meetings in order to decide on the agenda, organizational framework, time-table and other modalities for these Meetings.
    (iii) *Other functions*
    The Committee may, in addition and as appropriate, meet in order to exchange views on matters of common interest to the participating States concerning the aforementioned tasks and the Chapter on the Follow-up to the CSCE,
3. The meetings of the Committee will, as a rule, be held 3–4 times in the interim period between the Follow-up Meetings of the participating States and their duration should preferably not exceed 1–2 weeks, or in the case of a Preparatory Meeting of the Follow-up Meetings 4–6 weeks.

PART THREE

HUMAN RIGHTS IN THE SHADOW OF MILITARY RIVALRY: FROM MADRID TO VIENNA

ACCENT ON MILITARY SECURITY

Soviet Interest in "Military Détente"

78

What Is Behind Soviet Insistence on Military Détente?
by Vladimir Lomeiko.
"Realities and Prospects of Détente as Seen in Moscow
after the Belgrade Conference," in Cornelis C. van den
Heuvel and Rio D. Praaning (eds.), *The Belgrade
Conference: Progress or Retrogression* (Leiden: New
Rhine, 1978), pp. 33–37.

Political détente cannot endure parallel with an arms build-up for too long. Unless the arms race is stopped, it will stop all progress of détente. This is what lies behind Moscow's invariable insistence on political détente being constantly supplemented with military détente measures. In all disarmament forums, at the UN, in the Disarmament Committee in Geneva, at the Vienna talks on the Reduction of Armed Forces and Armaments in Central Europe, and the SALT-talks, the Soviet Union has been following a constructive approach, taking into account the balance of forces and the principle of equality and identical security.

The objective realities of the present world, with a parity of forces between East and West, demand respect for the principles of equality and identical security. What is required in order to prevent détente from being destabilized is to desist from all attempts at gaining unilateral advantages, let alone strategic superiority.

Whenever any of the parties involved attempts to obtain unilateral advantages, this inevitably shakes the partner's confidence and the stability of their relations. This has been particularly manifest in the Soviet-American talks on limiting strategic armaments (SALT-2), where the American side has shown itself intent on getting unilateral advantages.

The problem of SALT-2 is not so much one of the Washington SALT-2 supporters coming to terms with their Russian partners as one of overcoming their opponents at home, for, indeed, there are three, rather than two, partners at the negotiating table.

Whereas Moscow speaks with one voice, and, what is more, one and the same voice, what it hears in reply is a chorus of discordant voices. The point is not only that in the early stages it had Ford to deal with, and now Carter, it is that while Brezhnev has a united and, what is no less important, consistent-minded Soviet Union behind him, the American President has his doves and hawks.

The USSR has no military-industrial complex that would have self-seeking interest in war orders and a private stake in war profits. In the US, on the other hand, as experience indicates, the development of new military technology is outside the control of the White House. The cruise missile and the neutron bomb had been both offered to the American President as ready-made weapons destined to assure US world supremacy. The whole world has seen President Carter come under massive pressure from vested interests to whom new types of armaments mean billions-of-dollars' worth of orders and political leverage both at home and far outside.

Moscow is alarmed and alerted by intensified activities of the US forces working against an early SALT-2 agreement and for the introduction of new weapons systems, particularly such dangerous ones as the neutron bomb.

The neutron bomb story is particularly noteworthy, for it shows that President Carter must have failed to understand the Russians. There is nothing else to account for the fact that he did not reply to Leonid Brezhnev's Christmas proposal for a mutual renunciation of the production of neutron weapons. Conceding that he could have failed to understand it, Moscow repeated its proposal in March, 1978, and its willingness to negotiate the matter with Washington.

A further refusal, tacit or public, can have hardly calculable consequences, not only for Soviet-American relations, but for the international situation as a whole. In all probability, this is also something the White House does not understand in full, nor do its counterparts in some West-European capitals. One can see that from the counter-arguments of Western politicians and journalists in reply to the Soviet proposal for a mutual renunciation of the production of neutron weapons. Some of our opponents argue in this way: since the Russians are uneasy, that means that the West has hit the mark. It is because of this misinterpretation of the Soviet proposal that there has even been a certain increase in the number of neutron arms advocates among Western politicians and military men. Others, on the contrary, feign surprise at the Soviet Union's reaction, and suggest that neutron weapons are no reason to be so uneasy about, as they are no more dangerous than any other. This brings them to the idea that this is the type of weapon to use to strengthen NATO or as a bargaining counter to talk the Russians into giving ground.

Either method of approach reveals a misreading of Moscow's attitude to neutron weapons and, in consequence, a grave miscalculation of the Western strategy of East-West relationship. If one acts on the assumption that the policy of détente is to rest on a global East-West strategic power balance and undiminished security, one has to admit that détente requires further agreements aimed at containing the arms race and at confidence-building. From this point of view, the neutron bomb cannot but affect adversely the policy of détente. Although it cannot upset the strategic East-West balance, it does upset the very spirit of détente by compelling the other side to take counter-measures, and that would mean yet another round of the nuclear arms race and a flare-up of mutual mistrust.

The main danger of the present situation resides in the Western failure to understand properly the political and psychological motives of Russian insistence in the neutron bomb case. The Soviet Union wants no further arms build-up, and not because it is incapable of sustaining it. It coped with similar tasks in far harder times. Now the Russians would not even have to tighten their belts to do so, the present Soviet military potential is enough to meet the challenge.

Moscow is opposed to neutron weapons because, above all, it sees them as an instrument whereby to force it into reversing its policy towards the West, that is: giving up the policy based on confidence and nuclear arms limitation in favor of one of spending more on new types of armaments. All this is bound to cause the Soviet people to mistrust their Western partners and to do much damage to the chances of détente.

Every succeeding President has to earn the trust, not only of his own people, but of other nations as well. President Carter's statement of the need to spare mankind the risk of nuclear disaster and of his desire to improve relations with the Russians has earned him the greater trust of many, the Russians included. However, considering that this trust is on the wane because of the long-drawn-out confrontation at the SALT talks, the neutron arms issue turns into an acid test of détente.

Whenever Moscow speaks of the special responsibility of the USSR and the US for the future of détente, it does not mean any special rights or privileges, but the heaviest burden of armaments, including nuclear and strategic, that the two powers have to bear. They are the biggest states, and a conflict between them, being inevitably global in scope, would as inevitably affect their allies and many other countries. Naturally, the future of détente does primarily depend on the success of the USSR-US talks about containing the arms race.

While attaching due significance to its relations with Washington, Moscow is just as keen on developing friendly relations with other countries. It is understood in the Soviet Union that relations between the USSR and the US cannot but tell on the overall international climate, but that does not mean that the efforts of other nations towards improving their relations with the Soviet Union and checking the arms race cannot positively influence the pursuit of international détente.

Just on the contrary, it is precisely the development of Soviet-French and Soviet–West German cooperation as well as improved relations between the USSR and other West European countries that have brought about an all-European Conference and a strengthening of détente in Europe and the rest of the world. Further prospects for international détente largely depend on the efforts of both the Soviet Union and the United States as well as West European countries to maintain stability in the world.

It is accepted in Moscow that destabilizing factors do undermine mutual trust and détente, and it is precisely because the USSR is interested in stability, parity of forces and cooperation that it wants a military-strategic balance between the Soviet Union and the US to stay. In Washington, on the other hand, the partisans of strategic parity with the USSR do not always gain the upper hand in their disputes with the adherents of a policy to win American superiority.

Current events in the world show that the US is balancing between their strategy of deterrence and the need to pursue détente. The only possible effect of such a shaky balance between these conflicting guidelines is destabilization of the international situation. Just as it causes the US allies to feel insecure, it compels Moscow to keep fit to deal with the "doves" and the "hawks" alike.

79

Hostages to Détente, by John Wilberforce.
Speech by the head of British delegation, reported by RFE
correspondent Roland Eggleston, Madrid, December 3, 1980.

Chief British delegate John Wilberforce referred to a linkage which he
said had become apparent in a working group dealing with co-operation
in the humanitarian field.

"A certain delegation has taken the line there that its government's
willingness to deal with humanitarian cases in accordance with its commitments under the Final Act will depend on progress in matters of
interest to it, including particularly a so-called conference on military
détente and disarmament in Europe. One would not have thought that
the conference on security and co-operation in Europe would witness
such a crude and unprincipled attempt at linkage," he said.

Wilberforce said: "The idea that individual human beings should be
held hostage to the political objectives of a certain government is
totally unacceptable."

The Impact of Afghanistan

80

The Hamburg Scientific Forum, by Morton Vonduyke.
Report by RFE correspondent, Hamburg, February 21, 1980.

The shadows of Afghanistan and Andrei Sakharov clouded the opening
days of the international conference of scientists in Hamburg this week.

Scientists from Western Europe clearly showed their anxiety over
the current East-West tension generated by the Soviet invasion of
Afghanistan and Moscow's repressive treatment of one of the Soviet
Union's leading scientists, human rights activist Andrei Sakharov. A
good many of the Western delegates directly mentioned their concern
over the fate of Sakharov in their opening statements to the conference
plenary session.

The East European delegates mentioned neither Sakharov nor the
invasion, but they joined wholeheartedly with their Western colleagues
in emphatically pleading for cooperation in their discussions for the
next two weeks. The very fact that virtually all the delegates hammered away at the need for cooperation was obvious proof that the

ramifications of the Soviet invasion and its repressive treatment of Sakharov and other scientists weighed heavily on their minds.

The delegates from Eastern Europe kept to general terms in their speeches, insisting on the need during the discussions for businesslike exchanges of scientific information and views free from political coloring.

But the very attitude of the Eastern European delegates—and most certainly that of the Western scientists—showed that it will be almost impossible to separate politics from science, just as it is impossible to separate politics from the Olympics. And especially after a conference opening at which American, British and Soviet delegates clashed over Soviet treatment of Sakharov, it will take a lot of filtering to keep the discussions concerning complicated medical and scientific subjects on a purely scientific level.

In fact, one influential delegation at the conference expects the scientists, who represent the 35 signatory states of the Helsinki Final Act, to accomplish much less at the conference than they would have had it been free from the taint of invasion and maltreatment of scientists.

The subject of restrictions on interchange of scientists and information will be unavoidable in virtually every topic they will discuss, for advancement of science in the world community depends on intercommunication of all sorts. These communications have been stifled in the Soviet Union, along with other violations of intellectual freedoms necessary to scientists. The Soviet actions against scientists—not only against Sakharov—have engendered a climate of displeasure and distrust within the conference hall.

The announced intention of several Western delegations is to send a strong signal to Moscow, through the Soviet scientists attending the conference, that the Soviet government must change its treatment of scientists and reinstate their freedom to work and think in the world scientific community, or else witness the unquestionable withering away of all scientific exchanges and communications with the major scientific and technological nations.

Some delegates feel much more can be gained from individual private visits or communications between scientists from different countries than can be achieved by a conference of this nature and size, especially when it is marred by political overtones. They feel the Hamburg forum is inherently more of a cosmetic nature for politicians of the participating states than a genuine scientific conference really intent on scientific achievement.

81

Science and Human Rights, by Philip Handler.
Speech by the President of the U.S. National Academy of
Science, Madrid, December 3, 1980, *World Affairs* 144
(1982): 342–43, 345–46, 351.

It is a deep irony that the subject of cooperation in science should be on the agenda of the CSCE. Communication and cooperation among scientists is a tradition of five centuries; indeed, it is the very essence of science because without communication, science is essentially pointless.

Accordingly, it is apparent that if the original provisions of the Final Act, all of them, were adhered to by the signatory countries, there would be little need to pursue the subject of scientific cooperation further within the CSCE context. But it was because that did not appear to be the case that the scientific forum at Hamburg assumed a character surely quite different from that anticipated when the provision for a scientific forum was written into the Final Act.

By the time we had gathered, it was apparent that the scientists of the West were primarily concerned with what they considered to be serious infringements of the human rights and freedoms of too many of their scientific colleagues in the East.

To be sure, none of the scientists who have been grievously injured have been so treated because of their scientific activities. In general, the seeming transgressions for which they have been penalized so excessively have been either to have participated in monitoring their own governments' adherence to the provisions of the Final Act or merely to have requested permission to emigrate—activities vouchsafed by the Final Act itself. And it was attention to that circumstance that dominated our time in Hamburg.

That time was not wasted. The report of the scientific forum, achieved by the same consensus process common to all CSCE meetings, contains several pregnant statements. Let me remind you of them: "It is observed that the present state of international scientific cooperation still requires improvements in various respects. Such improvements should be achieved bilaterally and multilaterally, at governmental and non-governmental levels, through intergovernmental and other agreements, international programs and cooperative projects. And by providing equitable opportunities for scientific research and for wider communication and travel necessary for professional purposes."

The word *equitable* was mine. I know that it does not have an exact equivalent in most other languages. As I recall, I referred to its dictionary definition as "fair, just and reasonable."

Further, the report states that: "It is furthermore considered necessary to state that respect for human rights and fundamental freedoms by all states represents one of the foundations for significant improvement of their mutual relations and of international scientific cooperation at all levels."

It was our understanding, Mr. Chairman, that those two statements in the report of the scientific forum constituted a statement of linkage between the strong endorsement of international cooperation in science and technology to be found in Basket II and the several profound statements concerning human rights and fundamental freedoms to be found in Baskets I and III. These several elements cannot, any longer, be discussed as issues apart because they are not issues apart—they are indissolubly linked.

Mr. Chairman, to American scientists the question of freedom of inquiry, freedom to write and publish, freedom to speak, to come and go across national borders, freedom to live where one's heart and conscience take one, are indissolubly bound to freedom of one's person. We cannot consider scientific communication as somehow distinct from other forms of human communication. We perceive no essential distinctions between pursuit of truth about the nature of man or of the physical universe and pursuit of truth about the human condition in the societies in which we live. We will continue to speak out for those whose rights have been denied, for the cost of silence is the abandonment of human rights, and that is a price we will not pay.

If I may quote a colleague: "Intellectual freedom is essential to human society—freedom to obtain and distribute information, freedom for open-minded and unfearing debate, and freedom from the pressure by officialdom and prejudices. Such a trinity of freedom of thought is the only guarantee against an infection of people by mass myths—freedom of thought is the only guarantee of the feasibility of a scientific democratic approach to politics, economy and culture." Mr. Chairman, those words were written by a foreign member of the National Academy of Science of the USA—Andrei Sakharov.

82

Soviet Scientific Exchanges Endorsed, by Oleh Zwadiuk.
Report by RFE correspondent, Washington,
November 20, 1980.

A group of American experts in the exchange and human rights fields says that private Soviet-American exchanges are a vital aspect of relations between the two countries and should not be altogether discontinued.

The recommendation appeared in a report issued by the Helsinki Watch Committee, a private American human rights group. It was based on a conference the committee sponsored in April attended by 27 experts "professionally concerned" with human rights and exchanges. It was issued to coincide with the Helsinki review conference currently underway in Madrid.

The conference was designed to discuss "developing common approaches for handling the broad range of human rights problems that have become a factor in the exchanges."

The conferees concluded, the report says, that Soviet science in most cases lags behind that of the U.S. and thus the exchanges in this field tend to be of greater benefit to Moscow. Nevertheless, they maintained, American scientists learned enough from their Soviet counterparts to justify continuation of the exchange programs "on purely scientific grounds."

Moreover, they said, "The exchanges are the United States Government's main source of information about the progress of Soviet science."

Other reasons mentioned in support of the endorsement were:

—Exchange programs in the social sciences and humanities have opened up areas of information previously unavailable to American scholars and they have contributed to American understanding of the Soviet Union.

—While the exchanges are not a panacea for speedy resolution of problems between the two superpowers, they do provide over the long-term "a viable medium for political accommodation" in making possible high-level informal contacts between Soviet and American delegates who have known each other over a period of years.

—The exchanges act as a lifeline to the Soviet dissident community. The conferees noted that Americans traveling to the USSR on exchange programs or officially sanctioned meetings often meet with Soviet colleagues who are dissidents. "These meetings are valuable sources of information for such persons who are often cut off from information about the latest developments in their professional fields and from news of friends and relatives in the outside world," they said.

—The conference participants also pointed out that cancellation of exchanges is contrary to the United States commitment to promote the free exchange of people and ideas. "Even though the Soviet Union has not adhered to this principle, it makes very little sense for the United States to respond by violation of its own principles," they said.

—Finally, the experts concluded that the exchanges can be used "as a lever to secure other concessions from Soviet officials or to express discontent over Soviet policies by temporarily reducing contact without abrogating existing exchange agreements."

The conferees noted that the U.S. is limited in its power to influence the Soviet Union. Nevertheless, they recommended "a pluralistic response" to Soviet abuses. They said that the more monolithic the American response the more likely it is to be perceived by the Soviet Union as "an officially orchestrated political propaganda by the United States Government."

The conferees said: "American actions which are seen by the Soviets as voluntaristic expressions of protest by private American organizations and individuals have the greatest impact."

83

Canadian Foreign Minister's Speech, by Mark MacGuigan.
Report by RFE correspondent Roland Eggleston,
Madrid, November 12, 1980.

The Canadian foreign minister, Mark MacGuigan, said tonight that "The shadow of Afghanistan" would chill détente as long as Soviet troops remained in that country.

He said the Afghan crisis could *not* be viewed as a purely local or regional issue or one which fell outside East-West relations.

MacGuigan said: "At a minimum, Soviet actions have challenged directly the principles in the Helsinki Final Act of sovereign equality, of refraining from the threat or use of force, inviolability of frontiers, the territorial integrity of states, non-intervention in internal affairs and equal rights and self-determination of peoples."

He pointed out that all the 35 states which signed the Helsinki accords had expressed their conviction that détente should be a comprehensive process, universal in scope.

They had agreed to refrain from the use of force against the territorial integrity or political independence of any state. They declared their intention to conduct their relations with all other states in the spirit of the principles of the Final Act. They had also expressed their common will to act in applying those principles in conformity with the purposes and principles of the Charter of the United Nations.

The Canadian Foreign Minister said, "History has taught us painfully that confidence and stability in one region of the world cannot remain unaffected by distrust and instability in another quarter of the globe.

"To ensure that confidence prevails in Europe, the participating states must accept that the same rules of conduct must apply elsewhere. In the absence of such an understanding, and of any clearly defined boundary between the pursuit of national interests and the practice of restraints, the policy that we have called détente will inevitably be undermined."

84

Egg and Figleaf, by *The Economist* (London), November 22, 1980, pp. 48–49.

"Don't look for any bones in an egg," said Mr. Leonid Ilyichov at the Madrid conference on Tuesday. Mr. Ilyichov was claiming that nobody need feel threatened by Russia. But his attempts to sweep aside the contrary evidence have been sadly unconvincing.

"The so-called Afghan problem," in his words, is no concern of the 35 governments represented at Madrid, and anyway the situation is "returning to normal"—a bizarre phrase to use about a country occupied by (but still resisting) a large Soviet army, where a puppet regime, installed after the killing of the head of state, is visibly both controlled and sustained by the invaders. Ilyichov has brusquely rejected western suggestions that the outlook for disarmament talks would be improved if the Russians withdrew from Afghanistan before the Madrid conference ends in March. On Monday the British representative urged him not to go on trying to cover up Russian embarrassment with the figleaf of claims that interference by other states was the sole cause of Afghanistan's woes. On Tuesday Mr. Ilyichov insisted on brandishing it again.

After two months of stone walling on procedural points, Russia's men at Madrid were obliged last week to allow this review conference on the 1975 Helsinki agreement actually to get on with reviewing the 35 governments' compliance with their 1975 promises. Since Russia has flagrantly violated those promises, in Europe as well as elsewhere, it is in for a sticky month. Its most familiar figleaf—the claim that its persecution of human-rights campaigners is a private affair which foreigners must not even comment on—has been blown away by the Helsinki agreement itself, which binds the 35 parties to meet periodically for "thorough" reviews of its implementation.

This week Mr. Ilyichov has been trying on a new figleaf. He now argues that Helsinki was not formally a treaty, so each signatory is free to flout its terms. This belated claim—more see-through than cover-up—sheds a curious light on the years of effort that Mr. Brezhnev put into bringing about the Helsinki agreement, and on the solemnity with which he personally signed that 25,000-word text, the fruit of long and arduous negotiation over the many specific commitments it includes. Has anybody dared to break the news to the Soviet president that his man in Madrid, driven desperate by finding himelf naked in the council chamber, has branded the whole thing as a huge and costly fraud?

Hands Off Poland

85

From Helsinki to Poland, by Vojtech Mastny.
*Newsletter, National Committee on American
Foreign Policy* 4, no. 1 (February 1981): 1–4.

Since World War II no event in Europe has evoked such a mixture of anxiety and hope as the recent Polish upheaval. By raising the specter of Soviet military intervention, with all its incalculable consequences for the East-West balance, the crisis has called into question the durability of the international order that, despite all its imperfections, has kept peace on the divided continent for a third of a century. The dramatic changes that have taken place in Poland have also opened up the prospect of a very different order resulting from the eventual demise of the Soviet empire—that affront to Europeans in an age of decolonization and national self-determination.

Détente took a turn for the worse almost immediately after Helsinki. It has continued to evaporate ever since. Six years later, the word détente, if used at all, is usually spoken of in the past tense. We know, or think we do, the reason for the West's disillusionment with that enticing but vague notion. The reasons for the Soviets' disillusionment are equally important. They may be summed up as the gradual distintegration of Moscow's Helsinki assumptions. This is not to suggest that the causes of the crisis are to be found solely or mainly in Europe. Enough developments elsewhere have nourished more conflict than European ones have produced. Nevertheless, from the Soviet point of view the evanescence of détente is primarily explicable by what has happened or failed to happen in Europe and in its eastern part especially.

To begin with, the coveted consolidation of Moscow's European domain did not take place. The ink had hardly dried on the Helsinki Final Act when its seemingly innocuous "Basket Three" provisions assumed political substance by giving impetus to dissent in Eastern Europe and in the Soviet Union itself. Since then repression has decimated opposition in some parts of the Soviet empire but not in others. In Poland riots flared up in 1976. Four years later, when individual dissent voiced by intellectuals merged for the first time with the mass discontent of workers, this cornerstone of the empire was shaken to its foundations.

The infusion of Western technology facilitated by détente has not succeeded in reversing declining growth rates and falling productivity in the Soviet Union and its dependencies. With few exceptions, inflation has increased, and the standard of living has declined. Russian leaders could take little comfort in the knowledge that the West was faced with many of the same problems, for the variety of strategies adopted by the West demonstrated its better capacity to cope with economic problems. In the Polish case, massive infusions of foreign funds not only failed to forestall but actually precipitated the crisis by exposing the regime's singular incompetence in putting the money to productive use. As a result, for the first time anywhere in the Soviet bloc economic change forced political change—an ominous development for its Marxist chiefs.

Beset by worsening internal problems, the Russians have also come nowhere near establishing themselves as the arbiters of Europe. Despite their apparent deftness, they have been unable to capitalize on the dissension that persists in the Western alliance. They failed to gain footholds in Western Europe, as evidenced especially by their aborted attempt to gain sway during the revolutionary turmoil in Portugal, where they overplayed their heavy hand. Among most Europeans, Moscow's resort to internal repression has generated revulsion rather than respect.

The Soviet Union's rising military power, superfluous by any reasonable standards, has not notably reduced its leaders' insecurity, the thrust of which continues to be internal rather than external. That insecurity has given birth to the appalling phenomenon of a runaway military machine in search of a purpose. Finding one in attempting to subjugate Afghanistan has been bad enough; finding another in Poland could be worse. In Sir John Hackett's fictitious but plausible account of a future World War III, the search for such a purpose triggered the war.

The Polish crisis has dramatized the peril looming in the shifting military balance. Theoretically, the balance can be redressed by applying the West's superior resources. But this countermeasure, although essential to stability, cannot alone ensure world order and can instead lead to the opposite condition by imposing on the Russians a timetable during which their putative military edge would have to be exploited lest it be forfeited. The challenge to Western statesmanship involves proceeding with the necessary alteration without putting any such timetable into effect.

As long as the Polish events follow their course without provoking the Red Army's intervention, they should provide the West with a respite by immobilizing a country vital to any forward Soviet strategy in Europe. Because of their involvement in Afghanistan and for too many other sound reasons, Soviet leaders have been inhibited from using force to discipline Poland. No matter how reluctantly, they have preferred to acquiesce in the imposition of effective constraints on the party's monopoly of power, even though such constraints have undermined the pillar on which their control of Eastern Europe has traditionally rested. In so doing, they have shown an ability to accommodate themselves, albeit under pressure, to the prospect that a radical transformation of their system of power may be inevitable.

Even though the West cannot claim the main credit for these momentous developments, which only the courage and the political acumen of the Polish workers have made possible, it possesses the means to influence their course on the economic, diplomatic, and moral levels. Some of the means are more readily available to America's European allies and nonaligned friends than to a superpower bearing the brunt of military competition with the Soviet Union.

By supplying Poland with some material assistance but not nearly enough to help it overcome its economic debacle, the Soviet Union has indicated that it expects the West to provide the necessary aid. This is a challenge and an opportunity that the United States, together with its allies, can best meet. The respective governments and bankers need to coordinate the further extension of credit to Poland by attaching the appropriate strings. By controlling the amount and the timing of the funds, they can help create in Poland the right conditions conducive to making the recent changes permanent. For example, they can insist on the participation of Polish union representatives in any negotiations conducted with the Warsaw government and make the aid dependent on specific economic reforms.

Unlike economic negotiations, efforts to deter the always possible Soviet intervention should proceed out of public sight. Through diplomatic channels, rather than by public proclamations, the United States and Western European governments can more effectively apprise Moscow of their intended responses—in specific rather than in general terms. Through such channels they can better persuade Soviet leaders that giving the Poles a chance will foster the interests of the Soviet Union as well.

The longer the trend in Poland remains uncertain, the greater will be the need for moral support, the limited but real effectiveness of which has been amply demonstrated by the aftermath of Helsinki. The tone of officially-sponsored broadcasts is an important measure of such support. By amplifying its private rather than by its governmental voices, the West can demonstrate that it is still committed to the values of freedom that the Poles are endeavoring to obtain. At issue is not any gratuitous promotion of instability in Soviet Eastern Europe. But neither should the West create the impression that it has acquired a vested interest in maintaining stability on Soviet terms alone.

The transformation of divided Europe since Helsinki has both increased the need and expanded the opportunities for deflecting the unavoidable East-West competition from potentially lethal military rivalry toward more rewarding nonmilitary pursuits. Even in the heyday of détente, Soviet leaders maintained that their brand of détente necessitates more vigorous political and ideological struggle. Since then the West has grown more capable of waging these struggles. Its capability can be translated into effective policies if it accepts the fact that the struggle may get worse before the prospects for a genuine détente can be realized.

86

French Delegate on the Polish Situation, by Benoît d'Aboville.
Report by RFE correspondent Roland Eggleston, Madrid,
December 17, 1980.

French delegate Benoît d'Aboville told the conference in Madrid today that the Polish situation proved the need for more and better military confidence-building measures in Europe.

"Many people have recently had their attention drawn to certain military movements in the heart of our continent," he said.

"According to the information we have obtained, a high number of divisions have been brought into play as well as the corresponding means of communication and command.

"Reservists have been called up, severe restrictions imposed and then lifted on the movements of accredited military attachés and missions. Units have been placed on a high alert.

"In short, we are led to believe that there is, objectively speaking, more going on than a series of small, successive and contiguous military maneuvers."

He said that all the talk and concern this had aroused proved conclusively the need for measures to increase confidence in Europe.

87

Afghanistan Is a Symbol Word, by Roland Eggleston.
Report by RFE correspondent, Madrid, April 3 and June 9, 1981.

Britain and France head those who believe that the invasion of Afghanistan should be brought to the fore again.

It should be realized that Afghanistan is a symbol word for the Western delegations in Madrid. It has become a cliché for them to say at press briefings that when they mention Afghanistan they are thinking of Poland. None of the Western spokesmen ever mention Poland by name during the conference sessions to avoid a confrontation which could be embarrassing for the Poles. But there is no attempt to hide where the interest really lies when debate turns to Afghanistan's sovereign rights and the violation of its frontier. . . .

Some Western and neutral delegates at the Helsinki follow-up conference in Madrid would like to have it well on its way toward a successful conclusion by the time the Polish party congress meets next month. They feel this would be a restraint on the Soviet Union.

Previously, Western delegates have said the conference should just be in session then in case of Soviet pressure on Poland during the Congress, which is scheduled to start on July 14.

But the head of one Western delegation told reporters today that "many of us now believe it would be better if the conference looked like being a success and close to agreement in areas favored by the Soviets, particularly if the agreement concerned the meeting on military security in Europe, which the Soviets want very badly. It would give them a stake in preserving the situation, or, put another way, it would give them something to lose if they did upset Poland."

Delegates from other Western countries and some neutral nations made the same point independently in separate talks with reporters. None of them wished to be identified.

All, however, stressed their recognition that if the Soviet Union did decide to intervene in Poland, it would not be dissuaded by concern about the reaction of the Madrid conference.

"If the USSR does do anything against Poland it will do so in the knowledge that it has burned its bridges with the West and the neutrals and the non-aligned for a long time," another Western delegation leader said. "The repercussions here in Madrid will just be a small part of an enormous reaction."

The Western and neutral delegates also said that informal discussions were going on about the value of holding the proposed military meeting in Poland, as the Warsaw Pact itself has suggested. It is felt the presence of a large number of Western, neutral and non-aligned delegations in Warsaw could act as a restraint on the Soviet Union.

The West generally favors a rival offer from Sweden to host the conference in Stockholm but some Western delegates believe it might help the Polish situation if the talks were convened in Warsaw instead.

88

We Are at a Critical Crossroads, by Alexander Haig.
Statement by U.S. Secretary of State, Madrid, February 9,
1982, in: *The Madrid CSCE Review Meeting* (Washington,
D.C.: Commission on Security and Cooperation in Europe,
1983), pp. 41–45.

We are at a critical crossroads in the postwar history of Europe. The first principles of the Helsinki Final Act are under attack. My purpose— and indeed the purpose of this conference—must be to defend the Act by speaking clearly about what is happening and why. For more than a year, the American delegation, ably directed by Ambassador Kampelman, has sought with others to build on the promise of the Helsinki Final Act. We have discussed our differences, and we have pursued new initiatives. Throughout, our purpose has been to strengthen security and cooperation in Europe. All of these efforts are now overshadowed by ominous events in the heart of Europe itself. The Polish people, whose destiny has always affected European security, are being denied their right to determine their own affairs. A forcible suppression of the Polish search for dignity in the workplace, for freedom, and for self-determination is underway. The generals of this war against the Polish people are none other than the Polish regime itself, acting under the instigation and coercion of the Soviet Union. How can these actions be reconciled with Polish and Soviet signatures on the Helsinki Accords?

Nothing endangers security and cooperation in Europe more than the threat and the use of force to deny internationally recognized rights. Nothing endangers the Helsinki Final Act and the Helsinki process more than this willful violation of solemn international obligation. We would be threatening the future peace of Europe if we ignored this dramatic attack on international principles.

Clearly, all countries interested in a more secure, united and open Europe—the work of this conference—have a responsibility to raise their voices here today. The American people, and other peoples as well, could never countenance a cynical attempt to place the Polish tragedy beyond the reach of the Helsinki Final Act. To the contrary, the Act justifies our concern and demands our protest. Put most simply the issue is whether we meant what we said in August of 1975.

In Principle I of the Final Act, the signatories said that the states had the rights to choose and develop their political, social, economic and cultural systems. Yet through intimidation and interference, the Soviet Union has conspired with the Polish military authorities to deprive Poland of this basic right.

In Principle II, the signatories said that participating states would refrain from the threat or use of force against the territorial integrity or political independence of any state. Yet Soviet and Warsaw Pact military demonstrations and the palpable fear of Soviet military intervention have been used to intimidate the Polish people in their search for reform.

In Principles IV and VI, the signatories said they would refrain from any action against the political independence of any other participating state and from any intervention in their internal or external affairs. Yet the Polish nation has been the victim of a long and vicious campaign. Official statements, some emanating from the highest levels of the Soviet Government, have warned of dire consequences if the Poles persisted in their pursuit of Polish solutions to Polish problems.

In Principle VII, the signatories said they would promote and encourage the effective exercise of civil, political, economic, social, cultural and other rights and freedoms. But the Polish military authorities, far from promoting and encouraging the exercise of these rights, are suppressing the most fundamental freedoms of the Polish People.

In Principle VIII, the signatories said they would respect the right of peoples freely to determine their political status, without external interference, and to pursue as they wished their political, economic, social and cultural development. Violation of this principle threatens the entire Final Act. Yet since the beginning of the reform movement in Poland, the Soviet Union has attempted systematically to deny the right of the Polish people to chart their own future.

In Principle X, the signatories said that "In exercising their sovereign rights, they will conform with their legal obligations under international law. . . ." The suppression of the civil and human rights of the Polish people violates the internationally recognized rights set forth in the U.N. Charter and the Universal Declaration of Human Rights, as well as the specific provisions of the Final Act.

What I have just described is the bill of rights which the Helsinki Final Act provided Western civilization. Thus, the Final Act sets forth basic standards by which to judge ourselves and each other. These principles were the product of laborious negotiations. They were solemnly undertaken. My own country's attitude was well expressed by President Ford, when he said: "We take this work and these words very seriously. We will spare no effort to ease tensions and solve problems between us. But it is important that you recognize the deep devotion of the American people and their government to human rights and fundamental freedoms and thus to the pledges that this conference has made. . . ."

We cannot accept the fallacious argument that legitimate security interests or alliance systems are threatened by a defense of the Helsinki principles. In fact, peaceful change is essential to any durable framework for security. No legitimate government is threatened by freedom and justice. Solidarity with the Polish people and our support for their rights are essential to the survival of the Helsinki process—and to our own self-respect.

—We look for the release from prison of those trade union leaders and others who seek to realize the objectives of the Helsinki Final Act for their people. Promises of good intentions or the mere movement of prisoners to model camps are not enough.

—We look for the lifting of martial law. This means the end of repressive conditions.

—We look for reconciliation in Poland. Restoration of internationally recognized rights and a resumption of the process of reform and liberalization provide the only basis for a constructive national dialogue, free from external coercion.

The American people, like those of so many lands, have a special and strong attachment to the people of Poland. No nation has suffered more, nor displayed such enduring courage. Relief from current oppression is not enough—the Polish people want more, need more, deserve more.

The United States has decided to join other concerned countries in offering a major program to help Poland overcome its economic problems, including agricultural shortages and massive external debt. This assistance will become available when the basic rights of the Polish people are restored and their quest for a more decent society resumed.

We will not aid tyranny. But if tyranny stand aside, we are ready to help. It is up to the Polish military regime and the Soviet Union to create and to maintain the conditions in which the Polish people can, with Western assistance, rebuild their economy.

As these conditions are restored, we also will be among the first to insist that we return to the job of reaching agreement on moving the Helsinki process forward in both the human rights and security areas. In the meantime, business as usual here at Madrid would simply condone the massive violations of the Final Act now occurring in Poland. These violations—part of a broader pattern of Soviet lack of restraint—threaten the very basis of this conference. We cannot pretend to build up the structure of peace and security here in Madrid while the foundation for that structure is being undermined in Poland. How can the United States return to negotiations on new words and new undertakings while existing obligations are being so blatantly ignored?

Confidence-Building and Disarmament

89

East and West Differ on CBMS, by Roland Eggleston.
Report by RFE correspondent, Madrid, December 3, 1980.

The Soviet Union, which pressed so hard for the Helsinki follow-up conference in Madrid to devote hours of debate to military security, now finds that it has walked into an ambush of its own making.

The West, led by the United States, Britain, Canada, Holland and West Germany, have criticized the Warsaw Pact's claims to have fulfilled the military security provisions in the Helsinki Final Act. Even neutral nations such as Austria and Switzerland have said the Warsaw Pact's performance is unsatisfactory.

Our correspondent in Madrid says the general tone of the criticism is that the Soviet Union and its allies have done no more than fulfill the minimum letter of the military accords in the Helsinki agreement. They have not honored the spirit.

The Helsinki Final Act contains only one major military confidence-building measure. That is that prior notification should be given of maneuvers involving 25,000 troops or more. In the case of the Soviet Union, notification has to be given only for maneuvers in border regions within 250 kilometers of another European country.

The Helsinki Final Act also suggests that countries conducting maneuvers could voluntarily invite foreign observers to watch them.

However, the Final Act also contains some recommendations which, it says, could strengthen confidence and increase security and stability. The most important point is that states can, if they wish, notify other countries of military maneuvers of less than 25,000 men. Another suggests that states can, at their own discretion, report other forms of major military movements.

In fact, since the Helsinki accords were signed in 1975, the Warsaw Pact nations have notified on only three maneuvers of less than 25,000 men. NATO nations have done so 20 times. Even the neutral and non-aligned participants in the Helsinki process have notified on a larger number of small-scale maneuvers than the Warsaw Pact.

The Warsaw Pact's boast that it had honored the call to voluntarily invite military observers to its maneuvers also got short shrift from non-Communist nations. It was pointed out that since the Helsinki Final Act was signed in 1975 the Warsaw Pact has invited observers to only seven of 13 major maneuvers. On the other hand, NATO has invited observers to a total of 22 large- and small-scale maneuvers.

Some of the countries invited to these Warsaw Pact maneuvers were scathing about the conditions. It was pointed out that NATO provides transport, binoculars, maps and detailed information and makes sure that the observers see actions of military significance.

In contrast, the Warsaw Pact provided few facilities and little information. Many delegates were particularly critical of the maneuvers which took place in the Soviet Union in July last year. They said there was a lot of travel, a lot of entertainment but less than four hours of actual observation of the maneuvers.

The observers also said they had a feeling they were watching staged demonstrations rather than actual exercise activity.

There was general agreement, not only from the West but also the neutral and non-aligned nations, on basic criteria for any new confidence-building measures.

The four major points which emerged are that the new measures must be binding on all signatories to the Helsinki Final Act and not voluntary, they must be of military significance, they must be verifiable and they must apply to all nations equally.

The last provision refers to the fact that the Soviet Union now only has to report maneuvers within 250 kilometers of its European borders. The non-Communist nations insist that it report maneuvers anywhere within the European part of the USSR.

In addition, most Western countries want a requirement to report maneuvers by as few as 10,000 men instead of the present 25,000. They also believe it would help European security if nations had to report all other out-of-garrison activity by troops. That includes movements of troops from one part of the country to another even when maneuvers are not involved.

The Soviet Union likes none of this. It argued this week that to make confidence-building measures mandatory instead of voluntary would involve a change in the wording of the Helsinki Final Act.

It also said the agreement in Helsinki to limit the Soviet Union's liability to report maneuvers only within 25 kilometers of its borders has been the result of a balance of interests. It said it would not accept any changes.

90

Six Proposals for a Meeting, by Roland Eggleston.
Report by RFE correspondent, Madrid, December 17, 1980.

Six proposals have been submitted to the Madrid conference from the West, the Warsaw Pact, the neutral and non-aligned nations, Sweden, Yugoslavia, and Romania. The general feeling in the conference hall is that sufficient support has been generated to hold a meeting on CBMS, although finding a compromise between the six proposals will not be easy.

The proposals range from a woolly, loosely-worded scheme put forward by Poland on behalf of the Warsaw Pact to much more specific proposals from France on behalf of the West. The proposals by the neutrals and non-aligned, Romania, and Sweden also contain very concrete suggestions on how military security could be improved in Europe through new confidence-building measures.

One major difference is that the paper put forward by France on behalf of the Western allies says that in future the Soviet Union should be obliged to report military maneuvers anywhere in its European territories. Under the Final Act signed in Helsinki in 1975 it only has to report those within 250 kilometers of its European borders. The Soviet Union and its allies have made clear in private conversations they will not accept this change.

The Warsaw Pact proposal, like some of the other proposals, says there should be two conferences, the first dealing with military confidence-building measures and the second with the limitation of military activity and the reduction of armed forces and armaments.

However, Western critics say the Warsaw Pact paper virtually brushes aside the first phase concerning confidence-building measures. It says they should reduce the danger of the outbreak of war in Europe but makes not one single concrete suggestion.

In contrast, the French paper makes definite suggestions for the dissemination of more information about military activities. So does the separate paper put forward by Romania on its own behalf and the paper submitted by the neutral and non-aligned nations.

The Romanian paper also calls for such detailed information about major military movements and wants both naval and air exercises included in the reporting process. It says European security would be helped if there were no multi-national maneuvers near the borders of other states.

Western delegates say the Romanian paper is carefully worded so that its implied criticisms of present procedures could be directed to either NATO or the Warsaw Pact. One of its other points calls for a freezing of military budgets until there is an agreement on their reduction and a ban on reinforcing troops on the territory of other European states.

The Yugoslav and Swedish papers are phrased in more general terms but also contain some interesting thoughts on new military confidence-building measures.

An important difference between the Western paper and most of the others is that the West is interested only in a meeting on strengthening confidence-building measures. There is no mention of this growing into a second conference on disarmament proper. The West feels there are already enough disarmament meetings in progress in Vienna and Geneva and little more would be achieved by holding one under the aegis of the Helsinki process.

91

Swedish Outline for a Disarmament Conference, by Carl-Johan Rappe. Statement by the head of Swedish delegation, Madrid, December 17, 1980. Politiska avdelningen, Enhet V, Ministry of Foreign Affairs, Stockholm.

SALT II is in deep trouble. Any renegotiation, supposing it is undertaken, is bound to be a lengthy process. TNF negotiations are at a very preliminary stage and are also likely to be most complicated and protracted. The MBFR-negotiations are struggling along on their eighth year without even a basic agreement on the numbers of troops involved.

There may be many reasons for this. One is, obviously, that in Europe as elsewhere military and defense interests carry greater weight than disarmament and peaceful settlements of disputes.

Another one, more fundamental and pervasive, is the lack of confidence between European States, between East and West. There is little reason to believe that the *peoples* of Europe today distrust each other. But the conflict of *ideologies* leads to suspicion and armaments beyond reasonable limits. And so action feeds counteraction. This pattern has been further complicated by recent events. Actual and threatened intervention in European and adjacent states have so much eroded confidence that one must look with anguish and despair at the possibilities of peace and disarmament.

But it is necessary to break out of this vicious circle of distrust and mounting confrontation and to demonstrate a new dedication and a new resolve to turn the tide.

This Conference offers one opportunity to do just this. Like most others, we believe that this meeting should decide on a detailed and concrete mandate for a Conference on Disarmament in Europe whose primary task would be to rebuild political confidence, to enhance security and, subsequently, to move towards arms limitation and reduction agreements. This is the gist of the document which Sweden has just circulated.

As can be seen from the Swedish proposal, it envisages a two phase conference, the first of which would concentrate on negotiating developed and enlarged CBM's and the second of which would deal with disarmament proper.

Mr. Chairman, the measures we have in mind should be seen as extended and enlarged measures as compared to the "first generation" CBM's of the Final Act for which we and other neutral and non-aligned States have already, at this meeting, proposed improved provisions. For instance, whereas our NN-proposal contains a specified and realistic measure for the notification of major military movements, we conceive in the present Swedish proposal of further developed similar measures with more specified and militarily significant parameters to be negotiated during the first phase of the Conference.

I want to stress further that we consider it difficult, not to say erroneous, to attempt to discuss CBM's in complete isolation from the prevailing or developing armaments situation in Europe. Whereas it can be argued that no disarmament is possible in a climate of distrust and that therefore CBM's must come first, it is equally difficult to imagine that CBM's can be negotiated and agreed without taking into account the armaments situation and the ongoing military competition in Europe. The two questions are closely interlinked and must both receive attention already during the first phase of the Conference. We agree, however, that the negotiating stress should be on CBM's.

In order to indicate, not least to our public opinion, that our efforts have an intention somewhat commensurate with the problems at hand, Sweden further considers it indispensable to spell out clearly that, in a second phase, the Conference would take up disarmament proper for negotiation, both in relation to conventional and, as appropriate, to nuclear weapons. We realize that any second phase must depend on progress in the first and we appreciate that certain nuclear matters are not likely to be treated in a 35-state context. The deployment and use of nuclear weapons are, however, of direct concern to all these states and are, therefore, certainly a matter to which they would have a right to address themselves in a European context.

I hasten to add that Sweden has no intention of upsetting other negotiations in these fields. We think it desirable, however, that, already during the first phase, Conference participants be empowered to exchange views on nuclear and conventional arms limitation and reduction in Europe and to express their opinions on the course of substantive negotiations in other fora.

During the second phase, which would not be likely to take place until a few years hence, the Conference will thus begin substantive negotiation on conventional forces and, as possible and relevant, also on nuclear weapons in Europe or aimed at it. It would, of course, be our hope and presumption that by that time MBFR, which would then have passed its tenth year, and perhaps TNF would have yielded first results. At that point it would appear logical and desirable to move the brunt of such negotiations to the wider forum of a Conference on Disarmament in Europe.

92

The United States Supports French Proposal, by Max M. Kampelman. Speech by the head of U.S. delegation, Madrid, February 16, 1981. In Max M. Kampelman, *Three Years at the East-West Divide* (New York: Freedom House, 1983), pp. 30–32.

On February 11, the United States in this plenary discussed aspects of European military security as that issue has been reflected in our discussions here and in the security proposals before us. As I noted then, it had been a constant desire of my government to expand and strengthen military confidence-building measures as a way of attaining that security we seek. But efforts to build confidence have floundered, and for good reason. Efforts to build confidence are greatly hindered if there is a weak underlying foundation of confidence to build upon. And, as has been noted here often, by us and by others, this underlying confidence has been severely damaged by actions of the Soviet Union in recent months and years.

A few here have argued that under these circumstances, our common interests are best served by beginning with CBMS of little significance—with voluntary measures or measures which cannot or will not be verified. The argument is made that such CBMS would be at least again a start; and that we can move on later to more significant measures.

My government disagrees. We join with many other participating states here who are convinced that unless this meeting mandates a negotiation with specific and firm criteria, those who dislike effective CBMS will keep us talking about words, about vague declarations, and about pious but meaningless pronouncements for generations to come; and all without coming to grips with the basic requirements for real security. For our part, we cannot depend upon security by pronouncement, by declaration, or by promise—unless those pronouncements involve specific obligations, unless we can be assured that those declarations will be honored, and unless there are means to verify that what has been promised will be done.

We have the opportunity starting here in Madrid and within our CSCE process to explore the new and promising field of confidence-building measures. Because this field is new, we must be sure to structure our discussions carefully. Because we are interested in genuine arms control, we view laxness and imprecision as contrary to our purposes and counterproductive to confidence building. And we will absolutely not lend our support in this meeting to a cosmetic and meaningless negotiation.

It was this clear requirement that any negotiations be carefully structured to make a real contribution to security that led the administration of President Reagan to give intensive and detailed study to RM.7, the proposal of France for a Conference on the Military Aspects of Security in Europe.

I would like now to describe to this plenary meeting the critical elements in our consideration.

First of all, the French proposal prescribes a mandate for a post-Madrid meeting which will focus discussion on confidence-building measures that are of true military significance. It is clear that measures which are not "militarily significant"—which would not deal effectively with military activities that could threaten the security of other states—are the kinds of cosmetic proposals that would contribute nothing to security and might well detract from it.

Second, the mandate in RM.7 calls for "provisions ensuring appropriate verification of commitments." Effective verification has been at the heart of the American approach to every arms control negotiation we have undertaken since World War II. We, therefore, agree with the emphasis which this proposal gives to verification. All forces in Europe must be covered, including, of course, our own. And I want to note here, in connection with some misleading comments and implications made by some delegations, that, outside the complete European area proposed to be covered by the French proposal, many more Soviet than American forces would be *exempted* from coverage.

Third, RM.7 places a strong political obligation on all the participants reliably to implement the confidence-building measures. We all know from our own experience regarding the implementation of discretionary measures that any new measures must be founded on a commitment to this full and consistent implementation, or they simply will not be lived up to.

Fourth, the French proposal lists specific categories of confidence-building measures to be examined or negotiated. We believe it concentrates attention on the three areas where productive results are most likely: on measures of information on the strength and positioning of the military forces of the parties; on measures to increase stability, such as by more stringent and precise prenotification of military activities of immediate security concern to the rest of Europe; and on measures of observation and verification. Moreover, a separate post-Madrid conference, as France proposes, would seem to provide the best forum for effective consideration of these measures.

Fifth, the French proposal will make confidence-building measures to ". . . strengthen confidence . . . and thus contribute to increasing stability and security in Europe." This statement means all of Europe, including the European areas of the Soviet Union. It makes no sense to us that CBMS should exempt some portions of Europe. CBMS will not build confidence if they ignore large portions of the European Soviet Union, where there are considerable military forces which have a direct and immediate potential threat to security in Europe.

Sixth, RM.7 clearly establishes a link between a post-Madrid conference and the CSCE process. It states that measures agreed at the conference would be referred to the next CSCE follow-up meeting. This procedure is indispensable for the continued vitality of the CSCE process, which must not be bypassed.

Finally, the French proposal specifies that further steps in the arms control area will be considered only after we have had the opportunity to evaluate the results of the CBM negotiation and to review other developments in the arms control field. We consider this course to be in the best interest of genuine security. The need is to concentrate on achieving a successful CBM outcome; we must not be distracted from the important immediate task of building confidence by diversionary attempts to lay out plans for a vague second phase sometime in the future in an atmosphere and under conditions we cannot now foresee.

Mr. Chairman, careful consideration of all the factors I have just cited has led my government to one conclusion: President Reagan has resolved to commit the full support of the United States government to the French proposal, RM.7. We support it because it offers the prospect of serious and productive negotiations to achieve security in Europe.

We stand with France and the many others here who have joined in opposing a post-Madrid security meeting unless it is determined in advance that there will be serious negotiations. For us this means negotiation of militarily significant, verifiable confidence-building measures applicable to all of Europe with a high degree of political obligation. To accept less than these criteria would be to fail to serve the interests of true security.

There is one additional criterion which cannot be included in a formal mandate, but it is important nonetheless. This is the criterion of balance. CSCE cannot survive in the future solely as a security negotiation. The genius of the Final Act is its recognition that true security depends upon a balance of progress on security, on human rights, and on economic cooperation. The post-Madrid conference on CBMS, as outlined in RM.7, is, as our French colleagues have pointed out, inherently linked to CSCE. This means that the progress we contemplate in the security area must be matched by significant steps forward in the other areas of CSCE if balance is to be maintained.

Mr. Chairman, recent occurrences have made progress on security a much more difficult task than it seemed only a few years ago. We all know the reasons for this; and we know where the responsibility lies. In this situation, we strongly believe that the burden of performance must be on those who have disturbed the peace and damaged the atmosphere of international trust. The French proposal offers an opportunity to discharge this burden, because it is designed to make more difficult the use of military power for intimidation or aggression. And it is designed to increase warning of surprise attack in Europe.

THE MADRID ACHIEVEMENT

A Struggle for Hearts and Minds

93

Three-Way Battle in Madrid, by Kenneth L. Adelman.
Christian Science Monitor, September 9, 1980.

Just what the world needs now—another arena for conflict. Madrid is the spot as delegates from 35 nations arrive in sunny Spain today (September 9) to plan for the review of the Helsinki accords. But the real battles open on November 11 and will be three-dimensional—between East and West, between the US and its allies, and among the US participants. However bitter the clashes become, the final outcome may well be salutary.

First the East-West dimension. When the accords were signed in 1975, the Soviets instantly pocketed their prize—moving to legitimize the postwar frontiers. But the West has had to keep collecting on its rewards—furthering human rights within signatory countries and human contact between them. Since then, however, the collecting has become tougher with increasing repression in the East and the squalid Soviet invasion of Afghanistan.

This year the US and West prepare for Madrid while their leaders are running for reelection against hard-line opponents. Propelled by such domestic politics as well as by the international climate, by President Carter's personal commitment to human rights, and by congressional pressure, the American delegation is certain to talk tough. Note the splendid appointments of ex-Attorney General Griffin Bell and Max Kampelman, a leading light of the Committee on the Present Danger, to head up the US team.

The Soviets are clearly worried, as there is much that is tough to talk about, including the imprisonment or exile of at least 43 Soviet monitors of the Helsinki accords. And the beat goes on: 75-year-old Oksana Meshko, mother of a political prisoner and survivor of Stalin's gulag, was recently shoved into a psychiatric ward. The Soviets tremble over many such tales getting out of Madrid into the USSR via foreign broadcasts. As the Marquis de Custine remarked 150 years ago after visiting there, "One word of truth hurled into Russia is like a spark landing in a keg of powder."

Afghanistan looms as a large topic in Madrid. The Soviet invasion violates at least half of the 10 principles in the Helsinki Final Act. Sensing vulnerability, the Soviets strive to divert attention towards a spanking new "Conference on Military Détente" in which to regurgitate a dollop of tired old proposals.

Western Europeans also wish to tilt from human rights perorations to security talk preparations. This is the second skirmish: between the US and its allies, who share *Le Monde*'s concern (August 1) that "Washington intends to turn the Madrid conference into a trial." Their diplomats spurn even naming countries which violate human rights, while American delegates plan also to name specific persons whose rights have been so violated.

The third clash is among the Americans. Henry Kissinger called for boycotting this gathering as the US did the Olympics, and Ronald Reagan expressed his own "uneasy feeling." He said, "If the athletes can't go, why should the diplomats go?"

Unlike the Olympics, though, this get-together cannot glorify the Russians either as hosts or as winners. This is a field open to clear Western victory. And what better arena than Spain where democracy flourishes, as in Portugal and Greece, after years of dictatorship? The reversibility of authoritarianism, so fresh in the air of Spain, is inconceivable to Soviet-dominated Czechoslovakia since 1968, Hungary since 1956, etc.

Other Americans wish to go, but to go gingerly. Alas, this is the quintessential approach of the State Department, which clings to the remnants, nay to the memory, of détente. Its European bureau, honchoing the Madrid meeting, reeks of clientism; it parrots the Europeans on major points. Besides, diplomats seek concrete accomplishments— lengthy communiqués, detailed agreements, commitments for more and more meetings—as their profession's prime product. These accrue from quiet, classical diplomacy.

But a conference need not produce tangibles to be successful, as the superb congressional Helsinki commission well realizes. Madrid should serve the West firstly as a ritual, a reminder of individual rights and of the shared values that bind a citizen to a country and to a larger community of free peoples. Anthropologists know the value of rituals; diplomats should learn.

Second, by striking the contrast between free and totalitarian societies, Madrid can bolster public awareness of the treasures at home and the threats at hand. This is particularly critical in Western Europe, whose press covers the Helsinki process in greater depth and whose citizens are more reluctant to augment defense than those in the US.

Third, the Madrid meeting helps those shorn of freedom. From banishment in Gorky, Nobel laureate Sakharov on August 11 smuggled another message past the KGB to urge that the West go to Madrid and fight vigorously. Helsinki is the repository of dissidents' hopes and has spawned private human rights groups—the Charter '77 group in Czechoslovakia, the now-prominent Workers Defense Committee in Poland, and the Helsinki watch committees in the Soviet Union. They work more courageously, more continually, and perhaps over time more effectively than anything Westerners can muster.

Lastly, Madrid can have an exhilarating impact for Americans. With the Vietnam war behind us and Iran and Afghanistan upon us, there burns a fiery pro-Americanism that cries out for manifestation. As the first post-détente conference of consequence, Madrid can nudge the emerging consensus—in tone if not in policy—that Americans face the Soviet challenge without illusions, all the while exuding pride rather than shame and extolling our virtues rather than fuzzing them.

94

Why We Negotiate about Words, by Max M. Kampelman.
Speech by the head of U.S. delegation, Madrid, July 18, 1983.
In Max M. Kampelman, *Three Years at the East-West Divide*
(New York: Freedom House, 1983), pp. 122, 124.

A first-page editorial in the July 14 issue of *Pravda* sharpens for us not only the real meaning of the Madrid agreement, but its decided limitations as well.

The editorial's theme is the speech made to the June plenum of the Communist Party Central Committee by the leader of the Soviet Union, during which he said: "There is a struggle for the hearts and minds of billions of people on this planet." Concerned that the U.S.S.R. may not be doing too well in that struggle, *Pravda* urges that Soviet citizens be "immunized" against hostile ideas. Specifically, it aims at religion in the U.S.S.R. as a danger.

The United States understands the profound seriousness of the inherent contradictions between the Soviet totalitarian system and the system of liberty and individual dignity which is a hallmark of democratic governments. Reaching agreements such as we did in Helsinki and now in Madrid, do not, by themselves, automatically minimize those differences or end the competition.

We intend to be in the competition for "hearts and minds" to which *Pravda* refers. We welcome a competition of ideas and values. In many ways the Madrid forum has been and remains a vehicle for that competition. What concerns us deeply, however, is that the Soviet Union may believe that it cannot win a competition of ideas and values without the threat and use of armed force and repression, both within and outside its borders.

The Helsinki Final Act and the Madrid agreement are efforts to channel the competition of values within civilized constraints, and at the same time to strive for understanding so that we can learn to live with one another in peace. The fact that these agreements continue to be violated, even during this very period of negotiation and agreement, is discouraging.

Our delegation believes in the importance of words. But we cannot permit an agreement on words to obfuscate unpleasant realities.

We have sought and welcome the agreement represented by our decision in Madrid. We do not wish to minimize the importance of that agreement. But we also do not wish to minimize the consequence of undermining such agreements when they are not complied with in letter and in spirit.

The question might well be asked, therefore, and many in my country understandably ask, why do we negotiate about words? Why do we seek to forge a concluding document? Why do we enter into an agreement at a time when the repression of human beings in the Soviet Union is greater than at any time since the Helsinki accords were signed in 1975?

Mr. Chairman, it is because the pursuit of peace is too vital, the need for understanding too indispensable, the importance of the Helsinki accords too great to permit us to be discouraged by the task or by the obstacles we face.

We are convinced that the Helsinki Final Act has within it a formula for peace which is indispensable in this age of potential nuclear devastation. It is our conviction, furthermore, that unless these principles are taken seriously, the accords will become historically irrelevant. We, therefore, continue to express ourselves on this issue, even during these closing days of our meeting, in order to help mobilize a wider moral and political insistence upon universal respect for the Act by compliance with its provisions. Anything less threatens the integrity of our process and of our relations with it.

95

Getting Out of Yalta, by Max M. Kampelman.
Speech by the head of U.S. delegation, Madrid, March 12,
1982. In Max M. Kampelman, *Three Years at the East-West
Divide* (New York: Freedom House, 1983), pp. 89–90.

A few days ago the distinguished head of the Yugoslav delegation made an impressive talk here, a portion of which made an important contribution to this discussion. In referring to the Yalta Agreement, he said that the Helsinki Final Act establishes a principle which rejects the notion of "spheres of influence." On New Year's Day, President Mitterrand of France in a similar message stated that it was time to consider "getting out of Yalta."

Historians frequently refer to the "myth" of Yalta. They say that to equate Yalta with spheres of influence is to misread history. The Yalta Agreement was based on the assumption that the peoples of Eastern Europe were to be guaranteed free elections so that they might choose their own governments and those governments would then be free to select their own alliances. That did not take place.

The partition of Europe along predetermined lines cannot and should not become a permanent part of our geopolitics. The myth of Yalta, together with its concomitant so-called "Brezhnev Doctrine" is a danger to peace. It stands in the way of necessary peaceful change and can only, if it remains, produce later upheavals which will threaten our stability, in the East as well as in the West. Change will come. Its winds will reach us as inevitably as do the winds of the seasons. It will come to the East as it comes to all of us, because life requires change. The great challenge is whether that change can come peacefully.

96

The Challenge of the Helsinki Process, by George Shultz.
Address by U.S. Secretary of State, Madrid, September 9, 1983,
Current Policy No. 508, Bureau of Public Affairs,
Department of State.

Experience has shown that no wall is high enough, no jamming station strong enough, to keep out ideas or to keep down the hopes of men and women who yearn for freedom. The division of Europe is today, as it always was, unnatural and inhuman. Therefore, the attempt to keep Europe divided by raw power is inevitably a source of instability. There can be no lasting security or cooperation in Europe as long as one government is afraid of its own people and seeks reassurance in imposing a system of force on its people—and on its neighbors.

In the most profound sense, the Helsinki process represents an historic effort to erode the cruel divisions between East and West in Europe. It is an effort that must continue because it embodies the most basic interests, deepest convictions, and highest hopes of all the peoples of Europe.

No Business As Usual

97

The CSCE's Worst Crisis, by Roland Eggleston.
Report by RFE correspondent, Munich, January 27, 1982.

The imposition of martial law in Poland in December, 1981, faced the Madrid conference with its worst crisis.

Martial law was declared on December 13, just as the neutral and non-aligned delegations were circulating a draft of a final document which they hoped East and West would accept as the best compromise possible, allowing the conference to end quickly after the Christmas recess.

These hopes died as civil liberties in Poland were suspended and its trade unionists and human rights activists hustled into detention camps. The final session before the adjournment, on December 18, heard harsh denunciations of martial law from France, Britain, West Germany and Belgium.

With the details of the oppression in Poland still sketchy, the then-head of the Spanish delegation, Javier Rupérez, a diplomat whose career had included a posting in Warsaw, warned in an emotional speech that: "What has happened in Poland is not an internal matter of that country. It has repercussions for peace in Europe and the world."

The chief American negotiator, Max Kampelman, put the blame on the Soviet Union and demanded that the Soviets honor the principles of the Helsinki Final Act pledging non-intervention in the affairs of another participating state and the non-use of either force or the threat of force.

Kampelman said these pledges had to be honored "so that Poland, that proud country, may strive successfully to resolve its problems and decide upon its destiny without further violence and bloodshed."

Under strong pressure from the Swiss and the Austrians, the neutral and non-aligned group agreed at a two-day meeting in Vienna this week that the debate on the Polish crisis was necessary because it was more than just a domestic issue.

98

Western Disagreements, by Michael B. Wall.
Report by RFE correspondent, Bonn, February 2, 1982.

A week before the resumption of the Madrid conference, West Germany and the United States have differing views on how to proceed.

The resumption of the Madrid meeting itself is not at issue. Both Bonn and Washington intend to use the first week to loudly protest the continuing suppression of human rights in Poland. The differences concern the approach to take toward the Madrid meeting thereafter. In a nutshell, American and West German sources in Bonn both say, the United States has suggested that the meeting be suspended until the autumn while the West Germans want it to continue now. Other countries are involved on both sides of the discussion, but it has come to be symbolized as one between Bonn and Washington, perhaps because they have taken very different approaches to the entire Polish situation.

The West Germans tend to give special emphasis to all East-West contacts, especially—as they often say—in times of crisis. They also want the Madrid meeting to agree on a concrete mandate for a European disarmament conference that would discuss confidence-building measures for all of Europe, including the Soviet Union up to the Urals.

Bonn places great value on the entire European security conference process. The West Germans point out that the civil rights activists in Eastern Europe have all cited the Helsinki agreement, and they think this contributes towards liberalization in Eastern Europe. They also say that keeping Madrid going provides a handy forum for complaining directly to Warsaw and Moscow about developments in Poland. Genscher has said Moscow should not be relieved of the responsibility for implementing the Helsinki agreement.

The Americans, on the other hand, say the repression in Poland makes a mockery of the Helsinki agreement. Their argument is that there is little point in continuing with Madrid if that repression goes on. American sources also say it would be wrong just to return to business as usual after having complained about Poland. They argue that such a seemingly cynical approach would run the risk of undermining public support for the Helsinki process.

99

An Extraordinary Spectacle, by Roland Eggleston.
Report by RFE correspondent, Madrid, February 9, 1982.

Foreign ministers from virtually all Western, neutral and non-aligned countries, including United States Secretary of State Alexander Haig, arranged to go to Madrid to show their outrage at the repression in Poland.

But the Warsaw Pact had its own plans. It was determined to hinder the foreign ministers' initiative and its efforts to do so produced one of the most extraordinary spectacles ever witnessed at an international conference.

By one of those chances which create good drama, the previously-arranged schedule had made Poland's Włodzimierz Konarski the chairman for the opening session of the resumption. Twenty-one speakers were scheduled, among them 13 Western and neutral foreign ministers, including Haig.

The session began as usual shortly after 1100. The conference heard a barrage of criticism of events in Poland from Haig and the foreign ministers of Canada, Belgium, Italy and West Germany.

At 1330 Konarski banged his gavel on the table. It was the usual time for the lunch break. But instead he announced he was ending the session for the day. Only eight of those on the list had spoken—the non-Westerners being Hungary, the Soviet Union and Poland itself.

This announcement provoked uproar. Shouts and jeers rang across the hall. Among the angriest was French foreign minister Claude Cheysson, who had been about to speak when the Pole imposed the guillotine.

Konarski banged his gavel again. He sought to justify himself by saying that before the recess the delegates had agreed to a morning meeting on the first day of the new session but had not mentioned an afternoon one. When Ireland tried to rectify this with a proposal that all speakers on the list be allowed to have their say, the Soviet Union and Czechoslovakia refused consensus, saying it would change the rules.

The argument raged on for seven hours, with the West refusing to grant consensus to end the meeting and the Warsaw Pact refusing to permit it to carry on. The session finally ended when the chief Austrian negotiator, Franz Ceska, whose years of experience in the Helsinki process had earned him special respect from East and West, persuaded both sides to adjourn for the night. The French foreign minister stormed out telling reporters the whole performance had been "shameful and comic." The Swiss foreign minister, who had also been prevented from speaking, described it as a circus.

The Norwegian foreign minister, Svenn Stray, drew applause from Western and neutral delegates tonight by saying that "You people of Eastern Europe, I tell you you will never with all your tactics be able to silence the voice of the free world."

And nothing was gained by the Communist tactics. Those who had been prevented from speaking by the Polish chairman were able to do so the next day when Portugal, a NATO country, was in the chair. And more Western and neutral foreign ministers had their say later in the week.

100

Attempts to Adjourn, by Roland Eggleston.
Report by RFE correspondent, Madrid,
February 10 and 16, 1982.

The Soviet Union and its allies would like the conference to return to discussing a final document summarizing all that has been done in the past 14 months in Madrid. It keeps pressing the virtues of the draft final document presented by the neutral and non-aligned nations just before the Christmas recess. Conveniently forgotten are the criticisms of the neutral paper which were heard at the time it was presented.

But the draft document is aimed at improving the human rights provisions in the Helsinki Final Act, at allowing more freedom of information and at helping family reunification.

One of the authors of the paper, Switzerland, told the heads of delegations meeting today that it could not sign its own document while the situation remains as it is in Poland. If Switzerland feels that way, it makes the Soviet Union and its allies appear ludicrous as they try to pretend that the conference can discuss the paper in a business-as-usual atmosphere.

The lead in the moves for an early closure is being taken by Switzerland, one of the strongest supporters of the Helsinki process. It believes that the imposition of martial law in Poland has done serious damage to the international atmosphere and for the meeting to continue in such an atmosphere can only damage the Helsinki process. Its foreign minister, Pierre Aubert, said today that Switzerland's belief that the talks should recess had been given a new impetus by what he called yesterday's spectacle." . . . The Austrians, Finns, Swedes, Maltese and Cypriots told reporters they could not agree to the Swiss initiative calling for an immediate recess because the angry tone of the debate in Madrid was damaging the Helsinki process. They said they believed the discussions should continue for a few more weeks. In the circumstances, the Swiss have apparently dropped their plan to present a formal motion on a recess.

The problem now is going to be what to talk about in the coming weeks. The head of the American delegation, Max Kampelman, made clear today that if the meeting does continue for a few more weeks the United States will make these weeks as uncomfortable as possible for the Soviet Union.

101

The Eloquent Silences, by Roland Eggleston.
Report by RFE correspondent, Madrid, March 2 and 5, 1982.

The chief U.S. delegate, Max Kampelman, told Western correspondents on March 1 that there would be no normal negotiations regardless of how long the Soviet Union kept the conference in session.

Kampelman said the West was determined that at the twice-weekly plenary sessions it would speak only about the situation in Poland or about Soviet violations of the Helsinki Final Act. And it would say nothing at the other meetings, which are theoretically supposed to discuss the draft final document. This has been the Western attitude since this phase of the Madrid conference resumed three weeks ago and he said nothing would change it.

He went out of his way to emphasize that the West was united in this strategy even if not all members of NATO took an active part by speaking in the plenaries. He said all Western countries agreed with the basic tactic and it also enjoyed the support of many of the neutral and non-aligned nations. . . . Instead of agreeing, as on every other Friday, to a schedule of meeting for next Monday, Tuesday and Wednesday the West on March 5 declared it would not accept any more sessions of the so-called drafting committee. It said it would agree only to a schedule of plenary meetings.

The drafting committee is the sole survivor of all the working groups which used to exist at the conference. Its theoretical task is to negotiate an agreement on a final document. But in practice it has done nothing since the Madrid conference resumed nearly a month ago after the Christmas recess.

The West has refused to negotiate in the thrice weekly sessions of the committee as part of its protest against the imposition of martial law in Poland. All the Western states attend the meetings but simply sit there in silence.

In a typical session, the Soviet Union and some of its allies—particularly Bulgaria and Czechoslovakia—begin with a demand for negotiations. The West sits in silence. Possibly one of the neutral and non-aligned, usually Malta, makes a one minute statement about how something should be done. Then there is silence again and the meeting breaks up.

On March 5 the West told the Soviet Union that this situation was going to continue and so there was no point in scheduling any more meetings of the drafting group. The Soviet Union, of course, refused to accept the Western demand. It said it would never accept a schedule made up only of plenaries. It insisted that the drafting committees not only be retained but in fact increased in number.

That is where the situation rested late this afternoon. Our correspondent says that no one is sure how it will be resolved.

Theoretically, unless there is agreement on more meetings, today's session could go on indefinitely until some sort of agreement was reached on how to end it.

In practice, this session will probably reach an agreed end after a few hours. But the West feels that it will have made its point.

It is telling the Soviet Union that unless there is an agreement on a recess, the West will adopt similar tactics the next time the schedule has to be arranged.

Another purpose of today's demonstration was to reaffirm in a dramatic fashion the West's refusal to join negotiations on a draft document. Diplomats said there had been signs that the Soviet Union thought the West's unity on this point was weakening. Today was intended to dispel any such illusions.

102

The West Wins Recess, by Jan Sizoo and Rudolf Th. Jurrjens.
In Jan Sizoo and Rudolf Th. Jurrjens, *CSCE Decision-Making:
The Madrid Experience* (The Hague: Nijhoff, 1984),
pp. 203–8.

The NATO caucus had considered what the consequences would be if by the end of the last day of the week, 5 March, no agreement had been reached on the program of work for the following week. Would it mean the end of the Madrid Meeting? The answer was: no. The Madrid Meeting had been set up by consensus in Belgrade and could only be terminated by another consensus. Without this the conference would go on forever, with or without the grid. In Belgrade the practice had been that if a Plenary failed to reach agreement on the work program for the following days it would meet again on the next working day in order to continue discussing the program.

The Plenary session which began on 5 March was chaired by the Czechoslovakian representative, in response to whose enquiry the Swiss delegate had to reply that no agreement on a work program had yet been reached in the corridors of the building. After the representatives who had put their names on the speakers' list had spoken (the main theme was once more developments in Poland), at the beginning of the afternoon, again the Swiss delegate had to report that still nothing had been agreed in the corridors on the program of the next week, and as far as he could see there was no prospect of agreement. This led to the first silence: despite appeals from the chairman none of the delegations was prepared to come forward with concrete proposals for a work program. The Maltese representative finally drew the conclusion that the Plenary ought to be closed, and reassemble on the next working day to continue discussing the work program. To this the Soviet delegate immediately replied that there was no reason why the discussion on a grid should not begin at once, for as long as there was no work program there was also no fixed time and date for the next Plenary. The coffee-break which followed brought no improvement: no-one would budge. After the coffee-break there was a further long silence which led the chairman to propose yet another coffee-break. The GDR then proposed going on with the work program of the past week which would mean that there would be two Drafting Group meetings, whereupon the Belgian representative (Belgium was President of the Ten) proposed a work program consisting exclusively of two meetings of the Plenary.

A verbal battle now followed between some East European representatives and the West over whether the Purple Book required the work program to include a Drafting Group meeting or not. There was at this time only one Drafting Group, set up in December 1981 to replace all the Drafting Groups which had been instituted according to the Purple Book a year earlier. The Soviet delegate claimed that the present Drafting Group was legal successor to the Drafting Groups referred to in the final paragraph of article 4 of the Purple Book and these had been given the explicit task of assisting the Plenary in drafting the concluding document of the Meeting. Now the Plenary was still officially occupied with item 8 on the agenda: "drafting of a concluding document," and the

Plenary had no right to dispense with the Drafting Group until all its item 8 work was completed. A work program with no Drafting Group was subversive of the Purple Book and the CSCE in general, for to liquidate this group would be a blow to any prospects of adopting a substantive concluding document. Western delegations replied by observing that the Drafting Groups referred to in the Purple Book had long ceased to exist and the Plenary, as the main body of the Meeting, was entitled to organize its own work and to decide for itself whether or not it needed the assistance of a Drafting Group.

After a silence and yet another coffee-break (during which the NATO caucus decided to go on keeping silent) East European delegations repeated their arguments but, in the absence of any reactions from the West, were forced to come to a halt. The silence which followed was broken by the representative of Malta: "Procedures have already been seen to have political implications but now keeping silent has also acquired political meaning. We just sit, and look, and stare! Another coffee-break? Even coffee-breaks are no more use." Nevertheless a coffee-break followed and directly after it the Maltese once more put his view that the meeting ought to be closed and reconvened on the next working day, which was Monday, following Belgrade practice in cases when agreement on a work program had not been reached. To this, however, the Soviet delegation now explicitly refused its consent; it was determined to hold out against closure of the session as long as no consensus was forthcoming for the GDR delegation's proposal for a program including two meetings of the Drafting Group. In doing this the Soviet delegation took up a position opposite to the one it had occupied on 9 February for it now recognized a consensus as necessary for the closure rather than the continuation of the meeting.

When midnight had passed another problem arose. Was the Czechoslovakian representative, who was the current chairman, to make way for the next day's chairman who was from the Turkish delegation? He did not do so. In Belgrade, if meetings went on for long, beyond midnight, it had been the custom for the chairman sometimes to remain in office and sometimes to change, according to the meeting's consensus. On this occasion the Czechoslovakian did not find it necessary to follow the "daily rotation" rule from the Purple Book. The Soviet delegation devised the following argument to support him: rule (70) of the Blue Book asserted that the chairmanship changed with each meeting but here there was no question of a new scheduled meeting because it was the same meeting which was in progress; so it was also unnecessary to have a new chairman. The insertion of a coffee-break did not mean that the ensuing period constituted a new meeting. It followed that after a fresh coffee-break the chairman in office had to continue to fulfill his duties. It was the same problem as has already been described as contributing to the events of 11 November 1980 after the clock had been restarted and the Hungarian chairman refused to make way for his successor. But this time the chairman's refusal to stand down brought a sharp reaction from NNA countries who argued that daily rotation meant that the chairmanship had to change with the day: when the day changed so must the chair. The CSCE principle of equality demanded daily rotation of the chairmanship because otherwise the unallied countries would be to an important degree dependent on the whims of the two military pacts which together constituted a large majority.

A fresh coffee-break produced no further results; informal discussions in the corridors only led to a hardening of positions. Once more the chairman asked who wished to speak and met with no reply; it was now 2:40 A.M. This time the silence lasted for fifty minutes. The interpreters must have thought that the hundred or so diplomats in the chamber had taken leave of their senses. Fifty minutes of silence in a full chamber is a long time. Some diplomats read the paper, some nodded off and some gossiped with their neighbors. Silence may speak louder than words. The British representative called it "an eloquent silence." Its effect may be to raise the tension more than any discussion. Finally the chairman announced that the Executive Secretary had managed to get the coffee bar re-opened. It had been shut for several hours but the attendants had been fetched from their beds. Did anyone object to a coffee-break? The answer being a silence, so it was decided and it was during this interval that the negotiators from the various caucuses agreed on a formula for putting an end to the night's performance. The meeting would not be closed, for this the Warsaw Pact countries refused, but a coffee-break would be called extending until 11 A.M. on the following Monday. It was then 5:30 A.M. on Saturday morning so the coffee-break would last 54½ hours. On the Monday morning the meeting would continue. Whether the Czechoslovakian or the Turkish representative, as next in alphabetical order, would then preside over the meeting, was left undecided.

During the weekend Western delegates realized what a strange situation they were in, thanks to the inexorable consensus rule. The Soviet delegation was not willing to consent to the Plenary session's being closed unless the GDR proposal for the work program was accepted. But the West was not willing to accept this proposal. So the session would go on for ever and ever, perpetually under the chairmanship of the Czechoslovakian representative since he refused to stand down until the session ended. And this situation could continue for as long as the Soviet delegation wanted.

The same weekend saw negotiations taking place in the hotel rooms of Madrid on the initiative of NNA countries; representatives from the caucuses took part and agreement was reached on a package deal. The most important elements of this agreement were that it was agreed to have a working program for one week which would include some meetings of the Drafting Group as proposed by the GDR, but at the end of the week the Madrid Meeting would go into recess until the beginning of November, which fulfilled the wishes of Western countries. In November, drafting of a concluding document would be continued and therefore the first work program in November would also include meetings of the Drafting Group. Western and NNA countries had achieved their most important aim, an agreed recess until the autumn. East European countries had succeeded in having the appearance kept up that the Madrid Meeting's Drafting Group was still negotiating a substantive concluding document, in spite of the situation in Poland, and would continue negotiations in November. Throughout the three meetings of the Drafting Group held in the last week before the recess the West maintained its silence. Some NNA countries did speak but there was no question of serious negotiations on the concluding document.

Filling the Third Basket

103

Family Reunification, by Roland Eggleston.
Report by RFE correspondent, Madrid, December 17, 1980.

The West today introduced proposals for speeding procedures in the Soviet Union and Eastern Europe for family reunification and marriage between citizens of different states. They are intended to tighten up the vague language in the Final Act. This says that applications regarding personal contacts should be considered "within reasonable time limits" or "as expeditiously as possible."

The Western proposal says that applications should normally be granted. If they are not, there should be an immediate explanation in writing and the people concerned should be allowed to renew their application. Nor should they suffer any discrimination regarding their job, housing, residential status or access to social, economic or educational benefits because of submitting the application.

The Western proposal, sponsored by Canada, the United States and Spain, is for a separate meeting of experts to consider the whole issue of human rights.

The paper makes clear that the three sponsors want to discuss not just the right of the individual to the fundamental freedoms expressed in the Helsinki Final Act but also the effect the non-observance of these can have on the development of friendly relations and cooperation among states.

Some non-Communist spokesmen have told our correspondent it might be possible to make a trade-off with the Soviet Union and its allies on the proposal for a meeting on military security in exchange for a meeting of experts on human rights. But they said they had not formulated their ideas sufficiently to give an example of what could be offered. Other non-Communist spokesmen were skeptical that any such trading would be possible.

104

Flow of Information, by Roland Eggleston.
Report by RFE correspondent, Madrid, December 2, 1980,
and February 3, 1981.

Spain, Austria and Switzerland today tabled a proposal aimed at giving the people of Eastern Europe better access to foreign newspapers and periodicals.

The paper also calls for better working conditions for journalists, including direct access to sources, whether public bodies or private individuals. It says that neither the journalist nor his informant should be punished as a result of obtaining or communicating information.

The first proposal is that newspapers and journals from other participating states should be available at points of sale accessible to the public. Non-Communist states have charged previously that the few foreign papers allowed into the Soviet Union and Eastern Europe are usually only available in luxury hotels inaccessible to the local public or in closed libraries.

The proposal also says that the foreign newspapers and periodicals allowed into a country should show a diversity of opinion. It has been charged that in many Communist countries the only foreign newspapers available are Communist publications.

A Swiss contribution to the paper suggests that reading rooms should be set up in national capitals and other big towns with a representative selection of foreign daily and weekly newspapers and other periodicals. It is emphasized that these should be readily accessible to everybody.

Poland has the best record in making the foreign press available to its citizens. Foreign newspapers and periodicals are available in many reading rooms and also in some cafés.

The paper says none of the signatory countries should withdraw a journalist's accreditation, expel him or refuse him a visa. Nor should any action by members of his family living with him lead to such measures being taken.

The Austrian delegation chief told reporters his country had assembled what he called a "heavy dossier of statistics" about Soviet and East European restrictions on foreign correspondents to back up its arguments.

The paper says journalists should not be obliged to be accompanied by a government guide in travelling around a country and should be allowed to carry personal notes and other documents needed for the job. This was a reference to several cases in which personal notes taken by Western journalists in interviews in Eastern Europe have been confiscated when they left the country.

The paper says that journalists should not have to notify official bodies when they travel around a country or obtain permission to do so except in clearly-defined military zones. Nor should they have to obtain authorization for interviews and investigations. . . .

The Soviet Union and its allies, on the one hand, and the West, neutrals and the Vatican, on the other, have such fundamentally different outlooks that it is hard to see a compromise emerging.

The aim of both the Western and neutral papers is to allow the fresh air of different opinions to blow through closed societies, to open minds to new ideas and new thoughts. The rival paper submitted jointly by the Soviet Union and East Germany could scarcely be more different.

There is no mention in its four pages of making foreign newspapers and journals available, even though this is mentioned in the Helsinki Final Act. There is no discussion of free access to contacts. And, of course, there is no mention of radio jamming because none of the broadcasts of Radio Moscow or any of its allies are jammed in the West.

The Soviet–East German paper is more a recital of the duties of a journalist coupled with the penalties which await him if he fails to fulfill these obligations.

The Soviet–East German paper says it is the duty of the foreign correspondent not to disseminate disinformation, tendentious information, lies or imputations. It is the duty of a foreign correspondent to obey the laws and regulations of the host country and not to interfere in its internal affairs. It is the duty of a journalist to help strengthen peace and security and to enhance mutual understanding and trust among peoples.

These are all worthy goals which the average Western correspondent maintains anyway as his personal code. But the Soviet Union and its allies have their own definition of all these terms.

As delegates pointed out, Western journalists who maintain contacts with dissidents have been accused of violating almost all of them. The same applies to those correspondents who wrote stories some months ago about reported strikes at the Togliatti motor works or passed on reports about mysterious deaths in the town of Sverdlovsk. Yet by Western standards these are all legitimate stories to be filed. As several delegations pointed out, Soviet correspondents would report them if they happened in the West.

In keeping with this approach, the Soviet–East German paper calls for the establishment of press centers which, among other helpful activities, will "provide support in arranging interviews, visits to enterprises etc." There is no provision for a journalist to get his interviews on his own.

For foreign correspondents who stick to the rules, the Soviet–East German paper holds out the attraction of official help in finding living and working accommodation and obtaining health care. Permanent correspondents are offered complete exemption from taxes.

Those who don't stick to the rules, however, are warned that noncompliance can lead to restriction even of the rights granted them under the Helsinki Final Act and eventually to expulsion.

The Soviet–East German paper, of course, has no chance of being accepted by the Western and neutral nations which put forward the more liberal proposals.

Nor does a separate Romanian paper, which also offers seemingly worthy goals, such as calling on governments to outlaw fascist and neo-fascist organizations and prohibit propaganda inciting to violence and war.

The problem, as non-Communist delegates have tried to explain, is once again the old one of terminology. What one country terms fascist propaganda can be considered truth in another. As an American delegate told a recent working group, not even political scientists have been able to find an acceptable definition of fascism in years of trying, so how is it possible to expect the Madrid conference to succeed.

That brought a torrent of abuse from the Soviet delegate Sergei Kondrashev, who claimed that it insulted the millions of dead in the Second World War. But he failed to offer any definition of his own.

105

Radio Free Europe Defended, by Roland Eggleston.
Report by RFE correspondent, Madrid, February 4, 1981.

The broadcasts of Radio Free Europe and Radio Liberty have been defended against Soviet and East European attacks.

At today's session an American spokesman denied Soviet allegations that war criminals are employed at the Radios. The U.S. delegate, Guy Coriden, was replying in a working group to allegations made earlier this week by the third-ranking member of the Soviet team, Sergei Kondrashev.

The Soviet Union and Czechoslovakia are co-sponsors of a resolution calling on nations which finance or provide facilities for the two American-financed stations to stop doing so. The right of the Radios to continue broadcasting has been defended by most of the Western allies, including the U.S., Luxembourg, Spain, Turkey, and Holland speaking for the European Common Market.

Coriden said today that "A war criminal is someone convicted of war crimes. It is not someone who has been the subject of slander, lies and tendentious information in the Soviet press.

"There is no one under the first definition working at either Radio Free Europe or Radio Liberty. But there are a number of people in the second category."

Coriden then turned to a comment by the Czechoslovak spokesman in the working group, Dr. Rudolf Kožušník. Kožušník had noted the number of Western delegations which had supported RFE/RL and said these did not know the content of the broadcasts from the two stations and should not comment on them.

"This would not be a valid objection even if we were a group of individuals representing only ourselves," Coriden said. "But of course we are not. We are official delegates representing our governments and the governments are informed about the contents of those broadcasts.

"I repeat, however, that it would not be valid even if we were personally uninformed. Because jamming is still a violation of the Helsinki Final Act, the United Nations Declaration of Human Rights and the provisions of the International Telecommunications Union, so we must object to it."

He said the Soviet Union and its allies had several times criticized the quality of the broadcasts from the two stations. If they were so poor, he asked, why was the Soviet Union spending so much money trying to jam them?

The Soviet delegate, Sergei Kondrashev, claimed in his statement that RFE/RL's objective was to undermine the countries of Eastern Europe.

"They are engaged in a systematic attempt to substitute truth with the fruits of their imagination, with lies and slander," he said. "This is contrary to détente and to the Final Act."

In the latest working group, Turkey criticized the Soviet-Czechoslovak resolution and also the fact that the two Radios are jammed by the Soviet Union and some of its allies. Turkey said this was a violation of the Helsinki Final Act.

"Turkey is also the object of a radio station broadcasting from somewhere outside our borders," its spokesman said. "We, too, consider it to be an annoying, lying, tendentious operation. But we do not jam it. We trust our people to be able to distinguish for themselves fact from fiction."

Spain also spoke against the Soviet-Czechoslovak resolution. Spain is one of the countries where RFE/RL has transmitters.

Jorge Fuentes, who is normally a member of the Spanish delegation to the United Nations, recalled that during the Franco dictatorship a station called Radio España Independiente had broadcast from Piteşti, in Romania. It was unpopular with the regime governing Spain at that time. But now it had disappeared because the reason for its existence had disappeared and no one had listened to it anymore.

106

New Western Proposals, by Roland Eggleston.
Report by RFE correspondent, Madrid, November 9 and 11, 1982.

The conference resumed on November 9 under the shadow of continued martial law in Poland and the repression of human rights activists in the Soviet Union.

Neither the United States nor the Soviet Union spoke at today's opening plenary session. But both issues were pressed strongly by members of NATO and the Common Market, and also by neutral Sweden whose chief delegate, Björn Skala, spoke out very strongly on them.

The Common Market took the lead for the West by tabling three new proposals aimed at protecting the rights of the individual, particularly in Poland.

Of the three tabled today, the first and most important concerns the right to free trade unions and is a reflection of Western anger and concern at the banning of Solidarity in Poland.

It demands that the 35 states which signed the Helsinki accords in 1975 guarantee "the right of everyone freely to form and join trade unions of his choice."

It goes on to say that trade unions should have the right to strike and the other normal rights laid down in the convention of the International Labor Organization. The measures call on the 35 states to repeal any laws which are incompatible with the free exercise of these rights.

Another Western measure on the rights of peoples to determine their own political status was also aimed at the situation in Poland. However, as Western delegates told our correspondent, it also referred to other countries suffering various forms of Soviet pressure.

It refers to the right of all peoples "to determine in full freedom their internal and external political status and to pursue as they wish their political, economic, social and cultural development."

The third Western measure put forward today concerns the repression of the groups established in the Soviet Union and Eastern Europe to monitor how those governments are living up to the commitments they made in the 1975 Helsinki accords.

It says the activities of citizens to promote and protect the implementation of the Final Act are legal. Therefore all the countries which signed the accords should take measures to ensure that individuals have the freedom to express their views about the way governments are treating the accords.

The Norwegian delegate, Leif Mevik, also took the Soviet Union sharply to task for the repression of the Helsinki monitoring groups in the Soviet Union and for the virtual elimination of direct-dialling telephone communication with the West. He said the cuts in telephone services were contrary to the letter and spirit on the Helsinki Final Act, which called for the promotion of contacts between people and better working conditions for journalists and business people. . . .

The West's new initiative at Madrid this week was intended to make the negotiations reflect the real world outside the conference hall, particularly in Poland.

Denmark and Canada, supported by the rest of the Common Market and NATO countries, tabled 13 new proposals which ranged from the right to free, independent trade unions through a rejection of radio jamming to the right to have access to foreign embassies.

The purpose, as the head of the Canadian delegation, Lou Rogers, told reporters, was to demonstrate that the Helsinki accords are not just intangible but are meant to benefit ordinary people.

The West also took other moves, some of which were intended to demonstrate its rejection of what appears to be the Communist approach that the Helsinki accords are just words which can be ignored as desired.

This took the form of cutting out statements from the half-finished final document which bear no reality to what the Soviet Union and its allies are doing.

For instance, the West wants to remove from the final document a paragraph which says that all 35 states in the Helsinki process "express their determination to refrain from the use of force, or the threat to use force."

The West's view is that it is a farce to leave this statement in the final document in view of the Soviet invasion of Afghanistan and the pressure it has imposed on Poland.

For similar reasons, the West wants to remove another paragraph in which the 35 states express their determination to stop the arms buildup. The West accuses the Soviet Union of also violating this by its massive military buildup of the last few years.

The most important of the other Western proposals emphasizes the right to freedom of religion without any kind of interference from the state. This was already a part of the draft final document tabled by the neutral and non-aligned states in December last year but the new Western proposal strengthens its language.

The need for it was demonstrated to the delegates during the week by members from the evangelical Baptist faith from the Soviet Union who now live in the United States. One of them, the mother of the Pastor Georgi Vins, passed around pamphlets, documents and photographs describing the fate of those who try to practice a religion not approved by the authorities.

Another Western proposal calls for a ban of the jamming of radio broadcasts. It is deliberately tied to a statement already contained in the Helsinki Final Act in which the 35 states commit themselves to the wider dissemination of information. This is also expected to be hotly contested by the Soviet Union, Poland, Czechoslovakia and Bulgaria, all of which have criticized Western broadcasting in the past. Poland's martial law authorities have been particularly angered by Polish-language broadcasts from the West and in August made a formal protest to the United States, Britain, France and West Germany. The complaints were rejected by all four countries.

The West has also called for two experts meetings to discuss the deteriorating situation in human rights and in the field of human contacts, which includes such things as family reunification and marriages between people of different countries.

The Canadian Ambassador, Lou Rogers, told reporters the West was deeply distressed at the decrease in the number of people allowed to leave the Soviet Union and Eastern Europe to join their families in other countries. He said this applied not only to Jewish emigration from the Soviet Union but also to the emigration of ethnic Germans, Armenians and others.

Several of the Western European diplomats who framed the new proposals have gone out of their way to tell reporters that they are an expression of the West's determination to make the Madrid conference successful despite all the disappointments of the past two years. Our correspondent says that in fact the number of diplomats who still believe something can be achieved is quite remarkable considering the wide differences which still exist on key East-West issues.

107

Debate on Monitoring Rights, by Roland Eggleston.
Report by RFE correspondent, Madrid, November 25, 1982.

The conference today began debating a proposed statement by the West emphasizing the rights of individuals in the Soviet Union and Eastern Europe to check on whether their governments are honoring the 1975 Helsinki accords.

But the Soviet Union and Czechoslovakia argued that the Helsinki accords did not provide a legal basis for the monitoring groups.

They claimed that the accords concerned only governments and not individuals. It was up to separate governments to worry about their own citizens.

The West, led by the United States, Canada, Britain, and Holland, replied in strong terms that the whole purpose of the Helsinki Final Act and of international relations generally was to benefit the individual.

Our correspondent says that at one point Soviet delegates Viktor Chikalov and Sergei Kondrashev accused the West of trying to "subvert" the Helsinki accords by placing such emphasis on individuals.

Czechoslovak delegate Rudolf Kožušník supported them in claiming that the West was trying to get the Madrid conference to interfere in the relationship between the state and the people in the Soviet Union and Eastern Europe.

During the debate, Western delegates stressed that private citizens had also formed Helsinki monitoring groups in the United States and Western Europe but were treated much differently. American delegates said that in the U.S. the Helsinki monitors are regularly invited to appear before Congressional committees to report on their complaints and opinions.

108

Bid for Soviet Concession, by Roland Eggleston.
Report by RFE correspondent, Madrid, December 13, 1982.

Soviet negotiators at Madrid will go home this week with a warning from the West that the USSR must make a major human rights concession if it wants Western agreement to a key meeting on military security.

NATO sources told our correspondent that this message had been repeated to the leaders of the Soviet delegation several times in the past ten days at private meetings with Western negotiators.

The West's stand is that, as much as it wants the meeting as a major step towards enhancing security in Europe, it has to be balanced by an equally significant move on human rights.

The NATO sources told our correspondent that they had not spelled out in the private meetings with the Soviet delegates exactly what would be considered an acceptable human rights concession, but they said it must be more than what is offered in the draft final document which is being negotiated in Madrid.

The Making of a Compromise

109

A Matter of Words, by Roland Eggleston.
Report by RFE correspondent, Madrid, May 24, 1983.

The East-West problems involved in bringing the conference to a close are largely a matter of words.

Most of the improvements the West is seeking in the draft final document consist of what seem to be minor changes in wording. However, the hostility shown by the Soviet Union and its allies is a tip that the changes are not as unimportant as they appear. It explains why the Soviet Union is ready to accept the draft final document exactly as it stands and is unwilling to accept any changes.

The ordinary person might see little reason for the West to quibble about a sentence which reads: "The participating states express their determination to encourage genuine and positive efforts to implement the 1975 Helsinki Final Act. . . ."

The West however, wants the words "genuine and positive" removed before it will approve the sentence.

The reason is that they have become distorted in Soviet and East European dictionaries.

The intention of the neutral countries which drew up the draft final document is that the sentence should demonstrate support for those who are trying to put the Final Act into practice—for instance, the Helsinki monitoring groups in the Soviet Union.

However, the Soviets argue that these groups are not making "genuine and positive" efforts but the reverse. They claim, therefore, that the agreement will not be broken if these groups are persecuted.

Another deceptive sentence is contained in the agreement to convene an international conference of human rights experts in Canada in 1985.

The present text in the draft final document says the Madrid conference has agreed "to convene a meeting of experts of the participating states on questions concerning respect—in their states—for human rights and fundamental freedoms."

The loaded words here are "in their states." Western diplomats say there have already been broad hints from the Soviet Union and some of its allies—particularly Czechoslovakia and Bulgaria—that this can be interpreted as meaning that diplomats will have to limit their discussion of human rights problems to their own countries. The U.S., for instance, would not be able to talk about the persecution of Charter 77 in Czechoslovakia.

Therefore the NATO and Common Market countries want to alter the three key words to "in those states." It seems an unimportant change but what a difference it makes. It will open up the 1985 meeting to enable the diplomats to talk about events in the other countries.

The West also sees a trap in the present wording about trade union rights.

As it stands, the draft final document says that workers have the right freely to establish and join trade unions. It also says these unions have the right freely to exercise the activities laid down in relevant international instruments.

But it then goes on to say that "These rights will be exercised in compliance with the law of the state—and—in conformity with the state's obligations under international law."

Western diplomats believe this puts too much emphasis on saying that the rights will be subject to the state. They want to correct this by dropping the word "and." In its place they would put a comma.

The sentence then reads that trade union rights will be "exercised in compliance with the law of the state, in conformity with the state's obligations under international law."

It is a subtle change which may seem pointless to an outsider. But in the precise niceties of diplomatic language the effect is to give equal weight to the state's laws and to its international obligations.

When considering this movement of words one has to keep in mind that the diplomats are thinking of those who will follow them.

Few of those drafting the final document in Madrid will be present at the next Helsinki follow-up conference in about three years' time when there will be an examination of how the 35 states have honored their pledges.

There will be few who will be able to say "This is what we meant by such and such a line." Therefore the wording has to have precise meanings which can be understood exactly by those who come later.

But East-West political difficulties hinder diplomats making some of the wording as clear as they would like.

For instance, one of the improvements sought by the West in the draft final document stresses that international radio broadcasting encourages understanding among peoples.

The West and the Warsaw Pact both understand what this implies: that jamming of international radio broadcasts is therefore a bad thing. But there is no mention of jamming in the text because that would bring an automatic rejection from the Soviet Union and the East European countries which jam Western radio broadcasts.

The sentence may still be rejected by them. But it has a slim chance of winning approval this way. After all, the Soviet Union and all the East European countries also have extensive international broadcasts.

It is this weighing of the meaning of words which has taken up most of the time of the 31-month-old Madrid conference and which is now delaying its end. At present the talks are at a virtual standstill because of Soviet reluctance to negotiate on the words the West is seeking. But the non-Communist nations are confident that it will eventually do so so that a final agreement can be achieved.

110

Soviets Find Amendments Unacceptable, by Roland Eggleston.
Report by RFE correspondent, Madrid, June 15, 1983.

Sergei Kondrashev, who is listed number three in the Soviet delegation, told the conference he was speaking because he saw a need to dispel some doubts and illusions.

Kondrashev listed the four Western amendments, which consist of two changes in the text of the final document and two new paragraphs to be included in the document. One of them calls for an international meeting on family reunification and the other notes the benefits of international broadcasting.

"In order to be perfectly clear, these amendments have been, are, and will remain totally unacceptable."

Kondrashev noted that the Soviet Union had accepted the final document as drafted by the neutral and non-aligned group in March although it had reservations about some of its provisions.

"If other people would demonstrate a similar feeling of responsibility the meeting could be concluded in the very near future," he said.

The head of the East German delegation, Peter Steglitz, supported Kondrashev and said the Soviet Union had taken an important step by deciding to accept the draft final document as it stood.

"We have exhausted the maneuvering room and it is now a matter of political will," he said.

Steglitz discussed particularly the Western proposal for an international conference in Switzerland in 1986 to discuss problems of family reunification and marriage between people of different states.

He argued that these sort of conferences depended on the general political situation and it would be better to see how the climate developed. He would not exclude such a meeting out of hand, but the situation had not matured sufficiently at this time. Steglitz also said that questions regarding human contacts were very sensitive and difficult and it could be more effective to discuss them at a bilateral level.

He said the draft final document was already tilted towards the West in many of its provisions but East Germany was prepared to accept that. However convening an experts' meeting on human contacts to discuss family reunification and similar issues would unbalance it to an unacceptable degree.

111

The Spanish Proposal, by Felipe González.
Speech by Spanish Premier, reported by RFE correspondent
Roland Eggleston, Madrid, June 17, 1983.

Spain understands that it has a special function to fulfill at this
Madrid meeting. We are an active participant in the deliberations, but
we also have a singular responsibility as the host country. We want to
fulfill that responsibility with fairness and equal concern for the rights
and interests of all the 35 participating states here.

We are, therefore, making specific proposals today on how to end this
meeting on a positive note. Our proposals comprise a package. We are
convinced there is no room for further negotiations because that would
only open up the process to additional delays, arguments and new tensions.

We present our package to you in the hope that it will be accepted in
its totality.

We fear that if it is not accepted, then in June 1983 the issue is simply not ripe for a conclusion.

The basis for our proposals is RM-39 (revised) which was tabled by
the neutral and non-aligned countries in March. We propose that it be
adopted as the final concluding document with all of us agreeing to the
three following points:

First, in the humanitarian area, I am informed by the government of
Switzerland that it wishes to invite all the participating states to a meeting of experts to explore how best further to achieve the objectives of
the human contacts provisions of the Helsinki Final Act. They propose
the date of April 16, 1986 in Bern. The meeting will adapt to the rules
of procedure of CSCE.

We believe it would strengthen the Helsinki process for the Madrid
meeting to accept that invitation on behalf of all the states. In that
connection, we note that one of the resolutions unanimously adopted at
the recently concluded Budapest meeting of the interparliamentary
union recommended the convening of such a meeting "in the not too
distant future." Those supporting that resolution, of course, included
leading parliamentarians from the East and the West, the USSR and
the US. What was agreed upon unanimously in Budapest can certainly
be implemented in Madrid.

Second, we are also aware that controversy exists on the wording of
a sentence designed "to encourage . . . efforts to implement the Final
Act." Since the words "genuine and positive" used to describe those

efforts appear to be duplicative, we urge as a compromise that the word "genuine" be permitted to remain in the text and the reference to "positive" be dropped.

Finally, let me turn to the security provisions of the final document. We are taking a major step toward peace by agreeing to begin, in 1983, the convening of a conference of confidence and security measures and disarmament in Europe. Even though two months have elapsed since the recommended April 27 date for ending the Madrid meeting, we believe the preparatory meeting for that conference should begin on October 25th of this year, even though the formal convening, in view of the lack of time for adequate preparation, will now have to be scheduled for January 17th, 1984.

One outstanding issue remains. Efforts to resolve it linguistically have not succeeded. It is obvious to any reader of the paragraph describing notifiable activities in the sea area and air space adjoining the whole of Europe that the word "such" before "activities" is not only ambiguously imprecise in English, but there is no clear understanding as to what it refers. Rather than attempting to define it and after consulting with some of the authors of the provision, we believe a solution to the impasse is to drop the word "such" from the text.

With agreement on these few points, the Madrid meeting is prepared to come to a successful close. Any additional substantive amendments at any other place in the document would seriously jeopardize success.

I speak as the head of the Spanish Government and I respectfully suggest that each of you, on my behalf, forward this message to the heads of each of your governments, for their consideration.

It is my final recommendation that you agree, once a formal consensus is arrived at, to recess your meetings for two or three weeks, at which point to reconvene with concluding statements by your foreign ministers. At that time, let us all rededicate ourselves to the cause of peace.

Thank you. The next step is yours to take.

112

The Minimal Acceptable Outcome, by Jörg Kastl.
Address by the head of West German delegation, reported
by RFE correspondent Roland Eggleston, Madrid,
June 24, 1983.

The solution proposed by the Spanish Prime Minister in his endeavor to reach a consensus on the concluding document does not cover all the issues the governments of the Ten still regard as highly desirable. They cannot consider as unreasonable their desire to give the document fuller balance in the human dimension.

Their people will have difficulties in understanding the refusal of such amendments.

These governments together with their friends, in a spirit of compromise and led by their sense of responsibility towards the viability of the CSCE process, have already made far-reaching sacrifices at the outset of this phase of our meeting. Their former proposals for improving the concluding document and for rendering it more realistic have been considerably cut down in number and scope. Therefore, it will surprise nobody that the Ten have serious difficulties to regard as fully satisfactory the substance of the Spanish package proposal.

The delegations of the Ten have declared themselves ready to negotiate proposed improvements in whatever form or forum and are still prepared to do so. Unfortunately, this offer has been flatly rejected for the last seven weeks by some few delegations.

However, in order to overcome the present dangerous impasse, in the interest of reaching consensus now, and as a minimal acceptable outcome to the Madrid meeting, the Ten would be prepared to accept the Spanish proposal in the terms formulated by Prime Minister González, on the understanding that all other participating states do the same.

113

Qualified U.S. Agreement, by Roland Eggleston.
Report by RFE correspondent, Madrid, June 24, 1983.

The United States told the Soviet Union in Madrid today that it would reluctantly accept the compromise final document proposed by Spain but would not negotiate on it.

The deputy chief of the American delegation, Edward Kilham, told the conference that if the Spanish compromise was not accepted, the United States would return to demanding acceptance of the four improvements in the final document which the West had demanded before Spain presented its compromise.

The Spanish proposal either drops or weakens several of these Western amendments but maintains the key demand for an international conference on the problems of East-West family reunification. The American attitude was supported by Canada and the ten West European members of the Common Market who also said the Spanish compromise had to be accepted as a package.

The American delegate Kilham told reporters later the Spanish proposal was the "absolute rock bottom" of what the West would accept.

He agreed that the U.S. and the West had previously compromised on several of its goals in the hope of reaching agreement but said: "The striptease is over. We will not give up anything more."

114

Soviets Ready to Act, by Anatolii Kovalev.
Speech by Soviet delegation leader, reported by RFE
correspondent Roland Eggleston, Madrid, July 1, 1983.

In Moscow, a conference has just concluded of the party leaders and political heads of Bulgaria, Hungary, East Germany, Poland, Romania, the USSR and Czechoslovakia.

This conference emphasized the significance and necessity of an early conclusion to the Madrid meeting with positive results meeting the expectations of peoples of Europe and providing for the convocation of a conference on confidence-building measures and security and disarmament in Europe.

This would be, as is further stated in the joint communiqué, an important contribution to the affirmation of the policy of peace, détente and cooperation.

As everyone is aware, the Soviet delegation agreed to the draft of the revised final document of the neutral and non-aligned states in which it was tabled by its authors.

The Soviet delegation is ready to act within the framework of the initiative of the Spanish government, to act in such a manner that mutually acceptable possibilities might be found through joint efforts.

115

The Remaining Differences, by Roland Eggleston.
Report by RFE correspondent, Madrid, July 1, 1983.

The belief that the conference can be brought to a quick and successful end in the next few days is based not on what Kovalev said in his speech at today's plenary session but on what he and other Warsaw Pact delegates have been saying behind the scenes in private meetings with the West. In other words, the public position has not gone as far as the private one. The West interprets this as meaning the Soviet Union has left itself an escape route if necessary.

In the private talks, the Soviet Union has said it will accept virtually all the compromise document drawn up by Premier González including the West's key proposal for an international conference in Switzerland in 1986 to discuss the problems of East-West family reunification and marriage between people of different states.

The Soviet Union has reversed itself and is now willing to accept this—but with a catch which both the United States and West Germany are reluctant to accept.

The Soviets don't want this agreement to be included in the main body of the final document of Madrid. They say it should be a so-called "Chairman's statement," which in practical terms means it would be an annex to the main document.

It would not affect the validity of the conference, but America and West Germany feel it would give it an inferior status to other meetings which are included in the main body of the final document.

These include a meeting of human rights experts in Canada in 1985, the meeting on military security in Europe which is to be held in Stockholm and other minor gatherings such as the seminar which is to be held in Venice at the end of next year to discuss economic and cultural co-operation in the Mediterranean.

116

A Fairly Substantial Document, by Roland Eggleston.
Report by RFE correspondent, Madrid, July 7, 1983.

Have all these months of East-West argument and wrangling, sometimes just over sentences or the placing of a word, been worth it?

Some critics say the agreements gained are small and insignificant, particularly at a time when East-West relations are at a low level. But the response from most of the negotiators from Western and neutral countries is that although many of them, particularly in human rights, are only small steps forward, it has been worth the efforts to get them and they are building blocks for more progress in the future.

One of the biggest achievements is the decision to convene an international conference in Stockholm, probably beginning next January, to discuss military security in Europe and devise measures to guard against surprise attack. This conference was sought, for different reasons, by both the West and the Soviet Union and its allies. It will last at least three years, because it is obliged to report on its progress to the next Helsinki follow-up conference in Vienna in 1986, but many expect it to continue for 10 to 15 years because of the difficult issues involved.

Western diplomats take for granted that Moscow will try to use the Stockholm conference as a permanent propaganda forum. It is expected to begin by using it as a platform to criticize the deployment of the new American medium-range missiles from the end of this year.

The West wants the conference because it believes it can eventually make a genuine contribution to military security in Europe.

The purpose of the talks is to discuss what are called confidence-and-security-building measures. In practice, this means trying to reach agreements under which nations will have to give advance warning of any major movements of troops or aircraft or declare what weapons they have in storage. Eventually the Soviet Union might even be required to give more details of its military budgets than it does now, although Western diplomats concede that is a very long-term goal. The West considers it won a victory in the plans for this conference. The terms proposed by the Soviet Union and its allies in the initial discussions back in 1981 were so vague that almost anything could have been raised. It was clear the Soviet Union was interested in nothing more than a forum where it could make its usual empty propaganda designed to create the impression that it is a peace-loving country.

But in months of weary negotiation the West, supported by the neutrals, forced agreement on a set of guidelines which say that all the confidence-building measures accepted by the Stockholm conference have to be of genuine military significance and politically binding on the governments which sign the agreements.

Western and neutral diplomats consider this a major improvement on the rather weak agreements on confidence-building in the Helsinki Final Act.

In another advance, these confidence-building measures will have to be applied across all Europe from the Atlantic to the Ural Mountains in the Soviet Union. In the Helsinki agreements, the Soviet Union was obliged to honor the agreements on confidence-building measures only in a narrow band along its European borders.

But the achievements reached in Madrid in the field of human rights are even more significant in the eyes of Western and neutral diplomats.

The struggle continued right up to the present, with the Soviet Union agreeing only in the past few days to accept an international conference in Switzerland in 1986 to discuss the obstacles it and some of its allies put in the way of family reunification and other basic human issues such as marriage when one partner lives in a Warsaw Pact country and the other in the West.

The Soviet Union remains unhappy about this conference and struggled to the last to try to whittle down the terms of its mandate but the

West is confident it will be able to bring up all the humanitarian issues it wants to.

Months before this, however, tough American, British, West German, French and other Western negotiators, backed vigorously by the Swiss, the Austrians and other members of the neutral and non-aligned group, had won approval of a series of agreements which bring slight improvements to those wanting to emigrate from the Soviet Union and other Warsaw Pact countries.

These agreements say that all 35 participating states will deal favorably with applications for meetings with family members in other countries.

It says that in emergency cases these will be decided as expeditiously as possible. When it is a matter of marriage between citizens of different states or non-emergency family meetings the decision should be taken in six months or less.

The agreement also says no one should be penalized by making applications to emigrate or to have these meetings with other members of the family. It says specifically that no one should lose his job or social benefits or housing rights.

Western and neutral negotiators have particular reason for satisfaction about these agreements. They also tried to get something similar at the last Helsinki follow-up conference in Belgrade in 1977–78 but failed because the Soviet Union and its allies refused to consider them.

And terms of the agreement achieved in Madrid are better than those sought in Belgrade.

Another of the Madrid agreements says the fees for visas and passports should be gradually reduced until they sink to a moderate level in relation to a person's average monthly income.

Western negotiators say this is important because there is little point in an East European country agreeing to apparently liberal emigration or travel practices if it then pushes up the cost of a visa or a passport to impossible levels.

The Madrid document also makes a minor, but in the eyes of many diplomats significant improvement in some of the human rights already enshrined in the Helsinki Final Act. The difference is that the new Madrid document obliges states to take the necessary action to see that these rights can be exercised.

For example, Principle Seven of the Helsinki Final Act sets out the obligations of the participating states to respect human rights and fundamental freedoms, including the freedom of thought, conscience, religion or belief.

An agreement in the Madrid document says the 35 participating states "will take the necessary action in their respective countries to effectively ensure this right."

The next paragraph in the same section refers to the freedom of the individual to profess and practice, alone or with others, a religion or belief in accordance with the dictates of his own conscience.

This, too, is similar to a text in the Final Act. But the Madrid document adds that the 35 participating states "agree to take the action necessary to ensure" this freedom.

It is another matter whether the Soviet Union and its allies will honor these new agreements any more than they have honored the commitments they made in the 1975 Final Act. But, as the head of the Austrian delegation in Madrid, Franz Ceska, told our correspondent, by accepting the Madrid agreements the Soviet Union is accepting an additional document for which it can be held accountable in world opinion.

As far as Ceska and most Western diplomats are concerned, this makes the long struggle worthwhile.

The Madrid document also contains a paragraph on trade union rights—which the Helsinki Final Act does not have.

It is nowhere near as strong as the statement on trade unions which the West proposed last November in a show of support for the Solidarity trade union in Poland. For instance, the reference to the right to strike has been dropped because it was rejected by the East Europeans.

It must be remembered that every agreement in Madrid requires the consensus of all 35 states. It takes only one objection for a proposal to fail.

But the agreement which was won says that "The participating states will ensure the right of workers freely to establish and join trade unions, the right of trade unions freely to exercise their activities and other rights as laid down in relevant international instruments."

It goes on to say that these rights "will be exercised in compliance with the law of the state and in conformity with the state's obligations under international law." Western diplomats know that this provides an opening for a state to clamp down on trade unions which demand too many of the rights they know they are entitled to possess in the modern world. But they consider it is a start. In Vienna in 1986 perhaps more can be achieved.

There are also minor advances on such points as having access to foreign missions.

A sentence in the Madrid document says that access by visitors to foreign missions "will be assured with due regard to the necessary requirement of security of these missions."

It seems a simple statement. But it took months and months of negotiations to get the Soviet Union and its allies to agree that the overriding consideration was the security of the missions themselves.

The Warsaw Pact countries had argued that access to foreign missions should be regulated according to the needs of state security.

The section on freedom of information in the Madrid document falls short of what non-Communist countries had sought. The neutral countries are particularly disappointed because this was a section in which they were particularly interested.

But there are some steps forward to improve the living and working conditions of journalists working in foreign countries.

There is also a minor improvement regarding the possibilities for obtaining foreign newspapers and journals. The document says the 35 participating states will encourage contacts with a view to concluding "long-term agreements designed to increase the quantities and numbers of titles of newspapers and other publications imported from other states."

This reflects the fact that in the Soviet Union and Eastern Europe firms and organizations may be able to import individual copies or limited numbers of foreign journals and magazines but find it difficult to get agreement on long-term import contracts because of officially-created obstacles.

The Madrid document also says that the 35 states agree to "further extend the possibilities for the public to take out subscriptions" to foreign journals and magazines according to the relevant provisions of the Helsinki Final Act.

These are not the only benefits of the final document in the eyes of its Western and neutral supporters. There is a strong statement on terrorism which ignores the oft-repeated Soviet thesis that terrorism conducted by national liberation movements is not really terrorism at all.

There is also what most Western diplomats consider at least an adequate statement on the first phase of the Madrid conference when the Soviet invasion of Afghanistan and its other violations of the Helsinki Final Act were denounced in strong terms.

Of course neither Afghanistan nor the Soviet Union is mentioned by name because Moscow and its allies blocked a consensus.

But the document says that "serious violations of a number of the Final Act's principles were deplored" and goes on to say that strict application of them is essential for the improvement of mutual relations.

No Western or neutral diplomat in Madrid would disagree that the steps forward are very modest. But they say the main thing is that there has been a step forward, particularly on human rights issues. It is seen as a new start after the failure of Belgrade.

117

Malta Withholds Consensus, by Evariste Saliba.
Address by the Maltese delegate, reported by RFE
correspondent Roland Eggleston, Madrid, July 14, 1983.

The essential value of the CSCE process lies in the real opportunity it offers to all participating states to play a direct role in discussing and resolving issues related to their security. It is an integral part of this process that our approach to security issues is not dominated exclusively by the concerns relating to superpower confrontation. Helsinki clearly established this principle and what was mainly a failure in Belgrade was precisely a failure at that point in time to raise our sights beyond the level of superpower politics. Here again in Madrid the nature of superpower relationships and the level of their confrontation has dominated our discussions for almost three years.

Malta has consistently made it absolutely clear that it will never connive at turning the CSCE into yet another forum for superpower politics—this time with the added advantage of a wide-ranging endorsement of their desires at the end of the day. Success in Madrid can only be measured in terms of how much the process of the CSCE retains all the essential elements forged out in Helsinki.

One of the elements concerns the linkage between security in the Mediterranean and security in Europe. Malta's insistence on this linkage has always been inspired by our conviction that concentrating our attention exclusively on the continental mass of Europe could only lead to the shifting of the center of confrontation to the periphery of the continent, particularly in the Mediterranean. This we can never accept.

Malta's proposals to convene an expert meeting on Mediterranean security is the minimum we can salvage to ensure our Belgrade commitment.

It should surprise no one, therefore, to see us insist on our position, reiterated as recently as last Friday, July 8, 1983: namely that Malta cannot give its consensus to the documents before us until acceptable formulae are found to meet our just request.

118

East and West United, by Roland Eggleston.
Report by RFE correspondent, Madrid, July 20 and 26,
September 5 and 6, 1983.

The West, the Soviet Union, the Warsaw Pact, and Malta's allies in
the neutral and non-aligned group decline to accept the meeting demanded by Malta because they believe it would bring the troubles and
tensions of the Middle East and North Africa into the Helsinki process
and blur its effort to resolve the problems of Europe.

By informal agreement, all of them have refused even to discuss the
issue with Malta. Now most of them have decided to withdraw their
leading delegates as a new mark of disapproval.

Apart from the political reasons, many of the old hands in the Helsinki process have personal feelings about allowing Malta to have
its way.

One of the few decisions of the last Helsinki follow-up conference in
Belgrade in 1977–78 was to hold a meeting on Mediterranean co-operation in Malta in February 1979. Malta obtained that concession by
using similar tactics to those it has adopted now—it refused consensus
to the final document until it won.

Apart from being irritated at this tactic, the older diplomats say that
when they got to Malta they were charged extraordinarily high fees for
virtually every service. They say they have no intention of submitting to
either situation again.

A solution will require the agreement of Malta's Premier Dom Mintoff and his Foreign Minister Alexander Trigona. And there are hints
that it will be several days before they will be ready for discussions.

The clearest came from Malta's delegate in Madrid, who confirmed
to reporters today that Dom Mintoff was on holiday sailing somewhere
in the Mediterranean.

His actual whereabouts is a mystery. Dom Mintoff's previous sailing
holidays have taken him to Tunis, around the coast of Italy or along
the Adriatic coast off Yugoslavia.

Even this story is familiar to the old hands. They recall that when
they were trying to arrange a compromise with Malta at the Belgrade
conference Dom Mintoff was said to be away hunting and could not be
disturbed. He finally met the negotiator, the West German Ambassador,
at 0300 one morning, still dressed in his riding clothes.

A story being told around the corridors in Madrid is that Malta was
equally difficult in the final days in Helsinki in 1975 before the Final

Act was signed. The Soviet Foreign Minister, Andrei Gromyko, is reported to have finally exploded and said: "Who needs Malta? The other 34 can agree to it without them."

Western diplomats say that Malta's refusal to allow the Helsinki follow-up conference in Madrid to close had cost 385,000 Swiss francs by July 26. Of this, Malta's share is only 770 francs.

This is the cost of keeping the conference going for the 11 days since July 15 when all other states except Malta agreed to the final document.

Diplomats told our correspondent that it costs 35,000 Swiss francs a day to keep the Palacio de Congresos in session with its heavy military guard, its interpreters, its personnel and necessary services such as electricity.

Malta pays only 0.2 percent of this under the sliding scale which remains the same for all meetings in the Helsinki process. The heaviest burden lies on the United States, the Soviet Union, Britain, West Germany, France and Italy, all of which pay 8.8 per cent. . . .

On September 5, the delegates in Madrid decided to implement all the agreements in the final document even if Malta continues to prevent its formal adoption. Their decision was contained in a document circulated at the conference that evening.

Diplomats said no formal action to implement the statement would be taken while negotiations with Malta were continuing. It will come into force only if Malta persists in refusing to accept the final document. . . .

On September 6, Maltese delegate Evariste Saliba told the conference he accepted a compromise declaration saying all states in the Helsinki process would support Maltese initiatives to strengthen peace in the Mediterranean—but only when they considered it appropriate to do so.

A second statement said these initiatives, whether from Malta or other states, had to be part of the Helsinki process and with the agreement of the other 34 states. This part of the declaration was included at the insistence of the United States which wanted to ensure that Malta did not act independently.

The agreements end the conflict which had cast a shadow over the East-West agreements reached in three years of East-West negotiations.

ACCOMMODATING THE INCOMPATIBLE

The Soviet View of Human Rights

119

An Appeal for Time, by Iulii Vorontsov.
Report by RFE correspondent Robert Tilley, Belgrade,
March 10, 1978.

The leader of the Soviet delegation at the Belgrade conference, Iulii
Vorontsov, says that by the next follow-up conference—in Madrid in
1980—the West may have reason to be more satisfied with Moscow's
record in the field of human contacts.

In a private meeting with a Canadian government minister, Vorontsov appealed for time and a let-up in what he claimed was a campaign
by Western countries—including Canada—on the human rights issue.

The meeting, last Wednesday, was between Vorontsov and Norman
Cafik, Canadian Minister of State for Multiculturalism. It lasted about
half an hour.

In a statement to the press, Cafik's office said: "Vorontsov argued . . .
that the West, including Canada, had in his view spoiled the Belgrade
meeting by trying to draw too direct a line between human rights and
human contact issues.

"Human rights," he said, were a matter of ideology and raised fundamental constitutional problems for the Soviet Union.

"Vorontsov said human contact issues were more a matter of administration practices, and in a country as vast as the Soviet Union, lack of
quick and easy communication between major centers and remote regions was obviously a problem.

"Claiming matters had improved since Helsinki and would continue to do so, he said the Soviet Union must be allowed time and not be put under the public pressure of a human rights campaign designed to force changes on them. He added he was confident that by Madrid there would be reason for Western countries like Canada to be more satisfied with Soviet practices, noting that in the next two years there will be many bilateral discussions of means of introducing improvements."

But the Soviet delegation leader added that "In the same interval, the West should be very careful about planning human rights campaigns such as had been mounted against the Soviet Union at Belgrade."

Vorontsov also suggested that human contacts problems, and family reunifications in particular, should be handled "in a more routine, low-key way which would not engage governments at parliamentary or senior political levels in such a public fashion."

120

Policy toward Dissidents Defended, by Leonid Ilichev.
Reported by RFE correspondent Roland Eggleston, Madrid,
May 9, 1981.

The head of the Soviet delegation at the Madrid conference, Leonid Ilichev, tonight described dissidents in his country as criminals.

Ilichev told a press conference there was a difference between a concern for human rights and a concern for dissidents.

He described dissidents as "people without shame or honor who choose the path of criminal deeds and then ask defenders in the West to help them get political capital out of their actions."

Ilichev also said the Soviet Union had a "socialist conception of human rights and we don't attempt to impose that on the United States. Nor do we want them to impose their conception on the Soviet Union or other countries."

121

Clash at Ottawa, by Roland Eggleston.
Report by RFE correspondent, Ottawa, May 15, 1985.

Yesterday saw the most bitter East-West arguments at the Ottawa Human Rights Conference since the talks began three weeks ago. The main row in the three-hour debate involved the Soviet Union, Britain and West Germany.

Western diplomats told reporters afterwards they believed the Soviet

Union had used most of the arguments it had developed for the conference during the debate. They also charged that many of the Soviet accusations were factually incorrect and easily disproved. One Western diplomat described most of them as "rubbish" and said he was surprised the delegation had not done better.

The row took place behind closed doors because of the Soviet and Warsaw Pact refusal to open the sessions to the press. But Western diplomats kept slipping out to give reporters a running account.

It began with a speech by the British negotiator, Anthony Williams, condemning the Soviet human rights record. He was immediately answered by the head of the Soviet delegation, Vsevolod Sofinskii, and for nearly three hours they took turn in taking the floor on points of order to answer the other's accusations.

The argument ranged over social problems in Britain, the struggle against the Irish Republican Army terrorists in Northern Ireland and moved into the use of Yiddish and Hebrew in the Soviet Union and Gaelic in Scotland. Western diplomats who listened to the argument said the Soviet diplomat made no attempt to answer any of the specific charges of human rights violations.

He began his response to Williams by attacking Britain's social record, claiming that maternity leave granted pregnant British women was inadequate and did not match the rights accorded in the Soviet Union or anywhere in Eastern Europe. He also said there were 3.6 million unemployed in Britain, which was a violation of the basic right to work. In addition he said two million adult Britons were illiterate.

From there, Sofinskii moved on to attack Britain's war against the Irish Republican Army terrorists in Northern Ireland. He described them as fighters for civil rights. Sofinskii claimed that British troops had killed several thousand Irish people—most of them women and children—when firing the rubber bullets used for crowd control. But his main argument concerned a young man named Bobby Sands who was one of several members of the IRA who starved themselves to death in a British-controlled prison in 1981. Sands was 31 years old.

Sofinskii said it could turn out that Bobby Sands was one of the 20th century's greatest heroes. Without explaining this comment he then went on to draw a parallel between Sands and the Soviet human rights activist Andrei Sakharov. Sofinskii said the Western world had celebrated Sakharov on his 60th birthday but Bobby Sands had never had a chance to reach that age. He suggested that Sands could have become an equally famous figure—perhaps a writer or a musician. Sofinskii then sat down. He had spoken for 37 minutes.

The British diplomat immediately took the floor again to answer him.

He said Bobby Sands was a self-confessed terrorist. He said a few years ago the Soviet Union executed three Armenians for allegedly placing a bomb in the Moscow subway but the West had never described these people as fighters for civil rights.

Later a new argument developed between the British and Soviet diplomats over the rights of Jews in the Soviet Union to publish newspapers and other journals in Hebrew and Yiddish. Sofinskii said the Jews could do so and supported his argument by referring to the newspaper of the Birobidzhan Jewish Republic, the *Birobidzhan Stern*. He followed up by saying that in Britain Scots and Welsh were unable to use their own language.

Williams, who had a Scottish adviser sitting behind him, rejected this argument by pointing out that Gaelic is sometimes used in the courts in West Scotland. He also told Sofinskii that there is an active movement in Wales to preserve the Welsh language.

The Soviet diplomat did not reserve his attack for Britain. He also sharply criticized West Germany's level of unemployment and also its treatment of its Turkish and other foreign workers. The attack was apparently prompted by a speech earlier in the day by the West German delegation leader, Ekkehard Eickhoff. He had concentrated on criticizing the limits the Soviet Union places on the emigration of ethnic Germans.

Sofinskii did not answer the specific complaints. But he said freedom of movement existed in Warsaw Pact countries. He claimed that Canada alone had "received" 250,000 Germans made up of people from East Germany and ethnic Germans from the Soviet Union.

But again, Sofinskii's main response was to attack West Germany's social record, saying its rate of unemployment violated a basic human right. He put the figure at 2.6 million and said it was easy to remember because it was close to the 3.6 million unemployed which he claims is the figure for Britain. He claimed that because of the economic situation foreign workers were being forced to leave West Germany without compensation although they had worked there for years. He also claimed that West Germans discriminated against Turkish workers.

The West German ambassador responded with a strong statement that in his country the trade unions were free and they ensured that the rights of the Turkish workers were protected. And he added that whenever discrimination appeared the West German authorities took steps to overcome it.

The final row on this day of angry words involved a Dutch defense of the nonofficial groups established in Eastern Europe to monitor violations of the human rights commitments of the Helsinki Accords.

The head of the Dutch delegation, Bob Croin, said the Helsinki Accords guaranteed their right to do so and he strongly condemned the Soviet Union and its allies for violating its own commitments. Croin also emphasized what he called the natural right of peoples to criticize their own government. He said that if Holland began imprisoning people for criticizing the government it would soon have the entire population behind bars.

122

KGB General on Human Rights, by Sergei Kondrashev.
Report by RFE correspondent Roland Eggleston,
Ottawa, May 17, 1985.

The deputy leader of the Soviet delegation at the Ottawa Human Rights Conference Thursday gave it his view of the human rights situation in the Soviet Union. Sergei Kondrashev, who is a KGB general, was responding to Western accusations about Soviet violations of the human rights provisions of the Helsinki agreement.

One of Kondrashev's points was that no one was prosecuted for teaching Hebrew in the Soviet Union. Western diplomats told reporters this was technically correct but was not the full story. They said that in the Soviet Union a license is needed to teach and few are granted to those who wanted to teach Hebrew. So those who do teach are prosecuted for doing so without a license.

Kondrashev cited the case of Iosif Begun, a Jewish electrical engineer who began teaching Hebrew when he lost his job after applying for an exit visa in 1971. In 1982 Begun was arrested on charges of anti-Soviet agitation and propaganda and sentenced to seven years in a strict labor camp to be followed by five years in internal exile.

Kondrashev acknowledged that Begun had applied for a visa in 1971 and been refused. Without explanation, he said Begun later lost his job and then began organizing underground publications. "Over the next seven years he did not work but carried out the instructions he received from abroad," Kondrashev claimed. "He was supposed to be teaching Hebrew. But could he exist on that for seven years? He had only four students."

Later the head of the Dutch delegation, Bob Croin, took the floor to ask Kondrashev why the Soviet Union refused an exit visa to Begun. "He would have been happy and you would have had no more problems," he said, "Why not let him leave?"

Kondrashev's only answer was to say he was prepared to meet Croin privately to tell him more about the case.

Kondrashev also said that in the past few years 1,544 new "religious associations" had been created in the Soviet Union, including 35 Orthodox churches, 54 Catholic chapels and more than 700 institutions for the Baptists, Evangelicals and Seventh Day Adventists. Kondrashev said that alone in 1983–84 there had been 282 new "religious associations." Without explanation, he then added: "To give an objective picture, 502 have disappeared."

Kondrashev strongly denied there was anti-Semitism in the Soviet Union. He said Jews made up only 0.7 per cent of the population but they provided more than five per cent of the numbers engaged in scientific work, about six per cent of the lawyers and legal experts and about six per cent of those engaged in culture, arts and the media. They also provided about three per cent of those engaged in medicine. Kondrashev added: "As for Jewish students, they have the top position in the country."

Kondrashev said the Soviet Union recognized the cause of family reunification and large numbers of Jews had been given exit visas to go to Israel to join family members. "But 90 per cent of those who supposedly wanted to go to Israel either remained in Europe or went over the ocean," he said. "What kind of reunification is that? They neglected their relatives."

Afterwards Western diplomats said many of Kondrashev's statistics were invented. They described this as standard anti-Western propaganda. But they said they could not understand why Kondrashev had resorted to it when addressing a meeting of international diplomats who knew the truth.

A British diplomat told reporters: "It was a clumsy propaganda effort directed at people who knew better."

The U.S. View of Human Rights

123

The Key Words of This Call for Our Meeting, by Richard Schifter. Introductory statement by the head of U.S. delegation, Ottawa, May 10, 1985.

The key words of this call for our Meeting, "human rights and fundamental freedoms," had been the subject of detailed discussion at the

Helsinki Conference which produced the Final Act. They were defined in Principle VII.

These paragraphs, Mr. Chairman, constitute recognition by all signatories to the Final Act of the close link between respect for human rights and the development of friendly relations among nations, the interrelationship between a government's respect for the rights of its own citizens and its regard for the inhabitants of this globe who live beyond its borders. There was a time, not long ago, when the great majority of the citizens of our respective countries did not pay a great deal of attention to what it was that was happening beyond the limits of their villages or towns and most assuredly did not pay attention to occurrences in other countries. It was the world's experience with the Nazi system that brought about a fundamental change in outlook. As Pastor Martin Niemöller observed, if you ignore the misdeeds done to your neighbors, there will be no one around to assist you once misdeeds are done to you. Increasingly, in recent decades men and women across the face of this earth have come to understand the validity of the thoughts of John Donne, who authored the words made famous by Ernest Hemingway:

> No man is an iland, intire of it selfe; every man is a peece of the Continent, a part of the maine; if a clod bee washed away by the Sea, Europe is the lesse, as well as if a Promontorie were, as well as if a Mannor of thy friends or if thine owne were; any mans death diminishes me, because I am involved in Mankinde; and therefore never send to know for whom the bell tolls; It tolls for thee.

In my country, Mr. Chairman, as I am sure is the case in other countries as well, these words of John Donne have increasingly been reflected in the general attitude of people toward world events. In the United States this general attitude has through the electoral process been transmitted to the President and the Congress. The President and the Congress, in turn, have seen to it that the attitude to which I have referred is reflected in the formulation of our foreign policy. Our people care about the manner in which the governments of other countries deal with their own citizens and they insist that the Government of the United States make known the views of the American public on this vital issue and interact with other countries in keeping with these views. Thus, the link established in Principle VII between respect for human rights and friendly relations among States is not an invention of the drafters of the Helsinki Final Act, but the codification of a relationship which the authors recognized as existing.

The point I am making, Mr. Chairman, let it be clearly understood, is that in our view respect for human rights in individual states contributes to the improvement of international relations. By the same token, disrespect for human rights contributes to the deterioration of international relations.

The distinguished representative of the Soviet Union, in his opening speech two days ago, also spoke of this linkage between human rights, on the one hand, and relations between states, on the other. However, he reversed the cause-and-effect relationship which I have just described. In his view, if I understood him correctly, détente leads to greater respect for human rights and international tension leads to a clamp-down on human rights. Through its distinguished representative the Soviet Union told us that if we cooperate with it in international affairs, it is prepared to cooperate with us in the area of human rights.

We have, Mr. Chairman, some problems with the logic of this proposition. When we use the term "human rights," we describe the relationship between a government and its own citizens. Does it stand to reason that if foreign countries establish friendly relations with a particular government that government, in turn, will—so to speak—reward the foreign countries by dealing kindly with its own citizens? And does it further stand to reason that if international relations are tense, the foreign countries will be punished by the government in question through the adoption of repressive measures against its own citizens? Would this not mean that a government holds its own people hostage, treating them well or poorly depending on the way other countries treat it in international affairs?

Nor need we deal with this problem as an abstract, philosophic proposition. We have empiric evidence in recent history that sheds light on this issue.

After the long dark night of Stalinism, the dawn of greater respect for human rights in the Soviet Union arrived in the spring of 1956, following Chairman Khrushchev's address to the 20th Congress of the Communist Party of the Soviet Union. That dawn came in a period often referred to as the Cold War. International crisis succeeded international crisis, to reach a terrifying crescendo in October 1962. Yet, during this very period of international tension domestic controls in the Soviet Union were eased, causing the era to become known as that of the thaw. What is clear is that the thaw came first, followed ultimately, in the wake of the Cuban Missile Crisis, by significant relaxation of international tension.

We witnessed the same sequence, that of domestic change being followed by international change, not the other way around, in the Nineteen Seventies. At the very time that East-West relations improved further, bringing on the period of détente, the Soviet Union began its campaign to suppress political dissidents. To use the phrase which so frequently appeared in Soviet theoretical journals in those days, "the correlation of forces was tilting in favor of the Socialist camp." And as it kept tilting throughout the Seventies, as détente continued, the tilt in the domestic sphere was against the exercise of human rights. The thaw having long since ended, freedom of expression was returned to the deep freeze. At the very time that United States and Soviet negotiators met to complete the SALT II negotiations, in 1979, reports of a wave of new arrests of Helsinki monitors cast an ominous shadow over the new agreement. There were many reasons as to why the United States Senate failed to ratify SALT II, but the least that can be said of the repressive measures taken by the Soviet Union in the late Seventies is that they did not help maintain the spirit of détente and most assuredly did not win Senate votes for SALT II.

The point I am making is, I am sure, clear. We must all learn from history. And the one lesson taught by the events I have just described is that respect for human rights leads to a relaxation of international tension, not the other way around.

There once existed the notion, to be sure, that what a potentate did to his subjects is his business and not anyone else's. An American protest against human rights violations delivered during the Administration of President Theodore Roosevelt to the Government of Czar Nicholas II was rejected on that ground. But the world has moved on since then. Immediately following World War II the international community reflected on the horrors for which the Nazi regime had been responsible, horrors which were first visited upon the country's own citizens, on persons persecuted for political dissent or ethnic origin or both, horrors which later enveloped most of the European continent. It was in light of these reflections that the Universal Declaration of Human Rights was drafted and adopted and that 27 years later Principle VII was incorporated into the Helsinki Final Act. Both documents elevated the issue of a government's respect for the human rights of its own citizens from the domestic to the international plane.

In his presentation to us the other evening, our distinguished Soviet colleague offered one other reason why we should not be discussing each other's human rights problems at this meeting. The point he made was that the Madrid Concluding Document mandated each of us merely to report on human rights conditions in his own country and not elsewhere. In quoting from the Madrid Document he said that it provides for a review of respect for human rights "v svaikh stranakh," which, I am told, indeed means in Russian in "their own countries." If that were a correct quotation from the Concluding Document, our colleague might very well have a good argument. But it is not a correct quotation. The official Russian text of the Concluding Document calls for a review of respect for human rights "v ikh gosudarstvakh," which, I am further told, means in Russian "in their states," thus encompassing all of them, not limiting each of us to speak only about his own country. I am confident that after checking his version against the official Russian text of the Concluding Document, our colleague will take due note of the discrepancy and recognize the difference in meaning.

124

The U.S. and International Covenants, by Richard Schifter.
Statement by the head of U.S. delegation, Ottawa,
June 4, 1985.

I shall now turn to the Polish proposal OME 11, calling inter alia for ratification of the international Covenants on Economic, Social and Cultural Rights and on Civil and Political Rights by participating States which have not done so heretofore. According to my calculations, 26 of the participating States have ratified the Conventions; nine have not. The United States is one of these nine.

In an earlier intervention, Mr. Chairman, I explained why we do not consider it appropriate to discuss the issue of ratification at this meeting. As I noted then, we have come here to examine the question of the extent to which there are shortfalls in performance on the promises heretofore made to respect human rights, not how often we should promise again what we have promised earlier. However, as Poland has decided to raise this issue, let me explain, on behalf of one of the nine participating States which have not ratified the conventions, what the serious obstacles are that stand in the way of ratification.

As many of the delegations know, reflecting the decision of the executive branch of our Government, the United States has signed the Conventions. Ratification requires, however, the affirmative vote of two-thirds of the United States Senate and that has not been obtained. There was a time, Mr. Chairman, when a good many students of this subject strongly urged Senate ratification of the Covenants and recommended that the legal problems that Senators had with a few of their provisions be resolved with appropriate reservations. By today, however, weighty and most serious additional concerns exist as to the appropriateness of these Covenants. To illustrate these problems, let me suggest the following imaginary dialogue that might take place if I were to testify before the Senate Foreign Relations Committee in support of ratification of the Covenants.

A Senator might ask me: "Mr. Ambassador, I want to draw your attention to Article 8, Section 1(a) of the Covenant on Economic, Social and Cultural Rights and Article 22, Section 1 of the Covenant on Civil and Political Rights. The first of these reads as follows:

" 'The States Parties . . . undertake to ensure . . . the right of everyone to form trade unions and join the trade union of his choice . . . for the promotion and protection of his economic and social interests.' The second reads as follows: 'Everyone shall have the right to freedom of association with others, including the right to form and join trade unions for the protection of his interests.' "

"Now, Ambassador, isn't it true that Poland signed both of these covenants? And isn't it true that a free union movement was formed in Poland, called Solidarity, with which almost half of the adult population of Poland affiliated itself? And isn't it also true that this free union movement has been ruthlessly suppressed? How does that square with the sections from the Covenants which I have just read to you?"

I suppose I would answer the question as follows: "Senator what you say is true. But the Polish Government is relying on escape clauses in the Covenants. In the Economic, Social and Cultural Covenant the escape clause reads as follows: 'No restrictions may be placed on the exercise of this right other than those prescribed by law and which are necessary in a democratic society in the interests of national security or public order or for the protection of the rights and freedoms of others.' In the Civil and Political Covenant, the escape clause is quite similar. It just adds the protection of public health or morals as justification for restricting the rights of labor unions."

The Senator's response in this imaginary conversation might be as follows: "What kind of quibble is this, Ambassador? Solidarity was a peaceful, unarmed movement, trying to exercise nothing but traditional labor union functions, and not even all of them. It was no threat to national security or public order or to public health or morals. And how do you protect what the Covenants call a democratic society by suppressing democratic rights? Or can the Covenants be construed to allow suppression of a peaceful labor union in the interest of national security if the threat comes not from the union but from abroad?"

I could answer as follows: "Well, Senator, Poland notified the United Nations Secretary General of its temporary derogation of the provisions of the Civil and Political Covenant by stating the following:

" 'Temporary limitation of certain rights of citizens has been prompted by the supreme national interest. It was caused by the exigencies of averting civil war, economic anarchy as well as destabilization of the

State and social structures. The purpose of the measures thus introduced has been to reverse an exceptionally serious public emergency threatening the life of the nation and to create conditions for an effective protection of Poland's sovereignty and independence.' "

The Senator's response might be as follows: "Those are a lot of fancy phrases, Ambassador. From what I know about the situation in Poland in 1981 I am sure there was no threat of civil war or economic anarchy or threat to the stability of the state. What the phrase destabilization of the social structure means I simply don't know. As for the threat to the life of the nation, sovereignty and independence, as I asked before, do you mean that you can suspend all these rights under the Covenant if the threat comes from abroad? and in the case of Poland, which is entirely surrounded by its allies in the Warsaw Pact, where could such a threat originate?

"Let me ask you another question. Article 18 of the Civil and Political Covenant guarantees freedom of expression. But I see that Michnik, Lis and Frasyniuk have been arrested again. How do you explain that?

"And what about free labor unions in some of the other countries in that area of the world? And what about Article 12 of the Civil and Political Covenant, which allows people to move freely within their countries, to leave their countries and to return? And what about the freedom of religion as guaranteed by Article 20 and about the right of peaceful assembly as guaranteed by Article 21? Are any of these provisions observed by any of those countries, all of which have signed the Covenant on Civil and Political Rights? And let me ask you, Ambassador, if all these provisions are either being violated by the countries that signed them or can be rendered meaningless by those loopholes that are big enough to drive a truck through, can you tell this Committee what useful purpose is served by our recommending that the Senate ratify these documents?"

Mr. Chairman, as of now I can't think of a good answer to this last question. And because I cannot give a good answer, because there is no good answer, I cannot possibly agree to the Polish proposal.

125

U.S. and Soviet Quality of Life Compared, by Richard Schifter.
Address by the head of U.S. delegation, Ottawa, May 22, 1985,
Current Policy No. 713, Department of State.

Ever since this conference began, we have returned, from time to time, to a discussion of what is perceived to be the distinction between political and civil rights on one hand and economic and social rights on the other hand. I shall, therefore, at the outset of this statement, set forth the thoughts of the U.S. delegation on this issue.

Rights of the individual

Those of us who trace our views of government to the writings of the English and French thinkers of the 18th century Enlightenment subscribe to the proposition that government derives its mandate from the consent of the governed, such consent being expressed in free elections. The government, thus, reflects the will of the majority. In this context of majority rule, the philosophers on the subject defined certain rights of the individual which are so basic that no government may deprive him of them, irrespective of the size of the popular majority by which it was installed in office. These rights of the individual are what we understand principally under the term "human rights." They define and clarify the fundamental relationship between the individual and his government, and they consist, essentially, of limitations on the powers of government. Like the biblical "Thou shalt not," the beginning phrase of the first amendment to the U.S. Constitution, the beginning phrase of our Bill of Rights, is "Congress shall make no law"—a phrase followed by the subjects on which Congress shall make no law, such as abridgment of freedom of speech or the press.

When we use the term "right," we think of a claim which can be enforced in the courts. The rights guaranteed in the U.S. Constitution, which in CSCE terminology are referred to as political and civil rights, are rights which every citizen can call upon the courts to protect.

We view what are here referred to as economic and social rights as belonging in an essentially different category. They are, as we see it, the goals of government policy in domestic affairs. Government, as we see it, should foster policies which will have the effect of encouraging economic development so as to provide jobs under decent working conditions for all those who want to work at income levels which allow for an adequate standard of living. These goals should be attained in a setting which allows freedom of choice of his work to everyone. For those who are unable to find jobs we provide unemployment compensation and, if that is unavailable, other forms of social assistance. The economic system which is now in place in our country is fully in keeping with the relevant articles of the Universal Declaration of Human Rights.

The U.S. delegation, in selecting issues for discussion at this conference, decided deliberately to limit itself to problems which, though of great concern to the American public, would not require systemic changes in the Soviet Union to effect correction. Every one of the problems we have raised so far about conditions in countries which describe themselves as Marxist-Leninist could be eliminated while staying within the system.

It so happens, therefore, that the Soviet human rights problems of greatest concern to the American public are the problems which could be most easily solved by the Soviet Union. They concern, as we have pointed out, the incarceration of persons guilty only of giving expression to their thoughts, the persecution of religious believers, the commitment of sane persons to institutions for the mentally ill, cultural repression, and discrimination against certain people on the grounds of ancestry. The Soviet State could, as I have said, correct these problems without effecting fundamental structural change.

We had not intended to engage in discussions of economic and social conditions in the Soviet Union, both because the American public is not as deeply aware of or concerned about them and because correction of any shortcomings which we would have to point out would, indeed, require systemic change in the Soviet Union. We see such changes occurring gradually in some other countries which had initially adopted the Soviet economic model. However, we did not think this meeting to be an appropriate forum for a discussion of such issues. Nevertheless, as the Soviet delegation has clearly insisted that we engage in a discussion of social and economic issues, let me say that we are prepared to join in that debate. To begin with, I shall respond in detail to the concerns expressed by the Soviet delegation as to social and economic problems in the United States.

U.S. social and economic problems

Unemployment. First of all, let me discuss the problem of unemployment in the United States. Our present unemployment rate is 7.3%. It reached a peak of 10.5% in 1982 and has declined significantly since then. Millions of new jobs have been created in recent years, offering new opportunities to the unemployed as well as to persons newly entering the job market. While we agree that an unemployment rate of 7.3% is still too high and further efforts need to be made to reduce the unemployment level, we believe that any person analyzing our unemployment rate should note the following:

About two percentage points are attributable to so-called frictional unemployment, i.e., persons in transit from one job to another.

A significant number of the job opportunities which are available in the United States at any one time go unfilled because no one in the locality in which the jobs are available is interested in doing the kind of work available át the wages which are being offered; as we don't have a system under which people can be compelled to work, unfilled jobs thus exist side by side with unemployment.

We do not have an anti-parasitism law; some persons prefer to draw unemployment insurance payments or welfare benefits rather than take jobs which they deem unsuitable.

The percentage of our adult population looking for work in the productive sector of the economy is enlarged by the fact that we have significantly fewer people than the Soviet Union in our military forces, in our police forces, and, for that matter, in prison or performing forced labor; specifically, though the Soviet population is only 12% greater than that of the United States, its military forces are almost 200% greater, its police forces more than 100% greater, and its prison population, including forced labor, over 1,100% greater than the corresponding figures in the United States.

I have made these points only to explain what the 7.3% figure means, not to suggest that it can and should be ignored. Our government is committed to the proposition that everyone who wants to work should have an opportunity to do so. Government policy is dedicated to the stimulation of economic growth, to the creation of more jobs, to the raising of standards of living, to the reduction of poverty. In a country such as ours, there is often disagreement as to what might be the best policy to effect economic growth. Different political groupings advocate different solutions to the problems we face. But there is an overwhelming consensus that unemployment must be reduced and that it should be reduced within our present economic framework.

When we compare our economic model to alternate approaches, we must note that, to some extent, unemployment in our country is a consequence of our ideas of individual freedom. We do not assign people to jobs or prosecute them for parasitism if they fail to take an available job. As I have noted, there are people in our country who pass up job opportunities because they don't like the jobs that are being offered or consider the wage offers too low. There are others who are unemployed and might be able to get a job of their liking and at a satisfactory wage at a substantial distance from their home, but they are loath to move.

Much of the latter kind of unemployment is created by the fact that the economy adapts itself to market conditions. Uneconomic enterprises are thus compelled to close, sometimes causing serious dislocation in the communities dependent on them. In the long run, such adjustments enable the economy to adapt itself to change and to increase its overall productivity. But in the short run, it creates serious hardships for the people directly and adversely affected. To deal with these hardships and to bridge the periods of difficulty is a continuing challenge to our Federal, State, and local governments. We recognize it for the problem it is and seek to deal with it. For reasons which I shall state later, the overwhelming majority of our people are not at all attracted to the solution to this problem which the Soviet Union offers.

There is one other point that needs to be made with regard to the issue of employment. We need to emphasize the role which a free labor movement has played in the United States in strengthening the role of the worker, achieving increases in wages and improvements in working conditions. The existence of a free labor movement, accountable only to its members and not under the control of employers or governments, is, we believe, essential to the protection of the interests of working people. It has succeeded in the United States in setting standards not only for its own members but for unorganized workers as well. As I noted yesterday, workers in certain states which profess to have been founded for the benefit of the working people are deprived of the ability to assert their interests through the operation of free and independent labor unions.

Homelessness. The distinguished Soviet representative has raised the issue of homelessness in the United States. We recognize the existence of homelessness in our society. This is a complex and difficult problem for us, in large part because in recent years our laws have not allowed us to incarcerate or commit to mental institutions persons who insist on living on the sidewalks of our cities as long as they are not threats to themselves or society. Many of these people refuse to make use of the wide range of accommodations available to them. In some societies they would be charged with vagrancy, parasitism, or forced into mental institutions. In our cities they remain on the streets, quite understandably causing many visitors to wonder whether there is, in fact, no housing available for them.

The fact is that our Federal Government and our State governments have spent and continue to spend hundreds of millions of dollars to provide shelter for the homeless. Those who cannot be self-sufficient, such as the elderly, are given priority in assistance programs. Furthermore, the tradition of voluntarism in the United States has resulted in the creation of a great number of nonprofit groups which have specialized in helping those in need of what our laws call safe and sanitary housing. Particular efforts have been made to assist the elderly.

I should also make it clear that there are quite a number of people in our country who live in housing which we deem substandard. We are interested in improving such housing, though we know that what is substandard in the United States may be standard in countries which are among our severest critics.

Discrimination. We readily concede that persons were for a long time discriminated against in our country on the grounds of their ancestry, and we recognize that government at all levels shares culpability with regard to this problem. However, beginning 40 years ago, policies on the subject of race began to change in our country and have changed at an ever-accelerating pace. Over this period the Federal Government as well as State and local governments have succeeded in stamping out all officially sanctioned forms of discrimination based on ancestry. Beyond that, laws have been enacted that require the private sector to conform to fundamental principles of nondiscrimination.

What I have just said does not mean that we can overnight overcome the results of generations of discrimination and disadvantage. I have not carefully checked all the statistics which our distinguished Soviet colleague has recited, but they may very well be correct. What is important to note is the change in the figures in recent years, as groups of our population which were previously discriminated against have seen the barriers fall and have used the opportunities which have been afforded them.

Nothing that I have said is designed to suggest that we have eliminated racial and ethnic antagonisms within our population. They do exist, and government is not able to change that fact. But here, too, we have witnessed change. Through the activities of various institutions—including, particularly, religious organizations—younger people have increasingly been imbued with a commitment to human brotherhood. We, therefore, have reason to believe that over time these antagonisms will continue to diminish.

My remarks about nondiscrimination generally apply to Indians as well, but our Indian people have a special problem, which they share with indigenous peoples elsewhere in the world—indigenous peoples whose culture and economies differ markedly from those of the surrounding society. Many of our Indian reservation residents are only a few generations removed from a hunting and fishing culture. They have found it much more difficult to fit into industrial society than do the descendants of families engaged in agriculture.

The unusually large unemployment rate on Indian reservations is related to this problem. It is, let me emphasize, the unemployment rate not of Indian people but for Indian reservations. Indian people who have decided to leave the reservations can find and have found jobs elsewhere in the country. But there is no doubt that Indian reservations have found it difficult to attract industry and thereby create job opportunities for Indian people at reasonable wage levels in their home communities. It happens to be a problem with which our government has concerned itself and continues to concern itself. I readily concede that the problem has not been solved. In fact, I have personally worked and written on this subject.

I shall complete this discussion of discrimination by noting again that the United States has served as a magnet for immigrants of all races to achieve a higher standard of life for themselves and for their children. The fact that a majority of recent immigrants to the United States are nonwhites from non-European areas and that they have integrated into our society at a truly amazing speed is clear evidence of the strength of the well-recognized American acceptance of a variety of ethnic groups into our social and economic system.

The role of women. Much has also been said here as to the role of women in the United States. As to the point made concerning the Equal Rights Amendment, let me note again that the courts of the United States have construed the 5th and 14th amendments to the U.S. Constitution so as to require legal equality between the sexes.

Admittedly, what is required by law takes time to be translated into reality in day-to-day life. The entry of women into our economic life on a basis of parity occurred only quite recently, after 1970. It has, however, progressed at amazing speed. To cite one item of statistics that comes to mind, in 1970, 2% of all law school students were women. Today they are 50%.

But new entries do not come in at the very top. That is why we find average women's wages to be below the average earned by men. It was 60% in 1980; it is 64% today and is expected to continue to rise as the years go by. Here, too, we do not suggest that we have reached our goal of full actual rather than purely legal equality, but we are clearly on our way toward that goal.

Soviet economic progress since the October Revolution

As I said earlier, we had not intended to engage here in a debate on the respective advantages of the U.S. and Soviet models, but as the Soviet Union has initiated this discussion, we want to make it clear that we are not inclined to shrink from it. Let me say also that we recognize that the Soviet Union started to industrialize later than we did and that the Soviet Union suffered devastation during World Wars I and II. But let us also remember that we recalled earlier in this session that the war in Europe ended 40 years ago. How far has the Soviet Union been able to travel in this period on the way to its economic goals?

In the early 1960's, Nikita Khrushchev predicted that the Soviet Union would surpass the United States in living standards by 1980. Yet studies of comparative per capita consumption conducted by University of Virginia professor Gertrude Schroeder and others show that today, 25 years after Khrushchev spoke and 67 years after the October Revolution, the Soviet standard of living remains barely one-third of the U.S. level. These same studies show that Soviet living standards are much lower than in any developed Western country.

The average Soviet citizen, in fact, lives less well than someone living at the official U.S. poverty line. An American family living at that level, for example, lives on an income which is 41% of the U.S. average. About 15.2% of our population lives at or below that level. By comparison, as indicated, the average Soviet citizen lives at about one-third of the U.S. average, which gives us some idea of the percentage of the Soviet population which lives below the U.S. poverty line. As suggested earlier by our distinguished Spanish colleague, equally dramatic comparisons can be made between the average Soviet citizen and the average unemployed worker in the West. In the recession year of 1982, for example—the worst since World War II—the median per capita income for unemployed workers in the United States was about $5,000. The average income of a family with an unemployed worker was $20,000. We do not deny that such an income in many cases reflected a substantial decline in living standards. But a Soviet family living on the equivalent of $20,000 a year would be quite well off, even after we have adjusted for differences in the cost of basic needs.

In making these comparisons, I do not mean to suggest that the Soviet Union has made no economic progress since the October Revolution. But the limited success the Soviet economy has enjoyed in the past was dependent on constant additions to the labor force and on the availability of plentiful and inexpensive resources. Now that the Soviet Union has used up its surplus labor pool and its resources are more costly, its growth rates have plummeted. The Soviet Union, in fact, is no longer closing the gap between itself and the developed West. The per capita consumption comparisons I cited earlier have remained constant over the last decade. Given low Soviet labor productivity, the gap can reasonably be expected to widen in the future.

Shortcomings of the Soviet economic system

Consumer shortages and corruption. The Soviet economy today is characterized by pervasive shortages of consumer goods and the widespread corruption these shortages generate. These features, moreover, are not temporary problems which will solve themselves through continued progress over time. Rather, they are problems endemic to the Soviet system of centralized economic planning. This system, based on the notion that a small group of planners can efficiently allocate resources for an entire economy, has created instead an economy of bottlenecks, shortages, and waste.

In the Soviet Union, unlike anywhere in the developed West, the most basic consumer goods are in continuous short supply and rationing remains a common fact of Soviet life. The situation has been so bad in some localities in recent years that food riots have reportedly occurred. In 1981, *Izvestiia* reported the introduction of rationing in 12 major Soviet cities, including Irkutsk, Kazan, Tbilisi, Vologda, and Naberezhnye Chelny (now called Brezhnev). We have learned that meat and butter have both been formally rationed in the closed city of Sverdlovsk and its surrounding villages for several years. Presumably, the same is true of many other areas closed to foreign visitors.

The long lines of people lining up for scarce items on Soviet city streets have become famous throughout the world. The production and distribution system is so capricious that it is impossible to tell what will be available from one day to the next. This is why Soviet housewives frequently join lines without inquiring what is for sale. They simply assume they had better get whatever it is while it's available. This is also one important cause of Soviet productivity problems, since working people are typically obliged to take unauthorized absences from their jobs to chase after scarce necessities. These endless shortages force the average Soviet family to spend 2 hours shopping every day just to obtain the basic necessities of life.

The endless waiting is bad enough, but the Soviet consumer often finds that the product waiting for him at the front of the line is hardly worth the wait. The quality, variety, and design of the consumer goods available in the Soviet Union are, in fact, notoriously poor by both Western and East European standards, and retail trade and personal service facilities are scarce, primitive, and inefficient.

As one might expect, the chronic shortage of basic consumer goods has fostered the creation of an enormous black market in scarce items. This, in turn, has led to widespread official corruption as persons with administrative control over scarce commodities divert them for personal gain. Corruption exists in all societies, but in the Soviet Union it is a pervasive and normal part of life. Stealing from the state is so common that the Soviet people have come to take it for granted. Anecdotes about corruption and bribery have become a staple of Soviet humor.

The leaders of the Soviet Union are aware of the problem, of course.

It has been frequently raised at party plenums, and the Soviet media are replete with stories of corruption, bribery, and the executions of those unfortunate enough to be selected as examples of equal justice under law. What the Soviet leadership seemingly fails to realize or simply will not face is that an economy of shortages inevitably breeds corruption. Some estimate that as much as 25% of the Soviet gross national product (GNP) is diverted to the black market every year.

It must be emphasized once again that the chronic shortages and widespread corruption which characterize contemporary Soviet life are fundamental features of the Soviet economic system. They reflect the systemic inflexibility of a centralized economic planning system which breeds bottlenecks and inefficiencies.

The Soviet consumer is further disadvantaged by the Soviet preference for spending on defense and heavy industry at the expense of the consumer sector. Soviet per capita spending for defense, for example, is, in relative terms, at least twice as high as in any developed Western country. Though we have heard a great many reminders from some of our colleagues here of the importance of the right to life and appeals for an end to the arms race, let us remember that in the 1970's the Soviet Union was the only runner in that arms race, continuing its buildup while the United States was, in effect, engaging in unilateral arms reduction. Today, the Soviet Union spends at least 14% of its GNP on defense, compared to only 7% for the United States. Given the Soviet Union's systemic economic problems and its emphasis on heavy industry and weapons procurement, it is little wonder that Soviet authorities and press commentators chronically complain about the evils of "consumerism" and against the excessive accumulation of material goods.

Effects of agricultural collectivization. The Soviet system of collectivized agriculture also contributes to the harshness of Soviet life. Much of the problem in food supply stems from the collectivized nature of Soviet agriculture. As is well known, the forced collectivization of agriculture in the early 1930's divested Soviet farmers of their land. What is not so well known is that the forcible confiscation of grain supplies that accompanied it resulted in a widespread famine that killed as many as 6 million in the Ukraine alone. Collectivization not only killed 6 million people but it permanently crippled Soviet agriculture.

The Soviet Union—in prerevolutionary days the world's largest grain exporter—is now the world's largest grain importer. Twenty percent of the Soviet work force works in agriculture, compared to 3% in the United States. Yet the Soviet Union often has had to import up to 25% of its grain. American farmers, who own their own land, are 10 times more productive than their Soviet counterparts. Each year, approximately 20% of the grain, fruit, and vegetable harvest, and as much as 50% of the Soviet potato crop, perishes because of the poor storage, transportation, and distribution system.

Soviet farmers have not lost their ability to grow crops. They just lack the incentive to do so on a *kolkhoz* [collective farm]. By contrast, even though private plots, which are farmed by individuals in the early morning and late evening hours, occupy only 4% of the Soviet Union's arable land, they produce 25% of the Soviet Union's total crop output.

Housing shortages and deficiencies. Housing in the Soviet Union is in as short supply as most consumer goods. At least 20% of all urban families must share kitchen and toilet facilities with other families. Another 5% live in factory dormitories. Young married couples are typically forced to live with their parents and must wait years for housing of their own.

The housing that does exist is extremely cramped, more so than in any other developed country in the world. The average Soviet citizen has 14 square meters of living space, for example, compared to the 49 square meters available to the average American. This means that there are approximately two people for every room in the Soviet Union, compared with two rooms for every person in the United States. Soviet statistics reveal that in 1983, 32% of all urban housing had no hot water, 23% was without gas, 19% without indoor baths, 12% without central heating, 11% without sewage facilities, and 9% without water.

The housing situation is much worse in the countryside and contains many features reminiscent of the 19th century—or even the 18th. There, for the most part, heating is with fireplaces, food is cooked on wood stoves, outhouses provide the toilet facilities, and water frequently is from a well.

Although there has been much new housing built in the Soviet Union in recent years, almost all of it consists of poorly constructed high-rise apartment buildings, which are even more poorly maintained. At the current rate of construction, the per capita space available to Soviet citizens will begin to approach the Western standard in approximately 150 years. Soviet housing woes should come as no surprise, given the fact that the Soviet Union spends less than one-fifth as much on housing as the United States and well under half of what is spent in Spain and Japan.

Status of Soviet women. Women in the Soviet Union usually occupy the lowest status and lowest paying jobs in Soviet society. One-third of all working Soviet women, for example, are employed as agricultural laborers. By contrast, only 1.5% of American women are so employed.

Soviet authorities often point to the liberal maternity benefits accorded to Soviet women. Yet the Soviet Union is currently suffering from a severe labor shortage brought on by declining birth rates. This reduction in birth rates, in turn, is due to the extraordinarily high abortion rate. Many women have a history of five or more abortions. The fact is that the low Soviet standard of living compels women to work to supplement the family income. Maternity benefits, with extra mouths to feed and bodies to clothe, are, in many instances, simply not enough to encourage a family to let a child be born.

Unlike Soviet men, the working day of a Soviet woman does not end as she leaves the field or factory. Soviet women are expected to do the cooking and the housework and the waiting in line.

In the West, women have effectively banded together to fight discrimination and sexism, but Soviet women have no access to effective political power. In its entire history, only one woman has ever served on the Politburo; none serves there now. Fewer than 5% of Central Committee members are female. Interestingly, only one-fourth of Communist Party members are female.

Medical care and health problems. Soviet authorities are often fond of pointing out that health care in the Soviet Union is free. As with so much that is free or subsidized in the Soviet Union, however, you often get what you pay for. Although there are plenty of beds in Soviet hospitals, the people who lie in them frequently receive substandard care. One-third of them, for example, develop postoperative infections due to unsanitary conditions. Most of the doctors who care for them, moreover, are poorly trained by Western standards. Medicine is not a high-prestige occupation in the Soviet Union, and doctors are among the lowest paid workers in Soviet society. Significantly, 70% of these low-paid physicians are women.

Soviet medicine is not immune to the same shortages that afflict the rest of Soviet society. Medical equipment and many medicines are in extremely short supply. One-third of all Soviet hospitals, for example, do not have adequate facilities for blood transfusions. Basic items such as bandages, aspirin, and syringes are often difficult to find. Food rations are so small that patients must supplement their diet with food from home. In Novosibirsk, for example, which is home to many leading Soviet academic institutes and where one would expect supplies to be significantly better than normal, only 11% of the 216 standard drugs to be prescribed for specific illnesses are actually available. These shortages are not surprising in light of the fact that Soviet per capita expenditures on health care are less than one-third the U.S. level.

Although the problems in the Soviet health care delivery system are serious, they are not the most serious medical problem facing the Soviet Union today. Dramatically, over the course of the past two decades a significant deterioration has occurred in the overall health status of the Soviet population. Recent studies show that there has been an increase in Soviet death and morbidity rates over the past 20 years. The life expectancy of Soviet males has decreased during the same period by a little over 4 years, from 66 in the mid-1960's to just under 62 years today. In the United States during the same period, male life expectancy increased from 66 to 71 years. Infant mortality in the Soviet Union has increased from 26.2 per 1,000 live births in 1971 to about 40 per 1,000 today. U.S. infant mortality during the same period has decreased from 24.7 per 1,000 to 10.7.

The Soviet figure for infant mortality is necessarily an estimate since Soviet authorities stopped publishing infant mortality statistics after 1974 when the rate had risen to 31.9 per 1,000. This rate was already much higher than in any developed Western country. The Soviet Union also has stopped publishing life expectancy figures. The reason why this has been done is obvious enough. The decrease in male life expectancy and the increase in infant mortality in the Soviet Union are historic events. Never before has a developed, industrialized nation suffered a decline in these demographic indicators in time of peace.

The reasons for this decline are even more disturbing for anyone tempted to look to the Soviet Union as a model for social and economic development. Factors such as poor health care, increased smoking, and frequently unregulated industrial pollution are important, but perhaps the most important contributor is alcohol. This would appear to be the view of Soviet authorities themselves.

The Soviet Union leads the world in the per capita consumption of hard liquor. Much of it is consumed in the form of home-brewed moonshine known as *samogon*. Alcohol consumption in the Soviet Union has more than doubled over the past 25 years. The death rate from alcohol poisoning in the Soviet Union is 88 times the U.S. rate, and alcohol and its effects may be the leading cause of death among Soviet males.

Alcohol abuse in the Soviet Union is not simply a male problem. Alcohol abuse is the third leading cause of illness among Soviet women and is a key factor in both the alarming rise in birth defects and the increased infant mortality rate. By 1980 the net social cost of alcohol abuse in decreased labor productivity in the Soviet Union amounted to a staggering 8%–9% of the total national income.

Much of the heavy drinking in the Soviet Union occurs in the work place. Professor R. Lirmyan of the Soviet Academy of the U.S.S.R. Min-

istry of Internal Affairs, writing in a 1982 issue of *Molodoy Kommunist,*
reported that 37% of the male work force is chronically drunk. Not surprisingly, drunkenness is the leading cause of industrial accidents.

A poll cited in a March 1984 edition of a Soviet journal, *Sovetskaya
Rossiya,* revealed that half the Soviet population regards drunkenness as
the number one social problem in the Soviet Union. Seventy-four percent said they were alarmed over the extent of public drunkenness.
These statistics make clear that the Soviet Union now suffers from an
alcohol abuse problem of epidemic proportions, serious enough to cause
a significant rise in the national death rate.

As I remarked earlier, even the Soviet leadership concurs with this
assessment. Vitaly Fedorchuk, the Soviet Minister for Internal Affairs,
interviewed in the August 29, 1984, issue of *Literaturnaya Gazeta,* can-
didly acknowledged that Soviet mortality and sickness rates have been
on the increase, and he specifically cited alcohol abuse as the cause.

We note with interest that the Soviet authorities only last week announced yet another campaign against the abuse of alcohol. Production
is to be cut back, the drinking age raised, and penalties against the man-
ufacture of home brew increased. While it is possible that these measures may meet with some limited success, we note that similar campaigns have always failed in the past. Our suspicion is that alcohol abuse
in the Soviet Union will remain an alarmingly serious problem until
the Soviet leadership begins to come to grips with the profound social
malaise that gave rise to the problem in the first place. In saying this,
I do not mean to deny that there are drug and alcohol problems in the
United States and in other countries which deserve our serious attention. But I am suggesting that in the Soviet Union we are dealing with
a problem of an entirely different order of magnitude.

Egalitarianism in the Soviet Union

I have been talking at length here about some serious difficulties in the
Soviet social and economic system. But there is one more problem I
would like to discuss. As we know, Marxist-Leninist ideology claims to
be based on the notion of egalitarianism. This, we are told, is what the
great October Revolution was all about. One would, therefore, expect
that whatever problems the Soviet Union might have, the Soviet authorities would ensure that no class or group of individuals would ever
be accorded privileges not available to other members of Soviet society.

But the truth is that certain groups in Soviet society (the party, the military officer corps, the diplomatic corps, the scientific-technical intelligentsia, the cultural and sports establishments) have deliberately shielded themselves from the social and economic hardships faced by the rest of the population. A privileged 5% of the Soviet population, known as the *Nomenklatura*, has access to special "closed" stores that are specially stocked with foreign goods not available in regular stores, as well as bountiful supplies of Soviet goods that are in short supply elsewhere. The average Soviet citizen is forbidden from entering these stores, which are unmarked and have opaque windows to prevent the curious from looking in. Housing space is allocated by state authorities on the basis of social status. Many leading Soviet organizations have their own housing facilities, which are of good standard and centrally located.

The Fourth Directorate of the Ministry of Health runs a closed system of hospitals, clinics, and dispensaries for the *Nomenklatura*, providing far better services than those available to the general population. The Soviet ruling oligarchy also has access to such special benefits as foreign travel, automobiles, admission to the best schools, country houses, access to cultural events, and paid vacations in choice resorts, which are not available to the average citizen. Even the center lanes of certain roads are closed off for their exclusive personal use. To quote from George Orwell's *Animal Farm*: "All animals are equal, but some are more equal than others."

Conclusion

In an earlier intervention, the distinguished Soviet representative suggested that we were reluctant to discuss social and economic issues in this forum. I hope that I have succeeded in dispelling this impression. Despite our many problems, we believe that we in the West, with our pluralistic, mixed-market economies, have gone further toward meeting basic human social and economic aspirations than has the system now in place in the Soviet Union.

More than 35 years ago, there was published a collection of essays authored by prominent former communists or fellow travelers, including Ignazio Silone, André Gide, Richard Wright, and Arthur Koestler. The book was entitled *The God That Failed*. Each of these prominent writers explained in his own words why he had concluded that the price in terms of personal freedom was not worth paying to attain the promised goal of a future paradise. The decades that passed have demonstrated that the image of paradise off in the distance was only a mirage.

The Balance Sheet of Ottawa

126

Assessment of the Meeting of Experts, by Ekkehard Eickhoff.
"Das KSZE-Expertentreffen über Menschenrechte in Ottawa—
eine Bewertung," *Europa-Archiv* 19 (1985): 573–80.
Translated from the German by Carol Herrmann.

The necessity of the debate

The purpose of the meeting in Ottawa, according to the mandate from
the follow-up meeting of Madrid (1983), was to look into "questions
concerning respect, in their States, for human rights and fundamental
freedoms, in all their aspects, as embodied in the Final Act." It should
"draw up conclusions and recommendations to be submitted to the
governments of all participating States." The meeting of experts did
indeed deal in a lively and in-depth manner with the respect or disrespect for human rights and fundamental freedoms for participating
States. A critical dialogue with a frank and sober explanation of the
human rights question in Europe was a matter of political credibility.

This dialogue has taken place. That was not to be taken for granted.
The Soviet Union and its allies at first took the position, in an arbitrary
and absurd interpretation of the mandate, that each country was to
report only on the human rights situation at home. They also resolutely
refused to discuss individual cases of human rights violations. But after
the West, including the neutral countries, did not let itself be swayed
from dealing with flagrant human rights abuses in the Warsaw Pact
countries, and when the United States successively brought up serious
individual cases in detail, the Soviet Union turned to a critical counter-
attack. Thus developed a comprehensive debate, from May 8 to
June 4, 1985, over the respect for human rights in the participating
countries, including discussion of individual cases. In the process, a
realistic, differentiated and in many areas depressing panorama of the
human rights situation in Eastern Europe was depicted.

Although only the opening and final sessions of the meeting were
public, the texts of the most important interventions from both sides
nevertheless constantly found their way into the media. In this way this
discussion and its echo in the press and in broadcasting—which was
liveliest in Central Europe and in the American East Coast press—contributed to a shaping of opinion that reached all of Europe. It strengthened the awareness that human rights apply to everyone despite all vio-

lations, even if compliance cannot be forced—a fate that they share with the Ten Commandments.

Human rights and political goals

The Western delegations endeavored to advance beyond this unavoidable, even necessary, controversy to at least the initial stages of a dialogue about human rights problems. With this the individual participating countries had in mind especially those human rights which most concern their citizens: for example, freedom of religion and of conscience for France, and freedom of movement for the Federal Republic of Germany. The Soviet delegation offered the opportunity for an initial movement beyond the controversy when it pointed to the separations which arise through family reunifications between those individuals leaving the country and the friends and relatives left behind. The Federal Republic of Germany acknowledged this: family separations over long periods of time and great distances lead to the development of new circles of personal ties around the separated members on both sides, one of which will be forsaken when the family reunion has finally been effected. That was the beginning of an exchange of practical arguments about a significant and concrete human rights problem. The interest of the West in a continuing dialogue demanded that even objective criticism from the Eastern side, for instance due to the non-guarantee of the right to work, be examined in detail. Conversely, it was necessary to differentiate as precisely as possible in the criticism directed at other countries. So, for example, the delegation of the Federal Republic of Germany, in the pursuit of its main concern, the realization of the right to freedom of movement, also recognized with praise human rights advances in the GDR in particular (visitor and exit statistics). In this part of the debate the unanimous defense in the plenary of the right to freedom of movement by all friends of the Federal Republic of Germany, including the neutral countries, made a lasting impression.[1]

A noteworthy beginning to a constructive East-West dialogue on the rights of minorities developed out of the criticism that the Turkish delegation directed at Bulgaria due to its assimilation campaign with regard to Muslim, Turkish-speaking citizens. This criticism was, to be sure, strictly rejected by Bulgaria. But a broad debate unfolded from this controversy, a debate which dealt with the complex minority problem of the Danube countries in informative and sophisticated assessments from both parts of Europe.

From the course of the four-week discussion on the respect for human rights, one can draw the positive and unequivocal conclusion that it not only left the character of the concluding records as the basis of a call for the fulfillment of human rights obligations in other CSCE countries untouched, but indeed strengthened it.

The Soviet Union and its allies in no way limited themselves in this debate to the defensive. In fact, all participants had expected that the East would put the social, economic and cultural human rights—such as the right to work, right to health care, right to education—in the forefront and would accuse the West of massive violation of these rights. Such was indeed the case. The West confronted this criticism willingly, but described these rights as self-evident political goals of every modern democratic country—quite apart from the fact that most of the participating countries are obligated by their signing of the United Nations Human Rights Pact of 1966 to respect these "human rights of the second generation" and that the Final Act also refers to them. But the Soviet Union was obviously following a strategy which proceeded from a defense through diversion. In its opinion, in the Final Act and the Madrid Concluding Document there is an imbalance between the classic individual human rights and basic freedoms on the one side, and the economic, social and cultural human rights on the other, and the Soviets are trying to shift this relationship in favor of the latter. As battering ram for breaking into the human rights edifice of the CSCE, they made use of a so-called "human right of the third generation," the "right to life in peace."[2] By claiming with their allies that in the nuclear age this "right to life in peace" is the fundamental prerequisite for fulfillment of all other rights, and by insisting with great obstinacy almost to the end of the negotiations on the introduction of this right into a concluding document of the meeting of experts, they made clear that they are seeking to give the human rights obligations of the CSCE a new weight and orientation.

Human rights and international relations

The formula of "right to life in peace" as a human right was in this context totally unacceptable to the West. As a prerequisite for the fulfillment of individual human rights, it pushes the primary and indisputable obligation of the participating countries to a policy of peacekeeping onto a false level, and the human rights rules of conduct of the Final Act onto an inappropriate one. For the West, respect for the classic individual rights and liberties, which the state owes to its citizens, to the individual, is the basis of every civilized authority of the state, the prerequisite for the fulfillment of political goals such as full employment or the efficiency of the health service and educational system.

In contrast to these political obligations, which also include the obligation to a policy of constructive maintenance of peace, the primary, individual human rights and basic liberties are precise in content and for the citizen legally recoverable in court. They stand at the head of the Universal Declaration of Human Rights of the United Nations of 1948 and of the Final Act (Principle vii). Those human rights obligations described in the Final Act and Madrid Concluding Document, as formulated there, are the result of a long negotiation process and part of a balanced whole—and a central part. Any attempt to retroactively shift the relative weights would be risky. It would be, as the Swiss Foreign Minister, Pierre Aubert, explained in Helsinki, "dangerous, if one attempted to revise indirectly those postulates of the Final Act, whose application causes vehement debates such as those experienced by our experts in Ottawa. Since it concerns a text of very delicate balance, the attempt to reinterpret certain postulates in it would have unfortunate consequences." Such an attempt at revision in a central part of the Final Act would have to give rise to mistrust, rather than serving the main purpose of the entire process, namely to create trust and secure peace.

Finally, the discussions in Ottawa have clarified another point. The Warsaw Pact countries came into the meeting of experts with the thesis that the issue at hand in Ottawa concerned international cooperation in the area of human rights; the realization of these rights was therefore to be ensured above all by first providing for good relations between countries (best on the terms proposed by the East). As long as this did not happen, fulfillment criticism would be harmful to détente and human rights. The West, including most of the neutral countries, resolutely opposed this assertion. It finds no support of any kind in the Madrid mandate. Above all, it turns upside down the clear meaning of the Final Act in Principle vii, which states: "The participating States recognize the universal significance of human rights and fundamental freedoms, respect for which is an essential factor for the peace, justice and well-being necessary to ensure the development of friendly relations and cooperation among themselves."

This somewhat adventuresome Eastern interpretation of the relationship between human rights and international relations within the framework of the csce, which degrades human rights to the hostage of good political behavior, was put aside by the conference. But the Soviet Union and its allies then weakened their thesis to the extent that human rights topics may not be introduced as the subject of ideological differences into the relations between countries of differing social orders and may not be misused for increasing tension in international relations. They remained with this version without imposing excessive restraint on their polemics because of it, in particular against the United States.

Preliminary work for future conferences

Even though the conference of experts could not agree on a final report, it nevertheless:
—thoroughly portrayed human rights abuses,
—contributed to the clarification of opposing viewpoints,
—reduced extreme reinterpretation attempts ad absurdum and rejected them,
—maintained undiminished the validity of the human rights obligations as the basis of appeal and the integrity of the human rights section in the general context of the CSCE,
—and allowed along with open polemics concrete and constructive discussions among the participating countries.

These discussions were carried on above all in bilateral contacts outside the plenary sessions. They permitted the continuing treatment of numerous problems and individual cases, particularly the fostering of exit applications.

The meeting of experts was not actually unable to agree on the subjects of some recommendations for further treatment during the following meeting. In the intensive negotiations of the last weeks a fundamental agreement to a series of topics emerged. But since the Soviet Union insisted until the end upon introducing the "right to life in peace" into the recommendations, and since it refused to agree to the recommendation to hold an additional CSCE meeting on human rights, the considererable degree of agreement on other topics (such as the banning of torture, equal rights for men and women and rights of migrant workers) could not be incorporated into recommendations.

Finally, the meeting of experts produced well-formulated preliminary work which the participating countries in Vienna 1986 can take up. The delegations of the European Economic Community and of the Atlantic Alliance presented in the last stage of the conference document OME 47 (Ottawa Meeting of Experts), the draft of a report true to the mandate with conclusions and recommendations. When one considers the very diverse main interests, nuances and expectations for success with which they came to Ottawa, it is noteworthy that all 17 Western delegations could at the end agree on such a moderately formulated yet substantial text. It contains precise recommendations on a wide range of topics: on the right to refer, individually or in groups, to the CSCE documents, to promote them and to act according to them and on the republication of CSCE and UN human rights documents as well as on the access to these texts; on freedom of movement, freedom of conscience and of religion; on the rights of minorities, equal rights for men and women, union rights and international cooperation of individuals, groups and institutions in the area of human rights; on the carrying through with human rights into the area of criminal law, namely through the banning of torture, admission of trial observers, reduction of solitary confinement, visiting rights for humanitarian reunions in penal institutions and the banning of the misuse of psychiatry; finally, recommendations on terrorism, on information by governments on human rights inquiries, and on an additional meeting of experts on human rights.

The OME 47 document also takes into account some important proposals of the neutral and nonaligned countries. For the West, therefore, the joint formulation of texts on these human rights on such a broad base is an achievement of some worth.

Under the same date, June 14, the Warsaw Pact countries also submitted the draft of a report (OME 48). The now traditional stopping of the clock over the weekend at CSCE functions (Friday, June 14, was according to the agenda the last working day of the meeting before the final public session on the afternoon of June 17) would still have allowed for intensive negotiations. But a comparison of the moderately formulated Western proposals OME 47 with the Eastern draft OME 48, whose proposal section is almost without exception controversial and largely objectionable, as well as the experience of the last round of negotiations make every further attempt at agreement on such a broad base appear hopeless.

The neutral countries thereupon introduced OME 49, an extremely short and modest draft of a final report aimed at mediation, in order to find a consensus on a bare minimum of political statements. In addition to the descriptive section of the report, this draft contains only a single conclusion: that it is necessary to strengthen efforts for the promotion and encouragement of an effective exercise of human rights and fundamental freedoms contained in the Final Act without regard to the political, economic and social systems. It also contained only a single recommendation: that the participating countries in the follow-up meeting in Vienna should take into consideration the calling of an additional meeting of experts on the respect for human rights. In addition, it emphasized the importance of the task to realize the relevant precepts of the Madrid Concluding Document, referred to the human rights obligations of the participating countries also from Principle VII, and repeated verbatim the paragraph from this principle which relates the respect for human rights to peace, justice and well-being as well as to the development of friendly relations among states. It also noted that "a number of participants had expressed their alarm over serious violations of human rights and basic liberties in some of the participating countries."

The countries of the European Economic Community and of the Western Alliance adopted this mediation proposal without any cuts. The Soviet Union and its allies, on the other hand, were not ready to accept even the one, carefully formulated recommendation which it contained for an additional meeting on human rights and in turn submitted the (last) proposal for a shortened report (OME 50). This followed the neutral mediation text of OME 49, but avoided its recommendation as well as any mention of human rights violations. For the West, as well as for the neutral and nonaligned countries, it was, however, unacceptable to give up this single recommendation.

Thus the conference ended with a constellation in which the Warsaw Pact countries opposed the entire West including all neutral and nonaligned countries, from Finland to Yugoslavia and Malta, from Sweden to Cyprus. All these last-named countries were brought together by a common fundamental system of values in which they will tolerate no diminution.

Tasks for the follow-up meeting in Vienna

This is certainly noteworthy as a clarifying event. But the West cannot have the slightest interest in the construction and strengthening of ideological fronts cutting across Europe. It therefore appears no less noteworthy that in the shortened final positions of OME 49 and OME 50 the lively efforts of both sides toward a compromise and a fulfillment of the mandate became evident. The Warsaw Pact document OME 50 refers to the compulsory nature of the Final Act and of the Madrid Concluding Document with the same words as OME 49 and contains the same conclusion. It likewise uses the wording of the Final Act on the relationship between human rights, peace and relations among states. In a commentary published since then, the leaders of the Soviet delegation, Ambassador Vsevolod Sofinskii and Envoy Sergei Kondrashev, described the fulfillment debate as useful and clarifying.

The debate might also appear useful to the representatives of the Soviet Union because they could present in such detail their criticism of the alleged inadequate guarantee of social, economic and cultural human rights in the West. Useful above all also because they could push forward the "human right to life in peace" with verbal force like a mine under the bastion of the classic human rights—namely as a right (so asserted the Soviet delegation) that actually precedes all others, since by its nonfulfillment this bastion collapses.

Here we must warn against the misapprehension that the West is taking a stand in the CSCE, in the United Nations or elsewhere with the classic individual human rights against the new social human rights of the East. There is no question of that. The West recognizes its obligations arising from the social, economic and cultural human rights as they are formulated in the United Nations human rights pacts of 1966. East and West agree in recognizing the precepts laid down in these treaties. The safeguarding of these rights is a binding political goal for the state. Only through political measures can they be meaningfully guaranteed. That also holds true for the "right to life in peace." Peace-keeping is the primary political goal of the Atlantic Alliance. The threat of total destruction of human life in the nuclear age can only be averted politically. The classic individual human rights and basic liberties, however, unite all three powers of the state. They should be legally available and even enforceable from the state by every individual, as is the case today in the member nations of the Council of Europe.

The debate in Ottawa was not about the—undisputed—content of the here named human rights of the "first, second and third generations," but concerned rather their realization and their rank. The raising of ever-new political goals to the rank of human rights serves no one. But it can indeed offer the state a tool with which to bury under other demands those human rights which it finds inconvenient and finally to subordinate these rights to political goals. This danger is evident.

It has often been lamented that the meeting of experts in Ottawa could not reach a closing consensus and has therefore left no trace of its existence in the concluding documents of the CSCE process. In this case, all Western participants agreed with the viewpoint of the neutral countries that it is better to discharge no document at all than to discharge a meaningless or ambiguous one. But above all, Ottawa has not only brought clarification and revelation, has not only left us valuable experiences and insights but, with the final proposals submitted, it has also produced conference material which already reduces many diverse viewpoints to a common denominator.

NOTES

1   Here, as on many other topics of the debate, the GDR delegation under Ambassador Wolfgang Kiesewetter led a moderate, relevant discussion.
2   See Christian Tomuschat, "Recht auf Frieden: Ein neues Menschenrecht der dritten Generation?," *Europa-Archiv*, September 1985, pp. 271ff.

Culture and Insecurity

127

Differing Conceptions of Culture, by Mihajlo Mihajlov.
"The Budapest Cultural Forum: Heritage, Diversity,
Freedom," *Radio Free Europe Research*, RAD Background
Report/117, October 11, 1985, pp. 2–3.

Differing Eastern and Western conceptions of culture had already given
rise to heated exchanges at the preparatory meeting for the forum, which
was held in Budapest late in 1984. The Western negotiators proposed
that the agenda of the forum should be divided into three parts: dealing
with the creative process, the dissemination of culture, and international
cooperation in the arts. The East European diplomats wanted the
agenda to be divided into different forms of culture, without qualifica-
tions, a procedure calculated to diminish the possibility of raising the
matter of cultural freedom. The West also proposed that delegations to
the forum should include eminent practicing writers and other artists,
while the communist negotiators wanted the delegations to be composed of state bureaucrats. The final agreed agenda divided the forum
into four categories: the plastic and applied arts (including the preservation of cultural and historical monuments); the performing arts (including film, radio, and television); literature (including translations, especially of less widely spoken languages); and mutual cultural knowledge.
The delegations will comprise both government officials and leading
artists. All meetings will be closed to the public except for the opening
and closing sessions.

128

The Arts, the Individual, and Society, by Norman St. John Stevas.
Address by the head of the British delegation, reported by
RFE correspondent Roland Eggleston, Budapest,
October 16, 1985.

Our cultural forum today is not an isolated phenomenon, a *jeu d'esprit*
which has sprung out of a void, but it is an essential development of
the agreements reached at Helsinki.

Some people ask what has Helsinki achieved over the last decade—to
which I reply it has at least succeeded in bringing about the recognition
of the concept of individual human rights in theory, however much

there may be shortcomings in practice. Perhaps the time has now come to make a new start and achieve new practical objectives in the field of culture, which with defense and economics, are given equal prominence in the Helsinki accords.

Right from the outset we should recognize the differences that lie between us. The truth of the matter is that in Western countries we have one idea of culture; in socialist countries there is another. Let me make this crystal clear. The Western idea of culture is essentially one based on the freedom, liberty and autonomy of the individual. The socialist idea of culture, on the other hand, gives pride of place to society as a collectivity rather than to the individual person. As the Soviet Minister of Culture, Mr. Petr Demichev, said earlier this month, "artists concentrate their efforts on socialist work and on strengthening the principles of social justice." I entirely reject that view of art. There is no such thing as socialist art or capitalist art, there is good art or bad art, that is all.

We are not here to gloss over our differences as if they did not exist, papering over the cracks between the rival ideologies. We are not here for self-congratulation and meaningless cultural rhetoric. Neither are we here to engage in a series of polemics and confrontations.

The palm for a definition of culture which is fruitful and still bearing must I think be carried off by the 19th century writer, Matthew Arnold. He commends culture "as the great help out of our present difficulties. Culture being a pursuit of our total perfection by means of getting to know, on all the matters which most concern us, the best which has been thought and said in the world, and, through this knowledge, turning a stream of fresh and free thought upon our stock notions and habits." We may supplement it by what Coleridge said, supported by John Henry Newman, that culture is nothing less than "the harmonious development of those qualities and faculties that characterise our humanity."

It follows therefore that the freedom of the individual is the seminal idea that lies at the heart of the European idea of culture. As soon as you say the word itself you are in the realm, not of fantasy, but of practical reality, of freedom to read, to write, to compose, free from any kind of fear or censorship, the writer choosing freely what to write, guided not by state dictation but by interior standards of goodness and truth, and the reader following the same path.

What hope of engagement can there be with an idea of culture—the socialist one—that is anti-individualist, centered on society, and regards culture as a reflection of economics?

The chances are better than one might think. Marx himself never developed a fully consistent cultural theory. Lenin himself is inconsistent. Having said that "every artist has a right to create freely according to his ideals," he goes on to say "we must guide this process according to a plan and agree on its results." It is through these inconsistencies that a way through may be found for a real dialogue.

I would reject the view that arts are wholly dependent on society and equally deny that the arts determine social reality through creating categories and perceptions.

The truth is, I believe, that the arts in part reflect the structure of society and in part change, develop and create it.

How then do the arts do this? The arts are not the messiah, neither are they in Gautier's caustic phrase, "un chemin de fer." They do, however, put us in touch with the highest human values and achievements, and in a society whose technical richness and material plenty are matched only by its spiritual starvation, they play something of the role discharged by religion in past ages. The arts have now come to age and have their own autonomy, but their roots lie in religion.

It was in Moscow this year that Mr. Ponomarev said to me that the Soviet Union is a part of European civilization. I entirely agree with that. At the foundation of European civilization lies a religious ideal. That is why we are so interested today in the future of the great Russian Orthodox Church which played such an important role in the survival of the Soviet Union in its most testing hours in 1941. That is why we ask legitimately what contribution can it make in Soviet society? And what of other religions? And what of the position of the Jews whose enhancement of our civilization has been so profound, and persistent?

What can the state do for the arts and culture? It should not seek, as the representative of the United States so rightly stressed, to control culture. It is not the function of the Minister of Culture or the Minister for the Arts to direct them. His task is an important but humble one. It is to help to create and to preserve a framework within which the arts can flourish. He is a trustee of the possibilities of civilization.

So what can we do here at this forum to assist in these great matters? The first thing we can do is to lay down our arms and take up the real issues and arguments. We are not to make decisions—that is the prerogative of next year's meeting of our governments in Vienna—but we are here to put forward proposals and they should be proposals which have some chance of being adopted.

Since example is always more important than precept, let me put forward some ideas of my own which may be discussed in detail of course in the smaller groups. There are still far too many administrative and bureaucratic obstacles in the path of cultural cooperation between states. We should start to reduce them or better still get rid of them altogether.

There are delays in granting visas for cultural exchanges; visits are cancelled or postponed at the last minute with no rational explanation being offered.

Other obstacles arise from an apparent lack of trust of regimes for the political reliability of the intellectuals and cultural figures whose talents are necessary to those very states. Privileges of travel, and the opportunity to communicate with their peers is often arbitrarily and haphazardly denied. Objective norms might be drawn up by this forum to govern such matters.

We should seek to abolish the restrictions on the import of books, particularly religious books and publications which should be able to pass freely between individuals in different states. We should have many more exchanges, particularly in the sphere of music and the performing arts. The representative of Czechoslovakia made a most moving speech in favor of cultural freedom. I would commend to him the jazz section of the union of musicians in his country which is at present under a cloud. Oratorical support is one thing, implementation is another.

Finally, the libraries and archives of all signatory countries should be opened to "bona fide" scholars. We want to create a "conspiration"—in the original Latin sense of the term a breathing together—so that the major works of the authors of the individual countries concerned are made available freely. And there is one small but crucial point as a token of our sincerity: the jamming of foreign language broadcasts should stop.

129

The Independent Cultural Symposium, by Janet Fleischman.
Testimony by Assistant to the Executive Director of the
U.S. Helsinki Watch Committee before the Commission
on Security and Cooperation in Europe, Washington,
December 11, 1985.

On October 15–17, Helsinki Watch and the International Helsinki Federation for Human Rights (IHF), a nongovernmental organization with national committees in ten countries, sponsored an independent cultural symposium in Budapest. The meeting was held at the same time—but separate from—the opening of the CSCE Cultural Forum in Budapest. Despite the fact that nongovernmental organizations had staged public events without obstruction at Helsinki meetings in the

Western capitals of Madrid and Ottawa, the Hungarian government forbade the IHF to use the public facilities that had been reserved for its meetings. In our view, the Hungarian government's action violated the 1975 Helsinki accords, which it signed, and the Concluding Document of the 1980–83 Madrid Conference, which it approved.

With the help of many Hungarian intellectuals, however, our meetings were relocated to private apartments and went ahead without further obstruction. This was the first time that private citizens from both East and West had met openly in a Warsaw Pact country to discuss such topics as "writers and their integrity" and "the future of European culture."

In many respects, the Helsinki spirit was as alive as it has ever been for those few days in Budapest. Our independent symposium drew attention both to the official Cultural Forum and to the limits of official Hungarian tolerance. The outcome was therefore contradictory: on one side, the Hungarian government violated its commitments under the Helsinki accords and the Madrid Concluding Document by denying us permission to use the facilities we had reserved to hold our citizens' cultural forum; on the other side, we were not prevented from going forward with our meetings and succeeded in injecting life and meaning into the Helsinki process. Without the existence of this only ongoing East-West forum, our independent symposium could never have taken place. The lifeline we were able to bring to the members of the Hungarian opposition gave them the encouragement of international attention to continue with their activities. In addition, in an effort to demonstrate its good will just before the opening of the Forum, the Hungarian government lifted George Krasso's house arrest and informed János Kis and János Kenedi that they could have passports.

An essential part of the Helsinki process involves the contact between citizens of the participating states. The signatories of the Madrid Concluding Document recognized this when they committed themselves "to ensure satisfactory conditions for activities within the framework of mutual co-operation on their territory, such as sporting and cultural events, in which citizens of other participating States take part." In our view, the citizens' cultural forum that we planned is just the kind of activity contemplated in the agreements reached at Helsinki and Madrid.

Moreover, the fact that our meetings did go forward without further hindrance raises another issue; those meetings would probably not have been allowed to take place in any other Warsaw Pact country, and despite our problems with the Hungarian authorities, they were allowed to take place in Budapest. Due to the Cultural Forum, an opportunity was provided for Hungarian citizens to talk openly about the complicated system of censorship in their country and about the persecution which the Hungarian minority is subjected to in neighboring Romania. Writers and intellectuals from East and West discussed writing under repression as well as in exile, ethnic identity, censorship and the future of European culture. By any standards, it was an extraordinarily dynamic intellectual exchange, but given the fact that it was happening in a place where such discussion is rarely permitted, the event took on even greater importance.

Nevertheless, any importance that the independent forum may have acquired must be viewed within the context of the Helsinki process. The process was given meaning because Hungarian citizens were willing to take considerable risks for the sake of Helsinki—a process that they obviously do not think of as futile. The Committee of Culture of Underground Solidarity prepared a report for the Cultural Forum; Charter 77 addressed an appeal to the Forum and worked to compile a book on culture in Czechoslovakia; Hungarian activists wrote reports about culture in Hungary and about the situation of the Hungarian minority in Romania—none of these human rights activists in repressive countries felt that the process was futile. To them, Helsinki is a framework for hope. Accordingly, it is our responsibility as people concerned with human rights in the West to support their efforts, to call attention to their plight and to devise ways to open channels of communication and exchange.

130

Free Flow of Information, by David O. Ives.
Interview with the chairman of wGBH, Boston public
television, reported by RFE correspondent Roland Eggleston,
Budapest, November 1, 1985.

U.S. television executive David Ives today replied to a series of questions posed yesterday by East German art historian Lothar Bisky about the American approach to the free flow of information.

"1. What is meant by "free flow of information?"

"Answer: Literally, just what it says. The U.S. believes that greater understanding among peoples can only be achieved when there is the maximum possible freedom for the citizens of all countries to obtain the information they happen to want—whether it is in the form of books, newspapers, magazines, technical journals, films, poems, religious tracts, radio and television broadcasts, or anything else, whether its source is domestic or foreign and whether or not the information is agreeable to those who govern the country in which the citizens live."

"2. Does not every country have the right to choose its own flow of information?"

"Answer: We believe that every citizen of every country has the right and that no government should impose on any citizen any limit on information he may seek. It is the right of the individual we support, not the right of the government."

"3. If there were free flow of information, would this not lead to 'intellectual imperialism,' presumably because there would be a greater flow of information in one direction than in another?"

"Answer: That is entirely a question of what the individuals in any country happen to want. If citizens from a country want more information from outside their borders, that is their free choice. If not, it is also their free choice."

"4. What information would flow back from the GDR to the US?"

"Again, it is up to the free choice of individuals. Whatever they want is what they should be able to obtain."

"5. Is the information to be used to impose on our country your ideals?"

"Answer: By no means. It is to be used only as each individual from your country wants to use it. Our goal is only freedom of individual choice."

"6. Are you denouncing our form of communication?"

"Answer: Only if and to the extent that the individual in your country is not free to choose the information he wants. If he is free to choose, then we think his understanding will be advanced. If he is not, then his understanding will be more difficult."

"7. Is this free flow only a way to expand the American market for information?"

"Answer: That is a choice to be made by individual decision. If the individual wants more information from the U.S. he should be allowed to obtain it. If he wants less, that is entirely his business."

"8. And last, are you not just bandying about the words 'free flow of information'?

"Answer: Most emphatically not. Freedom of speech, freedom of though, freedom of information—and their corollaries—absence of censorship, absence of restrictions, absence of any official orthodoxy—are absolutely basic to our American ideals and we are convinced that all men in any part of the world also want such freedoms, and that when these freedoms are available to all, understanding among all peoples will be within our reach."

131

One Europe and Writers' Duty, by Roland Eggleston.
Report by RFE correspondent, Budapest, November 4, 1985.

This morning's session of the Budapest Cultural Forum began with a
plea by the West German writer Günter Grass for the meeting to take
up the concept of Europe adopted by the Hungarian dissident writer
György Konrad.

Grass, who came to Budapest for only one day, said he had been
reading an essay by Konrad. Grass said that instead of speaking of East
Europe or West Europe the forum should take up Konrad's dream of
one Europe which was unfortunately divided by Yalta and Potsdam.

Grass also called for the establishment of a European Cultural Institute based in Budapest with branches in Vienna and Amsterdam.

The West German writer was followed by N. T. Fedorenko, who is
editor-in-chief of the Soviet foreign literature review *Inostrannaia Litera-
tura* and secretary of the board of the Soviet Writers' Union.

Fedorenko said it was the writer's duty to work for peace. At one
point he said: "Nothing else is worth writing about except peace."

He set the tone of his speech at the beginning by noting that this
year marked the 40th anniversary of the victory over fascism. Fedorenko
said that U.S. and Soviet soldiers had waged a common struggle against
the threat to humanity and argued that many American writers were
concerned at the possibility of nuclear war.

"The role of the writer is to tell the truth about war and about the
rising threat of nuclear disaster," Fedorenko said.

132

The Crux of the Problem, by Sol Polansky.
Plenary speech by the deputy head of U.S. delegation,
Budapest, November 8, 1985.

Mr. Chairman, we have all heard the clichés: art is truth. The pen is
mightier than the sword. Yet, we have seen how courageous individuals,
armed only with the force of ideas and a determined pen, have fought
at great risk for their artistic integrity. At another distinguished forum
last month a panel of writers offered eloquent comments on the nature
of the creative process and of the problem of cultural repression.
Timothy Garton Ash, author of a moving book on Solidarity, put the

crux of the problem in stark perspective by quoting Polish poet Cyprian Norwid:

> Gigantic armies, valiant generals,
> Trusted men and women of the police.
> And whom do they pursue?
> Just a few ideas;
> Nothing new.

Visions of the Future at Stockholm

133

A Report on the First Year of the Conference, by James E. Goodby. Remarks by head of the U.S. delegation to Conference on Confidence- and Security-Building Measures and Disarmament in Europe, Institut Français des Relations Internationales, Paris, December 3, 1984.

I. *The stakes*

Last July Pierre Lellouche wrote in *Newsweek* magazine that "The Soviets are quietly turning the Stockholm forum into a deadly machinery to alter to its advantage the postwar political and strategic order in Europe." Their method, he wrote, was to influence Western public opinion through "empty but nice sounding declarations"; their objective was to establish a "Pan-European security order from which the United States would ultimately be expelled." And he argued that "Western weakness . . . makes for the steady success of Moscow's strategy."

It is too seldom noticed that the Stockholm Conference, in fact, is addressing matters which could lead to profound changes in the present system of European security. Because the Conference is dealing with some of the most fundamental issues of Western security, it is no exaggeration to say that the essential agenda of Stockholm is the future political and strategic order in Europe. Stockholm is a part of the struggle between contending visions of the future. Ideas which are being discussed there must necessarily be seen as potentially contributing to the success of one or the other of these visions.

The Soviet vision we know well. As practiced in the past it has required limitations on the sovereignty of neighboring states; it is based on the expectation of endless confrontation and an impulse towards hegemony, as the ultimate requirement of security. The Western vision hopes that despite deep and persisting ideological differences, the walls which now divide the community of European nations can give way to a system more tolerant of diversity; that security can be found in balance and restraint. Of course, we are speaking of long historical processes, and, of course, the Stockholm Conference is only one of the arenas in which this "long twilight struggle" is being conducted. But when one hears of the seemingly trivial debate in Stockholm over obscure or arcane points, it is well to recall, as Mr. Lellouche has done, that the ultimate stakes are very high indeed.

II. *The balance sheet*

If the stakes in this "Great Game" are so fateful, we must weigh what the Soviets have done to create a new strategic order in Europe and what degree of success they have achieved. As Pierre Lellouche suggests, some Soviet proposals at Stockholm are "empty but nice-sounding declarations." Others have more content, but it is of a nature designed to disadvantage the West. Some proposals, such as those relating to chemical weapons and military budgets, would cut across useful and promising work being done elsewhere. In these categories fall the following Soviet proposals: a pledge not to be the first to use nuclear weapons; nuclear-free zones; a freeze and reduction of military budgets; and a ban on chemical weapons in Europe. And, indeed, as Mr. Lellouche suggests, these proposals have the potential for altering the global balance of power.

But the fact is that there is no ground swell of support at Stockholm for this Soviet program nor for any individual proposal in it. The neutral and non-aligned countries have introduced a series of proposals, the thrust of which is quite different from the direction taken by Moscow. The countries of the Atlantic Alliance have patiently exposed the shortcomings in each of these Soviet proposals. No one can credibly contend that the Soviets have succeeded in turning Stockholm into a propaganda platform which has deceived public opinion. The press, when it covers Stockholm, quite sensibly has found the stock items of the Soviet program to be not very interesting. Moscow has tried hard to steer Stockholm towards a polemical debate about nuclear weapons. As the party which last year chose to turn its back on nuclear negotiations, however, the Soviet case has not seemed very plausible.

Now we should ask how Western ideas are faring at Stockholm. Norway's Johan Holst wrote recently that "Confidence-building measures should be viewed as elements in a process for peaceful change of the post-war political order." These words elegantly sum up the larger aims of the proposals which the Atlantic Alliance has introduced in Stockholm. The West has held that Stockholm can be a place for serious arms control business and that this should be based on the principle of cooperation among all participants on an equal footing. An approach based on mutual, rather than unilateral, advantage in the building of confidence and the enhancement of stability implies a relationship among all the nations of Europe which is antithetical to the instinct for hegemony. Among other things, the proposals of the Atlantic Alliance emphasize the need for accurate perceptions of the intent of military operations, as a remedy for miscalculation and a deterrent against surprise attack. This objective requires positive cooperation, since it concerns the act of reassurance. And that means greater openness, or as the Belgian Ambassador at Stockholm nicely put it, the "de-mystification" of military activities on the continent of Europe.

In contrast to the polite but rather indifferent reaction to the supposedly eye-catching wares of the Soviet Union, the down-to-earth ideas which have been advanced by the countries of the Atlantic Alliance are in the mainstream of the Conference. The neutral and non-aligned group has presented very similar proposals. The debate in the Conference has been focused primarily on the theme of how to strengthen the practical confidence-building measures first developed in the Helsinki Final Act of 1975. The press in Western Europe almost unanimously has seen the purpose of the Stockholm Conference as that of reducing the risk of war through implementing practical measures designed to prevent crises and foster practical forms of cooperation. In short, Western ideas and the specific methods of implementing those ideas seem to be accepted as the real business of Stockholm.

I turn now to a description of some of the specific Western proposals and objectives in Stockholm and to a few of the key developments of the year just passing.

III. A new approach to arms control

Stockholm is not only about political visions; it is also and most immediately about a new approach to arms control. In the last quarter of a century very few arms control efforts have been aimed at eliminating the proximate causes of war, such as crises arising from misperceptions. Arms control negotiations typically have dealt with reducing the perceived *threat*, whether that be the threat perceived from arsenals of nuclear warheads or from the levels of conventional forces in Central Europe. The few arms control attempts to deal directly with the "proximate" causes of war have been important but limited in scope and objectives, the Moscow-Washington "hot line" and the United States-Soviet "incidents at sea" agreement being two examples. No comprehensive negotiation has yet succeeded in putting into place arrangements designed to prevent crises or to contain or resolve them should they occur. This is, however, the aim of the Western nations represented at Stockholm. Success in achieving this goal would encourage natural and normal relations among the countries comprising the whole of Europe.

Another way of considering the difference between "classical" arms control and the new ideas being discussed in Stockholm is that the former has dealt with the *levels* of forces whereas the latter deals with the *operations* of military forces. "Classical" arms control negotiations typically try to establish long-term stability, for example, by providing greater predictability about the types and levels of strategic forces that will be maintained over a future span of time. But in Stockholm, the Allies are urging agreements which will promote short-term stability, that is, during periods of intense and possibly turbulent international political developments which might require urgent attention. The aim would be to have procedures in place which would prevent misunderstandings possibly leading to dangerous escalation and which would assist nations in keeping potentially dangerous situations under control. How well the West has done in rallying support for this point of view may be seen in the following review of other proposals introduced in Stockholm.

During 1984, five sets of proposals were submitted to the Stockholm Conference. In addition to those of the Atlantic Alliance, proposals were advanced by Romania, by the neutral and nonaligned countries, by the Soviet Union, and by Malta.

Romania's proposals were important for several reasons. Its ideas included elements based on the Warsaw Pact's political proposals, but also included were interesting approaches to confidence-building designed to strengthen the measures agreed to in the Helsinki Final Act. One of the Soviet Union's proposals also provided for improvements in "Helsinki-style" confidence-building measures. The proposals submitted by the neutral and nonaligned countries deserve special attention because they have helped to define the "center of gravity" of the Stockholm Conference. Nine of the twelve proposals included in their approach were similar to those introduced by the Allies. Three of them went beyond the Alliance's approach, in that they called for specific limitations, or constraints, on the way military forces could be deployed. In so doing, the neutral countries identified a "gray zone" that lies between the stabilizing intent of the Alliance's proposals and the arms reduction aims of "classical" arms control. Their approach deserves—and is receiving—serious study.

The point which emerges from this is clear: there is a significant degree of convergence between all of these proposals and those made by the Allies.

IV. *The mechanics of underwriting stability*

The nations of the Atlantic Alliance have used as their common point of departure the confidence-building measures of the 1975 Final Act of Helsinki. Those measures were modest experiments; they needed to be improved substantially. In their proposals, the Western countries are seeking to negotiate agreements that will, among other things, build on the rudimentary notification and observation procedures in the Helsinki Final Act. By mandate, the Stockholm Conference is already advancing significantly from the Final Act: by mutual agreement of all the countries, Stockholm is dealing with the *whole of Europe*, from the Atlantic to the Urals, whereas the Final Act exempted most of the European part of the Soviet Union.

The countries of the Atlantic Alliance are seeking to extend notification of maneuvers to include alerts, amphibious operations, and mobilization. They are urging that military *units*, specifically the division rather than levels of manpower, should be the basis for notifications. They are proposing an exchange of information as a standard against which to judge the significance of out-of-garrison military activities. On-site inspection to clear up questions arising from implementation of this agreement and to defuse potential crises should be a part of a strengthened regime for enhancing stability. Means for urgent communications among the participants in this system could also serve to deter or resolve crises. The Allies are seeking longer advance notice of military activities and a lower threshold for notification than was provided in the Helsinki Final Act. In addition, the Western countries are proposing to exchange annual forecasts of military operations within the zone. This annual forecast will have a constraining effect, in that it will be more difficult for a military exercise suddenly to be mounted for the purpose of political intimidation. Together with mandatory observation of all notified military activities, these measures would exert pressure for stability in Europe. By establishing normal patterns of military activities for military operations in Europe and arrangements for reacting jointly to situations outside these "norms," we would create conditions which could facilitate the resolution of potential crises.

Johan Holst has suggested that "We should look at confidence-building measures as management instruments designed to reduce the pressure from arms on the process of politics during peacetime and on decision-making in crisis and war." The Alliance's proposals are designed to do exactly that. If a system can be established which promotes stability, which damps down potential crises, which discourages the use of military force for political intimidation, and in which crises can be contained and quickly resolved, we will indeed have "reduced the pressures from arms on the process of politics."

V. *Some perspectives on 1984*

The Foreign Ministers of the thirty-five participants opened the Conference in January 1984, a period that marked, in retrospect, the beginning of a transition in Soviet-American relations. President Reagan's major policy statement on Soviet-American relations was delivered on January 16; it was followed immediately by talks between Secretary Shultz and Foreign Minister Gromyko. Although icy winds from the East were lowering temperatures everywhere, the seeds of future negotiations were even then being planted.

Perhaps the most important political impetus which the Stockholm Conference received during the year was President Reagan's speech of June 4 in Dublin. In that speech the President, in effect, outlined the shape of an ultimate agreement when he mentioned the possibility of discussing a Soviet-sponsored proposal regarding non-use of force if the Soviets would negotiate concrete confidence-building measures such as those which the Alliance and the neutral countries had been advocating.

In the four sessions which were held during 1984, however, the Soviets showed little inclination to accept the Alliance's invitation to a negotiation. But just today, December 3, all participants, including the Soviet Union, have agreed on a working structure which should encourage serious and detailed negotiations. This could be a turning point. The opportunity now exists, more than ever before, for the "flexible give-and-take negotiating process" President Reagan called for in September. The portents are increasingly favorable, and we hope that the Soviets will use this new opportunity to work out agreements within the range of proposals which are truly negotiable at Stockholm. There has existed for some time a substantive "point of departure" for negotiations which many delegations have already discerned; now there is available to the negotiators a structure to facilitate detailed comparison of proposals and to begin the process of bridging the gaps.

It should be noted that many delegations in Stockholm have remarked that all the problems to which individual nations attach high priority cannot possibly be dealt with in Stockholm. But these matters need not go unattended, quite the contrary. For example, President Reagan in speaking before the United Nations on September 24 offered some ideas which would help to build confidence *bilaterally* between the United States and the Soviet Union. It is obvious that the Stockholm Conference is not the universe. Many things can be done bilaterally or in other forums to improve confidence between states; these could reinforce measures agreed in Stockholm.

VI. *Summing up*

Today, as we near the end of the Conference's first year, it seems that the West is not doing too badly, as measured against the basic thesis of Pierre Lellouche. The weakness to which he referred has not been in evidence. Perhaps we may even be permitted to say that the restoration of America's sense of strength, purpose, and confidence had something to do with this.

The Conference appears to have accepted a Western concept of security. Plenty of declarations have been heard from the East, but the majority of the Conference participants appear firmly committed to serious negotiations on practical measures designed to enhance stability in Europe. A consensus-building process has been at work which points to an outcome based on combining a reaffirmation of the renunciation of force with practical confidence-building measures intended to give real expression to that principle. And the idea of a more open continent is even more firmly entrenched than ever.

The Soviets, even if they use the new working structure to begin to hammer out a consensus, certainly will continue to offer the West self-serving panaceas for Europe's security problems. The temptation to seize easy results at the expense of meaningful results will always be there and it will always be exploited to the disadvantage of the West, if possible. But the first year of discussions suggests that if the West remains united, meaningful results are possible in Stockholm.

Détente, Arms Control, and Human Rights

134

Human Rights in East-West Relations, by Ministry
of Foreign Affairs of the Netherlands.
Memorandum presented to the Lower House of the States
General of the Kingdom of the Netherlands, May 3, 1979,
Human Rights and Foreign Policy (The Hague: Ministry
of Foreign Affairs, 1979), pp. 111–13, 121–22.

The human rights issue plays an important part in East-West relations.
The main reason is that the attitude to the individual in the communist
countries differs fundamentally from that in the democratic countries.
In itself, such a difference of approach would not need to have any great
influence on international relations were it not that the existing human
rights situation in Eastern Europe is felt by large sections of the population there to be more or less unsatisfactory, and precisely in comparison with the situations in the West, while moreover the grave abuses of
human rights in the Eastern European countries also cause offense in
the Western world and thus are a source of tension in the relationship
between East and West.

At the same time this issue must be viewed in conjunction with the
compelling necessity of avoiding a military confrontation between East
and West. For an armed conflict between East and West could cause
death and havoc on a scale totally unacceptable to both parties, in consequence of the destruction potential of the superpowers. In this situation the Netherlands and its allies pursue a policy directed towards
stability, arms control and détente, a policy in which the promotion of
human rights has a place of its own.

The policy of détente (including here the promotion of arms control
and of forms of cooperation which are useful for both sides) is directed
towards preventing deterioration of the political climate between East
and West, reducing the mistrust between the two sides, and building
up a community of interests going beyond the common interest in preventing a war of extermination. However, this policy cannot remove
the fundamental opposition between the two groups of States. In particular, it cannot in the short term lead to an alteration in the profound
differences of viewpoint between East and West with regard to the
most desirable organization of society and the place of the individual in
that society. Not only is individual freedom subject to drastic restric-

tions in the Soviet Union and its allied States, but to a certain extent these restrictions of freedom constitute an essential part of the ruling system in those countries. Full realization of the classic freedoms would accordingly endanger the very existence of those systems. If the West were to insist upon full political freedom for the people in the communist countries, the governments of those countries would inevitably feel this as a direct threat to their existence. Since the policy of détente aims at giving those governments no reason to feel threatened but on the contrary aims at reducing such feelings, the West will have to exercise due restraint on this point. Besides, the striving for freedom itself would presumably not benefit if the communist governments were to feel that their existence was threatened, as this would induce them to draw the reins tighter within their countries.

Set against these sobering observations, however, there is the other important aspect of the human rights problem in East-West relations, namely that disregard of human rights in the communist countries is itself a cause of tension both within those countries and between those countries and the West. This of course particularly applies to such grave forms of terror as characterized the Stalinist period, but also for example to the violent methods by which inhabitants of the German Democratic Republic are prevented from leaving their country and to the way in which the Soviet Union has repeatedly intervened in order to oppose internal political developments in Eastern European countries. It follows that liberalization and greater security of the individual before the law within the communist countries would themselves contribute to détente in East-West relations. The same applies to freer movement of persons, ideas and information between those countries and the West. The policy of détente can only contribute towards a lasting rapprochement if one ensures that recognition of the political configuration which came about in Europe after the Second World War does not result in cementing the isolation of the Eastern European peoples which this configuration has caused. This realization was one of the points of departure for the position adopted by the West at the Conference on Security and Cooperation in Europe (1973–1975).

In taking this approach, the West by no means seeks to endanger the existing stability in Europe, if only since doing so could threaten its own security. The Government believes that it is possible, without endangering that stability, to pursue a policy in which there is a positive interaction between the promotion of détente and the promotion of human rights, on the one hand because greater respect for human rights in the communist countries could remove certain sources of tension between East and West, and on the other hand because a more relaxed international climate could improve the chances of a less tense domestic policy being adopted in those countries.

The necessity of maintaining the existing stability does not however mean that the West should always avoid friction of every kind with Eastern European governments when championing respect for human rights. Even if championing these rights gives rise to temporary frictions in East-West relations, it is not a foregone conclusion that it will not have a beneficial influence on those relations in the long term. In this connection it should also be borne in mind that the internal stability of the Eastern European countries might benefit as well from liberalization and greater security of the individual before the law. Moreover, in the Government's view stability within Europe as a whole would benefit from the coming about of more natural relations between the Soviet Union and its allies, that is to say relations based more upon voluntary cooperation than upon power. The ultimate aim of policy on East-West relations should therefore be to achieve an order in which all the peoples of Europe will be able to live together without fear of violence or coercision and in greater harmony than is now the case.

It has been claimed that with its insistence on respect for human rights and observance of the humanitarian clauses in the Final Act, the West provokes defensive reactions from the Eastern European governments, which not only do not serve the cause of human rights but also endanger détente. Recent sentencing of dissidents appears to support this view. The following can be said in reply to this.

In the first place it could be asked whether, if détente has really experienced a setback because of this, this should be ascribed to the activities of those who are working for a more humane society in the whole of Europe or to action by those who oppose such a development. But in addition to this, one should guard against putting matters in too absolute terms. Not every abuse of human rights endangers the process of détente, nor will every protest against such abuses lead to reactions injurious to the future of this process. It is unmistakably true that the Final Act lays down norms which for the time being cannot be achieved in view of the ruling system in the communist countries. It must equally be recognized that the appreciable increase in Western involvement with human rights policy in Eastern Europe as a result of Helsinki has created a new situation for the governments of those countries, which they have not yet learned to live with, as evidenced by their invoking the principle of non-intervention and by the intensification of repression here and there. The Western governments have always realized that it will take time before the commitments made at Helsinki will have positive results in the communist countries.

As we have indicated, in the present situation the communist governments cannot realistically be expected, in response to pressure from outside, to take measures which would seriously threaten their existence. Nonetheless, there are still considerable margins within which those governments can implement the pledges which they made at Helsinki without endangering their own existence. These margins will not be the same in every country; besides it is not impossible that such margins will become broader in the future. As it is not reasonable to assume that the existing margins will be used without any encouragement from outside, the West must continue to press for greater respect for human rights. Incidentally, the people in the Eastern European countries who are working for improvements in this field do not expect any less of the West. For their part, in their efforts to bring about improvements the Western countries must be guided by the consideration of what is most likely to produce results under the circumstances. This need not always and under all circumstances lead to the same policy. However disappointing the recent measures against dissidents are, it remains a gratifying fact that in the CSCE the Eastern European countries recognized the importance of human rights policy for relations between States. If the Western countries wish to preserve the process of détente from erosion, they will have to hold fast to this attainment.

Meanwhile, in all this it should be borne in mind that the CSCE exercise and the process of détente are not synonymous. Although the Final Act contains numerous rules of conduct which are of importance for détente, there are also various questions which it leaves unmentioned but which also affect the process of détente. First among these are the military aspects of détente. Accordingly, the Western countries have always attached great importance to achieving a more even balance of military power between East and West. In view of these questions, which are essential for East-West relations, the policy of détente must also be pursued against the background of developments outside the scope of the CSCE. However, championing respect for human rights will continue to play an important part in determining this policy, and has since Helsinki become inseparable from it, even if great importance will sometimes have to be attached to other considerations.

135

Human Rights and Security Are Inseparable, by James E. Goodby.
Address by the head of the U.S. delegation, reported by RFE correspondent Roland Eggleston, Stockholm, September 18, 1984.

The United States delegation has repeatedly emphasized that this conference is an integral part of the Helsinki process, that all aspects of the
Final Act are of equal importance. The United States holds that human
rights, peace and security are inseparable, and that it is only on this
basis that the spirit of the Helsinki accords truly can be realized.

If I cite this principle here today, it is not to seek to inscribe the subject of human rights on our agenda, but to note that confidence can be
undermined and tension can arise from failures in this area, and not
only from issues of military security. Ambassador Max Kampelman's
visit to Europe on behalf of President Reagan was an expression of this
truth. Our current discussions are affected by this truth, because it is
one of the elements of the overall political conditions surrounding the
conference.

We all know that when the progress of our conference is reviewed in
Vienna in 1986 it will be judged in a context which inseparably links all
of the obligations included in the Helsinki Final Act.

To make this point crystal clear, I invite my colleagues to consider
once again the issue which I raised in a letter which I sent directly to
each head of delegation over my signature last May 22. That letter, you
will recall, brought to your attention a resolution adopted by both
houses of the United States Congress. It involved a question of obligations assumed under the Helsinki Final Act, an issue which continues
to affect the integrity and prospects for continued progress in the Helsinki process. I can assure you that concerns about the Sakharovs expressed in that resolution last spring are as strongly felt today as they
were then.

Just as Foreign Minister Gromyko was correct to say that this conference cannot "be artificially isolated" from developments outside this
hall, so he was also right to say in his address of January 18 that "one of
the urgent tasks is to build confidence among nations—confidence both
political and military."

136

Congressmen Dismayed by Soviet Attitudes, by Roland Eggleston.
Report by RFE correspondent, Ottawa, May 11, 1985.

Six American Congressmen who conferred with the Soviet delegation to
the Ottawa Human Rights Conference say they are "dismayed" at the
Soviet attitude.

The Congressmen had a 90-minute meeting with Soviet chief negotiator Vsevolod Sofinskii and other members of the delegation in a private room at the conference center. They were led by Senator Alfonse
D'Amato, Chairman of the U.S. Commission on Security and Cooperation in Europe, and Representative Steny Hoyer, the co-chairman. The
others in the group were Senator James McClure, Representative Sandor
Levin, Representative John Edward Porter and Representative Tom
Lantos.

The Congressmen gave the Soviets the names of about 30 human
rights cases and asked for them to be given immediate attention. But
they said they got no response at all; there was no sign that the Soviet
delegation was prepared to act on individual cases. And when the Congressmen tried to hand over a letter addressed to General Secretary
Mikhail Gorbachev it was rejected by Sofinskii, who said he was not a
postman. The Congressmen displayed the letter at the press briefing and
said it would be passed on to the Soviet Union through the U.S. Embassy in Moscow.

Instead of answers to their statements and questions, Sofinskii criticized the United States, particularly for its alleged policies towards
women and minorities.

Representative Levin said the Congressmen found the Soviet lack of
knowledge about real conditions in the United States to be "appalling
and frightening." He added: "They went into wild flights of fiction
about what is happening in the United States and showed an ignorance
that was truly shocking."

Senator D'Amato began a press briefing after the meeting by saying:
"We view the issue of human rights as more than rhetoric. We think it
is absolutely essential in our dealings with the Soviets and others that
they demonstrate to us their commitment to live up to those obligations
which they are signatories to."

He said the Congressmen had tried to impress upon the Soviet delegation that their attitude towards future cooperation with the Soviet
Union in any field—economic, trade or mutual security would be guided
by how the Soviets lived up to their human rights undertakings in the

Helsinki Final Act. "If they can't live up to these accords on freedom of expression, on freedom of religion, of basic human rights, then they cannot blame us if we are very sceptical about other promises they make," he said.

137

The Message We Are Trying to Send, by Richard Schifter.
Press statement by the head of the U.S. delegation, reported by
RFE correspondent Roland Eggleston, Ottawa, May 14, 1985.

The chief American negotiator at the Human Rights Conference, Richard Schifter, says his job in Ottawa is to send a message to the Soviet leadership. Its essence is that if General Secretary Mikhail Gorbachev wants better relations with the United States in any field he must improve the Soviet human rights record because that is increasingly being used as a standard to measure the relationship.

At a meeting with the press this week, Schifter especially emphasized the link between better trade relations and such issues as Jewish emigration, religious freedom and the rights of minorities. But he said the human rights record could also affect the way the United States Congress reacts to whatever agreement is eventually worked out at the Geneva arms control talks. Schifter said that when it came to ratifying an arms agreement there would be questions in Congress over the value of the Soviet signature on the treaty.

"The message we are trying to send is that if the Soviet Union wants better relations it must be ready to pay a price by honoring its human rights commitments," Schifter said. "By publicizing names and specific cases we are in effect drawing a map for the Soviet Union and its allies of what they have to do."

Schifter has conveyed the message personally to the Soviet delegation in private talks in Ottawa.

The Enduring Process

138

Soviet Interest in the CSCE Process, by Robert Rand.
Report by RFE correspondent, Washington, February 22, 1982.

The Soviet Union's interest in promoting the CSCE process, in spite of the embarrassment and aggravation that the process has periodically created for the Kremlin, can be explained by five factors. Heading the list is the personal stake that Soviet President Leonid Brezhnev has in the Helsinki accords.

The Conference on Security and Cooperation in Europe, as the media in the USSR are fond of pointing out, originated as a Soviet policy initiative. The idea was incorporated into Brezhnev's "peace program," and has been identified with the Soviet leader ever since.

With Brezhnev's name and reputation so closely tied to the Helsinki agreement, the USSR has little choice but to support the continuation of the CSCE process. To do otherwise would be akin to admitting that the détente, as formulated by L. I. Brezhnev, had failed. As long as the current Soviet president is alive and in power, Moscow's backing of the CSCE process is unlikely to wane.

A second factor behind the USSR's continued interest in CSCE lies in Moscow's ability to utilize Helsinki as a vehicle to promote various Soviet peace initiatives. By its own admission, the Kremlin's main interest in the Madrid Conference is to gain agreement for a post-Madrid meeting on security and disarmament in Europe. By promoting measures such as this, the USSR hopes to enhance its reputation—both at home and abroad—as a responsible world power. It also hopes to convince the world community that the Soviet approach to CSCE is positive and forward-looking, while that of the United States and its allies is not.

The relationship between Washington and its West European partners provides the backdrop for the third factor behind the USSR's desire to promulgate the CSCE process. The Kremlin views Helsinki as a mechanism in which differences among the NATO alliance can be exploited. Cognizant of the lack of unity which the West has shown from time to time over various Helsinki-related issues—for instance, over how harshly to criticize Moscow for its human rights practice—the USSR has sought, via CSCE, to drive a wedge between Washington and its European partners.

As a result, Soviet diplomats have utilized Helsinki forums to urge West European signatories to disregard the American view of CSCE for the greater good of Europe. In this manner, Moscow has pursued what can be characterized as a bifurcated approach to détente, in which cooperation between the USSR and Western Europe is expounded, while Soviet-American détente, once seen by Moscow as the cornerstone of peaceful coexistence, is left to flounder.

A fourth factor that underlies the USSR's continued interest in the Helsinki process relates to the issue of human rights. While the Kremlin by no means favors a dialogue about Soviet human rights practices at

Helsinki forums, Moscow has nonetheless grudgingly come to accept the topic as an aspect of the CSCE process.

This represents an evolution of the Soviet position, for in the early days of Helsinki the mere mention of the name of a Soviet dissident at a CSCE conference would evoke considerable fuss in the USSR, and would generate concern over whether the Kremlin would tolerate what it viewed as interference in its internal affairs. Now, however, American delegates at Madrid commonly refer to the plight of dozens of imprisoned Soviet activists without commotion. The USSR does not see Western criticism of its human rights policies as an intolerable threat, and for that reason Moscow is willing to endure such attacks in order to protect its greater interest in the viability of the CSCE process.

One should add that the USSR's success in cracking down on internal dissent over the past seven years has eased Moscow's burden of enduring public criticism over its human rights policies, with so many of the USSR's leading dissidents imprisoned, exiled, or otherwise silenced, there is little danger that Western critiques of KGB activities will embolden Soviet dissidents and produce new waves of anti-government activism within the USSR.

A fifth and final factor behind the USSR's policy of promoting Helsinki lies in the future. Moscow may well believe that with the passage of time, the CSCE process will evolve into a forum more hospitable to Soviet policies than is now the case. According to this view, the countries of Western Europe will tire of the human rights aspects of the Helsinki dialogue, and come to see CSCE almost exclusively as a mechanism to discuss trade and security matters. This trend has already been discernible to American specialists who have watched the Helsinki process develop, and it is argued that the continuation of this tendency conforms fully with Moscow's interest in promoting Soviet–West European relations.

Commenting on this scenario, one CSCE expert, a member of the U.S. delegation to the Madrid Conference, speculated that the USSR would ultimately like to see Helsinki emerge as a "United Nations surrogate in Europe," i.e. a permanent forum in which East-West issues can be discussed, and in which American influence is minimal.

While the USSR has, from its perspective, good reason to favor the continuation of the CSCE process, Moscow's original enthusiasm for Helsinki has been tempered by dimmed expectations of what the process can realistically be expected to produce. The Soviet Union originally saw CSCE as a tool that could be used energetically to expand cooperation between East and West. The Soviet delegation to the Belgrade Conference, for instance, devoted much of its attention to lobbying for numerous new proposals to enhance bilateral and multilateral links between the Final Act's 35 signatory states.

But as the CSCE process grew into a human rights forum, Soviet eagerness began to wane. Moscow's enthusiasm for Helsinki, while still intact, dropped perceptibly. CSCE vanished as one of the foreign policy slogans of the CPSU. Helsinki appeared less frequently in the speeches of Soviet leaders. Although the USSR doubtless wants the CSCE process to continue, the Kremlin's expectations for Helsinki surely have not been met.

139

A Neutral's Plea, by Richard Müller.
Speech by the head of Finnish delegation, Madrid, December 10, 1980, dispatch no. 13/4535, December 11, 1980, Foreign Office, Helsinki.

The Finnish government considers the follow-up process as a vital, integral part of the entire Final Act, and attaches particular importance to the fact that the chapter of the Final Act on the follow-up is implemented in a proper and meaningful way.

We do not believe there can be any disagreement about the fact that there has been progress in the CSCE process, or that the follow-up meetings would not be considered a central—indeed vital—part of our mutual endeavors.

We, on our part, can reach no other conclusions than that all the CSCE states—without exception—wish to continue the multilateral CSCE process in a serious manner, in the spirit which our respective heads of governments indicated through the signatures they put on the final document in 1975.

Apart from the progress, and the resolve of the participating states with respect to the follow-up in general, we have to admit that there exist shortcomings, questions yet unanswered, matters of fact from which we should try to learn and benefit.

When assessing our performance and the experiences to be drawn from that, we feel that we should try to apply a longer term perspective. 'Here and now' in the CSCE performance is not enough.

In Geneva we spoke of the concepts of 'technical' or 'sectoral' follow-up on the one hand, and of the need to continue 'political consultations,' on the other. We were, at the same time, trying to find the right and meaningful expressions for both those concepts in the final text. Our objective was to secure for the implementation process the necessary element of growth and development. At the same time, we realized that the 'political contacts' that we had established were of central importance and that a joint exchange of views, performed on a multilateral basis, would be the best solution—as far as it was possible for us at that time—to anticipate the requirements of the future.

The Finnish delegation, on its part, feels that we must ask ourselves to what extent we might have come to make the well-known concept of a 'thorough exchange of views' the sole motivation of our follow-up meetings. In other words, whether we have extracted this exchange of views—the idea of consultations—from its original context in the Final Act.

It is right that the Final Act avoids setting any conditions for that discussion—and this is of course in itself the very prerequisite for a constructive and meaningful exchange of views. On the other hand, it does formulate at the same time in a positive manner the aims and objectives for the continuation of this multilateral process itself.

It is, therefore, we believe not enough to say that we must safeguard the continuity of the follow-up process. We must find ways and means to secure that it has a positive substance and purpose as well.

With respect to multilateral implementation, the experts' meetings are given a rather substantial role in the Final Act.

When the signatories to the Final Act were considering these forms for multilateral implementation, it was not their intention, as we understand it, to make the experts' meetings into some kind of a substitute mechanism for implementation—a device, by which to 'put away' unpleasant, difficult or simply unimportant matters. The intention was rather to create a pragmatic form for continued multilateral cooperation between the participating states. And there was, we believe, no intent to restrict their number in principle or in practice.

We believe we must recognize, more readily perhaps than hitherto, that, although there are and will be no doubts or disagreement with respect to our commitment to the Final Act itself, the follow-up process is meant to be, fundamentally, a dynamic process. It needs constantly new attention, new emphasis, the search for new concepts.

It is not an end in itself, nor was it meant to exist in a political vacuum, happily unaware of the realities of change. It must, therefore, respond to the changes in the international situation, and it must address itself to the question of how the CSCE process itself can influence that situation in a positive manner.

We must also, in our view, critically assess whether the implementation process that we envisaged in the beginning has in fact been evolving too much around the few moments of 'review of implementation' every third year, instead of becoming at the same time a part of our normal, everyday interaction, and a natural part of our continuous mutual efforts to solve our problems.

140

U.S. View of the Helsinki Anniversary, by Oleh Zwadiuk.
Report by RFE correspondent, Washington, July 29, 1985.

The United States views the tenth anniversary this week of the signing of the Helsinki Accords with a sense of sobriety and realism and not as a celebration.

"We go there with a very specific approach, which is to point out the gap between commitment and implementation," said Mark Palmer, Deputy U.S. Assistant Secretary of State for European Affairs. He said it is "very much not a celebration."

Palmer's views were supported by others, including Richard Schifter, the U.S. representative to the Human Rights Experts' Meeting in Ottawa, and James Goodby, the U.S. representative to the Conference on Confidence-Building Measures and Disarmament in Europe.

But the three experts expressed strong support for the Helsinki process at a special briefing on the accords at the White House Friday. They spoke to about 100 invited guests, many of whose former homelands are in Eastern Europe and the Soviet Union.

"I think the fact that the *Baltic Star* is pulling into Helsinki, carrying with it the most vivid possible demonstration of commitment to the freedom for the three Baltic states is a testimony to the continuing importance of the CSCE process," Palmer said. He was scheduled to leave this morning with U.S. Secretary of State George Shultz for Helsinki where the tenth anniversary meeting of the 35 signatory countries is taking place.

Palmer said that when Shultz meets this week with Soviet Foreign Minister Eduard Shevardnadze, "He will do what he has done in every single meeting with Gromyko, which is to make human rights his number one concern." Palmer said he has never seen a man more personally committed "to making sure that the Soviets understood how important that is to our relationship." He said Schultz is "very determined to not only leave Mr. Shevardnadze in no doubt about the fact, but also to try to persuade him . . . that there is a necessity for them to change their policies."

"We go with a sense of sobriety and realism because of course the record is so depressing, particularly in the Soviet Union," Palmer said. He added: "The trends today are almost universally negative. In fact, there are some areas in which it is objectively fair to say that since Stalin died, things have not been worse."

Ambassador Schifter, who was born in Austria and came to the U.S. in 1938, said in his remarks that the human rights provisions of the Helsinki accords "have done some specific harm" because many dissidents believed they could rely on them in their activities. Schifter said each one of the dissidents, particularly the Helsinki monitors, has paid with years of deprivation of liberty and other serious consequences. "Today, the fact that you cannot rely on these provisions is known," he said.

Schifter recalled that in Ottawa he had suggested that if the provisions were to be republished, they should carry a warning similar to the kind that appears on American cigarettes "which is that the use of these particular rights may be injurious to your health."

But Schifter said that no particular advantage would be gained by repudiating the accord. He said: "We simply have to keep holding them to it. We have to recognize that it is a difficult task to persuade the Soviets to change their pattern of behavior. At the same time, the process is there for us to use." Schifter said that while the effects in the Soviet Union are not encouraging, "at least some of us are under the impression that over time there is a chance of making some progress" in the smaller Warsaw Pact countries.

Goodby discussed progress in negotiations on the confidence building measures. He said there is a prospect of negotiations "which might lead to some results," but he added "don't get your hopes too high."

He said there isn't likely to be an agreement "much before another year of very, very hard work." He said that much depends on whether the Soviet Union is prepared to make "a lot of changes that so far they have appeared rather unwilling to make."

Michael Hathaway, Director and General Counsel of the U.S. Helsinki Commission, said debate about the value of the Helsinki accords "is alive and well" today.

He said there are significant numbers of people who believe that the Helsinki process "is a sham." Hathaway said, however, it should not be abandoned to the Soviet Union.

141

Meetings without Agreements, by Roland Eggleston.
"The Budapest Cultural Forum," *Radio Liberty Research*,
RL 392/85, November 26, 1985, pp. 1–2.

The failure of the Budapest Cultural Forum to produce a final document caused some observers of the meeting to ask anxious questions about the future of the Helsinki process. It is the second time this year that a meeting constituting part of the follow-up process to the Helsinki accords of 1975 has ended without any kind of final statement. The first was the human rights conference in Canada this year.

Besides this, a meeting in Greece last year on the peaceful settlement of disputes ended in virtually the same way. Frantic last-moment diplomacy produced a five-paragraph statement saying that the delegates had met, discussed the subject, and failed to find a common ground. In other words, that meeting in effect also ended without a final agreement.

The eyes of those who believe in the Helsinki process are now turned to the meeting on family reunification scheduled to be held in Switzerland next spring and the slow-moving conference in Stockholm on improving military security in Europe. It is possible that they too could end without a final document. In fact, of the many diplomats in Budapest who will also be in Switzerland and Stockholm, a lot of them believe it is possible that one or the other of these meetings could likewise end without a closing document. That would be unfortunate, because both are important meetings at which meaningful results are needed, but the diplomats deny that it would threaten the existence of the Helsinki process.

The head of the US delegation, Walter Stoessel, said so at a press briefing today. His comments have been echoed by West German, French, Dutch, Swiss, Swedish, and Austrian delegates. All say that the discussions are useful even if they do not produce a document but that it would of course be preferable to have one.

Perhaps significantly, there was also support for the future of the process by a senior member of the Soviet delegation, Sergei Kondrashev. He was tackled in the conference coffee shop yesterday by Western reporters who were outraged by a vicious attack on the United States at a Soviet press conference earlier in the day. He was told that the tone of the attack was unbelievable in the immediate wake of the Gorbachev-Reagan summit and could only mean that the Soviet Union scorned the Helsinki process.

Kondrashev responded mildly even if he did not apologize. The most interesting part of his remarks was, though, an expression of strong support for the Helsinki process. The Soviet Union believes in these multilateral discussions, he said, and does not want to see them fade away. Almost echoing Western spokesmen, he said that it was a pity there had been no results in Budapest but that this did not mean the end of the Helsinki process. Most delegates do appear to believe that Budapest has been one of the more successful meetings in the process despite the failure to produce a document.

142

Looking beyond the Moment, by Johan Jørgen Holst.
Revue roumaine d'études internationales 17, no. 2 (1983):
115–19.

The Helsinki process is an important element in the pattern of East-West relations, but it is not the core element. It has been important therefore to define a context for assessment, shedding light on the interrelationship among the various political issues which structure developments and define the scope for what can be achieved through the Helsinki process.

East-West relations are passing through a difficult period, not because of the Helsinki process, but rather because of actions undertaken and events unfolding both outside and inside Europe in a manner which provides conspicuous examples of a regretful failure of states to exercise restraint in their use of force or accumulation of armaments. Events in Poland involving an open-ended imposition of martial law and the eventual dissolution of the Solidarity union have contributed to a growing erosion of the credibility and relevance of détente in general and the Helsinki process in particular.

The basic theory behind the Helsinki process has not, however, been invalidated. The assumption that governments may be constrained from resorting to the use of force against other states or their own citizens by the existence of a web of multilateral commitments and transactions, a system of interdependence, still provides a reasonable working hypothesis. The theory did not purport to provide a recipe for how to prevent the threat to use force or the actual use of force, but suggested a way to make such transgressions more costly. However, the web of cooperative arrangements never became as dense and resilient as was envisaged in the mid-seventies. Structural obstacles to East-West trade combined with the economic crisis in the West to delay and constrain the development of economic relations. Détente may have stimulated rising expectations for increased freedom at the individual level which some Eastern governments were not prepared to accommodate.

The nature of the Helsinki process

The Helsinki process encompassed something much broader than the relations among states; it extended to the relations among societies. The condition of man as a citizen was made a matter of international concern. The Final Act did not provide a blueprint for interference into the internal affairs of other states, but it did reflect a recognition of the fact that in the latter half of the twentieth century traditional international relations have been overtaken by international communications. We live in a global village. Human identification, compassion and solidarity transcend borders among states and will inevitably and rightly exert pressure on governments. Hence, the CSCE process also affects relations between the state and the individual, between the state and society. The era of cabinet policy is gone, it has been overtaken and transformed by mass politics and the democratization of the social order.

The CSCE process addressed the military aspects of security in but a marginal manner. It focused on the issues of security in a broader context relating the military factor to the broader pattern and rules of international relations in Europe. Cooperation and increased transactions should cause the military confrontation to lose saliency and sharpness. The CSCE addressed the military issues in an indirect manner, but it could develop only if the direct attempts at dealing with the arms issues produced results as well.

The CSCE process is still in its feeble beginning. The current pessimism is a result in part of the confrontation of expectations with the stubborn realities of the remaining political conflicts. It was, as already observed, not the core process for shaping East-West relations. But in a period when the other processes ground to a halt, it was asked to do too much, to become the symbol and vehicle for East-West negotiations at a time when the subjects for negotiation became dominated by East-West differences in a manner which overloaded the CSCE. It became an arena for marking positions and demonstrating displeasure. When the political situation does not provide openings for new initiatives or expanded cooperation, diplomatic attention is focused on contentious assessments of the record of implementation. The CSCE may add to the crisis rather than ease and constrain its impact on the overall conduct of East-West relations. Nevertheless, talking is always better than shooting and out of talking may grow a greater understanding of the perceptions which govern the behavior of other states.

The existing alliances provide an essential part of the infrastructure of the present political order in Europe. However, the political order in Europe is not defined only by the two alliances. The texture is more complex. The nature of the alliances may change as a result of a reconstruction of the military confrontation in a manner which could broaden the scope for peaceful political change, leading to a softening of the bloc quality of the alliances. Eventually the alliances may wither away, but that is not on the short- or medium-term agenda. The alliances are necessary and vital pillars of the present structure of security in Europe.

In a very real sense the csce process has become a process protecting the rights and interests of the smaller powers. The multilateral system of rules, obligations and commitments raises thresholds against transgression and imperial behavior. The protection provided by such thresholds is fragile and marginal but it suggests another aspect of interdependence, protection through participation in a system based on prescribed norms and the assumption of mutual restraint.

The commitments contained in the Final Act are essentially political commitments. They were designed not as final benchmarks but rather as takeoff points, a standard of minimum requirements beyond which states should attempt to move by unilateral action. The Final Act provides scope for a process of mutual example; it embodies the notion of momentum through practice. However, in many areas states, and particularly some of the Eastern states, have failed to respond to the challenge of "walking the extra mile." This is certainly true in the area of confidence-building measures. Instead, discussion has come to center on the interpretation of literal commitments. Therefore calls are now made for juridical obligations and reliable verification.

The elusive détente

Any analysis of the course of East-West relations necessarily involves reference to complex and elusive concepts. Ambiguity can sometimes be constructive; in other circumstances it will becloud vision and hamper progress toward accommodation and a resolution of outstanding disagreements. Sometimes disagreement cannot be eradicated. States do pursue different and sometimes incompatible interests. They want different things with respect to the distribution of goods and advantage, influence and position; they entertain different visions concerning the management of international relations and the rules for international behavior. Nevertheless, we all know that international relations are not an anarchic social process. Political order results from the pursuit and recognition of shared interests. The immediate and urgent task is one of creating a basis for the pursuit of common security, cutting across the divisions in international relations.

That elusive French term, "détente," has been a key concept in the analysis of recent history. It is a shorthand term for a complex notion encompassing a situation of reduced tension, a goal of defused confrontation and a process of international relations dominated, or at least permeated, by the normative perspective of avoiding unintended conflict and identifying and broadening shared interests.

The ground rules governing the process of détente were supposed to provide a basis for the evolution of a viable and equitable political order particularly in Europe. These ground rules are at present in a rather inchoate state; states are still in search of a viable concept of common security, but some of the basic principles have emerged. They may be summarized in four basic clusters: (1) States must exercise mutual restraint in their pursuit of the national interest and, as a minimum condition, abstain from the use or threat to use force. (2) The equal rights and obligations of states must be respected. Their sovereign rights cannot be constrained or circumscribed by reference to particular and limited notions of internationalism which are essentially claims for a right to limit the sovereignty of certain states, or by reference to geopolitical circumstances; contiguity does not confer special rights on the stronger neighbor. (3) States should pursue negotiations about arms reduction and limitation with a view to preventing the military factor from dominating international relations and, most particularly, from driving events across the precipice of war in crises. (4) States should abide by a respect for the rights of the individual vis-à-vis the state. It should be recognized in this connection that the relationship between the individual and the state, between society and the state, is viewed in different perspectives in the various political cultures which exist also in Europe. At the same time states must abstain from the willful interference into the internal affairs of other states with a view to altering their political system. Difficult and contentious trade-offs must be made in this field of tension. The issues are not liable to find resolution through negotiation.

Détente, unfortunately, has come into a certain disrepute; primarily because delivery did not, and probably could not, live up to expectations. Hopes were pegged unrealistically high, the search for a new dawn could not bring about a structural transformation of the East-West conflict without addressing the substance of the outstanding political issues. CSCE encompassed procedures, rules of engagement and a code of conduct, the framework for international relations, rather than a resolution of the substantive issues which determine the patterns of conflict. Europe has not been made whole again, but the texture and quality of interstate relations as well as societal relations in Europe have changed profoundly. The Europe of the early eighties is qualitatively different from the Europe of the early seventies, not to speak of the early sixties. In spite of setbacks and disappointments we have a more open and a more cooperative political order in Europe today than in the previous decades of the postwar era.

Détente did not produce an end to the cold war, but it did transform it, by reducing the chill as well as the expectation of war. It was based on an acceptance of the territorial and political realities which were the results of the Second World War and the immediate postwar era as facts, and of the norm that those facts should not be altered by force. This particular point of departure is imbedded in the principles about the inviolability of frontiers and noninterference in the internal affairs of other states. Détente did not and could not imply the absence of conflict. Conflict persists and continues to constrain the scope for international cooperation. However, the facts created by nuclear weapons make obsolescent the traditional approaches to security and the avoidance of war.

One difficulty with the promulgation of détente, with the vagueness of its conceptualization, was that it stimulated expectations which were unrealistic, particularly the expectation that we could envisage the end of conflict. Conflict is endemic to international relations, but it is neither general nor unbounded. The process of détente is in many ways one of conflict management, of superimposing upon the international competition a commitment to mutual restraint and common security. In this connection a code of conduct must be developed, certain basic rules of engagement observed. But we have to recognize that the rules will harbor ambiguities. Clarity is in some connections of critical importance to real progress in the process of détente. But the search for clarity and codification may in other circumstances prove counterproductive, as it may highlight differences and convert them into obstacles. There is in diplomacy such a phenomenon as constructive ambiguity. Clarity often must evolve through practice and diplomatic consultation rather than being hammered out in negotiated, legally binding covenants.

Détente cannot be served à la carte. Interdependence is a fact of international life. As a general proposition the process of détente in Europe will be penetrated and shaped by other processes, involving developments outside Europe, the global military engagements and political commitments of the major powers which determine the shape of the political order in Europe, as well as the arms competition outside and inside Europe. Nevertheless, the art of diplomacy is also one of dividing conflicts, separating issues and limiting the implications of conflict.

The influence of political perspectives

General linkage then is a fact of international life and will inevitably color and influence the course of events and atmosphere of international deliberations. However, a recognition of such facts is different from the deliberate construction of links between general international behavior and, for example, negotiations and agreements on arms control. Such negotiations and agreements should be viewed as vehicles for promoting shared interests, rather than as gifts or rewards for good behavior.

It is too early to make up a balance sheet of détente, and like the balance sheet of imperialism in the nineteenth century, it will in any event not be a simple account to tally.

The benefits and costs look different to the various powers involved. The seventies did bring some substantial and a multitude of intangible changes to intersocietal as well as interstate relations in Europe. Expectations were not fulfilled but expectations should always be ahead of reality, only then will they be able to mold the reality of the future. Progress in international relations is never unilinear, developments follow a zigzag pattern. It is important, however, to assure that the general thrust is a forward thrust.

From the point of view of the United States the balance sheet looks different from what it does from Europe. The 1970s constituted a decade when the direct nuclear threat against the North American continent grew massively. It was the decade when the Soviet Union emerged as a global power with the means and apparent will to project military power to distant areas.

The small and medium powers in Europe must share a continent with the Soviet Union. There is no alternative to peaceful coexistence. That term has been, however, as elusive and ambiguous as "détente." The vocabulary in which East-West relations are discussed and defined needs a refinement and precision which has been lacking hitherto if the scope for misperception and miscalculation is to be narrowed. Because of an inescapable common destiny the states in Europe emphasize the need for continuity in the conduct of East-West relations. Here is a basic reason why economic warfare looks dangerous and unacceptable as a means of preventing military warfare, or of punishing transgression of the rules of behavior. Economic sanctions raise tricky issues about the long-term management of political relations, about the criteria for assessing performance, the difficulties of reentry into normal intercourse, about the relationship between ends and means. In the American political culture there is a stronger belief in a new beginning, in the discontinuity of history, in engagement by choice rather than by necessity. Somehow, the two conflicting visions and propensities must be reconciled, the twains must meet, for East-West relations to be put on a steady course.

The Eastern states must recognize that the political culture of open societies constrains and molds the range of policy choice for governments in such societies. Government policy must be viewed as responsible to the basic attitudes and norms which permeate the Western bodies politic. Popular concern about the right and fate of their fellowmen in distant lands impels governments to engage in their protection. There is an inevitable spillover of domestic values into the arena of foreign policy. A more open world, penetrated by the eyes of the medium, generates new constraints on the conduct of international relations. In the same manner the propensity for value projection in democratic societies tends to constrain the options for military power projection to distant areas.

The military factor

The situation in Europe is inescapably wrapped into the military competition between the two alliances and the two superpowers. However, Europe will be unable to develop a viable order if it is relegated to the constricted role of being treated as an incidental extension of the Soviet-American rivalry. It is important to prevent Europe from becoming a hostage zone for the nuclear forces of the Soviet Union and the United States. Zero-option encapsulates a real challenge to political vision in the 1980s. But the other elements in the military situation must be transformed as well in order to prevent the military dispositions from driving and unduly constraining political developments.

The Helsinki process collided with the persistent extension of the military competition on the continent of Europe. It will progress only if the trends are stemmed and reversed. This must be undertaken outside the CSCE as such. The level of armaments in Europe is unprecedentedly and dangerously high. The preeminent role of nuclear weapons exacerbates tensions and contributes to the divorce of military strategy from foreign policy. There is a need to break the trends toward a militarization of the political order in Europe. The Helsinki process is important because it highlights other and less violent and destructive means for shaping political relations on the continent of Europe, pointing beyond confrontation to a more "normal" and mixed order of cooperation and contained conflict.

Helsinki was an important departure, a new beginning encompassing the aspirations and hopes which permeate our societies for a better tomorrow. The journey has only just begun. It is a common journey. Governments have the responsibility to make possible that which is necessary.

APPENDIXES

A. CSCE Meetings, 1977–85

Helsinki Commission: The First Eight Years (Washington, D.C.: U.S. General Accounting Office, 1985), pp. 20–21.

Helsinki International Meetings

Belgrade Review Meeting

Preparatory meeting	June 15 to August 5, 1977
Main meeting	
Phase I, opening session	October 4 to November 14, 1977
Phase II, introduction and discussion of new proposals	November 15 to December 22, 1977
Phase III, Concluding Document	January 17 to March 9, 1978

Experts meetings

BONN, FRG

Meeting to prepare for scientific forum	June 20 to July 28, 1978

HAMBURG, FRG

Scientific forum	February 18 to March 3, 1980

MONTREUX, SWITZERLAND

Peaceful settlement of disputes	October 31 to December 11, 1978

VALLETTA, MALTA

Cooperation in Mediterranean	February 13 to March 26, 1979

MADRID REVIEW MEETING

Preparatory meeting	September 9 to November 10, 1980
Main meeting	
Phase I, opening session	November 11 to December 19, 1980
Phase II, consideration of new proposals and drafting work	January 27 to July 28, 1981
Phase III, review of implementation	October 27 to December 18, 1981
Phase IV, impasse over military security and human rights issues	February 9 to March 13, 1982

Phase V, complete work on Concluding Document based on RM-39	November 9 to December 18, 1982
Phase VI, adopt Concluding Document	February 8 to July 15, 1983
Phase VII, concluded with speeches of foreign ministers	September 7 to September 9, 1983

Follow-up Meetings to the Madrid CSCE Review Meeting

Date	Place	Meeting
		1983
October 25	Helsinki	Preparatory meeting to Stockholm meeting
		1984
January 17	Stockholm	Conference on Confidence and Security Building Measures and Disarmament in Europe (4 sessions in 1984; 4 in 1985)
March 21	Athens	Experts Meeting on Peaceful Settlement of Disputes in the Mediterranean
October 16	Venice	Venice Seminar on Economic, Scientific and Cultural Cooperation in the Mediterranean Within the Framework of the Valletta Meeting of Experts
November 21	Budapest	Preparatory meeting to the cultural forum
		1985
April 23	Ottawa	Preparatory meeting to the Experts Meeting on Human Rights
May 7	Ottawa	Experts Meeting on Human Rights
August 1	Helsinki	Commemorative meeting on the tenth anniversary of the Helsinki Final Act
October 15	Budapest	Cultural forum
		1986
April 2	Bern	Preparatory meeting to Experts Meeting on Human Contacts
April 16	Bern	Experts Meeting on Human Contacts
September 23	Vienna	Preparatory meeting to the Vienna CSCE Review Meeting
November 4	Vienna	Vienna CSCE Review Meeting

B. Concluding Document of the Belgrade Meeting 1977 (March 8, 1978)

Nils Andrén and Karl E. Birnbaum, eds., *Belgrade and Beyond: The CSCE Process in Perspective* (Alphen aan den Rijn: Sijthoff & Noordhoff, 1981), pp. 161–63.

Concluding Document of the Belgrade Meeting 1977 of Representatives of the Participating States of the Conference on Security and Cooperation in Europe, Held on the Basis of the Provisions of the Final Act Relating to the Follow-up to the Conference

The representatives of the participating States of the Conference on Security and Cooperation in Europe, appointed by the Ministers of Foreign Affairs of those states, met at Belgrade from 4 October 1977 to 8 March 1978 in accordance with the provisions of the Final Act relating to the follow-up to the Conference.

The participants received a message from the President of the Socialist Federal Republic of Yugoslavia, Josip Broz Tito, and were addressed by Mr. Miloš Minić, Vice-President of the Federal Executive Council and Federal Secretary for Foreign Affairs of the Socialist Federal Republic of Yugoslavia.

Contributions were made by the following nonparticipating Mediterranean States: Algeria, Egypt, Israel, Lebanon, Morocco, Syria and Tunisia.

The representatives of the participating States addressed the importance they attach to détente, which has continued since the adoption of the Final Act in spite of difficulties and obstacles encountered. In this context they underlined the role of the CSCE, the implementation of the provisions of the Final Act being essential for the development of this process.

The representatives of the participating States held a thorough exchange of views both on the implementation of the provisions of the Final Act and of the tasks defined by the Conference, as well as, in the context of the questions dealt with by the latter, on the deepening of their mutual relations, the improvement of security and the development of cooperation in Europe, and the development of the process of détente in the future.

The representatives of the participating States stressed the political importance of the Conference on Security and Cooperation in Europe and reaffirmed the resolve of their governments, to implement fully, unilaterally, bilaterally and multilaterally, all the provisions of the Final Act.

It was recognized that the exchange of views constitutes in itself a valuable contribution toward the achievement of the aims set by the CSCE, although different views were expressed as to the degree of implementation of the Final Act reached so far.

They also examined proposals concerning the above questions and the definition of the appropriate modalities for the holding of other meetings in conformity with the provisions of the chapter of the Final Act concerning the follow-up to the meeting.

In conformity with the relevant provisions of the Final Act and with their resolve to continue the multilateral process initiated by the CSCE, the participating States will hold further meetings among their representatives. The second of these meetings will be held in Madrid commencing Tuesday 11 November 1980.

A preparatory meeting will be held in Madrid commencing Tuesday 9 September 1980 to decide on appropriate modalities for the main Madrid meeting. This will be done on the basis of the Final Act as well as of the other relevant documents adopted during the process of the CSCE.*

It was also agreed to hold, within the framework of the follow-up to the CSCE, the meetings of experts of the participating States indicated below.

In conformity with the mandate contained in the Final Act and according to the proposal made to this effect by the Government of Switzerland a meeting of experts

---

* The other relevant documents adopted during the process of the CSCE are: The Final Recommendations of the Helsinki Consultations; The Decisions of the Preparatory Meeting to Organize the Belgrade Meeting 1977; this Concluding Document.

will be convened at Montreux on October 31, 1978, charged with pursuing the examination and elaboration of a generally acceptable method for peaceful settlement of disputes aimed at complementing existing methods.

Upon the invitation of the Government of the Federal Republic of Germany, the Meeting of Experts envisaged in the Final Act in order to prepare a "Scientific Forum" will take place in Bonn starting on June 20, 1978. Representatives of UNESCO and the United Nations Economic Commission for Europe shall be invited to state their views.

Upon the invitation of the Government of Malta, a meeting of experts on the Mediterranean will be held within the framework of the Mediterranean Chapter of the Final Act, convened on February 13, 1979, in La Valletta. Its mandate will be to consider the possibilities and means of prompting concrete initiatives for mutually beneficial cooperation concerning various economic, scientific and cultural fields, in addition to other initiatives relating to the above subjects already under way. The nonparticipating Mediterranean States will be invited to contribute to the work of this meeting. Questions relating to security will be discussed at the Madrid meeting.

The duration of the meetings of experts should not exceed 4–6 weeks. They will draw up conclusions and recommendations and send their reports to the governments of the participating States. The results of these meetings will be taken into account, as appropriate, at the Madrid Meeting.

All the above-mentioned meetings will be held in conformity with paragraph 4 of the Chapter on "Follow-up to the Conference" of the Final Act.

The government of the Socialist Federal Republic of Yugoslavia is requested to transmit the present document to the Secretary-General of the United Nations, to the Director-General of UNESCO and to the Executive Secretary of the United Nations Economic Commission for Europe. The government of the Socialist Federal Republic of Yugoslavia is also requested to transmit the present document to the governments of the Mediterranean nonparticipating States.

The representatives of the participating States expressed their profound gratitude to the people and government of the Socialist Federal Republic of Yugoslavia for the excellent organization of the Belgrade Meeting and the warm hospitality extended to the delegations which participated in the meeting.

C. Concluding Document of the Madrid Meeting 1980 (September 6, 1983)

The Madrid CSCE Review (Washington, D.C.: Commission on Security and Cooperation in Europe, 1983), pp. 64–102.

Concluding Document of the Madrid meeting 1980 of representatives of the participating states of the Conference on Security and Cooperation in Europe, held on the basis of the provisions of the Final Act relating to the Follow-up to the Conference

The representatives of the participating States of the Conference on Security and Cooperation in Europe met in Madrid from 11 November 1980 to 9 September 1983 in accordance with the provisions of the Final Act relating to the Follow-up to the Conference, as well as on the basis of the other relevant documents adopted during the process of the CSCE.

The participants were addressed on 12 November 1980 by the Spanish Prime Minister.

Opening statements were made by all Heads of Delegations among whom were Ministers and Deputy Ministers of Foreign Affairs of a number of participating States. Some Ministers of Foreign Affairs addressed the Meeting also at later stages.

Contributions were made by representatives of the United Nations Economic Commission for Europe (ECE) and UNESCO.

Contributions were also made by the following nonparticipating Mediterranean States: Algeria, Egypt, Israel, Morocco and Tunisia.

The representatives of the participating States stressed the high political significance of the Conference on Security and Cooperation in Europe and of the process initiated by it as well as of the ways and means it provides for States to further their efforts to increase security, develop cooperation and enhance mutual understanding in Europe. They therefore reaffirmed their commitment to the process of the CSCE and emphasized the importance of the implementation of all the provisions and the respect for all the principles of the Final Act by each of them as being essential for the development of this process. Furthermore, they stressed the importance they attach to security and genuine détente, while deploring the deterioration of the international situation since the Belgrade Meeting 1977.

Accordingly, the participating States agreed that renewed efforts should be made to give full effect to the Final Act through concrete action, unilateral, bilateral and multilateral, in order to restore trust and confidence between the participating States which would permit a substantial improvement in their mutual relations. They considered that the future of the CSCE process required balanced progress in all sections of the Final Act.

6. In accordance with the mandate provided for in the Final Act and the Agenda of the Madrid Meeting, the representatives of the participating States held a thorough exchange of views both on the implementation of the provisions of the Final Act and of the tasks defined by the Conference, as well as, in the context of the questions dealt with by the latter, on the deepening of their mutual relations, the improvement of security and the development of cooperation in Europe, and the development of the process of détente in the future.

7. It was confirmed that the thorough exchange of views constitutes in itself a valuable contribution toward the achievement of the aims set by the CSCE. In this context, it was agreed that these aims can only be attained by continuous implementation, unilaterally, bilaterally and multilaterally, of all the provisions and by respect for all the principles of the Final Act.

8. During this exchange of views, different and at times contradictory opinions were expressed as to the degree of implementation of the Final Act reached so far by participating States. While certain progress was noted, concern was expressed at the serious deficiencies in the implementation of this document.

9. Critical assessments from different viewpoints were given as to the application of and respect for the principles of the Final Act. Serious violations of a number of these principles were deplored during these assessments. Therefore, the participating States, at times represented at a higher level, considered it necessary to state, at various stages of the Meeting, that strict application of and respect for these principles, in all their aspects, are essential for the improvement of mutual relations between the participating States.

The necessity was also stressed that the relations of the participating States with all other States should be conducted in the spirit of these principles.

10. Concern was expressed about the continued lack of confidence among participating States.

Concern was also expressed as to the spread of terrorism.

11. The implementation of the provisions of the Final Act concerning Confidence-Building Measures, Cooperation in the field of Economics, of Science and Technology and of Environment, as well as Cooperation in Humanitarian and other fields was thoroughly discussed. It was considered that the numerous possibilities offered by the Final Act had not been sufficiently utilized. Questions relating to Security and Cooperation in the Mediterranean were also discussed.

12. The participating States reaffirmed their commitment to the continuation of the CSCE process as agreed to in the chapter on the Follow-up to the Conference contained in the Final Act.

13. The representatives of the participating States took note of the reports of the meetings of experts and of the "Scientific Forum," and in the course of their deliberations took the results of these meetings into account.

14. The representatives of the participating States examined all the proposals submitted concerning the above questions and agreed on the following:

Questions Relating to Security in Europe

The participating States express their determination

—to exert new efforts to make détente an effective, as well as continuing increasingly viable and comprehensive process, universal in scope, as undertaken under the Final Act;

—to seek solutions to outstanding problems through peaceful means;

—to fulfill consistently all the provisions under the Final Act and, in particular, strictly and unreservedly to respect and put into practice all the ten principles contained in the Declaration on Principles Guiding Relations between Participating States, irrespective of their political, economic or social system, as well as of their size, geographical location or level of economic development, including their commitment to conduct their relations with all other States in the spirit of these principles;

—to develop relations of mutual cooperation, friendship and confidence, refraining from any action which, being contrary to the Final Act, might impair such relations;

—to encourage genuine efforts to implement the Final Act;

—to exert genuine efforts toward containing an increasing arms buildup as well as toward strengthening confidence and security and promoting disarmament.

Principles

1. They reaffirm their determination fully to respect and apply these principles and accordingly, to promote by all means, both in law and practice, their increased effectiveness. They consider that one such means could be to give legislative expression—in forms appropriate to practices and procedures specific to each country—to the ten principles set forth in the Final Act.

2. They recognize it as important that treaties and agreements concluded by participating States reflect and be consonant with the relevant principles and, where appropriate, refer to them.

3. The participating States reaffirm the need that refraining from the threat or use of force, as a norm of international life, should be strictly and effectively ob-

served. To this end they stress their duty, under the relevant provisions of the Final Act, to act accordingly.

4. The participating States condemn terrorism, including terrorism in international relations, as endangering or taking innocent human lives or otherwise jeopardizing human rights and fundamental freedoms, and emphasize the necessity to take resolute measures to combat it. They express their determination to take effective measures for the prevention and suppression of acts of terrorism, both at the national level and through international cooperation including appropriate bilateral and multilateral agreements, and accordingly to broaden and reinforce mutual cooperation to combat such acts. They agree to do so in conformity with the Charter of the United Nations, the United Nations Declaration on Principles of International Law concerning Friendly Relations and Cooperation among States and the Helsinki Final Act.

5. In the context of the combat against acts of terrorism, they will take all appropriate measures in preventing their respective territories from being used for the preparation, organization or commission of terrorist activities, including those directed against other participating States and their citizens. This also includes measures to prohibit on their territories illegal activities of persons, groups and organizations that instigate, organize or engage in the perpetration of acts of terrorism.

6. The participating States confirm that they will refrain from direct or indirect assistance to terrorist activities or to subversive or other activities directed toward the violent overthrow of the regime of another participating State. Accordingly, they will refrain, *inter alia*, from financing, encouraging, fomenting or tolerating any such activities.

7. They express their determination to do their utmost to assure necessary security to all official representatives and persons who participate on their territories in activities within the scope of diplomatic, consular or other official relations.

8. They emphasize that all the participating States recognize in the Final Act the universal significance of human rights and fundamental freedoms, respect for which is an essential factor for the peace, justice and well-being necessary to ensure the development of friendly relations and cooperation among themselves, as among all States.

9. The participating States stress their determination to promote and encourage the effective exercise of human rights and fundamental freedoms, all of which derive from the inherent dignity of the human person and are essential for his free and full development, and to assure constant and tangible progress in accordance with the Final Act, aiming at further and steady development in this field in all participating States, irrespective of their political, economic and social systems.

They similarly stress their determination to develop their laws and regulations in the fields of civil, political, economic, social, cultural and other human rights and fundamental freedoms; they also emphasize their determination to ensure the effective exercise of these rights and freedoms.

They recall the right of the individual to know and act upon his rights and duties in the field of human rights and fundamental freedoms, as embodied in the Final Act, and will take the necessary action in their respective countries to effectively ensure this right.

10. The participating States reaffirm that they will recognize, respect and furthermore agree to take the action necessary to ensure the freedom of the individual to profess and practice, alone or in community with others, religion or belief acting in accordance with the dictates of his own conscience.

In this context, they will consult, whenever necessary, the religious faiths, institutions and organizations, which act within the constitutional framework of their respective countries.

They will favorably consider applications by religious communities of believers practicing or prepared to practice their faith within the constitutional framework of their States, to be granted the status provided for in their respective countries for religious faiths, institutions and organizations.

11. They stress also the importance of constant progress in ensuring the respect for and actual enjoyment of the rights of persons belonging to national minorities as well as protecting their legitimate interests as provided for in the Final Act.

12. They stress the importance of ensuring equal rights of men and women; accordingly, they agree to take all actions necessary to promote equally effective participation of men and women in political, economic, social and cultural life.

13. The participating States will ensure the right of workers freely to establish and join trade unions, the right of trade unions freely to exercise their activities and other rights as laid down in relevant international instruments. They note that these rights will be exercised in compliance with the law of the State and in conformity with the State's obligations under international law. They will encourage, as appropriate, direct contacts and communication among such trade unions and their representatives.

14. They reaffirm that governments, institutions, organizations and persons have a relevant and positive role to play in contributing toward the achievement of the above-mentioned aims of their cooperation.

15. They reaffirm the particular significance of the Universal Declaration of Human Rights, the International Covenants on Human Rights and other relevant international instruments of their joint and separate efforts to stimulate and develop universal respect for human rights and fundamental freedoms; they call on all participating States to act in conformity with those international instruments and on those participating States, which have not yet done so, to consider the possibility of acceding to the covenants.

16. They agree to give favorable consideration to the use of bilateral round-table meetings, held on a voluntary basis, between delegations composed by each participating State to discuss issues of human rights and fundamental freedoms in accordance with an agreed agenda in a spirit of mutual respect with a view to achieving greater understanding and cooperation based on the provisions of the Final Act.

17. They decide to convene a meeting of experts of the participating States on questions concerning respect, in their States, for human rights and fundamental freedoms, in all their aspects, as embodied in the Final Act.

Upon invitation of the Government of Canada, the meeting of experts will be held in Ottawa, beginning on 7 May 1985. It will draw up conclusions and recommendations to be submitted to the governments of all participating States.

The meeting will be preceded by a preparatory meeting which will be held in Ottawa upon the invitation of the Government of Canada, starting on 23 April 1985.

18. In conformity with the recommendation contained in the Report of the Montreux Meeting of Experts, another meeting of experts of the participating States will be convened, at the invitation of the Government of Greece. It will take place in Athens and will commence on 21 March 1984, with the purpose of pursuing, on the basis of the Final Act, the examination of a generally acceptable method for the peaceful settlement of disputes aimed at complementing existing methods. The

meeting will take into account the common approach set forth in the above-mentioned report.

19. Recalling the right of any participating State to belong or not to belong to international organizations, to be or not to be a party to bilateral or multilateral treaties including the right to be or not to be a party to treaties of alliance, and also the right to neutrality, the participating States take note of the declaration of the Government of the Republic of Malta in which it stated that, as an effective contribution to détente, peace and security in the Mediterranean region, the Republic of Malta is a neutral State adhering to a policy of nonalignment. They call upon all States to respect that declaration.

Conference on Confidence- and Security-building Measures and Disarmament in Europe

The participating States,

Recalling the provisions of the Final Act according to which they recognize the interest of all of them in efforts aimed at lessening military confrontation and promoting disarmament,

Have agreed to convene a Conference on Confidence- and Security-building Measures and Disarmament in Europe.

1. The aim of the Conference is, as a substantial and integral part of the multilateral process initiated by the Conference on Security and Cooperation in Europe, with the participation of all the States signatories of the Final Act, to undertake, in stages, new, effective and concrete actions designed to make progress in strengthening confidence and security and in achieving disarmament, so as to give effect and expression to the duty of States to refrain from the threat or use of force in their mutual relations.

2. Thus the Conference will begin a process of which the first stage will be devoted to the negotiation and adoption of a set of mutually complementary confidence- and security-building measures designed to reduce the risk of military confrontation in Europe.

3. The first stage of the Conference will be held in Stockholm commencing on 17 January 1984.

4. On the basis of equality of rights, balance and reciprocity, equal respect for the security interests of all CSCE participating States, and of their respective obligations concerning confidence- and security-building measures and disarmament in Europe, these confidence- and security-building measures will cover the whole of Europe as well as the adjoining sea area* and air space. They will be of military significance and politically binding and will be provided with adequate forms of verification which correspond to their content.

As far as the adjoining sea area and air space is concerned, the measures will be applicable to the military activities of all the participating States taking place there whenever these activities affect security in Europe as well as constitute a part of activities taking place within the whole of Europe as referred to above, which they will agree to notify. Necessary specifications will be made through the negotiations on the confidence- and security-building measures at the Conference.

---

* In this context, the notion of adjoining sea area is understood to refer also to ocean areas adjoining Europe.

Nothing in the definition of the zone given above will diminish obligations already undertaken under the Final Act. The confidence- and security-building measures to be agreed upon at the Conference will also be applicable in all areas covered by any of the provisions in the Final Act relating to confidence-building measures and certain aspects of security and disarmament.

The provisions established by the negotiators will come into force in the forms and according to the procedure to be agreed upon by the Conference.

5. Taking into account the above-mentioned aim of the Conference, the next follow-up meeting of the participating States of the CSCE, to be held in Vienna, commencing on 4 November 1986, will assess the progress achieved during the first stage of the Conference.

6. Taking into account the relevant provisions of the Final Act, and having reviewed the results achieved by the first stage of the Conference, and also in the light of other relevant negotiations on security and disarmament affecting Europe, a future CSCE follow-up meeting will consider ways and appropriate means for the participating States to continue their efforts for security and disarmament in Europe, including the question of supplementing the present mandate for the next stage of the Conference on Confidence- and Security-building Measures and Disarmament in Europe.

7. A preparatory meeting, charged with establishing the agenda, timetable and other organizational modalities for the first stage of the Conference, will be held in Helsinki, commencing on 25 October 1983. Its duration shall not exceed three weeks.

8. The rules of procedure, the working methods and the scale of distribution for the expenses valid for the CSCE will, *mutatis mutandis*, be applied to the Conference and to the preparatory meeting referred to in the preceding paragraph. The services of a technical secretariat will be provided by the host country.

Cooperation in the Field of Economics, of Science and Technology and of the Environment

1. The participating States consider that the implementation of all provisions of the Final Act and full respect for the principles guiding relations among them set out therein are an essential basis for the development of cooperation among them in the field of economics, of science and technology and of the environment. At the same time they reaffirm their conviction that cooperation in these fields contributes to the reinforcement of peace and security in Europe and in the world as a whole. In this spirit they reiterate their resolve to pursue and intensify such cooperation between one another, irrespective of their economic and social systems.

2. The participating States confirm their interest in promoting adequate, favorable conditions in order further to develop trade and industrial cooperation among them, in particular by fully implementing all provisions of the second chapter of the Final Act, so as to make greater use of the possibilities created by their economic, scientific and technical potential. In this context and taking into consideration the efforts already made unilaterally, bilaterally and multilaterally in order to overcome all kinds of obstacles to trade, they reaffirm their intention to make further efforts aimed at reducing or progressively eliminating all kinds of obstacles to the development of trade.

Taking account of the activities of the United Nations Economic Commission for Europe (ECE) already carried out in the field of all kinds of obstacles to trade, they recommend that further work on this subject be directed in particular toward identifying these obstacles and examining them with a view to finding means for their reduction or progressive elimination, in order to contribute to harmonious development of their economic relations.

3. On the basis of the provisions of the Final Act concerning business contacts and facilities the participating States declare their intention to make efforts to enable business negotiations and activities to be carried out more efficiently and expeditiously and further to create conditions facilitating closer contacts between representatives and experts of seller firms on the one hand and buyer as well as user firms on the other at all stages of transaction. They will also further other forms of operational contacts between sellers and users such as the holding of technical symposia and demonstrations and after-sales training or requalification courses for technical staff of user firms and organizations.

They also agree to take measures further to develop and improve facilities and working conditions for representatives of foreign firms and organizations on their territory, including telecommunications facilities for representatives of such firms and organizations, as well as to develop these and other amenities for temporarily resident staff including particularly site personnel. They will endeavor further to take measures to speed up as far as possible procedures for the registration of foreign firms' representation and offices as well as for granting entry visas to business representatives.

4. The participating States declare their intention to ensure the regular publication and dissemination, as rapidly as possible, of economic and commercial information compiled in such a way as to facilitate the appreciation of market opportunities and thus to contribute effectively to the process of developing international trade and industrial cooperation.

To this end and in order to make further progress in achieving the aims laid down in the relevant provisions of the Final Act they intend to intensify their efforts to improve the comparability, comprehensiveness and clarity of their economic and commercial statistics, in particular by adopting where necessary the following measures: by accompanying their economic and trade statistics by adequately defined summary indices based wherever possible on constant values; by publishing their interim statistics whenever technically possible at least on a quarterly basis; by publishing their statistical compilations in sufficient detail to achieve the aims referred to above, in particular by using for their foreign trade statistics a product breakdown permitting the identification of particular products for purposes of market analysis; by striving to have their economic and trade statistics no less comprehensive than those previously published by the State concerned.

They further express their willingness to cooperate toward the early completion of work in the appropriate United Nations bodies on the harmonization and alignment of statistical nomenclatures.

The participating States further recognize the usefulness of making economic and commercial information existing in other participating States readily available to enterprises and firms in their countries through appropriate channels.

5. The participating States, conscious of the need further to improve the conditions conducive to a more efficient functioning of institutions and firms acting in the field of marketing, will promote a more active exchange of knowledge and techniques required for effective marketing, and will encourage more intensive relations among such institutions and firms. They agree to make full use of the possibilities offered by the ECE to further their cooperation in this field.

6. The participating States note the increasing frequency in their economic relations of compensation transactions in all their forms. They recognize that a useful

role can be played by such transactions, concluded on a mutually acceptable basis. At the same time they recognize that problems can be created by the linkage in such transactions between purchases and sales.

Taking account of the studies of the ECE already carried out in this field, they recommend that further work on this subject be directed in particular toward identifying such problems and examining ways of solving them in order to contribute to a harmonious development of their economic relations.

7. The participating States recognize that the expansion of industrial cooperation, on the basis of their mutual interest and motivated by economic considerations, can contribute to the further development and diversification of their economic relations and to a wider utilization of modern technology.

They note the useful role bilateral agreements on economic, industrial and technical cooperation, including, where appropriate, those of a long-term nature, can play. They also express their willingness to promote favorable conditions for the development of industrial cooperation among competent organizations, enterprises and firms. To this end and with a view to facilitating the identification of new possibilities for industrial cooperation projects they recognize the desirability of further developing and improving the conditions for business activities and the exchange of economic and commercial information among competent organizations, enterprises and firms including small and medium-sized enterprises.

They also note that, if it is in the mutual interest of potential partners, new forms of industrial cooperation can be envisaged, including those with organizations, institutions and firms of third countries.

They recommend that the ECE pursue and continue to pay particular attention to its activities in the field of industrial cooperation, *inter alia* by further directing its efforts toward examining ways of promoting favorable conditions for the development of cooperation in this field, including the organization of symposia and seminars.

8. The participating States declare their readiness to continue their efforts aiming at a wider participation by small and medium-size enterprises in trade and industrial cooperation. Aware of the problems particularly affecting such enterprises, the participating States will endeavor further to improve the conditions dealt with in the preceding paragraphs in order to facilitate the operations of these enterprises in the above-mentioned fields. The participating States further recommend that the ECE develop its special studies pertaining to these problems.

9. The participating States recognize the increasing importance of cooperation in the field of energy, *inter alia* that of a long-term nature, on both a bilateral and multilateral basis. Welcoming the results so far achieved through such endeavors and in particular the work carried out by the ECE they express their support for continuing the cooperation pursued by the Senior Advisers to ECE Governments on Energy aiming at the fulfillment of all parts of their mandate.

10. The participating States reaffirm their interest in reducing and preventing technical barriers to trade and welcome the increased cooperation in this field, *inter alia* the work of the Government Officials Responsible for Standardization Policies in the ECE. They will encourage the conclusion of international certification arrangements covering where appropriate the mutual acceptance of certification systems providing mutually satisfactory guarantees.

11. The participating States recommend that appropriate action be taken in order to facilitate the use and enlarge the scope of arbitration as an instrument for settling disputes in international trade and industrial cooperation. They recommend in particular the application of the provisions of the United Nations Convention

on Recognition and Enforcement of Foreign Arbitral Awards of 1958 as well as a wider recourse to the arbitration rules elaborated by the United Nations Commission on International Trade Law. They also advocate that parties should, on the basis of the provisions of the Final Act, be allowed freedom in the choice of arbitrators and the place of arbitration, including the choice of arbitrators and the place of arbitration in a third country.

12. The participating States recognize the important role of scientific and technical progress in the economic and social development of all countries in particular those which are developing from an economic point of view. Taking into account the objectives which countries or institutions concerned pursue in their bilateral and multilateral relations they underline the importance of further developing, on the basis of reciprocal advantage and on the basis of mutual agreement and other arrangements, the forms and methods of cooperation in the field of science and technology provided for in the Final Act, for instance international programs and cooperative projects, while utilizing also various forms of contacts, including direct and individual contacts among scientists and specialists as well as contacts and communications among interested organizations, scientific and technological institutions and enterprises.

In this context they recognize the value of an improved exchange and dissemination of information concerning scientific and technical developments as a means of facilitating, on the basis of mutual advantage, the study and the transfer of, as well as access to scientific and technical achievements in fields of cooperation agreed between interested parties.

The participating States recommend that in the field of science and technology the ECE should give due attention, through appropriate ways and means, to the elaboration of studies and practical projects for the development of cooperation among member countries.

Furthermore, the participating States, aware of the relevant part of the Report of the "Scientific Forum," agree to encourage the development of scientific cooperation in the field of agriculture at bilateral, multilateral and subregional levels, with the aim, *inter alia*, of improving livestock and plant breeding and ensuring optimum use and conservation of water resources. To this end, they will promote further cooperation among research institutions and centers in their countries, through the exchange of information, the joint implementation of research programs, the organization of meetings among scientists and specialists, and other methods.

The participating States invite the ECE and other competent international organizations to support the implementation of these activities and to examine the possibilities of providing a wider exchange of scientific and technological information in the field of agriculture.

13. The participating States welcome with satisfaction the important steps taken to strengthen cooperation within the framework of the ECE in the field of the environment, including the High-Level Meeting on the Protection of the Environment (13–16 November 1979). Taking due account of work undertaken or envisaged in other competent international organizations, they recommend the continuation of efforts in this field, including, *inter alia,*

—giving priority to the effective implementation of the provisions of the Resolution on Long-Range Transboundary Air Pollution adopted at the High-Level Meeting,

—the early ratification of the Convention on Long-Range Transboundary Air Pollution signed at the High-Level Meeting,

—implementation of the Recommendations contained in the Declaration on Low and Non-Waste Technology and Reutilization and Recycling of Wastes,

—implementation of Decisions B and C of the thirty-fifth session of the ECE concerning the Declaration of Policy on Prevention and Control of Water Pollution, including transboundary pollution,

—support in carrying out the program of work of the ECE concerning the protection of the environment, including, *inter alia*, the work under way in the field of the protection of flora and fauna.

14. In the context of the provisions of the Final Act concerning migrant labor in Europe, the participating States note that recent developments in the world economy have affected the situation of migrant workers. In this connection, the participating States express their wish that host countries and countries of origin, guided by a spirit of mutual interest and cooperation, intensify their contacts with a view to improving further the general situation of migrant workers and their families, *inter alia* the protection of their human rights including their economic, social and cultural rights while taking particularly into account the special problems of second generation migrants. They will also endeavor to provide or promote, where reasonable demand exists, adequate teaching of the language and culture of the countries of origin.

The participating States recommend that, among other measures for facilitating the social and economic reintegration of returning migrant labor, the payment of pensions as acquired or established under the social security system to which such workers have been admitted in the host country should be ensured by appropriate legislative means or reciprocal agreements.

15. The participating States further recognize the importance for their economic development of promoting the exchange of information and experience on training for management staff. To this end they recommend the organization, in an appropriate existing framework and with the help of interested organizations such as, for example, the ECE and the International Labor Organization, of a symposium of persons responsible for services and institutions specializing in management training for administrations and enterprises with a view to exchanging information on training problems and methods, comparing experiences and encouraging the development of relations among the centers concerned.

16. The participating States welcome the valuable contribution made by the ECE to the multilateral implementation of the provisions of the Final Act pertaining to cooperation in the fields of economics, of science and technology and of the environment. Aware of the potential of the ECE for intensifying cooperation in these fields, they recommend the fullest use of the existing mechanisms and resources in order to continue and consolidate the implementation of the relevant provisions of the Final Act in the interest of its member countries, including those within the ECE region which are developing from an economic point of view.

17. The participating States, bearing in mind their will expressed in the provisions of the Final Act, reiterate the determination of each of them to promote stable and equitable international economic relations in the mutual interest of all States and, in this spirit, to participate equitably in promoting and strengthening economic cooperation with the developing countries in particular the least developed among them. They also note the usefulness, *inter alia*, of identifying and executing, in cooperation with developing countries, concrete projects, with a view to contributing to economic development in these countries.

They also declare their readiness to contribute to common efforts toward the establishment of a new international economic order and the implementation of the Strategy for the Third United Nations Development Decade, as adopted. They recognize the importance of the launching of mutually beneficial and adequately prepared global negotiations relating to international economic cooperation for development.

Questions Relating to Security and Cooperation in the Mediterranean

1. The participating States, bearing in mind that security in Europe, considered in the broader context of world security, is closely linked to security in the Mediterranean areas as a whole, reaffirm their intention to contribute to peace, security and justice in the Mediterranean region.

2. They further express their will

—to take positive steps toward lessening tensions and strengthening stability, security and peace in the Mediterranean and, to this end, to intensify efforts toward finding just, viable and lasting solutions, through peaceful means, to outstanding crucial problems, without resort to force or other means incompatible with the Principles of the Final Act, so as to promote confidence and security and make peace prevail in the region;

—to take measures designed to increase confidence and security;

—to develop good neighborly relations with all States in the region, with due regard to reciprocity, and in the spirit of the principles contained in the Declaration on Principles Guiding Relations between Participating States of the Final Act;

—to study further the possibility of *ad hoc* meetings of Mediterranean States aimed at strengthening security and intensifying cooperation in the Mediterranean.

3. In addition the participating States will, within the framework of the implementation of the Valletta report, consider the possibilities offered by new transport infrastructure developments to facilitate new commercial and industrial exchanges, as well as by the improvement of existing transport networks, and by a wider coordination of transport investments between interested parties. In this context they recommend that a study be undertaken, within the framework of the ECE, in order to establish the current and potential transport flows in the Mediterranean involving the participating States and other States of this region taking account of the current work in this field. They will further consider the question of introducing or extending, in accordance with the existing IMO regulations, the use of suitable techniques for aids to maritime navigation, principally in straits.

4. They further note with satisfaction the results of the Meeting of Experts held in Valletta on the subject of economic, scientific and cultural cooperation within the framework of the Mediterranean Chapter of the Final Act. They reaffirm the conclusions and recommendations of the report of this Meeting and agree that they will be guided accordingly. They also take note of efforts under way aiming at implementing them as appropriate. To this end, the participating States agree to convene from 16 to 26 October 1984 a seminar to be held at Venice at the invitation of the Government of Italy, to review the initiatives already undertaken, or envisaged, in all the sectors outlined in the report of the Valletta Meeting and stimulate, where necessary, broader developments in these sectors.

Representatives of the competent international organizations and representatives of the nonparticipating Mediterranean States will be invited to this Seminar in accordance with the rules and practices adopted at the Valletta Meeting.*

Cooperation in Humanitarian and Other Fields

The participating States,

Recalling the introductory sections of the Chapter on Cooperation in Humanitarian and other Fields of the Final Act, including those concerning the development of mutual understanding between them and détente and those concerning progress in cultural and educational exchanges, broader dissemination of information, contacts between people and the solution of humanitarian problems,

Resolving to pursue and expand cooperation in these fields and to achieve a fuller utilization of the possibilities offered by the Final Act,

Agree now to implement the following:

Human contacts

1. The participating States will favorably deal with applications relating to contacts and regular meetings on the basis of family ties, reunification of families and marriage between citizens of different States and will decide upon them in the same spirit.

2. They will decide upon these applications in emergency cases for family meetings as expeditiously as possible, for family reunification and for marriage between citizens of different States in normal practice within six months and for other family meetings within gradually decreasing time limits.

3. They confirm that the presentation or renewal of applications in these cases will not modify the rights and obligations of the applicants or of members of their families concerning *inter alia* employment, housing, residence status, family support, access to social, economic or educational benefits, as well as any other rights and obligations flowing from the laws and regulations of the respective participating State.

4. The participating States will provide the necessary information on the procedures to be followed by the applicants in these cases and on the regulations to be observed, as well as, upon the applicant's request, provide the relevant forms.

5. They will, where necessary, gradually reduce fees charged in connection with these applications, including those for visas and passports, in order to bring them to a moderate level in relation to the average monthly income in the respective participating State.

6. Applicants will be informed as expeditiously as possible of the decision that has been reached. In case of refusal applicants will also be informed of their right to renew applications after reasonably short intervals.

7. The participating States reaffirm their commitment fully to implement the provisions regarding diplomatic and other official missions and consular posts of other participating States contained in relevant multilateral or bilateral conventions, and to facilitate the normal functioning of those missions. Access by visitors to these missions will be assured with due regard to the necessary requirements of security of these missions.

---

* The organization of the Venice Seminar is set forth in the Chairman's statement of 6 September 1983 (see Annex I).

8. They also reaffirm their willingness to take, within their competence, reasonable steps, including necessary security measures, when appropriate, to ensure satisfactory conditions for activities within the framework of mutual cooperation on their territory, such as sporting and cultural events, in which citizens of other participating States take part.

9. The participating States will endeavor, where appropriate, to improve the conditions relating to legal, consular and medical assistance for citizens of other participating States temporarily on their territory for personal or professional reasons, taking due account of relevant multilateral or bilateral conventions or agreements.

10. They will further implement the relevant provisions of the Final Act, so that religious faiths, institutions, organizations and their representatives can, in the field of their activity, develop contacts and meetings among themselves and exchange information.

11. The participating States will encourage contacts and exchanges among young people and foster the broadening of cooperation among their youth organizations. They will favor the holding among young people and youth organizations of educational, cultural and other comparable events and activities. They will also favor the study of problems relating to the younger generation. The participating States will further the development of individual or collective youth tourism, when necessary on the basis of arrangements, *inter alia* by encouraging the granting of suitable facilities by the transport authorities and tourist organizations of the participating States or such facilities as those offered by the railway authorities participating in the "Inter-Rail" system.

Information

1. The participating States will further encourage the freer and wider dissemination of printed matter, periodical and nonperiodical, imported from other participating States, as well as an increase in the number of places where these publications are on public sale. These publications will also be accessible in reading rooms in large public libraries and similar institutions.

2. In particular, to facilitate the improvement of dissemination of printed information, the participating States will encourage contacts and negotiations between their competent firms and organizations with a view to concluding long-term agreements and contracts designed to increase the quantities and number of titles of newspapers and other publications imported from other participating States. They consider it desirable that the retail prices of foreign publications are not excessive in relation to prices in their country of origin.

3. They confirm their intention, according to the relevant provisions of the Final Act, to further extend the possibilities for the public to take out subscriptions.

4. They will favor the further expansion of cooperation among mass media and their representatives, especially between the editorial staffs of press agencies, newspapers, radio and television organizations as well as film companies. They will encourage a more regular exchange of news, articles, supplements and broadcasts as well as the exchange of editorial staff for better knowledge of respective practices. On the basis of reciprocity, they will improve the material and technical facilities provided for permanently or temporarily accredited television and radio reporters. Moreover, they will facilitate direct contacts among journalists as well as contacts within the framework of professional organizations.

5. They will decide without undue delay upon visa applications from journalists

and reexamine within a reasonable time frame applications which have been refused. Moreover, journalists wishing to travel for personal reasons and not for the purpose of reporting shall enjoy the same treatment as other visitors from their country of origin.

6. They will grant permanent correspondents and members of their families living with them multiple entry and exit visas valid for one year.

7. The participating States will examine the possibility of granting, where necessary on the basis of bilateral arrangements, accreditation and related facilities to journalists from other participating States who are permanently accredited in third countries.

8. They will facilitate travel by journalists from other participating States within their territories, *inter alia* by taking concrete measures where necessary, to afford them opportunities to travel more extensively, with the exception of areas closed for security reasons. They will inform journalists in advance, whenever possible, if new areas are closed for security reasons.

9. They will further increase the possibilities and, when necessary, improve the conditions for journalists from other participating States to establish and maintain personal contacts and communication with their sources.

10. They will, as a rule, authorize radio and television journalists, at their request, to be accompanied by their own sound and film technicians and to use their own equipment.

Similarly, journalists may carry with them reference material, including personal notes and files, to be used strictly for their professional purposes.*

11. The participating States will, where necessary, facilitate the establishment and operation, in their capitals, of press centers or institutions performing the same functions, open to the national and foreign press with suitable working facilities for the latter.

They will also consider further ways and means to assist journalists from other participating States and thus to enable them to resolve practical problems they may encounter.

Cooperation and exchanges in the field of culture

1. They will endeavor, by taking appropriate steps, to make the relevant information concerning possibilities offered by bilateral cultural agreements and programs available to interested persons, institutions and nongovernmental organizations, thus facilitating their effective implementation.

2. The participating States will further encourage wider dissemination of and access to books, films and other forms and means of cultural expression from other participating States, to this end improving by appropriate means, on bilateral and multilateral bases, the conditions for international commercial and noncommercial exchange of their cultural goods, *inter alia* by gradually lowering customs duties on these items.

3. The participating States will endeavor to encourage the translation, publication and dissemination of works in the sphere of literature and other fields of cultural activity from other participating States, especially those produced in less

---

* In this context it is understood that import of printed matter may be subject to local regulations which will be applied with due regard to the journalists' need for adequate working material.

widely spoken languages, by facilitating cooperation between publishing houses, in particular through the exchange of lists of books which might be translated as well as of other relevant information.

4. They will contribute to the development of contacts, cooperation and joint projects among the participating States regarding the protection, preservation and recording of historical heritage and monuments and the relationship between man, environment and this heritage; they express their interest in the possibility of convening an intergovernmental conference on these matters within the framework of UNESCO.

5. The participating States will encourage their radio and television organizations to continue developing the presentation of the cultural and artistic achievements of other participating States on the basis of bilateral and multilateral arrangements between these organizations, providing *inter alia* for exchanges of information on productions, for the broadcasting of shows and programs from other participating States, for coproductions, for the invitation of guest conductors and directors, as well as for the provision of mutual assistance to cultural film teams.

6. At the invitation of the Government of Hungary a "Cultural Forum" will take place in Budapest, commencing on 15 October 1985. It will be attended by leading personalities in the field of culture from the participating States. The "Forum" will discuss interrelated problems concerning creation, dissemination and cooperation, including the promotion and expansion of contacts and exchanges in the different fields of culture. A representative of UNESCO will be invited to present to the "Forum" the views of that organization. The "Forum" will be prepared by a meeting of experts, the duration of which will not exceed two weeks and which will be held upon the invitation of the Government of Hungary in Budapest, commencing 21 November 1984.

Cooperation and exchanges in the field of education

1. The participating States will promote the establishment of governmental and nongovernmental arrangements and agreements in education and science, to be carried out with the participation of educational or other competent institutions.

2. The participating States will contribute to the further improvement of exchanges of students, teachers and scholars and their access to each other's educational, cultural and scientific institutions, and also their access to open information material in accordance with the laws and regulations prevailing in each country. In this context, they will facilitate travel by scholars, teachers and students within the receiving State, the establishment by them of contacts with their colleagues, and will also encourage libraries, higher education establishments and similar institutions in their territories to make catalogs and lists of open archival material available to scholars, teachers and students from other participating States.

3. They will encourage a more regular exchange of information about scientific training programs, courses and seminars for young scientists and facilitate a wider participation in these activities of young scientists from different participating States. They will call upon the appropriate national and international organizations and institutions to give support, where appropriate, to the realization of these training activities.

4. The representatives of the participating States noted the usefulness of the work done during the "Scientific Forum" held in Hamburg, Federal Republic of Germany, from 18 February to 3 March 1980. Taking into account the results of

the "Scientific Forum," the participating States invited international organizations as well as the scientific organizations and scientists of the participating States to give due consideration to its conclusions and recommendations.

5. The participating States will favor widening the possibilities of teaching and studying less widely spread or studied European languages. They will, to this end, stimulate, within their competence, the organization of and attendance at summer university and other courses, the granting of scholarships for translators and the reinforcement of linguistic faculties including, in case of need, the provision of new facilities for studying these languages.

6. The participating States express their readiness to intensify the exchange, among them and within competent international organizations, of teaching materials, school textbooks, maps, bibliographies and other educational material, in order to promote better mutual knowledge and facilitate a fuller presentation of their respective countries.

Follow-up to the Conference

1. In conformity with the relevant provisions of the Final Act and with their resolve and commitment to continue the multilateral process initiated by the CSCE, the participating States will hold further meetings regularly among their representatives.

The third of these meetings will be held in Vienna commencing on 4 November 1986.

2. The agenda, working program and modalities of the main Madrid Meeting will be applied *mutatis mutandis* to the main Vienna Meeting, unless other decisions on these questions are taken by the preparatory meeting mentioned below.

For the purpose of making the adjustments to the agenda, working program and modalities of the main Madrid Meeting, a preparatory meeting will be held in Vienna commencing on 23 September 1986. It is understood that in this context adjustments concern those items requiring change as a result of the change in date and place, the drawing of lots, and the mention of the other meetings held in conformity with the decisions of the Madrid Meeting in 1980. The duration of the preparatory meeting shall not exceed two weeks.

3. The participating States further decide that in 1985, the tenth Anniversary of the signature of the Final Act of the CSCE will be duly commemorated in Helsinki.

4. The duration of the meetings mentioned in this document, unless otherwise agreed, should not exceed six weeks. The results of these meetings will be taken into account, as appropriate, at the Vienna Follow-up Meeting.

5. All the above-mentioned meetings will be held in conformity with Paragraph 4 of the Chapter on "Follow-up to the Conference" of the Final Act.

6. The Government of Spain is requested to transmit the present document to the Secretary General of the United Nations, to the Director General of UNESCO and to the Executive Secretary of the United Nations Economic Commission for Europe. The Government of Spain is also requested to transmit the present document to the Governments of the nonparticipating Mediterranean States.

7. The text of this document will be published in each participating State, which will disseminate it and make it known as widely as possible.

8. The representatives of the participating States express their profound gratitude to the people and Government of Spain for the excellent organization of the

Madrid Meeting and warm hospitality extended to the delegations which participated in the Meeting.

*Chairman's Statement, Venice Seminar on Economic, Scientific and
Cultural Cooperation in the Mediterranean Within the Framework
of the Results of the Valletta Meeting of Experts*

1. The Seminar will open on Tuesday, 16 October 1984 at 10 A.M. in Venice, Italy. It will close on Friday, 26 October 1984.

2. The work of the Seminar, guided by a Coordinating Committee composed of the delegations of the participating States, will be divided among three Study Groups devoted to Economics, Science and Culture respectively.

3. The first three days of the Seminar will be devoted to six sessions of the Committee.

4. The first session of the Committee will be public and will be devoted to the opening of the Seminar, to be followed by an address by a representative of the host country.

5. The second session of the Committee will decide whether to hold further sessions of the participating States to guide the work of the Study Groups and to take any other decisions necessary for the Seminar.

6. The following four sessions of the Committee will be public and will be devoted to introductory statements by the representatives of the participating States which so desire (in an order selected by lot in advance) and to introductory statements by the representatives of the nonparticipating Mediterranean States and the international organizations invited. The statements should not exceed 10 minutes per delegation.

7. Beginning on the fourth day and for the following three and a half working days, simultaneous meetings of the three Study Groups will be held.

8. The last one and a half days will be devoted to three sessions of the Committee. Two sessions will decide upon the most appropriate use for the documentation presented in the course of the work concerning the specific sectors indicated in the Valletta Report, such as publication of the introductory statements and distribution of the studies to the relevant international organizations, and will take any other necessary decisions.

The final session of the Committee will be public and will be devoted to the official closing of the Seminar with an address by a representative of the host country.

9. The Chair at the opening and closing sessions of both the Committee and the Study Groups will be taken by a representative from the delegation of the host country. Selection of the successive chairmen by lot will then ensure daily rotation of the Chair, in French alphabetical order, among the representatives of the participating States.

10. Participation in the work of the Seminar by the nonparticipating Mediterranean States (Algeria, Egypt, Israel, Lebanon, Libya, Morocco, Syria and Tunisia) and the international organizations (UNESCO, ECE, UNEP, WHO, ITU) invited will follow the rules and practices adopted at Valletta. This means, *inter alia*, that they will take part in the work of the three Study Groups and of the four sessions of the Committee on the second and third day as well as its opening and closing sessions.

11. Contributions, on the subjects for consideration in one or more of the work-

ing languages of the CSCE, may be sent through the proper channels—preferably not later than three months before the opening of the Seminar—to the Executive Secretary, who will circulate them to the other participating States, and to the non-participating Mediterranean States and to the international organizations which have notified their intention of taking part.

12. The Italian Government will designate the Executive Secretary of the Seminar. This designation should be agreed to by the participating States. The services of a technical secretariat will be provided by the host country.

13. Other rules of procedure, working methods and the scale of distribution for the expenses of the CSCE will, *mutatis mutandis*, be applied to the Seminar.

14. The arrangements outlined above will not constitute a precedent for any other CSCE forum.

Chairman's Statement, Bern Meeting of Experts on Human Contacts

The Chairman notes the absence of objection to the declaration made by the representative of Switzerland on 15 July 1983 extending an invitation by the Swiss Government to hold a meeting of experts on human contacts. Consequently, the Chairman notes that there is agreement to convene such a meeting to discuss the development of contacts among persons, institutions and organizations, with due account for the introductory part of the Chapter of the Final Act entitled *Cooperation in Humanitarian and Other Fields* and for the introductory part of section one (Human Contacts) of that Chapter, which reads *inter alia* as follows:

"The participating States,
Considering the development of contacts to be an important element in the strengthening of friendly relations and trust among peoples,
Affirming, in relation to their present effort to improve conditions in this area, the importance they attach to humanitarian considerations,
Desiring in this spirit to develop, with the continuance of détente, further efforts to achieve continuing progress in this field; . . ."

The meeting will be convened in Bern, on 15 April 1986. Its duration will not exceed six weeks. The meeting will be preceded by preparatory consultations, which will be held in Bern commencing on 2 April 1986. The results of the meeting will be taken into account, as appropriate, at the Vienna Follow-up Meeting.

The Swiss Government will designate the Executive Secretary of the meeting. This designation should be agreed to by the participating States. The services of a technical secretariat will be provided by the host country.

Other rules of procedure, working methods and the scale of distribution for the expenses of the CSCE will be applied *mutatis mutandis* to the Bern meeting.

The Chairman notes further that this statement will be an annex to the concluding document of the Madrid Meeting and will be published with it.

D. Western Draft Summary of the Results
of the Ottawa Meeting 1985 (June 15, 1985)

CSCE/OME.47/Rev. 1.

Proposal Submitted by the Delegations of Canada, Iceland, Italy,
Norway, Portugal, Spain, Turkey and the United States of America

Report of the Meeting of Experts Representing the Participating
States of the Conference on Security and Cooperation in Europe,
Foreseen by the Concluding Document of the Madrid Meeting of the
CSCE, on Questions Concerning Respect, in Their States, for Human
Rights and Fundamental Freedoms, in All Their Aspects, as Embodied
in the Final Act

1. In accordance with the relevant provisions of the Concluding Document of the Madrid Meeting of the Conference on Security and Cooperation in Europe, a Meeting of Experts representing the participating States took place in Ottawa, upon the invitation of the Government of Canada, from 7 May to 17 June 1985, on questions concerning respect, in their States, for human rights and fundamental freedoms, in all their aspects, as embodied in the Final Act.

2. The Meeting was preceded by a preparatory meeting which was held in Ottawa starting on 23 April 1985.

3. At the opening session, the participants were addressed by the Right Honorable Joe Clark PC MP, Secretary of State for External Affairs, on behalf of the Government of Canada.

4. The formal opening on 7 May and the formal closure on 17 June 1985, including concluding statements made by delegations wishing to do so, were held in open plenary meetings.

5. The participants adopted an agenda and had a frank discussion of implementation of the provisions of the Helsinki Final Act and the Madrid Concluding Document in the human rights field. Forty-five proposals for recommendations were submitted and considered by the participants.

6. During the discussion different and, at times, contradictory opinions were expressed as to respect, by the participating States, for human rights and fundamental freedoms, in all their aspects, as embodied in the Final Act and the Madrid Concluding Document. While certain progress was noted in a few States, grave concern was expressed at serious violations of human rights in some participating States. It was confirmed that this thorough exchange of views aimed at increased respect for human rights and fundamental freedoms constituted in itself a valuable contribution to the CSCE process.

7. This discussion was in conformity with the Final Act and therefore was not to be considered to be contradictory to the principle of nonintervention in the internal affairs of any State.

8. The participants reaffirmed that respect for human rights and fundamental freedoms is an essential factor for the peace, justice and well-being necessary to ensure the development of friendly relations and cooperation among their States as among all States. They expressed their concern that failure to achieve progress in respect for human rights and fundamental freedoms jeopardizes the credibility of the CSCE process as a whole.

9. They therefore emphasized the critical need to assure immediate and tangible

progress in the implementation of all the provisions of the Helsinki Final Act and the Madrid Concluding Document on the effective exercise of civil, political, economic, social, cultural and other rights and freedoms, thus ensuring the balanced development of the CSCE process.

10. The participants recognized the responsibility of each State to take prompt action to bring their practices and procedures into conformity with their commitments in the Final Act and Madrid Concluding Document, as well as other international declarations and agreements by which they may be bound, thus assuring the full exercise of human rights and fundamental freedoms.

11. They also emphasized that institutions, organizations and individuals have a positive and indispensable role to play in the achievement of the full exercise of human rights and fundamental freedoms. Furthermore, they recognized the importance of cooperation with and among institutions, organizations and individuals engaged as a matter of common concern in the protection of human rights in their own States or internationally.

12. They stressed the need, irrespective of their political, economic and social systems, to intensify their efforts to implement fully Principle VII (Respect for Human Rights and Fundamental Freedoms, including the Freedom of Thought, Conscience, Religion or Belief) of the Helsinki Final Act and the relevant provisions of the Concluding Document of the Madrid Meeting.

13. The participating States, recalling the right of the individual to know and act upon his rights in the field of human rights, as embodied in the Final Act and further reaffirmed in the Concluding Document of the Madrid Meeting, will take necessary action to remove legal and administrative measures so as to ensure in practice the right of all their citizens, individually or in groups, effectively to monitor the implementation of these documents. They will ensure the right of all their citizens freely to express their views on any question concerning implementation, in order to help ensure respect in their own country or in other participating States for these rights.

14. Further, they will, *inter alia*, publish or reissue the Helsinki Final Act and the Madrid Concluding Document, as well as the Universal Declaration of Human Rights and other relevant international instruments in the field of human rights by which they may be bound, disseminate these documents in their entirety, make them known as widely as possible and render them permanently accessible to all individuals in their countries. They will bear in mind particularly the possibility of drawing attention to these documents and other relevant CSCE documents on such occasions as the Commemoration of the Tenth Anniversary of the Signing of the Helsinki Final Act and further follow-up meetings.

15. They will fulfill their respective obligations concerning the fundamental right to freedom of movement in all its aspects as set forth in those international instruments by which they are bound.

16. With a view to strengthening implementation of the provisions of the Final Act and the Madrid Concluding Document concerning freedom of thought, conscience, religion or belief, and in compliance with the provisions of Article 18 of the Universal Declaration of Human Rights, Article 18 of the International Covenant on Civil and Political Rights, and the provisions of the United Nations Declaration on the Elimination of All Forms of Intolerance and Discrimination on the Basis of Religion or Belief, and any other international instruments by which they are bound, the participating States will pay special attention to the elimination of discrimination against the individual believer and religious communities wherever this occurs, on the grounds of religion or belief so as to ensure the equal

exercise of their rights. For this purpose, they will create an atmosphere of tolerance and respect for all matters relating to freedom to profess and practice religion or belief, alone or in community with others, in public or in private.

17. They will grant the status provided for in their respective countries for religious faiths, institutions and organizations, to religious communities of believers practicing or prepared to practice their faith, within the constitutional framework of their States, which apply for such status.

18. Further, they will engage in consultations with the religious faiths, institutions and organizations, in order to reach a better understanding of the requirements of religious freedom and to take action to ensure their fulfillment. For this purpose, they will act to guarantee, *inter alia:*

—the right of persons to give and receive religious education individually, collectively or through religious organizations, including the freedom of parents to transmit their religion or belief to their children;

—the freedom of the individual believer and communities of believers to establish and maintain contact and hold assemblies in common with fellow believers, including those of other countries;

—to produce, acquire, receive, import and make full use of publications and other materials concerning the profession and practice of religion or belief; to have access to and use the various media for religious purposes.

19. They will undertake the necessary measures and apply the provisions of their internal legislation and their international obligations emanating from agreements between States, as well as other international instruments by which they may be bound, contributing to the consequent realization and improvement of human rights and fundamental freedoms of members of national minorities, their legitimate interests and aspirations, thus refraining from discrimination against persons belonging to national minorities and safeguarding their national and cultural identity.

20. They stress the importance of ensuring equality of men and women in all spheres of life and will take appropriate measures in all fields to eliminate any discrimination against women in order to guarantee that all women and men may exercise and enjoy human rights and fundamental freedoms on an equal basis. Such measures shall ensure in particular the equally effective participation of men and women in political, economic, social and cultural life. Furthermore, they shall promote efforts to prevent violence against women.

21. The participating States, in fulfillment of their commitment in the Concluding Document of the Madrid Meeting in the field of trade union rights, will respect the right of freely established and joined trade unions and their freely chosen representatives to have direct and unrestricted contacts and communication among themselves.

22. They will authorize and encourage institutions, organizations and individuals to play their relevant role in monitoring the governments' respect for these provisions and in investigating individual complaints about alleged violations of them.

23. They will facilitate and support discussion and cooperation among individuals, groups and organizations engaged in the protection or promotion of human rights and fundamental freedoms such as humanitarian organizations, churches, relevant professional groups, cultural organizations, women's organizations and youth organizations. One useful purpose of such international cooperation could be to elaborate and adopt sets of common professional and ethical standards to ensure full protection of and respect for human rights and fundamental freedoms.

24. They will respond to inquiries and representations from governments of other participating States and from private individuals or groups on matters concerning human rights and fundamental freedoms within their respective States. Such inquiries or representations may be made to foreign ministries or to such other offices as the participating State may designate.

25. The participating States, convinced that torture and other cruel, inhuman or degrading treatment or punishment are among the most serious human rights violations and cannot be justified under any circumstances, and bearing in mind all relevant principles and provisions embodied in international instruments by which they may be bound, will take all necessary steps to eliminate such practice and take effective legislative, administrative, judicial, and other measures to prevent and punish such acts in the territory under their jurisdiction.

26. They will, to the maximum extent possible, respond positively to requests to observe legal proceedings. They will admit observers to such proceedings or provide full explanations as to why such observers may not be admitted.

27. They will work toward the reduction in length of incommunicado detention to a minimum.

28. They will also improve and increase the opportunities for representatives of nongovernmental humanitarian organizations to visit prisoners. Where possible, restrictions concerning the reasonable access of relatives and friends in privacy to individuals under detention or incarceration in prisons or other penal institutions will be progressively reduced.

29. They will ensure that individuals are protected from psychiatric practices which violate human rights and fundamental freedoms.

30. Noting that terrorism endangers or takes innocent human lives and is an intolerable violation of human dignity, the participants reaffirmed the relevant provisions of the Madrid Concluding Document on terrorism.

31. They will hold regular meetings in order to discuss questions of human rights and fundamental freedoms, including the freedom of thought, conscience, religion or belief, to encourage the implementation of the provisions of the Final Act and the Concluding Document of the Madrid Meeting in this field.

32. The participants expressed their deep gratitude to the Government of Canada for the excellent organization of the Meeting and to the Government and people of Canada for the warm hospitality extended to them during their stay.

E. Western Draft Summary of the Results of the Budapest Meeting 1985 (November 25, 1985)

CSCE/CFB.116

Proposal Submitted by the Delegations of Belgium, Canada, Denmark, France, the Federal Republic of Germany, Greece, Iceland, Ireland, Italy, Luxembourg, the Netherlands, Norway, Portugal, Spain, Turkey, the United Kingdom, and the United States of America

Report of the Cultural Forum of the Conference on Security and Cooperation in Europe

1. In accordance with

—the provisions of the Final Act of the Conference on Security and Cooperation in Europe,

—the relevant provisions of the Madrid Meeting,
—the report of the meeting of experts which took place in Budapest from 21 November to 4 December 1984,
the Cultural Forum took place in Budapest, Hungary, from 15 October to 25 November 1985. It was attended by leading personalities in the field of culture from the participating States.

2. After the formal opening of the Cultural Forum, participants were addressed by Mr. György Lázár, Prime Minister, on behalf of the Government of Hungary.

3. Under agenda item 2 of the Forum, opening statements were made in open plenary meetings by representatives of the participating States. The views of UNESCO were presented by a representative of that Organization.

4. Under agenda item 3 of the Forum, and in accordance with the mandate for the Forum, participants discussed, both in plenary and in subsidiary working bodies, interrelated problems concerning creation, dissemination and cooperation, including the promotion and expansion of contacts and exchanges in the different fields of culture.

5. The discussion of the above-mentioned interrelated problems was conducted in the context of the following fields:

—*Plastic and Applied Arts*
painting, graphic and photographic arts, sculpture, design, architecture, preservation of cultural and historical monuments;
—*Performing Arts*
theater, dance, folklore, music, film, cultural programs on radio and television;
—*Literature*
literature, publishing and translation, including reference to less widely spoken languages of the participating States;
—*Mutual Cultural Knowledge*
research, training and education in the arts, libraries, cultural heritage, preservation of and respect for the diversity and originality of the cultures of the participating States, museums, exhibitions.

6. The discussion covered a wide range of subjects in the cultural field. It also reflected the unique character of the Cultural Forum itself within the framework of the CSCE process and the vitality, strength and diversity of the various cultures of the participating States. The participants endeavored to contribute to the discussion with a view to promoting further creation, dissemination and cooperation in the fields of culture. During the discussion different and, at times, contradictory opinions were expressed not only on matters of substance but also on the procedure of the meeting.

7. A large number of proposals were presented under agenda item 3 both in the plenary and in the appropriate subsidiary working bodies.

8. As a result of its proceedings the Cultural Forum concluded the following:

—In the course of its history, Europe has developed a cultural identity of its own which is also part of the North American heritage. This identity is reflected in a basic unity of cultural values which has survived and had proved its cohesion and resilience despite present political and ideological divisions.
—Since the signing of the Final Act, cultural exchanges and cooperation have proved to be a stabilizing factor in relations between States participating in the CSCE. They contribute to a better understanding between individuals and

among peoples and thus help to promote conditions conducive to the building of confidence and the development of normal and friendly relations.

—International cooperation in the different fields of culture since the signing of the Final Act of the CSCE has been greater in some areas than in others. The present conditions for cultural creation and dissemination as well as for international exchanges and cooperation in the different fields of culture still require improvement in many respects.

—Such improvements should be sought and achieved by taking active steps to allow the full and unimpeded development of artistic creativity and the recognition of the role of individual artists and the integrity of their creation. They should also be sought and achieved by the unimpeded dissemination of cultural works through facilitating and supporting discussion and cooperation among individuals, groups and private organizations in the different fields of culture; through providing equitable opportunities for wider communication, more direct contacts and travel for personal as well as professional reasons. Similarly, improvements should be made at governmental and nongovernmental levels, bilaterally and multilaterally, through agreements between Governments and nongovernmental organizations and international programs, as part of a general expansion of cultural cooperation.

—This goal can, however, be reached only by respect for all the principles and by full implementation of the relevant provisions of the Final Act and the Concluding Document of the Madrid Follow-Up Meeting. It was stressed that there was a critical need to make immediate, tangible and balanced progress in such implementation, particularly with regard to creation, dissemination and cooperation in the different fields of culture. The participants in the Forum urged all participating States to observe the spirit and the letter of the Final Act and the Madrid Concluding Document in this respect.

—It is furthermore emphasized that full respect for human rights and fundamental freedoms, including cultural rights and freedoms, and including those of persons belonging to national minorities and regional cultures, by all States represents one of the basic principles for a significant improvement in their mutual relations, and in international cultural cooperation at all levels.

9. The participants in the Forum discussed, *inter alia*, the following specific problems relating to its mandate:

—The denial of opportunities in some participating States for individuals in the different fields of culture to form independent institutions and organizations and to play, as individuals or as members of these independent bodies, a full and unhindered part in the cultural activity of their own States and internationally;

—Limitations on access to and the use of information, publications and materials relating to culture;

—Restrictions on access to the cultural achievements of other participating States, e.g. through cultural institutes;

—The denial to persons belonging to national minorities and regional cultures of adequate protection, legal or otherwise, for the full development of their culture; and

—The need to support the efforts of individuals to reflect and promote the unity of European culture, which transcends the division of Europe.

10. The participants in the Cultural Forum urge the participating States to:

—Remove existing impediments which prevent individuals from forming or join-
ing independent institutions and organizations in order to pursue and promote,
as individuals or as members of these independent bodies, their interests in the
different fields of culture, including the protection and promotion of cultural
freedom and the respect shown by governments, including their own, for that
cultural freedom;

—Ensure unimpeded communication, direct contact, and cooperation, such as
the holding of meetings and exhibitions by private persons, institutions and
organizations active in the field of culture;

—Facilitate for humanitarian reasons the provision of the fullest information to
artists and others in the field of culture, who have attempted without success,
to contact their colleagues in another participating State;

—Remove legal and administrative measures, such as censorship, which constitute
barriers to creation and dissemination in the different fields of culture;

—Remove, while respecting intellectual property rights, restrictions on obtaining,
possessing, reproducing, publishing and distributing materials related to the
different fields of culture, including books, publications, films and videotapes, as
well as on the private ownership and use of and access to typewriters, word
processors and copying machines;

—Ensure unimpeded access of individual believers and communities of believers
to religious publications and related materials;

—Ensure unimpeded access to public archives, libraries, research institutes and
similar bodies for scholars, teachers, students and others who wish to undertake
research;

—Permit unimpeded reception of broadcasts and place no restrictions on the
right of individuals to choose freely their sources of broadcast information and
culture;

—Abstain from placing undue obstacles to access to direct broadcasting satellites
transmitting radio and television programs, including those of a cultural nature,
and allow individuals and groups to acquire the necessary equipment;

—Ensure that individuals engaged in the different fields of culture are free to
travel abroad, and, in particular, that those invited officially or privately to
travel to other participating States have the opportunity to do so;

—Make it possible, on the basis of bilateral arrangements, for each participating
State to establish cultural institutes on the territory of the other participating
States and to guarantee unhindered public access to them; and

—Protect the unique identity of national minorities and foster the free exercise
of cultural rights by persons belonging to them; ensure in practice unhindered
opportunities for these persons independently to maintain and develop their
own culture in all its aspects, including religion, cultural monuments, historical
artifacts, language, literature; and to ensure unhindered opportunities for them
to give and receive, individually or collectively, instruction in their own culture,
especially through the parental transmission of language, religion and cultural
identity to their children.

11. Therefore, the participants in the Cultural Forum recommend that the participating States encourage, facilitate and support the initiatives which official
institutes, nongovernmental organizations and individuals wish to undertake to promote the aims of the CSCE in the field of culture, e.g. meetings, symposia, exhibitions, festivals, research, training and coproduction programs in which scholars,
specialists and artists of the participating States may freely participate and to which

they may freely contribute, in order to realize progressively the objective of promoting knowledge and culture which transcend geographic boundaries.

12. In particular, the participants in the Cultural Forum recommend that the participating States:

—Facilitate the participation in international drama festivals of individuals, productions or companies chosen by the organizers and not replace them by any other individuals, productions or companies without prior consultation;

—Encourage invitations to conductors and individual performers from other participating States to perform with orchestras and choirs in their own States;

—Promote the exchange of members of art and music academies as well as of teachers and students of drama and dance schools;

—Take into account the important role that exchanges of teachers, students and material play in the education of young filmmakers, particularly through festivals and prizes;

—Remove barriers to participation in film festivals, including restrictions on public access to such festivals and censorship and control on what films may be shown;

—Might consider the possibility of a meeting of writers on the subject of "Liberty, Equality and Fraternity in Today's World"; a symposium on the subject of "The Impact of the Discovery of America on European Culture"; and a meeting of historians and cultural figures on "Transmission of Culture Through Emigration";

—Remove barriers to unimpeded participation in book fairs, displays and exhibits by prospective displayers; restrictions on public access to such book fairs, displays and exhibits; and censorship and control on what books or publications may be displayed;

—Consider the aesthetic aspects of the environment in the preservation, reshaping and building of cities;

—Might identify historic towns and cities for conservation and restoration projects in which other participating States might join;

—Might consider the possibility of establishing an international folklore center of States participating in the csce which would be responsible for the collection, systematization and publication of the folk heritage of the participating States for educational purposes;

—Explore the possibility of computerization and dissemination in standard form of bibliographies and of catalogs of cultural works and presentations, such as musical scores, contemporary public sculpture, films, videotapes, documentary programs shown on television, plays and the performances of artists and ensembles;

—Encourage the translation of research and literature, with special attention to bilingual editions as well as to the translation, publication and dissemination of literary works published in the less widely spoken languages in the participating States;

—Might consider proclaiming a city in a participating State "Capital of European Cultural Heritage" for one year. In the course of that year, the participating State in question would endeavor to make a special contribution to European culture in all its forms by organizing events and taking other initiatives in the city in question, including works by groups of artists. All other participating States would be invited to take part;

—Facilitate the holding of exhibitions which have a special reference to present everyday life;

—Encourage cooperation in protecting and preserving film material;

—Encourage the acquisition, coproduction and regular exchange of television and radio cultural programs;

—Encourage the appropriate national and international nongovernmental organizations to work out a general framework regarding cultural exchanges such as exhibitions, guest performances, etc., including general and administrative guidelines, the possible simplification of customs and other procedures, and ways of facilitating payment of fees to individuals and organizations where direct payments are rendered difficult by currency restrictions or economic constraints;

—Might consider the possibility of establishing a cultural foundation of States participating in the CSCE, which would aim at improving the conditions and opportunities of artistic creation; facilitating the dissemination of culture within and among States participating in the CSCE; and promoting cultural exchanges and cooperation among them.

13. The participants also considered a wide range of other proposals, not all of which have been reflected in this Report.

14. The participants expressed their appreciation of the effort which went into the preparation of these proposals, all of which will be recorded as they were submitted, annexed to this report, and sent forward for consideration in any further discussion of cultural questions within the framework of the CSCE.

15. The results of the Cultural Forum in Budapest will be taken into account, as appropriate, by the participating States at the next Follow-Up Meeting of the Conference on Security and Cooperation in Europe, scheduled for November 1986.

16. The participants expressed their gratitude to the Government of Hungary for the excellent organization of the Cultural Forum and for the warm hospitality extended to them during their stay in Budapest.

INDEX

Library of Congress Cataloging-in-Publication Data
Mastny, Vojtech, 1936–
  Helsinki, human rights, and European security.

  Includes index.
  1. Conference on Security and Cooperation in Europe
(1975: Helsinski, Finland)   2. Civil rights—Soviet
Union.   3. Civil rights—Europe, Eastern.   4. Arms
control.   5. Europe—Defenses.   I. Title.
JX1393.C65M38   1986   327.1′7′094   86–13560
ISBN 0–8223–0682–4